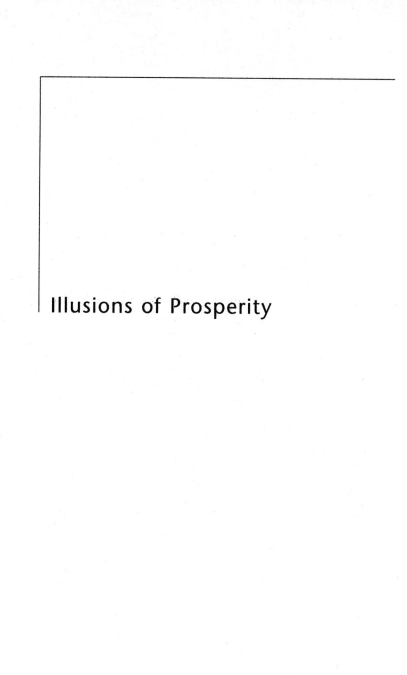

Illusions of Prosperity

Illusions of Prosperity

*America's Working Families
in an Age of Economic Insecurity*

Joel Blau

New York • Oxford • Oxford University Press • 1999

Oxford University Press

Oxford   New York
Athens   Auckland   Bangkok   Bogotá   Buenos Aires   Calcutta
Cape Town   Chennai   Dar es Salaam   Delhi   Florence   Hong Kong   Istanbul
Karachi   Kuala Lumpur   Madrid   Melbourne   Mexico City   Mumbaí
Nairobi   Paris   São Paulo   Singapore   Taipei   Tokyo   Toronto   Warsaw
and associated companies in
Berlin   Ibadan

Published by Oxford University Press, Inc.
198 Madison Avenue, New York, NY 10016

Oxford is a registered trademark of Oxford University Press

Cataloging-in-Publication Data
Blau, Joel.
Illusions of prosperity : America's working families in an age
of economic insecurity / Joel Blau.
p.   cm.
Includes bibliographical references and index.
ISBN 0-19-508993-6
1. Foreign trade and employment—United States.
2. Free trade—United States.
3. Unemployment—United States.
4. Public welfare—United States.
5. United States—Economic policy—1993–
6. Business relocation—United States.
7. Plant shutdowns—United States.
8. Wages—Developing countries.
9. Income distribution—United States.
I. Title
II. Title: American workers and their families
in an age of economic insecurity
HD5710.75.U6 B58   1999
331.1'0973—dc21   98-30262

1 3 5 7 9 8 6 4 2
Printed in the United States of America
on acid-free paper

In loving memory of my mother and father,
Helen and Raphael Blau,
who died during the writing of this book.

Contents

Acknowledgments

Before a book is published, authors usually ask friends and colleagues to read it in manuscript form. These friends and colleagues are the book's first public, the people who anticipate what a wider audience might say. Sometimes, this "first public" reacts contradictorily, and an author will have to decide between conflicting advice about the book's ideas, style, or organization. Apart from this exception, I have a rule: if you respect someone's opinion enough to show them a draft of the manuscript, you had better respond to their comments or have a compelling reason not to do so.

And so, I would like to thank the friends and colleagues who were the first public for this book. Although they bear no responsibility for its final form—for both the advice I did and did not take—they improved the manuscript in countless ways, and I want to express my appreciation for their time, wisdom, and expertise.

Ted Berkman and Christopher Dykema's comments on an early draft were particularly helpful. Both gave the whole manuscript a very careful reading, suggested improvements in language, and offered advice that guided me in later revisions. Each has had a significant impact on this book.

Subsequently, Mimi Abramovitz, Richard Cloward, Charles Noble, and Michael Reisch reviewed the manuscript. Saving me from errors of both fact and emphasis, they enriched the text and made it more readable.

Other people made helpful notes on individual chapters. I especially wish to recognize the assistance of Todd Boressoff, Ron Lehrer, Fred Newdom, Jerry Sachs, and Steve Slepian, each of whom made detailed and insightful comments. The chapters they read have been improved as a result of their efforts.

My colleagues at Stony Brook deserve a special note of thanks. For both the editorial advice and the support I have received from them for the last four years, I want to recognize Richard Adams, Ruth Brandwein, Paul Colson, Arthur Katz, Michael Lewis, and Abe Lurie.

My sincere appreciation goes as well to Sydelle Kramer, who edited, advised, and generally helped to keep me on track. Throughout the book's development, she smoothed the way.

And once again, I want to express my deep love and appreciation to my wife, Sandra Baron-Blau, for—well, for everything: her patience, her support, and not the least, her editorial skills.

Introduction

This book is about American workers, their families, and the political and economic consequences of America's growing reliance on the market. It is therefore, implicitly, about a great puzzle. The puzzle is why so many Americans welcome this growing reliance on the market when just a small percentage have actually benefited.

Americans think the market is their path to upward mobility. They have been socialized to believe that the free market is the best system of meeting human needs. Many are also convinced that government is an intolerable burden. Because all these beliefs have recently acquired a quasi-religious status in the United States, they are matters of faith, which despite the whisperings of a few dissenters, are not really open to public debate. As the faithful would have it, in the new global capitalism, there is no alternative.

This immunity from criticism has deep historical roots. Equating economic and political freedom, Americans have long associated markets with democracy. It is an equation that the downfall of communism and the "triumph" of capitalism have further bound together in the public's mind. Yet something crucial has been lost in celebrations of this linkage. Political freedom has always required the existence of political institutions to protect the relatively powerless from the relatively powerful. Defined as something besides the liberty to dispose of property, economic freedom has always required similar institutions to protect the great majority of the citizenry from the very wealthy.

Americans have often engaged in a spirited discussion about how economic and political institutions need to work together to preserve democratic freedoms and economic security for the majority, against the interests of powerful elites. The recent rhetoric about the "free" market has helped to undermine these institutions, because it has strengthened elites at the expense of both meaningful political participation and the living standards of the vast majority. By now, we have reached the point where an economic elite makes decisions about jobs and investment that define the fundamental conditions of

American life, and then, the electorate—or rather, the half of the electorate that still believes its opinion matters—gets to vote on some pertinent but necessarily secondary issues. As a result, the linkage of economic freedom and political democracy has been effectively severed.

Because the institutional mechanisms that protect the political and economic rights of Americans no longer fit the conditions of a changing world economy, we need to rethink carefully how these mechanisms might be reconstructed. In this book, I detail how the new rhetoric regarding free and hence "unrestrained" markets has undermined the protections that are necessary to ensure economic security for the population, and I suggest new mechanisms to prevent further downward mobility for American workers and their families. I contend that "democratic accountability" is the route to economic and political security, in both the economy, at the workplace and through protection for those unable to find work, and in the polity. Without this mechanism, free markets will increasingly come to mean the political and economic disenfranchisement of the majority, who will continue to pay the costs of the elites' unrestrained freedom.

These costs mount daily. Most Americans face a declining standard of living. They find it harder to get a raise, and they may well be fired when their company downsizes or moves elsewhere in search of cheaper labor. Income inequality skyrockets, the quality of our political life founders under the weight of private money, and families with ever fewer social supports strain to reconcile the competing demands of parenting and work. Although the market does have a long-standing immunity in this country, these costs put the clash between those who benefit and those who pay into ever sharper conflict.

The improving economy has certainly provided some political cover. As long as unemployment stays below 5 percent, and the stock market booms, the turn to the market seems to have paid off. The affluent prosper, and the media trumpets their prosperity as a total index of economic well-being. Yet even in these seemingly prosperous times, there is another undercurrent, one not captured in reports of the record construction of "starter-mansions" or the pace-setting sales of luxury yachts. Indeed, for the average worker, wages remain low, real income gains are scarce, and two jobs are often necessary to make ends meet. Even the unemployment figures disguise the true level of unemployment, which doubles with the addition of discouraged and involuntary part-time workers and reaches three to four times the national average in the inner city. And, of course, none of these economic figures touch on the social costs of the market. Whatever affluence it brings to the few, its ethos of Social Darwinism, narcissistic individualism, and a reverence for competition cannot forge a livable society.

I use the term "the economy" a lot in this book. The word "economy" traces its etymology to the Greek concept of a household, a single domestic unit whose fortunes rise or fall together. Since the widening split within the

American household constitutes one of the book's main themes, this usage is, in some sense, a misnomer. We no longer have a single American economy. Instead, we have at least two economies, one for a prospering business elite and the affluent professional-managerial classes, and another for everyone else. Both economically and politically, it is highly debatable whether such an arrangement is sustainable over the long term.

Besides, the one thing we know about economic booms is that they do not last. There is no telling what might trigger a recession—a regional crisis that spreads, a shift of currency allegiances or a glut of goods from global overproduction. Still, unless economic history has come to an end, and we have finally attained the free market utopia of an unending boom, there will be a recession. And as a result of the political and economic policies of the last twenty-five years, all the pieces are now in place to make the next recession a particularly nasty one.

For starters, the 1996 welfare law destroyed the safety net. This means that in any recession occurring after 2002, all those who have exhausted their five-year lifetime limit on public assistance will be left to drown. In this back to the future scenario, poverty in 2002 may begin to look a lot like poverty in 1932, before New Deal social policies offered some protection from the effects of the Great Depression.

Nor will the impact of the next recession be restricted to the poor. Many baby boomers own some stock—just enough to lift their hopes, but not enough to control the market. After the gains of the 1990s, they are counting on the appreciation of these stocks to buy a home, to pay for their children's college expenses, and to enjoy a comfortable retirement. In short, they are perfectly positioned for a big fall. If the stock market declines 44 percent over sixteen years as it did during the period from 1966 to 1982, there are going to be a lot of embittered people. Whether they are embittered to the right or embittered to the left, there will be large political consequences.

These large consequences are all the more probable because the next recession could well be international. In effect, globalization of the economy risks globalizing the business cycle, so that it becomes ever more difficult to contain recessions occurring in a single major country. If that country is the United States, the world's preeminent economic power, who else will pull the economy out of its tailspin? An international recession might therefore be quite a long one.

Of course, anyone can draft a long list of possible crises. It is not the purpose of this book to do so; its purpose is, rather, to show how our veneration of markets has lowered the living standards of most Americans and made us more vulnerable to the next, inevitable economic crisis. Americans need new ways to regain their upward mobility; they need a new path to economic security; and not the least, they are entitled as citizens to participate in the workplace and in a vibrant democratic public life. The increasingly market-based policies of the past twenty-five years have pushed these goals still further away.

Because these are almost fighting words in the United States today, Part I of this book begins by documenting what our faith in the market has wrought. The first chapter provides a broad overview of the effects of the turn to the market. Focusing on recent political history, it correlates the growth in income inequality with the imbalance of private and public power and the development of the garrison state. Since business mobility played an important role in these developments, the second chapter follows this analysis with an examination of globalization and the consequences of treaties such as NAFTA that seek to promote free trade. Unregulated free trade is closely tied to the preference of American business for a disposable labor force and a low-wage, low-skill strategy. The third and fourth chapters analyze these trends, which make it harder for so many Americans to earn a decent living and care for their families.

Part II examines the effect of the turn to the market on education (chapter 5), job training (chapter 6), and public assistance (chapter 7). Although Americans have usually relied on these programs to better their economic status, new economic conditions have undermined their effectiveness and caused them to falter. Now education no longer assures upward mobility, job training rarely offsets the financial loss from layoffs, and the old system of public assistance has been completely discarded. Whether it is education for profit, employment programs like the Job Training Partnership Act that prepare people solely for the private sector, or compulsory work for those on welfare, reforms of these programs have all been market based. And that is exactly the problem. As these three chapters show, reform on a market model either narrows or altogether restricts benefits, turning education, job training, and public assistance into ever less likely instruments of upward mobility. Amid all the euphoria about the market, we have somehow forgotten that programs modeled on the market can never be the remedy for the market's deficiencies.

If the market funnels its benefits to comparatively few, and market-based social policies are more likely to heighten than reduce the market's most inequitable tendencies, how can meaningful civic participation be encouraged? How can greater economic security be ensured? The answer to these questions is the subject of Part III. In chapter 8 on the workplace, chapter 9 on the government, and chapter 10 on "The Next Deal," I argue that the answer lies in increased economic and political democracy.

Economic democracy must begin at work, where the decline of trade unions and the mobility of business have reduced the influence of workers on the job. Many studies have shown, however, that worker participation increases productivity. Buffeted by changes at the workplace, employees also need a stronger voice in this critical part of their lives. In the past, assertions about democracy in the United States have always stopped at the office door. Applying the principle of democratic accountability, they will no longer.

Outside the workplace, ensuring economic security depends upon the adequacy of government social policies, and adequate social policies would require a substantial reworking of attitudes toward government. Americans have always been fearful of large institutions in general and big government in particular. Although the U.S. government actually plays a smaller role in the economy than in most other industrialized countries, this fact comforts few people. Indeed, most have only dropped their antipathy to government when, as in the 1930s and the 1960s, powerful social movements resulted in domestic social policies that worked on their behalf.

Nevertheless, since government is the only major institution that can possibly be counterposed to the market, hostility to government actually gives the market freer rein. From this perspective, the issue is not the size of the government, but rather its success in ensuring economic security. In the United States, the federal government has tended to be sprawling, decentralized, and ineffectual. Deferential toward business and hamstrung by the legacy of separation of powers, it has attended only fitfully to the population's needs. Under the principle of democratic accountability, we need to connect the vast majority of people to the government, give it an unambiguous mandate to act on their behalf, and hold it accountable if it fails.

Ensuring the economic security of the population is this mandate's guiding principle. Social policies that will ensure economic security include full employment, an insistence on wages sufficient to support a family, and social supports from universal programs for those who cannot work. The market thrives on economic insecurity. By obligating people to spend a lot of time meeting their most basic needs, it substitutes economic concerns for social concerns—the pursuit of a minimal standard of living for dynamic communities and an active civic life. The promise of economic security, then, goes far beyond economics. By freeing us to focus on how to live together, it could also animate our politics.

For now, market values define American life, and those values foster a society whose long-term viability is very much open to question. In the late nineteenth century, and again in the 1920s, the United States went through a period where economic elites successfully repelled most challenges. We are passing through such a period now. If history is any guide, this phase will come to an end in the not-so-distant future, and we will have to think once again about "first principles." When that happens, and our infatuation with markets wanes, we would do well to pursue the goals of economic security and democratic accountability. Unlike the market, at least they would make it easier for most Americans to work, earn a living, and raise their families.

Part 1

The Turn to the Market

The Triumph
of the Market

We got what we wanted. We got indications the economy wasn't
as strong as we had perceived. So the bond market took off and
the stock market followed.

—*Byron R. Wien, Morgan Stanley investment strategist,*
on the reasons for a Wall Street rally.

Mobil Oil reports first quarter profits of $636 million. One week later,
it eliminates 4700 jobs, and its stock rises to a new 52-week high.
Chemical forms the nation's largest bank by purchasing Chase Manhattan for $10 billion. Chemical then declares its intention to lay off
12,000 of the new bank's 75,000 workers, and its stock promptly jumps
11 percent. Kimberly-Clark, the Dallas-based producer of Kleenex tis-
sues and Huggies diapers, buys Scott Paper for $9.4 billion and fires
6000 workers. Two years later, when the deal does not work out, it lays
off another 5000 people.[1]

In the last quarter of the twentieth century, the United States embarked on a
great experiment. At work and in the national economy, Americans reembraced
the market as the key to improving their standard of living. In the workplace,
corporations deployed computer technology, revamped what nearly every
worker did, and laid off millions of people—including nearly 4.2 million
between 1993 and 1995 alone.[2] In the national economy, a chastened federal
government sought to become ever more marketlike: it downsized, deregulated,
and dismantled. With less government and fewer social protections, most Americans tried simply to catch the new wave. Now that a bona fide market economy
had been unleashed, surely it would bring prosperity to them, too.

Twenty-five years of this experiment have elapsed, and the results are in:
business has prospered, but American workers and their families have not. To

be sure, between 1973 and 1997, the economy did gain 45 million new jobs. Yet instead of diminishing income inequality, pay from these jobs helped drive it to a modern record. By 1996, despite five years of steady economic growth, median income remained 2.7 percent below its 1989 level. In fact, the decline in the median signified a much wider deterioration in living standards. In 1967, the bottom four-fifths of the population—roughly the poor and broad middle-class combined—had 56.3 percent of the national income. By 1996, however, their share had dropped to just 51 percent, leaving a near-record 49 percent to the top fifth. An extraordinary surge had boosted the affluent's windfall. Aided by a series of national administrations attentive to its well-being, the top fifth had garnered 97 percent of the 1979–1994 increase in total household income. Few experiments yield such clear outcomes. Although many had hoped to benefit from the new market economy, this affluent fifth is the only segment of the population that truly has.[3]

The turn to the market had other unsavory consequences. Markets are well-known for deftness and agility in getting prices right, but they are less commendable for their tendency to put a price on everything. Civic disengagement, health care and prisons for profit, the malling of suburban America, the epidemic of corporate advertising in public space, and the torrent of private money in public life all testify to a coarsening of American politics and culture. Competition to get the price right may be the hallmark of our economic system, but competition to put a price on everything produces a war of all against all. In this wartime condition, race and class tightly circumscribe communities, and the capacity to empathize with other people is fragile or nonexistent. No wonder that when people get angry, that anger often leads to bloody and senseless violence. In short, a limited conception of human potential defines the U.S. marketplace. Shoehorning most people into roles either as disempowered workers or impetuous consumers, it has ensured that the social losses also mount, until they easily match the economic.

Indeed, so small a percentage of the population has benefited from this turn toward the market that most Americans' willingness to tolerate it constitutes the great paradox of modern U.S. politics. Going along with the experiment just at the moment when the pace of globalization accelerated and technical skills became important, they mythologized the market as an even-handed distributor of benefits. For most, this judgment was badly mistaken. In the new, global economy, four-fifths simply did not possess the skills to realize much benefit for themselves.

Yet, from another perspective, the public response is no great mystery at all. In the twenty-five years after World War II, a market economy stimulated by military spending and, by international standards, a comparatively modest welfare state, produced a steadily rising standard of living. From 1945 to 1973, real wages grew 2.5 to 3.0 percent per year.[4] This postwar boom enriched the professional classes and brought industrial workers to the threshold of the middle class. Memories of the Depression dimmed. Sure, there were large pockets of poverty in Appalachia, the South, and the segregated inner cities. Still, in the popular mind, neither these facts nor the considerable stimuli of welfare spending and the Vietnam War could tarnish the image of a vibrant private sector.

During the next twenty years, wages stagnated, and the U.S. standard of living increased about one-quarter as fast as West Germany's and about one-seventh as fast as Japan's.[5] The experience of postwar prosperity, however, had left the American electorate with an ideological hangover. Although American businesses tried to make the U.S. competitive again by restraining wages, most American political leaders blamed the decline in living standards on an interventionist government. Since the postwar economy had recently delivered twenty-five years of prosperity, the electorate embraced this explanation, too. Quickly refined and applied to every possible public policy issue, the explanation was soon compressed into a neatly syllogistic argument. The market is dynamic and creates prosperity; the welfare state is burdensome and perpetuates poverty. Unshackle the market, and the economy will flourish once again, just as it did in the United States at the middle of the twentieth century.

Despite its seeming plausibility, this argument does have one major problem: it is not true. The confusion stems from a fundamental misconception. Amid all the talk about the dynamism of markets, we tend to forget that well-positioned people use their leverage in the market to create poverty, though the specific amount varies from country to country. In the United States at least, the beneficiaries of markets like to limit social benefits, fight increases in the minimum wage, contest the spread of trade unions, and welcome intervention from the Federal Reserve Bank when unemployment gets too low. Although some may bristle at the notion that anyone's use of their power in the private sector generates poverty, that is exactly what each of these policies does. The conventional argument links the market with prosperity and the welfare state with poverty. It needs reformulation. In this alternate and more accurate assessment, the welfare state merely manages the poverty that the private sector creates.

Nevertheless, as economic insecurity increased among American workers, they rejected this newer formulation for the conventional one that supposedly liberated the market. Global competition might be intensifying; employers might be increasingly stingy. Yet between reduced taxes and an increase in private investment, many Americans came to believe that they would be better off in the last quarter of the twentieth century with a less activist government and a smaller welfare state.

Unfortunately, American workers turned to the market just at the moment when the market caused the very problems they sought to address. They yearned for the marketplace of the postwar boom years, with rising wages, a secure job, and businesses that really tried to balance the claims of employees, shareholders, and communities. Instead, they got a marketplace with declining wages, massive layoffs, and companies that readily abandoned their communities in search of cheaper labor overseas. *This* marketplace could not cure the economic predicaments of American workers, but they chose it nonetheless.[6]

In the twenty-first century, American workers and their families will need a new approach to their economic difficulties, which recognizes that the market—especially, the contemporary global market—will only confer its benefits on a small minority. For everyone else who hopes to enjoy a decent standard of living, assured economic security, and participation in a thriving democracy, other policies will be necessary. These policies will not be nearly so reverential of the market, but there is very little reason to remain reverential when any honest analysis of the results of this experiment must reckon with all the damage the market has done to most people's standard of living.

The Market Experiment: Breaking the Social Contract

Over the last twenty-five years, there have been two phases in the return to the marketplace. In the first phase, lasting from the early 1970s to the collapse of Communism in 1989, corporations altered the old understandings about both the workplace and social policy. During the 1950s and 1960s at least, corporations and workers had preserved an implicit agreement: jobs were stable, workers were permanent, full-time employees, and the pattern of work itself was fixed. Companies valued loyalty and length of tenure, promoted workers internally, and sought to create shareholder value through slow, steady growth. Beginning in the 1970s, however, increased competition shattered this compact. Change replaced stability, and a constantly shifting workforce with a heavy influx of temporary labor replaced a workforce that looked to the company for a lifetime career. Instead of promoting workers internally, corporations purchased high-skilled workers on the open labor market. They valued performance and skills, not loyalty and tenure, and emphasized mergers as the most rapid method of augmenting the company's worth. Where the old contract stressed a fair day's work for a fair day's pay, the new understanding contained no such reciprocity. Instead, employees tried to satisfy personal needs; employers tried to maximize corporate growth; and hopefully, with some effort, these divergent goals could be reconciled enough to produce a saleable product or service.[7]

The first phase also undid the postwar understanding about social policy, which assumed that corporations remained in the United States, paid their taxes, and accepted the use of those revenues for the training of a healthy, skilled, and educated workforce. Veterans' benefits, which enabled veterans of World War II to attend college, were part of this social contract; so, too, were laws such as the 1962 Manpower Development Training Act, enacted out of concern about the effects of technology and automation on the workplace, as well as the full cavalcade of Great Society social programs—Job Corps, Medicaid, and the Civil Rights Act of 1964.[8] As corporations became more mobile, however, their need for a specifically American workforce declined, and the old contract about social policy became obsolete. Less willing to shoulder their share of the burden of operating the U.S. government, they succeeded in reducing taxed corporate profits as a percentage of the gross domestic product from 8.3 percent in 1967 to 2.3 percent in 1996.[9] The social safety net was similarly rent. There was no need for a healthy, skilled, and educated American workforce if less expensive employees in Mexico or Taiwan could do the job, and U.S. corporations did not have to contribute much toward their social benefits.

The second phase began with the collapse of Communism in 1989. By then, business had already accumulated considerable power over workers. As a result, once President Clinton's health care package failed to gain approval, a tattered public sector could no longer contain the rush toward the market.

In Europe, the collapse of Communism had meant the destruction of the Berlin Wall and the breakup of the Soviet Union. In the United States, Communism was never a real social force, but its collapse nonetheless changed the dynamics of public policy. Once Communism died, all nonmarket alternatives became suspect. Moreover, without any real political alternative, some of the more palatable nonmarket policies—including many social programs of the welfare state—were no longer quite so essential. After the market had triumphed completely, the beneficiaries of these programs and those sympathetic to them had no place else to go.

If the absence of nonmarket alternatives signified the political triumph of the marketplace, its economic triumph was evident in the financial market's increasing domination of the economy. By the 1990s, the financial sector had swollen to an annual trading volume thirty to forty times greater than the dollar turnover of the "real economy," where ordinary Americans earned their livelihoods.[10] As a result, in 1998, there were more than 7400 mutual funds in the United States, and their holdings had topped $5 trillion, an increase of 130-fold in less than twenty-five years.[11]

Since the top 10 percent of the population owns 88 percent of all stock and 90 percent of all bonds, the financial boom of the 1990s strengthened their hand. It is true that in historical terms, the boom may be illusory: despite increases of 33, 26, 22, and 16 percent from 1995 to 1998, stocks did not recover enough from the bear market of 1966 to 1981 to reach their long-term average appreciation rate of about 7 percent.[12] There is no doubt, however, that for the affluent, the boom was politically empowering.

The affluent used their ascendancy for many purposes, but one was certainly to combat the threat of inflation. Inflation has several possible causes. It could occur because too much money was pursuing too few goods, or alternatively, because too many employers were pursuing too few workers. In late twentieth-century America, the financial sector fretted mostly about the latter prospect. Concerned that a rapidly expanding economy would raise the cost of labor, allies of the financial sector consistently demanded that the Federal Reserve Bank keep the growth rate down. In their judgment, slow, steady growth was vastly preferable to a perilous cycle of boom and bust. The Fed was responsive to their concerns. When unemployment threatened to decline too much, it clamped down on the supply of money by hiking interest rates seven times in one year.[13]

Early in the second phase, then, political alternatives had vanished, and the economic dominance of financial markets was all but complete. Yet there was still one issue whose resolution might have pointed in other political directions. That issue was the need for health care, with its familiar litany of problems. Although the United States is the only major country besides South Africa without a national health care program, it spends more per capita than any other nation and still leaves about one-sixth of the population uninsured. It also fares poorly in most international comparisons on health indices such as longevity and infant mortality.[14] In his 1992 presidential campaign, Clinton had connected statistics like these with Americans' increasing discontent about their health care system. Confronted with the dilemma of proposing a solution emphasizing either the market or the government, Clinton chose the government. He did so, however, with a 1300-page long proposal for managed competition that soon impaled itself on one of the worst features of modern American liberalism, the clumsy and excessively bureaucratic effort to mediate between government and the market.

In managed competition, doctors, hospitals, and insurers would form partnerships. The uninsured would get government subsidies to join these partnerships, and the partnerships themselves would compete on the basis of price, success, and consumer satisfaction. There were two key problems with this plan: one an issue of policy and the other a matter of politics. As an issue of policy, managed competition created the need for a cumbersome federal bureaucracy, because it merely superimposed the government on top of the existing market institutions in the health care field. As a matter of politics, managed competition suffered from a crippling disability: divorced from any popular movement for health care reform, it was strictly the brainchild of a small policy elite.

The policy deficiency of managed competition flowed from its conception. Designed by Alain C. Enthoven of the Stanford Business School and Paul Ellwood, a health economist with strong ties to insurance companies, managed care was the health care business's model of national health reform, one which would employ the government to rationalize, but not challenge, the industry.[15] Instead of free health care on the English model, or full reimbursement for it on the Canadian, managed care charged the government with the enormously complex task of supervising the market. And while competition would surely restructure that market, all the stipulations about what government could and could not do in relation to that market necessitated exactly the kind of large, ineffectual bureaucracy that has given the federal government such a bad name.

Not surprisingly, the Clinton plan quickly vaporized when the inevitable opposition arose. As the airy invention of experts, the plan had no grass-roots support. That gave Republicans an opening. Led by neoconservative strategist William Kristol, they launched "an aggressive and uncompromising counter-strategy" to stop the health care bill and foreclose all possibility of future federal interventions. As Kristol wrote in a memorandum to Republican leaders,

> [the bill]'s rejection by Congress and the public would be a monumental setback for the president, and an incontestable piece of evidence that Democratic welfare-state liberalism remains firmly in retreat. Subsequent replacement of the Clinton scheme by a set of ever-more ambitious, free-market initiatives would make this coming year's health policy debate a watershed in the resurgence of a newly bold and principled Republican politics.[16]

The Clinton administration had missed a historic opportunity. There had been a movement for national health care patterned on the single-payer model. In place of that movement, they offered a sterile, technocratic proposal that tied the government up in knots. For such a fatigued conception of government, very few people were willing to fight.[17]

After the battle for national health care, just about every solution to a major domestic problem had to be geared to the market. The campaign had relied on a complex social program to cultivate a modest sense of solidarity among the American people. When the campaign failed, it signaled that the very goal of social solidarity was suspect, and narrow self-interest was to govern everything. That is when the dam broke. Powerful interests already kept a tight lid on the economy. With other political options seemingly foreclosed, there were no significant obstacles left on the path to a market-based public policy.

Only one discordant fact contravened this decision. The problems of U.S. workers and their families—declining wages, declining social supports, and fragmenting communities—originated in the same marketplace that policy makers were so eagerly embracing. Desperate for some solution to their social and economic problems, most workers embraced these policies, too. Yet amid the omnipresent paradox of market-based solutions to market-created problems, their decision had—for themselves more than for anybody else—the most far-reaching consequences.

The Consequences of the Turn to the Market

The consequences of the race to the market cut across every aspect of political and economic life, including disinvestment in the public sector, the resulting imbalance in power between the market and the government, record levels of wealth and income inequality, and a politics of both gridlock and instability. The inability to lessen the growing economic insecurity of U.S. workers has bred a barely suppressed rage, which expresses itself most flamboyantly on talk radio. In its less flamboyant forms, it is merely the quiet "common sense" of some neighborhoods: what is wrong has gone wrong because of gays, immigrants, racial minorities, women on welfare, and the poor generally. The effect of this rage on public life is corrosive, not the least because its targets are so badly misplaced. Even with their power inflated many times, the targets of this rage are not responsible for the transformation of the U.S. economy from a national to a global capitalism.

Disinvestment

The first principle of this transformation requires disinvestment in the public sector. The contraction of this sector withdraws the kinds of supports that would ease the transition to a new economy and further accelerates the decline in the standard of living. For much of the business community, however, this consequence is quite beside the point. To them, the public sector is increasingly peripheral, unless it is willing to tender assistance on their terms.

The state of California provides an instructive illustration of this process on the local level. There, as elsewhere, major changes have disrupted the marketplace. The defense sector, in particular, has downsized dramatically. Looking for cheaper labor, Hughes Electronics transferred its missile operations from southern California to Arizona and Colorado. This loss comes on top of overall reductions in military spending, which were projected to cost 125,000 jobs from 1993 to 1997, including 90,000 in the aerospace industry alone. Similarly, a good computer circuit board designer in California earns from $60,000 to $100,000, but since the going rate in Taiwan is $25,000, and employers can get a Ph.D. for $10,000 in India and China, an entire category of white-collar professionals is now underbid overseas. Then there is the competition from Mexico, which is devastating for agricultural labor. At Pillsbury's Green Giant frozen vegetable factory in Watsonville, California, 270 workers lost their jobs, including many to the company's factory in Irapuato. Born not far from Irapuato, Yolanda Navarro was a legal alien who worked at the Green Giant plant, spraying hot butter sauce on broccoli. After working her way up to $8.10 an hour after twenty years, she could not compete with her counterparts south of the border who earn $7.58 a day. Her husband, who also worked at Green Giant, changes tires for $7.00 an hour, with no benefits. Popular wisdom to the contrary, it is market forces far bigger than their presence as legal aliens that have triggered such profound turmoil in the Californian economy.[18]

As corporations loosen their ties to the state of California, they have even less reason to contribute to the development and maintenance of the local infrastructure. In 1960, when the California economy was still relatively insulated from competition, the value of its infrastructure—roads, school, sanitation systems, and utilities relative to population—was 40 percent higher than the national average and third in the country. Over the next thirty years, however, its value per capita grew more slowly than other states, so that by 1990, it was 11 percent below average and ranked thirty-sixth. Proposition 13 in the late 1970s was the first response to this trend, but it merely capped local spending and made the situation worse; despite a 27 percent increase in the state's population, county property taxes and general purpose revenues were lower, after adjustment for inflation, in fiscal year 1988–89 than in 1977–78. It was these fiscal constraints that set the context for what happened to Orange County. Eager to find a tax-free stratagem for raising more money, it gambled on high-risk securities and went bankrupt.[19]

As the downward spiral continued, the mix of public spending changed, reaching a new milestone when, in 1994, for the first time, the state spent more money on corrections than for higher education. California's higher education system has long been its pride; in fact, just ten years earlier (1983–84), higher education had led corrections 10 percent to 4 percent as a share of the state budget. Since then, however, corrections had added 25,900 employees, more than all other state departments combined, while education has actually lost 8100 employees. The state built nineteen prisons during this period—"the largest prison construction effort in the history of the world," according to one state senator. The decision to incarcerate rather than educate human capital puts the public infrastructure to a most novel and unfortunate use; for the cost of incarcerating one prisoner for a year, California could educate ten community college students, five state college students, or two students at flagship campuses such as Berkeley or UCLA.[20]

Statistics like these evoke an image of the garrison state, where disinvestment has led to a sharp reduction in human resource spending, and a growing proportion of revenues goes to protecting people from one another. Since American corporations are connected to everywhere and nowhere, they have an ever more tenuous relationship with specific localities. This tenuousness disrupts patterns of worklife and shatters social cohesion. It creates a vacuum that the garrison state must fill.

The Imbalance Between the Private and Public Sector

The turn to the market also unbalances the relationship between the private and public sector. Because capital mobility leads so readily to disinvestment, it tilts the balance of power away from the government and toward the marketplace. It is all part of the race to the bottom; with businesses free to move any-where they choose, state governments compete to woo private investment with outsized tax breaks and hefty direct subsidies. Although its Supreme Court ruled that Alabama failed to provide students with an adequate educa-tion, the state nonetheless assembled a $300 million, $200,000 per job deal to lure a Mercedes-Benz plant. Amazingly, it initially tried to pay for the package with money from the state education fund. Similarly, even though Owens-Corning Fiberglass Corporation had been in Toledo, Ohio for fifty-seven years, it only stayed there because the $90 million subsidy package that the city and state put together beat competing offers from Dallas, St. Louis, and Monroe, Michigan. Other packages include $32 million to keep the Pratt & Whitney aircraft engine factory in Connecticut, and $20 million to bring 150 of McCormick & Company's spice warehouse jobs from Maryland to Pennsylva-nia. Yet perhaps the most direct purchase of jobs occurred in Tulsa, Oklahoma, which paid for 25 percent of the cost of the Whirlpool plant with a temporary hike in its own sales tax.[21]

It has always been assumed that when private investment went on sale, there was some rough correspondence between the size of the public subsidy and the number of jobs produced. As long as business was relatively stationary and no one got too rich at public expense, the policy was flawed but defensi-ble. These flaws are magnified, however, when business is able to set the terms of investment, and the benefits accruing to private parties dwarf those going to the public. One of the starkest examples of these skewed benefits occurred in 1993, when Michael Eisner, head of Disney Enterprises, negotiated $163 million in tax subsidies from the state of Virginia for the development of a Civil War theme park located near the site of the Bull Run battlefield. In the face of intense opposition, Disney eventually canceled plans for the park. Still, amid all the debate about the propriety of "theme parking" the Civil War, few noticed that the same year, Disney paid Eisner $203 million. As Disney's chief executive officer, Eisner could therefore have funded the entire state subsidy out of his own pocket and still gone home with $40 million.[22]

Inequality of Wealth and Income

The growing inequality of private wealth is another consequence of embracing the market. It is, in some sense, the natural obverse of the poverty of the public sector: the richest 1 percent of Americans now have 39 percent of net national wealth. This level is almost unprecedented in the United States during the twentieth century, exceeded only by the period immediately prior to the Depression. The assets of the top group did decline between 1945 and 1976, by 10 percent, but this trend reversed once the United States turned to the market. The most recent gains spread especially unequally. Between 1983 and 1995, the top 1 percent's share rose by 3.8 percent, with the next four percent gaining very slightly, and the bottom 95 percent showing an absolute decline.[23]

The market has also fostered record modern levels of income inequality. Much discussed in recent years, this trend has been with us for so long that we tend to forget the pattern of postwar wage increases, which were supposed to last until the end of the twentieth century. Indeed, in 1967, at the height of the boom, *Fortune* magazine predicted wages would rise another 150 percent by the year 2000. Just five years later, however, income began to decline. The optimism faded quickly: by the mid-1980s, Wall Street economists were projecting that wages in the United States would erode for another quarter century.[24] This time, unfortunately, their prediction was right. Soon, pay raises became modest and scarce, replaced instead by one-shot bonuses, stock, and unbankable forms of recognition such as plaques, theater tickets, and thank-you notes like the 50,000 Federal Express sent in 1992 for a job well done. In one 1993 study, the number of companies relying on such practices tripled from 20 to 60 percent between 1988 and 1993.[25]

Median household income has suffered accordingly. The Census Bureau first determined median household income in 1967. From 1973 to 1994, it dropped by 2.2 percent, from $33,006 to $32,264. As the downward trend picked up speed, the typical American household lost income at an accelerating rate. Between 1989—the beginning of the second phase of the turn to the market—and 1994, it lost 6.3 percent or $2200 of its income. So steep was this slide that by 1994, the top fifth of the population was the only segment to have recovered from the 1990 recession. In fact, even as the economic recovery helped some employees make up lost ground, the earnings of the median worker in 1997 were still 3.1 percent less than in 1989.[26]

This decline in the middle, however, only partly captures what has happened at the extremes. In the late 1970s, no state yet had disparities so large that the top fifth of families with children received ten or more times the income of the bottom fifth. By the mid-1990s, however, this ratio existed in thirty states, and the ratio in New York, the state with the most unequal income distribution, approached 20 to 1. New York was, in fact, the only state where the top 20 percent of the population broke the 50 percent barrier—that is, one-fifth of the population garnered half of the income. During the same period, the income of the poorest fifth declined in forty-four states, including ten states where it plunged more than 30 percent. Arizona, with a 44 percent drop, led this race to the bottom.[27]

Amid all this data about income, nothing is more startling than the broad decline in wages. Between 1973 and 1997, the average hourly wage of production and nonsupervisory workers fell from $13.40 to $12.26. This long-term drop reached truly historic proportions, when, during one period from March 1994 to March 1995, average wages for civilian workers slumped 2.3 percent, and total compensation—both wages and benefits—slid 3 percent. According to Bradford DeLong, now a Berkeley economist and formerly assistant secretary for policy analysis at the Treasury, this outcome was possibly the largest one-year plunge since the introduction of power looms in the textile industry during the 1840s.[28]

Less skilled workers led this decline. Between 1979 and 1997, wages went down 30 percent for male high school dropouts, 17 percent for male high school graduates, 16 percent for female high school dropouts, and 3 percent for female high school graduates. At the bottom tenth of the wage distribution, real hourly wages dropped 15 percent between 1979 and 1997.[29] Racial disparities further steepened the downward slope. Although the mean earnings of white male high school dropouts fell by one-third between 1973 and 1989, the mean earnings of black male high school dropouts fell by nearly half.[30]

Among workers, one key factor depressing wages is the decline in union membership. In 1997, nonunion members received a median wage of $478 a week, while members of unions earned $640 or 25 percent more. Since unions now represent 14 percent of the labor force, down from the 27 percent they represented in the early 1970s, a much smaller percentage of workers are currently receiving the union differential. This trend accounts for about one-fifth of the growth in male wage inequality.[31]

For families at least, the entry of women into the labor force has partly mitigated the effects of this widening income gap. According to a survey by Louis Harris & Associates, employed married women provided 48 percent of their families' financial support in 1993. Since nearly 60 percent of women worked outside the home, the income of wives has accounted for two-thirds of the increase in the average income of couples. While taxes and work-related expenditures offset up to one-half of these additional earnings, and the absence of a full-time parent has transformed the internal dynamics of family life, the participation of women in the labor force is one of the few factors impeding the trend toward greater inequality of income.[32]

Among the upper reaches of income, the group whose remuneration has probably received the greatest scrutiny are chief executive officers. The real average after-tax income of American wage and salary workers may have fallen 13 percent in the 1970s and 1980s, but the real average after-tax income of CEOs rose 400 percent. In 1973–75, the CEOs of ten typically large companies earned forty-one times the wage of their average factory worker. By 1996, however, this ratio had risen to 209. In 1996, compensation for the ten highest paid CEOs ranged from $33.7 million for James Moffett of Freeport-McMoran Copper and Gold up to the $102.4 million received by Lawrence Coss of Green Tree Financial. Had workers' salaries inflated at the same rate during the previous fifteen years, the typical factory worker would now be earning $90,000 a year, and the income from a minimum wage job would yield $39,000 annually.[33]

Admittedly, these salaries often represent a relative pittance for a multibillion dollar corporation. Indeed, such sums have even been said to "purify decision-making": as Sherry Lansing, the head of Paramount Pictures stated, "The only way you can perform in a job is if you don't need it."[34] Quite apart from the issue of whether in an era of corporate restructuring, this principle constitutes a better personnel philosophy for a company's line workers or its CEO, the remuneration paid to chief executive officers correlates more closely with the salaries of the members of the compensation committee than it does with actual performance. And since chief executives often have a substantial influence in the selection of a board of directors who then in turn help to determine the CEOs' pay, the chief executives of large corporations have successfully created a small, self-enclosed market whose principles diverge quite noticeably from the market that ostensibly compels them to lay off so many employees.[35]

By comparison, foreign corporate executives receive much less. In France, England, and other European nations, CEOs generally get about one-third of their U.S. counterparts, or less than $1 million dollars. In Japan, CEOs earn under half of that sum, which yields a ratio of executive to worker income of just 17 to 1.[36] Once again, international competition may establish a market that drives down wages for workers, but it does not seem to affect executive salaries.

In reality, then, these compensation rates are only the most conspicuous example of the power of business over workers. Manifested most plainly in larger corporate profits and greater success in restraining wage growth, this power has produced the highest before-tax capital income since the 1960s. The shift upward has had portentous consequences. If the return on capital had been the same in 1994 and 1995 as it was during the average of the best years from 1959 to 1979, the hourly compensation of workers would have been 3.6 percent higher. The magnitude of this loss is equal in size to the presumed effect of factors such as the shift to services, globalization, or deunionization, and it is seven times stronger than the 0.5 percent that the Congressional Budget Office projects as the positive result of a balanced budget.[37]

This explosion of inequality has put conservatives on the defensive. Falling back on the old American belief in upward mobility, they insist that any individual can still climb rapidly upward despite the broad social trend. Former Federal Reserve Board Governor Lawrence Lindsey stated this position in its purest form when he said, "The rising share of the top 1% means that there was a lot of income mobility in America during the 1980s."[38]

Both research and common sense suggest otherwise. In any given year, two-thirds of poor people are likely to be poor next year, and another 26 percent are going to have incomes just one to two times the poverty level. Altogether, that means 91 percent of poor people are going to have incomes less than twice the poverty level, hardly a movement into the middle class. Similarly, there is, in any five-year period, only a 10 percent likelihood of vaulting from the poor to the middle class, that is, literally, from the bottom to the middle fifth of the income distribution.[39] Here is where common sense dovetails with research. In a global economy where high incomes generally require a high level of skill, the likelihood of much movement from below seems quite slight.

It is true that as the demand for skilled labor has swept through the global economy, it has exacerbated income inequality in nearly every country. In a study of the Organization for Economic Cooperation and Development (OECD) member nations, every country except the Netherlands experienced an increase in earnings at the eightieth and ninetieth percentiles. In Canada, the growth in the inequality of market income was even larger than the United States, but social policies helped buffer Canadian families from the effects of the market.[40] The United States has a much higher incidence of low pay than most other OECD countries, with more than one-quarter of all full-time workers earning less than two-thirds of the median income, and its poverty rate for nonaged households is over twice Sweden and Germany's, nearly double that of France, and 45 percent higher than the United Kingdom. Single mothers also fare much worse in this country.[41] With the United States doing so poorly in all these comparisons, it is hardly surprising that income inequality here is now greater than in any other major industrialized country.[42]

Although inequality is one of the most indisputable consequences of the turn to the market, public discussion of the issue has often veiled or obscured its import. Undoubtedly, many factors contributed to wage inequality: the increasing mobility of capital, corporate downsizing, declining unionization, trade deficits, and winner-take-all markets, where a few stars in every profession take a disproportionate share of the income.[43] Lists like these are very useful for discrete analyses of the individual factors contributing to the growth of inequality: an analysis that focuses on corporate downsizing or the mobility of capital alone is sure to be more finely grained. Still, singling out any one of these factors for closer examination sometimes fragments the picture so much that we forget they are all market-related phenomena. Academic treatments seldom mention this truth; popular discussions almost never do.[44]

In the popular media, a special issue of *U.S. News and World Report* typifies this approach. Organized around the theme of "Is the American Worker Getting Shafted? The Assault on the Middle Class," the magazine contains several articles on wage inequality. The articles include all the pertinent descriptive data—the number of Americans who have lost jobs, their difficulties obtaining employment that pays a comparable wage, even the danger that the widening gap between rich and poor might lead to a "worker backlash." Yet when the magazine talks about causes, the causes it cites are themselves largely descriptions rather than explanations of what has happened: the decline in the rate of productivity growth or the change in average earnings of poorly educated men. These may be manifestations of the growth in inequality, but they are not its cause. The overarching cause—a market-based economy with outcomes that social policy has been ever more strictly prohibited from modifying—is not mentioned. In this article, as in most other journalistic treatments, the market's invisible hand truly does remain invisible.[45]

Inequality squeezes workers and their families: they can sense the downward pressure. Yet the media treatment of this issue muddies the political implication of what they are experiencing. They desperately want someone in power to put a halt to their downward mobility, but all the prescribed remedies only seem to make their predicament worse. As their standard of living drifts lower, they do not know which political party to blame.

Political Instability

As Americans have turned toward the market, the economic condition of U.S. workers and their families has bred a political malaise that oscillates between instability and gridlock. A quarter of a century of downward mobility makes a huge political target: from election to election, the party out of power can always run on the slogan that things used to be better. It is true that they were better; it is also true that the position of the United States in the global economy is no longer unchallenged; but most important, it is true that this is a world-historical fact which no candidate can alter.

This is not to suggest politics makes no difference. It does, but sometimes political and economic forces outside the control of Congress and the president limit the difference it can make. When others have power, what American public officials do is still important, but no longer quite so decisive. In describing this loss of omnipotence, former Fed Chairman Paul Volcker quoted the words of an old friend of his from abroad. Volcker's career, the friend said, was really "a long saga of trying to make the decline of the United States in the world respectable and orderly."[46]

This decline in U.S. power further contributes to political instability. Not only is there growth in domestic income inequality, but the United States as a nation is also heading downward from controlling more than 40 percent of the world's wealth at the end of World War II, toward a more natural rate, based on geography, population, and natural resources, of 16–18 percent.[47] The top fifth of the U.S. population, which had skills of greater value in the global economy, succeeded in making the argument that a turn to the market was the best way to regain U.S. economic strength. Yet in making this argument, it also took for itself a bigger portion of what is gradually becoming a smaller share of total world income. This share is still significant, so that by 1997, 50 families and 150 individuals had become billionaires.[48] Nevertheless, when what is left must be divided among the other four-fifths, it strains the capacity of the entire political system.

Under these circumstances, it is hard to obtain a clear sense of political direction from the American electorate. The Clinton presidency follows the

Bush presidency, but then in 1994, the Republicans take over Congress. In 1996, Clinton is reelected, only to be threatened with impeachment two years later. Torn between a desire to regain the traditional values that the market has obliterated and an economic populism whose choice of targets varies between the government and an economic elite, the U.S. electorate thrashes about, quick to anger but unsure for more than one election cycle about its quarry.

Mutability of political sentiments among the electorate heightens the tendency toward gridlock. The U.S. political system is already significantly decentralized, with separation of powers dividing authority among institutions of the federal government and a two-century long history of contested power between the federal government and the states. When a shifting electorate fails to establish conclusively who exercises power, it accentuates this tendency toward decentralization and fuels conflict throughout the political system. By now, the parties are often too weak to resolve these conflicts, so politics assumes the form of a battle between institutions. Whether it is an independent prosecutor investigating the president, Congress questioning the usefulness of the federal bureaucracy, or the executive branch casting aspersions on Congress, all these institutions seek, in turn, to undermine each other. Inevitably, these attacks succeed in weakening the government, leaving it with a diminished capacity to govern and to address the political and economic issues that angered so many people in the first place.[49]

The Loss of Work and the "Loss" of China

The consequences of embracing the market have bewildered many Americans. They simply do not understand how they could have lost the old system of work relations. Once they had stable jobs, decent pay, and the likelihood of upward mobility. Then, in less than a generation, it all vanished without a trace. No one consulted them about this process, and few show much interest in what has happened to them afterward. They are, quite simply, in shock, and it is a loss that has shaken them and their system of belief to the core.

One has to go back to the aftermath of World War II for a comparable political trauma. The United States won the war, and despite an intensifying conflict with the Soviet Union in Europe, its dominance was assumed, perhaps as much in Asia as anywhere in the world. Then, in 1949, after victory over the Kuo-mintang, the Chinese Communists swept into Beijing. This event was totally inexplicable: How could the world's most populous country choose Communism over free enterprise? Although a serious analysis of China's political and economic history might have offered some insight, many Americans looked elsewhere for an explanation of why their world had turned upside down. The United States had "lost" China, Joseph McCarthy said, because there were 205 (or 150 or 79) Communists in the State Department.

For the next five years, the United States underwent a political paroxysm searching for those Communists in American society and government whose existence would explain why we could not enjoy a longer period of peace and serenity in the aftermath of such a hard-fought war.

Fast-forward forty years—the political paroxysm precipitated from the loss of work begins to look a lot like the political paroxysm precipitated from the "loss" of China. In both instances, a seemingly inexplicable event shattered assumptions that many held dear and launched a feverish search for culprits. This time, however, the search is not for Communists, but for those who are thought to deviate from "values" like stability, community, and responsibility that are said to embody an earlier set of work relations.[50] Like the political paroxysms of the 1950s, this search is diversionary: such values are going to be hard to come by in a new global capitalism that is neither stable, rooted in particular communities, nor responsible to anything much besides the dictates of the market. Nevertheless, the search does have one psychological advantage: unlike a distant and impersonal economy, its targets—gays, people of color, the poor, welfare recipients, immigrants, and single women with children—are people over whom others may exercise control, a control that cannot be so easily exercised over a powerful and resistant marketplace.

A recent survey of worker attitudes captures the psychopolitical implications of this phenomenon. Joel Rogers and Richard Freeman asked 2408 adult workers to choose between two hypothetical employee organizations. One organization had the cooperation of management in discussing issues, but no power to make decisions; the other had more power, but management opposed it. By a 63 percent to 21 percent margin, workers opted for the weaker organization. A remarkable 73 percent even said that employee organizations can only be effective if management cooperates.[51]

This study offers ready access to the minds of the American workers. They know that in the current political environment, employers have far more power and that if they wish, they can fire workers at will. No wonder eight out of ten employees agreed with the statement that "the average American business cares more about profits and less about people."[52] Steeped in consciousness of their own weakness, American workers nonetheless remain dependent upon employers for satisfaction of their material needs. It is, essentially, a hostage situation, and just as in many other hostage situations, it can make the hostages unnaturally solicitous about their captor's well-being. That is why they want employers to do well, even if they do not have much faith that they will benefit personally.

Still, since their anger about their own weakness must go somewhere, they scapegoat others. Scapegoating proves that even if they are dependent upon their employers, at least they have more power than some people. It also puts their trustworthiness on conspicuous display. Clearly, as long as they direct their anger at scapegoats, they will never strike the hand that feeds them.

Promises of Improvement: The Postwar Solutions to Economic Difficulty

In the past, whenever inflation threatened or recessions loomed, economists have soothed peoples' anxieties with talk of growth, greater productivity, or a heavier reliance on the market. Caught between their dependence on business and their alarm at the prospect of further downward mobility, American workers and their families have been receptive to the notion that at least one of these prescriptions would work. The talk may be reassuring, but the problem is that none of these remedies seems very likely to succeed now.

Promises of more rapid "economic growth" have long been the classic form of reassurance. If unemployment rose, or some groups of people were lagging behind, a faster rate of growth was supposed to solve the problem. More recently, however, the economic growth strategy has fallen on hard times. Fearful of triggering a new round of inflation, a large segment of the U.S. business community does not want the economy to grow any faster; when the economy does expand too rapidly, the Federal Reserve Bank simply tightens the reins. Faster economic growth also means a quicker transition to high-skilled labor and technology. Without programs tailored to their specific needs, such a strategy will certainly leave the unskilled poor further behind and may well speed downward mobility among a broad spectrum of the middle class.[53]

Once the economy began to slow in the 1970s and 1980s, greater productivity replaced growth as the ostensible path to prosperity for U.S. workers. Productivity growth had indeed slowed, from 2.8 percent between 1959 and 1973 to .9 percent from 1973 to 1990.[54] Still, for greater productivity to yield higher wages, business must pass the gains from that productivity to labor through larger earnings. In the 1990s, corporate downsizing and the introduction of technology has nudged the increase in real output per hour to 1.2 percent per year. Yet, because business has gained so much power over labor, real compensation per hour has lagged behind at just .6 percent.[55]

Because both growth and the need for increased worker productivity have lost their power to reassure, the promise of economic prosperity must take a new form. That new form is the turn to the market. Economic growth did bring a fairly high level of prosperity for awhile. Increased worker productivity would help, too, if the gains were more equitably shared. The turn to the market will bring more prosperity to already affluent Americans, but despite all the promises that are made for it, it will not bring much prosperity to anybody else.

Economic Security in the Global Marketplace

In addition to stagnation and downward mobility, the market has also made two of our oldest political conversations obsolete. The first political conversation held that middle-income Americans might occasionally have some economic difficulties, but if they worked hard and played by the rules, they would improve their standard of living. Theirs would be a triumph of diligence, resourcefulness, practicality, and character.

A second political conversation—about the poor—was also about character, except that *their* character was entirely the wrong sort. Lazy, dependent, and profligate, they were classified according to the language of the era as either undeserving, immersed in the culture of poverty, or members of a destructive underclass.[56] In essence, they failed because they lacked willpower, and they lacked morality.

Although each of these two conversations has the weight of history behind it, the economic basis for keeping them separate and distinct dwindles further every day. The U.S. economy has compressed the bottom four-fifths of the population, creating a common interest that bears down with increasing force. This interest may not be acted on or even perceived. There are, after all, many differences—social, cultural, and racial—from the top to the bottom of the group.[57] Still, actual economic conditions could nurture the perception that they share more in common than they do with an affluent elite. Now, for the first time in recent U.S. history, it may be possible to address both groups of people through the language of economic insecurity.

What to say, however, needs to be clearer. The old welfare state—that bedraggled child of the New Deal and the Great Society—is obsolete, because the mobility of business has severed the contract between it and the social needs of the American people. The power equation is not favorable, either: like the last decades of the nineteenth century, the first decades of the twenty-first century may be one of those historical periods in which economic elites prevail. Nevertheless, we must proceed, aware that any reconstitution of the social order is going to involve some constraints on markets as well as new roles for government and the corporation.

Education, job training, and income supports such as public assistance are the three policy areas that are particularly crucial to this reengineering. Education and job training once gave people hope; income supports once provided them with the minimal essentials for survival. By offering some possibility of upward mobility, these policies supplied much of the social glue that held the society together. In the new, global economy, however, they are less able to perform this function: when companies can move, and many U.S. businesses are committed to a low-wage, low-skilled strategy, social programs will flounder. The creation of a less hostile environment is therefore key to ensuring their success. And ultimately, that will mean empowering workers and making them secure, through democratization of the economy and more universalistic social policies.

2

Business Moves:
Markets, Nations,
and Inequality

> The countries that do not make themselves attractive will not get
> investors' attention. This is like a girl trying to get a boyfriend.
> She has to go out, have her hair done, wear makeup.
>
> —*David Mulford, undersecretary of the treasury*
> *in the Bush administration*

> Let's keep our factories and jobs here and move our corporate
> headquarters to Mexico, Korea, or wherever else we can get some
> reasonably priced chief executives.
>
> —*Jim Hightower*

The triumph of the market has eroded most Americans' standard of living. It
has rent the safety net and exacerbated inequality. If it had just happened in
the United States, the triumph of the market would have made these outcomes possible. In a global economy, the increasing mobility of business
made these outcomes likely.

Of course, the ability to move has always been a decisive factor in determining the relative power of employers and employees. Although they need
each other, it is generally easier for an employer to hire another worker than it
is for an employee to "hire" another boss. To nurture a stable relationship,
each must remain stationary. When one can move without the other, that
party is free to contract on better terms with somebody else and thereby gains
leverage. It was this fear that led employers to place strict regulations on the
movement of free laborers when the system of labor for wages first began to
spread in fourteenth-century England.[1]

Capital could always move, too, and it did, though usually toward new business enterprises. Profits from agriculture could be invested in industry; those from shipping in railroads. While shifts in capital investment from one industry to another still happen today, it is capital's new ability to shift production *of the very same product* from one place to another that so dramatically enhances employers' power. Employers once tried to keep their workers stationary; now, workers would like to keep their employers in the same place. In both the past and present, however, employers had the upper hand and could pursue the business strategy that best kept labor costs down.

Competitiveness drives mobility. In price-conscious markets, newly industrialized countries can undersell the United States, paying wages a fraction of our own. In quality-conscious markets, the increased capacity for diversity and customization of new microprocessor-based technologies has cut the cost-advantages of mass production.[2] Between competition on price and competition on quality, the impregnable fortress that once was the U.S. economy is no longer.

Part of the disorientation that U.S. workers experience stems from the speed of this change. In 1964, Lester Thurow, now professor of economics at the Massachusetts Institute of Technology and author of several best-selling books on economic issues, was a staff economist on President Lyndon Johnson's Council of Economic Advisors. Asked to prepare the forecast for the president's 1965 economic report, Thurow drafted his analysis and projections. The entire analysis did not mention the rest of the world.[3]

Such an omission would be impossible today. Not only has international trade expanded by 6 percent a year since 1950—more than 50 percent faster than the growth in world GDP—but the United States has led the way. Between 1970 and 1995, its proportion of trade to domestic output more than doubled, from 10 percent to 24 percent, the largest increase in any developed economy during that period, and well on the way to the 40 percent figure projected for 2006. Exports as a share of real GDP increased from under 5 to 11.6 percent from 1985 to 1992, or 95 percent in real terms; imports have likewise increased and now are at a postwar high of 13.2 percent. All together, these numbers mean that although domestic production for domestic use still accounts for about three-quarters of the economy, international trade has made significant inroads.[4]

In fact, the whole concept of international trade is really only one part of the process of globalization—trade in the actual manufacturing and assembly of goods. Facilitated by a raft of trade agreements like the North American Free Trade Agreement (NAFTA) and the General Agreement on Trade and Tariffs (GATT), this kind of globalization has lowered trade barriers and moved us all one large step closer to the establishment of a genuinely international marketplace. Under GATT, for example, the U.S. and Europe will cut tariffs by half on average on each others' goods. By 2000, according to the OECD, this reduction will bring about a $270 billion increase, or almost a 1 percent gain, in total world income.[5]

A second meaning of globalization is entirely different. It refers to "paper entrepreneurialism" and the growth of international financial markets. Dwarfing the growth of trade in manufactured goods, these financial markets draw on the $20 trillion of swaps, options, and other derivatives that circulate around the world. Investors speculate on minute spreads in global interest rates, as well as in foreign currency exchanges that are now trading $2.5 trillion a day. The technological revolution in banking has helped to propel this growth in speculative capacity. When Chemical Bank purchased Chase Manhattan, it acquired the $130 million center in Bournemouth, England that Chase had constructed to process transactions from around the world. A satellite network connects this 323,000-square foot facility to offices in New York, Hong Kong, Luxembourg, and Tokyo; the telecommunications lines to London can transmit the equivalent of the city's telephone directory in 90 seconds. The total value of all transactions it handles reaches trillions of dollars a year, and the money naturally tends to go where more of it can be made most rapidly. In essence, the financial markets are now so interlocked it is estimated that political and economic changes elsewhere account for 80 percent of the turbulence in a given market. As a result, a rise of interest rates in New York can easily spark a sell-off in Mexico.[6]

This search for the highest rate of profit often deprives some countries of funds. In the early 1990s, Sweden, Canada, Italy, and Spain were deeply in debt and faced a capital shortage. U.S. investors, however, were notably uninterested. Instead, from 1990 to the end of 1993, they absorbed a net $127 billion in the then-booming Asian and Latin American markets. In 1993, the Philippine market rose 133 percent, while Hong Kong, Indonesia, Malaysia, Thailand, and Brazil roughly doubled. Poland was up the most—718 percent, but Turkey gained 214 percent, and Zimbabwe rose 123 percent. Countries that were deeply in debt simply could not compete with speculative opportunities like these.[7]

As the capacity to speculate increases, however, so do the risks. Some of the major financial accidents have befallen Hedgefund manager George Soros, who lost $600 million by betting against a strong Japanese yen; Procter & Gamble, which lost $102 million on leveraged derivatives purchased from Bankers Trust Co.; and Nick Leeson, an unsupervised twenty-eight-year-old stock trader who bet a total of $27 billion, mostly on differences in futures contracts between Singapore and Osaka. Leeson lost $1.3 billion and bankrupted his employer, Barings P.L.C., a British investment firm that was 233 years old.[8]

Such losses are both symptoms and causes. They are symptoms of a speculative fervor that internationalizes the search for the most rewarding financial opportunities. This search leads to a winner-take-all phenomenon, where investment surges toward a few economic hotspots not only in one nation, but also around the world. Yet this phenomenon also has a downside: since the money cannot be in two places at the same time, the trend toward winner-take-all tends to foster inequality. Nations deemed to lack investment opportunities are left behind; companies whose bets turned out badly lay off workers. The judgment of the global marketplace is volatile, quick, and stern. Economically, it is the ultimate arbiter; politically, it is a threat to democracy, curtailing the independence and authority of the modern nation-state that has prevailed for the last two hundred years.

The Decline of the Nation-State

We must not romanticize the nation-state. In a century wracked by nationalism and war, millions of people have been killed in its name. Yet one characteristic of the nation-state may soon fill us with nostalgia: unlike the multinational corporation, votes could modify its behavior. That right has effectively been lost when General Motors' 1995 sales exceeded the gross domestic product of 169 countries, and the fifteen largest global corporations have gross incomes greater than the gross domestic product of 120.[9]

To be sure, economic status affected the citizen's political power within the nation-state. Although each had one vote, a major corporation's CEO always had more political power than a line worker in the same company. The global marketplace, however, transforms the absence of economic democracy within the nation-state into an overarching principle. Now citizens who have only some power have less, and those who used to possess greater power have much more. Finance capital can curb government's ability to tax, spend, borrow, or depreciate debt through inflation. As Nicholas P. Sargen, managing director of Global Advisors in Newark, New Jersey stated: "Who says you have to be elected to influence policy? The market is saying to policy makers, 'We're your watchdog.' "[10]

In effect, globalization of the economy has sharpened the conflict between the specifically national origins of social policies and the international scope of the economy that is supposed to provide the revenues on which those policies rest. The social democratic welfare state founders on this conflict. Without an assured and consistent source of funds, it must steadily diminish social protections. It can still raise an army, and it can still enact laws about violent crime. Nations, however, must be extremely cautious about enacting any law with significant economic restrictions, because someone, somewhere else, will surely be willing to perform the same task for less pay and with fewer burdensome regulations.

This need for the global marketplace's approval erodes the nation-state's sovereignty. If power no longer resides with governments, citizens cannot expect to hold them accountable. If governments have increasingly become "regulation-takers rather than regulation-makers," then agreements between them are pacts between subordinate rather than supreme powers. People still have an allegiance to their national governments, and it is possible that the loss of real control could foster a resurgence of tribal nationalism. What they really need, however, are international institutions that express the preferences of something other than major actors in the global marketplace. Unfortunately, these international institutions do not yet exist, at least partly because there is no widely recognized need for them in the conventional theory of free trade.[11]

Free Trade

In theory, free trade is like "free labor" or "free enterprise": a contractual agreement or understanding between parties to engage in some mutually beneficial economic activity with minimal interference from others. The key word, of course, is "free." Because "free laborers" contracted independently with their employers, they did not need a trade union.[12] Because "free enterprise" limits the role of the state, it assumes that people are free to enter into the economic activity of their choice. When nations adopt a policy of free trade, the trade that occurs "is a spontaneous reaction to different costs and prices, and to changes in income."[13] In "free trade," as in the parallel misnomers "free labor" and "free enterprise," politics and power are both absent.

This omission persists today. Perhaps the best known contemporary defender of free trade is Paul Krugman, professor of economics at the Massachusetts Institute of Technology. Krugman is the author of *Pop Internationalism*, a fierce rebuttal to those who in recent years have exaggerated the deleterious effects of free trade. Emphasizing that 70 percent of U.S. trade occurs with other high wage countries, Krugman disputes the contention that free trade is primarily responsible for declining U.S. wages. And summoning the full authority of the academy's understanding about international trade, he dismisses the pantheon of authors like Robert Reich, Lester Thurow, and Clyde Prestowitz who have worried at length and in public about its implications for the U.S. economy. For Krugman, "international trade is not about competition, it is about mutually beneficial exchange."[14]

Krugman's views constitute a useful corrective to the easy invocation of globalization as the primary cause of America's economic difficulties. Yet his refusal to acknowledge that international trade does contribute to some inequality has prompted criticism from supporters of free trade who believe we should address its problems more honestly. As the Council for Foreign Relations warns,

> economists are confident that the gains to the gainers generally exceed the losses to the losers. But that only guarantees that an economy's

mean standard of living rises. The problem is that the economy's median standard of living—the living standard of the most typical income earner in the very middle of the income distribution—may not rise. Defined this way, global integration may not benefit the typical citizen. And the broader economic problem is that global integration may not benefit middle-class citizens as a group.[15]

Krugman takes another approach. Confident that trade with foreign countries merely represents the international dimension of a self-regulating market, he adopts a narrowly econometric understanding of the data. The realities of power and conflict are missing from his numbers. When, for example, a corporation involved in labor negotiations threatens to outstation production, it gains leverage in its struggle with the union. If the union is then compelled to accept lower pay, the mere threat of imports has driven down wages without a single item ever passing through customs. Hence, notwithstanding the theory of some academic economists, it is both international trade and the threat of international trade that contributes to shrinking wages.

Histories of free trade have also excluded politics. In the past, nations have generally been loath to adopt a policy of free trade, unless they were sure of their comparative advantage. Comparative advantage, however, is constructed as well as inherent. As David Ricardo's classical theory contends, it may be genuinely inherent in a country, as a result of climate, geography, or resources. Unlike the classical theory, however, nations can also create comparative advantage, as Britain did when it used its political power to impede the growth of the Portuguese textile industry.[16] Obviously, much trade does occur between equally powerful countries. Nevertheless, nations that deploy the ideology of free trade are usually the ones that already have a distinct political edge.

Strip away the rhetoric of free trade, and it was clearly the desire to protect industries so that they might prosper and grow—not any interest in getting the prices right—that nurtured the development of most successful economies. Although this view, which lay clearly outside the boundaries of mainstream economics, has begun to make some inroads, it is still a minority opinion. Thus, McKinsey & Company, the international business consultants, concedes that while temporary trade barriers have not helped, except in one industry (cars in the U.S.), the Japanese did protect their infant auto, computer, metalworking, and consumer electronics industries until they could compete on their own. This acknowledgment is consistent with a larger revision in the history of free trade. Where once free trade was always assumed to benefit great economic powers like Holland, Britain, and the United States, now the evidence suggests it helps them on the upswing and also speeds their decline.[17]

The content of trade has changed in the new, global capitalism. Recent agreements to liberalize it go far beyond the traditional purpose of reducing quotas and tariffs for nonagricultural goods. Now they include categories like creation of international property rights for intellectual innovators and foreign investors. Since these agreements establish new restrictions on government intervention, they will have the clear effect of reducing transnational corporations' uncertainty and risk. National laws, policies, and customs that stand in the way of international investment are falling by the wayside. Under NAFTA, for example, no state can require a foreign investor to transfer a technology or mandate that a share of the materials used in production be purchased locally. Given their actual content and purpose, it is a misnomer to call such arrangements "free trade," when free capital would probably be a more accurate designation.[18]

The pattern of international trade has changed, too. Instead of firms in one country trading with firms in another, corporations have sought to reorganize on the basis of concentration without centralization. They make financial and technology deals with other corporations, with governments, and with legions of smaller firms who act as their suppliers and contractors. They create a complex of subsidiaries, networks, and alliances that transcend national borders. Major American corporations such as AT&T, for example, have paid tens of millions of dollars to leading business consultants like McKinsey & Company to find strategic parties abroad. As a forward-looking international consultant, McKinsey had prepared itself well for this task: between 1990 and 1994, it opened one new office in the United States and nineteen overseas.[19]

The expanding web of multinational networks means that 40 percent of trade is now intrafirm.[20] Inevitably, the growth of this trade has generated a vigorous debate about "who is us?" This debate has two dimensions. One dimension revolves around the increasing difficulty of determining the national content of any given product. Robert Reich puts the matter this way:

> Precision ice hockey equipment is designed in Sweden, financed in Canada, and assembled in Cleveland and Denmark for distribution in North America and Europe, respectively, out of alloys whose molecular structure was researched and patented in Delaware and fabricated in Japan. An advertising campaign is conceived in Britain; film footage for it is shot in Canada, dubbed in Britain, and edited in New York. A sports car is financed in Japan, designed in Italy, and assembled in Indiana, Mexico, and France, using advanced electronic components invented in New Jersey and fabricated in Japan.[21]

Planned, constructed, and assembled in many different places, these examples illustrate how fewer and fewer products have a single national origin.

Since the offshore divisions of U.S. companies have become increasingly lucrative, the diffusion of both production and profit would seem to strengthen Reich's argument that national origin is of little importance. Still, although the trend he identifies is certainly clear, Reich makes too much of its implications. As Laura Tyson, formerly Clinton's chair of the Council of Economic Advisers, has contended, most of the total output of U.S. multinationals continues to be produced within the United States. The component parts of multinationals may be proliferating rapidly, but they are not yet so interchangeable that the U.S. government should be giving direct aid in product sales to Japanese-based corporations.[22]

The second issue in the "who is us" involves a different, but related, matter. Here the question is not which multinational enterprise belongs to "us," but rather the whole concept of an undifferentiated "us," who will all benefit from free trade—either immediately, through cheaper prices, or from job growth over the longer haul. As confidence diminishes in the absolute certainty of this outcome, it is time to acknowledge that a policy of free trade may in fact be counterposed to a number of other worthy economic goals, including full employment at decent wages, maintenance of a skilled workforce, and rising levels of equitably distributed real income. We need some new theories about international trade to grapple with these issues.[23]

New strategic trade theory is an innovative, but flawed, start. Strategic trade theory tries to advance a national, rather than a merely corporate, interest. Even though the ties between transnational corporations and any one country are increasingly frayed, it assumes that improving some core businesses' trade position is still a worthwhile national goal. In this new strategic conception of international trade, there are two primary ways to use trade to advance a government's interests. One method tries to gain a larger share of the global market for oligopolistic industries. Since absence of competition already tends to increase their profits, some of these industries' global success will enhance national welfare by bringing more money home. The second method recognizes that because certain industries generate positive social gains far beyond what a single firm could capture, the national government should properly finance such research and development. High-tech industries that promote long-term growth, improved living standards, and scientific preeminence are probably the best candidates for this kind of investment.[24]

As an economic theory, the new strategic trade policy represents an improvement over an unyielding insistence on the value of free trade. By providing a role for government, the theory acknowledges that economic supremacy will not automatically spring from pure laissez-faire. The main focus of strategic trade policy, however, is its aggregate effect on nations, rather than its differential effect on groups. Yet these differential effects are crucial both within the United States and, by extension, to the prospects for greater international prosperity. Trade with low-wage countries exerts a centrifugal force on the U.S. wage structure, tearing it apart and breaking it down. At the same time, international economic disparities have serious consequences. They skew investment and trade patterns, with too much manufacturing moving away from high-wage countries, and low-wage manufacturing diminishing international aggregate demand. Low-wage countries cannot buy the products they produce, and with wages forced down by the competition, workers in the traditional manufacturing countries cannot buy goods either. The result of increased business profits is likely to be longer international stagnation.[25]

Because strategic trade theory does not pay much attention to these matters, it is ultimately not a very useful guide. After all, even on the national level, the issue is not the proportion of exports to imports: with a sufficiently favorable exchange rate, the poorest nation will still balance its accounts. The question is, instead, how can the United States compete in an open world economy with high and rising wages?[26]

Over the long term, our current low-wage strategy is sure to be counterproductive. As James Galbraith and Paulo Du Pin Calmon report, an analysis of six industries found relative wages never rose when trade performance declined, and trade performance never improved when pay was cut. "Wage givebacks not tied to capital renewal can forestall temporarily the loss of their jobs, but they cannot reverse competitive decline. Workers may better serve their industries, and their country, by fighting for their wages, and so forcing the choice between renewal and redeployment." Since trade advantage is, above all, a matter of technological position and not comparative pay, an insistence on high wages is key to forcing the kind of economic renewal that would make the United States more competitive in the future.[27]

Nevertheless, without international standards for labor, it will be easy to undercut American wage rates. That is why a global social market must ultimately define international trade policy. A social market that linked rising pay in foreign countries to their rising productivity would reduce the incentive for U.S. companies to cut and run. The crucial elements of this market include labor and environmental standards comparable to those in the United States. Implementation of these standards should be tied to the rate at which tariffs come down, and other policies should support them. Among these policies are the right to organize unions that members control democratically; the right to bargain about wages and working conditions; the right to strike; child labor laws; freedom from discrimination in hiring; and guarantees about occupational safety.[28] Without demonizing trade as the primary cause of eroding living standards in the United States, it is nonetheless a key consideration, one which probably accounts for at least one-quarter of the dramatic growth in wage inequality.[29]

Business Moves

With the fall of Communism, private capital can move nearly everywhere. Most business investment, however, has tended to follow one of several common routes. American companies seeking lower wages can relocate within the

United States and move to the nonunion southern states. For some firms, however, wages there may not be low enough. After the enactment of the North American Free Trade Agreement (NAFTA), they can now go even further south to Mexico. Then there are the opportunities in Eastern Europe as well as the turbulent economies of Southeast Asia. All these different regions are clamoring for investment. As the global marketplace becomes one, the shrewd investor of significant capital has ever more freedom to pick and choose.

Within the United States

The states of the Old Confederacy are the most frequent choice for some businesses. Between 1991 and 1993, the Northeast and West lost 450,000 manufacturing jobs, while the South gained 23,000. Among the major car manufacturers alone, Mercedes-Benz moved to Alabama, BMW went to South Carolina, Toyota invested in Kentucky, and Nissan joined Saturn by opening plants in Tennessee. While low wages and low rates of unionization are undoubtedly the key factors in this movement, the southern states have also benefited from the presence of some elite universities like Duke, as well as from a system of technical schools and community colleges. Quality of life issues such as low crime and affordable housing also contributed to their appeal.[30]

Although Pratt & Whitney, the Connecticut airplane engine manufacturer, merely threatened to move south, the arguments it made illustrate the advantages. Pratt & Whitney contended that Connecticut wages were $6 to $8 an hour higher: the average wage for a manufacturing worker in Connecticut was $513 a week, 38 percent more than in Georgia, where it is $372. Social benefits were also more generous in Connecticut, with maximum worker's compensation 240 percent higher at $769 than Georgia's $225. The effect of military cutbacks pervade these calculations. When the military procurement system signed cost-plus contracts, higher local costs were simply a factor of production, but as Pratt & Whitney sold fewer jet engines to the military, it became harder to pass local costs along.[31]

How much does the South benefit? Burgeoning investment has not significantly reduced poverty. Even though the West has replaced the South as the region with the highest poverty rate, more than 15 percent of Southerners in 1996 continued to live below the poverty line. The same pattern of changes at the workplace have kept wages down there. Since high school graduates in Memphis, Tennessee cannot get full-time jobs with International Harvester or Firestone Tire and Rubber any more, part-time jobs at Federal Express are all that is available. These jobs typically pay $8 an hour for a twenty-hour week. Chuck W. Thomson, vice president for personnel at Federal Express, says, "We tell them they should take this job with the understanding that it will be part-time indefinitely." Thomson is probably persuasive, because the alternative is still worse: stock clerks at Kroger Supermarkets begin at little more than the minimum wage, with a promotion from $7 to $8 an hour taking three to four years.[32]

Relocation to the South appeals to those companies wishing to remain within the United States who see the combination of low wages, willing workers, and short distances to market as a sufficient solution to their financial problems. NAFTA, however, eliminated many barriers to relocating outside the country. Now, if a company wants even cheaper, more compliant workers with still fewer protections, it can move to Mexico.

NAFTA and the Move to Mexico

The ease with which companies can move to Mexico has changed the business-labor relationship in the private sector. This change has not affected all companies equally. Some industries such as retail, nursing homes, and construction are relatively immobile: they can threaten to shut down their business, but realistically they cannot move. Nevertheless, the context for organizing has shifted. When workers organize now, employers have a potent new weapon at their disposal.

The most powerful documentation of this trend comes from a study sponsored by the Labor Ministries of Mexico, Canada, and the United States. Conducted by Kate Bronfenbrenner, Director of Labor Education Research at Cornell University, the report examined the effects of sudden plant closings on the rights of workers to organize. The report was an outgrowth of the effort to organize La Conexion Familiar, Sprint's San Francisco-based Hispanic marketing division. Sprint closed the division down just one week before a National Labor Relations Board vote that would have permitted employees to join the Communication Workers of America.

The study analyzed employer behavior in more than 500 organizing and 100 first contract campaigns. It found that 50 percent of all employers, and 62 percent of employers in mobile industries such as manufacturing, threatened to close at least part of their plant during the organizing campaign. Some of the threats were quite blatant. In Michigan, ITT Automotive parked thirteen flat-bed trucks in front of its plant, put production equipment on the trucks, and then posted signs on the side that read "Mexico Transfer Job." Others simply attached shipping labels to machinery with a Mexican address or posted maps of North America with an arrow pointing to the company's current site in Mexico. These threats made a difference. Unions won just 33 percent of the elections in plants, where the employers threatened to close down, as compared to 47 percent in those campaigns where no threat was made.[33]

When President Clinton signed NAFTA in 1993, proponents promised a better outcome. Drawing on the classic rhetoric of free trade, they contended that increased exports to Mexico would produce 100,000 new jobs. To be sure, there would be some structural adjustments, and a few jobs might even be lost. Still, the idea that employers would threaten workers with relocation to Mexico simply had no place in their conception of free trade. There is, after all, very little room for conflict in a transaction where the benefits must exceed the costs to produce a net social gain.[34]

Trade unionists and their allies looked at the Mexican wage scale and came to an entirely different conclusion. The average hourly wage in Mexico is $2.50, compared with $17.10 in the United States. Moreover, despite suggestions about a likely increase in Mexican wages, this differential is actually projected to widen by 2010 to more than $20 an hour ($4 an hour for Mexico in contrast to $25.40 an hour in the United States).[35] These numbers convinced opponents of NAFTA that the temptation to move to Mexico was just too great. Without minimum labor and environmental standards, they were sure that NAFTA would hurt thousands of American workers.

Jobs gained or jobs lost? In purely quantitative terms, it is difficult to judge who is right. Whether employers hire or fire does not usually have such a straightforward explanation. With the exception of a firm's immediate relocation to Mexico, or some additional hiring specifically for export to the Mexican market, too many unknowable factors determine the size of a company's labor force. Is the firm hiring because it sells more goods to another American company that has expanded its market in Mexico? Is it laying off workers because another product made in Mexico can now be substituted for its own? There is no hard statistical answer to these questions.

Still, the war about job numbers continued unabated. The Clinton administration claimed that after three years, NAFTA produced 90,000 to 160,000 new jobs. The Economic Policy Institute agreed that almost 160,000 jobs were created, but contended that more than 385,000 jobs were lost. The NAFTA Trade Adjustment Assistance Program has itself certified 132,000 workers who it says lost their jobs as a result of the agreement. Yet the office that certified these numbers is the subject of much controversy. Some claim it is understaffed and cannot keep up with the demand for certification, others, that layoffs without any connection to NAFTA have been improperly certified as NAFTA-related. Amid this morass of conflicting numbers, what is it, exactly, that we do know?[36]

We do know that a long list of companies promised additional hiring as a result of NAFTA. Despite their promises, these companies—Mattel, Zenith, Procter & Gamble, Allied Signal, and Scott Paper—all subsequently laid off U.S. workers. When Congress debated the North American Free Trade Agreement in 1993, for example, Fermin Cuza, vice president of the Mattel Corporation, testified before a congressional subcommittee that NAFTA would have a "very positive effect" on the 2000 employees of Mattel in the United States. Nevertheless, in less than two years, the Department of Labor certified that

520 workers at Mattel's Fisher-Price plant in Medina, New York were fired because of "increased company imports from Mexico."[37]

Then there is the 1994 devaluation of the peso. Most proponents of NAFTA either separate out the devaluation or treat it as secondary to any accounting of NAFTA.[38] In fact, the devaluation was a closely linked outcome. It occurred because the Mexican government pegged the peso at the artificially high rate of three to one dollar. Intended to buttress the arguments of NAFTA supporters, this rate made imported goods cheap and exports expensive, but it also brought about a 1994 trade deficit of $30 billion, the biggest in Mexico's history. As President Carlos Salinas de Gortari tried to conceal this crisis, Mexican currency reserves dropped from $25 billion to $6.5 billion. Once President Ernesto Zedillo Ponce de Leon took office, he allowed the peso to trade freely, and it promptly lost half its value. When U.S. holders of $35 billion in Mexican stocks panicked, Zedillo then announced a new economic program, whose real purpose—to boost exports and reduce imports—is directly contrary to NAFTA supporters' original promise that free trade would increase U.S. employment.[39]

The Goodyear Tire and Rubber Company illustrates the effects of this devaluation. Faced with a 3500 tire decline in daily domestic tire sales (down 23 percent), Goodyear's Mexican plant at Tultitlan shifted from exporting a single tire in 1992 to exporting half its production three years later. There had been a 20 percent U.S. tariff on tires, but with that tariff disappearing after NAFTA, competition would have ruined the Mexican plant. Goodyear reacted by firing 500 workers or one-fifth of its local workforce. The smaller workforce improved efficiency, until devaluation of the peso slashed workers' salaries and put the remaining jobs at risk. To protect their own jobs, Mexican workers once again boosted their efficiency. As a result, 62 cents of Mexican labor produces as much output as one dollar in the United States, and the jobs now at risk are American.[40]

This differential beckons constantly. In wages, a welder at Chrysler's Sterling, Michigan plant with seventeen years' seniority receives $16 an hour and substantial benefits; at Chrysler's Toluca, Mexico plant, a welder with five years' service gets $1.75 an hour, vacation pay, a Christmas bonus, and a subsidized lunch that costs about a penny.[41] Lighter environmental regulations are likewise appealing. In NAFTA's first year, Magnetek, a producer of light ballast, laid off 71 employees in Michigan and Indiana and transferred work to Mexico. In two of its Matamoros plants, where fumes from the tar necessary to create light ballast induce vomiting in some workers, it fired older workers and replaced them with younger ones who must work 45–48 hours a week for about $50 in pay.[42] Together, this combination of low wages and little environmental regulation makes it tempting to reallocate capital. Anheuser-Busch spent $447 million to purchase 18 percent of the Mexican brewer Cervecería Modelo at the same time that it announced a 10 percent cut in its U.S. workforce. Similarly, as part of a general restructuring, the First Chicago bank sought permission to open a subsidiary in Mexico while eliminating 600 jobs in Illinois.[43]

Perhaps the best criterion for a conclusive evaluation of NAFTA comes from its most sophisticated proponents. As one of them has argued,

> job gain/loss accounting methodologies should not be used to evaluate the relative benefits of trade. These methodologies should, however, be central to our understanding of the adjustment costs of the impacts of trade. In evaluating the relative benefits of trade, it is much more important to focus on understanding the long-term dynamic impacts on productivity growth and overall welfare gains, not merely on the short-term employment effects.[44]

The proponents are right. The issue of jobs gained or lost may well be secondary in evaluating NAFTA. So, too, in a larger sense, is the Mexican economy, which at one-twentieth the size, cannot, by itself, have much effect on the United States. The crucial issue is instead quite different: it is the capacity of global businesses to connect all the dots on the map and move, or threaten to move, wherever they want. NAFTA constitutes one important step toward establishing this dominance. Judged by this standard, it cannot make many claims to improvement of the general welfare.

Eastern Europe

Capital investment has also surged into Eastern Europe. East German labor costs are 5 to 10 percent of West Germany's. Since businesses have moved in pursuit of far smaller differentials, many companies are moving east. Some German firms have even opted out of their employers' federations as a way of escaping binding national labor agreements. Other companies have just cut jobs in more expensive regions and poured resources into Eastern Europe. Asea Brown Boveri, Ltd., a multinational engineering and electrical giant, has eliminated 40,000 jobs since 1990 in North America and Western Europe and created 21,150 jobs in the newly capitalist nations of Eastern Europe. Its employees in central Europe work four hundred more hours a year than the ones in Western Europe; its Polish workers get $2.58 an hour, instead of $30.33 an hour in Germany.[45]

American firms have participated actively in this shift of investment eastward. Hungary, which absorbed about half of all foreign investment in the first two years after Communism's collapse, got a General Electric light bulb facility. Schwinn invested in a Hungarian bike plant, and Levi's started a jeans factory. During a seven-month period between 1991 and 1992, U.S. firms also bought twenty-four former state enterprises in Czechoslovakia. Since Czechs smoke 30 billion cigarettes a year, Philip Morris made a profitable investment: it purchased a 56 percent interest in the state cigarette company.[46]

Despite this spurt in private capital, workers in Eastern Europe have experienced a decline in their standard of living even worse than their American counterparts. In fact, a UNICEF study of Eastern Europe reported that economic changes "have provoked a deterioration of unparalleled proportions in human welfare throughout most of the region." Russian conditions were the most distressing, with a tenfold increase in families living below the poverty line and a mortality rate up by 35 percent (from 1989 to 1994). By 1998, the cumulative effect of this decline had combined with deflation of the ruble to produce a total collapse of the Russian economy and an actual reduction in the size of the population. Similarly, between 1989 and 1994, wages also declined throughout East Europe: 28 percent in Poland, 18 percent in the Czech Republic, and 16 percent in Hungary. In some countries, a majority of the population was nonetheless satisfied with their living conditions, including, for example, 54 percent of the Czechs. At the other extreme, however, where the transition to the market has been most wrenching, 88 percent of the Ukrainians expressed discontent.[47]

To ease the transition to a market economy, some trade unions in Western Europe have tried to provide assistance to trade unions in the East. The Swedish metalworkers did help Hungarian labor to confront Electrolux, and IG Metal contributed two million deutsche marks to fight VW and Audi.[48] Although it takes some vision to offer this help, the self-interest is immediately apparent. Faced with the hypermobility of capital, other workers do not want to compete with the Eastern Europeans for the chance to offer the lowest wage. Like U.S. workers engaged in a similar competition with Mexican labor, they know it is a fruitless enterprise, one that depresses the wages of every participant.

Capital Moves West to Southeast Asia

In addition to moving into Eastern Europe, private capital has also emigrated to Southeast Asia. Aided by containment or, in some cases the outright suppression of trade unions, this investment spurred a growth rate, from 1985 to 1990, of 7.8 percent annually. In Southeast Asia as elsewhere, the lure was cheap wages—$5.30 an hour in South Korea and even less in Malaysia, Indonesia, and China. Once a group of underdeveloped third world countries, Southeast Asia became, in the language of the 1990s, an emerging market, until suddenly, in 1997, that market collapsed.[49]

This collapse suggested that a global capitalism might merely internationalize the severe cyclical patterns that have previously beset the economies of individual nations. It is, after all, altogether problematic how long companies can expand production in low-wage countries in order to sell in high-wage countries. Countries with high wages may be able to absorb the exports for awhile, but their capacity is not infinite, and indeed, the continual outstation-ing of production contracts it ever more sharply. Too much production for too little income is a recipe for a depression—only this time on a grand, interna-tional scale.

Since such an outcome seemed so improbable in the enthusiasm of the early 1990s, U.S. companies joined in the rush. In 1994 alone, Clinton announced a total of seventeen business agreements with Indonesia worth $40 billion. General Motors entered Indonesia, selling its Opel Vectra sedan assembled at its first Southeast Asian plant, located outside Jakarta. Likewise, Citibank opened the first Indonesian automatic teller machine. Other Ameri-can corporations include McDonald's, Procter and Gamble, Avon, and Levi-Strauss. Admittedly, Indonesia was still in a relatively early stage of economic development: just 10 percent of its 200 million people belong to a new middle class. Nevertheless, American corporations could not ignore an untapped mar-ket whose size exceeds the population of Australia.[50]

Once again, cheaper labor has proved inviting. Malaysia pays technical workers less than half of what Americans get. Western Digital makes most of its disk drives in Singapore and Malaysia, marketing 10 to 15 percent of this output in Asia and selling the rest in the United States and elsewhere overseas. Similarly, Malaysian engineers who used to work for Americans in Hewlett-Packard are now constructing their own production line, to make one million light-emitting diodes each day used for lighting cars, signs, and electronic dis-plays. Since it opened in 1972, the Hewlett-Packard plant has become steadily more autonomous, until now it solves engineering problems on the produc-tion line without help from the United States. Motorola and Intel have joined Hewlett-Packard in Malaysia; Intel, in fact, now makes three times as many chips as it did ten years ago with the same size workforce. All together, from 1988 to 1994, multinationals spent $20 billion on manufacturing in Malaysia. Such investments were appealing because suppliers and important Asian mar-kets are nearby, workers in a former colony of Britain speak English, the trade unions are weak, and the government hands out generous tax breaks.[51]

By 1997, however, the upsurge in Asian investment had produced too many unoccupied office towers, several inflated stock markets, and many overvalued currencies. A currency crisis in Thailand was first to burst the bubble. Then, within six months, the value of the Singapore stock market dropped 50 per-cent; in Malaysia, it plummeted 75 percent. So steep was this decline that in 1998, Malaysia withdrew from capital markets. Korea too had its economic problems. With equity to debt ratios of one to four in some chaebols (the fam-ily-run business groups that dominate the Korean economy), the Korean econ-omy could no longer expand itself out of debt. Soon, it joined Thailand and Indonesia in requesting an aid package from the International Monetary Fund. The spillover effects of this economic turbulence even extended to Japan, where Hokkaido Takushoku, one of the twenty largest banks, closed, only to be followed one week later by the failure of Yamaichi, the oldest Japanese securities firm, which left $24 billion in customer liabilities. As a result, by 1998, the Japanese unemployment had reached a record 4.1 percent, and the economy appeared to be tailspinning into a deeper recession.[52]

Despite the speculative boom, the explosive growth of the Asian economies was never endlessly sustainable. As Paul Krugman pointed out in 1994, most of the growth resulted from increasing the inputs—greater investment, more and better trained workers—than from any increase in efficiency. In Singapore, for example, the employed share of the population doubled once (from 27 percent in 1966 to 51 percent in 1990), but since it cannot double again, the rapid rate of growth could not be maintained.[53] When overbuilding and excess production did slow the growth rate, global financial markets turned what would have previously been a local downturn into an economic crisis with international implications.

Korea represents another illustration of this trend. In 1994, Korea submitted to pressure from the United States and agreed to pay the price of admission to the Organization of Economic Cooperation and Development—the deregulation of all financial institutions. Admission to the OECD requires open financial markets and carries with it the assumption that there can be no defaults on bank loans to member nations. As a consequence, between 1994, when it first received approval to join the OECD, and 1996, when its membership became official, foreign banks doubled their Korean loans from $52 to $108 billion. In essence, by guaranteeing the loans, the United States, together with other OECD nations, adopted the American savings and loan crisis of the 1980s as a policy model and exported it to other countries.[54]

It is the absence of regulation—over both the flow of goods and the flow of money—that shadows the growth of free trade. Free trade is always beneficial in the abstract, and sometimes it may even be beneficial in actuality. When it is not, however, the "adjustment costs" are no longer limited to "overpaid" workers in a particular industry, but may in fact involve the economic well-being and prosperity of entire nations. In these dire straits, the International Monetary Fund's rescue package then further contracts the economy, causing masses of workers to lose their jobs while largely indemnifying the losses of the financial elite. This scenario is certain to become more common, because without an international institution to prevent turbulence in the financial markets, no nation's economic standing can be assured, and the position of workers in every country gets steadily less secure.

The Pressure on the European Welfare States

Nothing better illustrates the impact of globalization on economic security than its effects on the European welfare states. Admittedly, this is a case of relative retrenchment: most European countries continue to have larger public sectors, better social benefits, lower rates of poverty, and less income inequality than the United States. Still, if the global market is powerful enough to squeeze social benefits in countries such as Germany and Sweden, the acquiescence of a reluctant welfare state like the United States becomes much more understandable.

Most European countries are proud of their social benefits, because they provide a reassuring measure of security. Policies like national health care, children's allowances, and parental leave are part of the social fabric, reflecting popular sentiment that rejects both the upside likelihood of entrepreneurial success and the downside prospect of unprotected poverty. These sentiments have real social consequences: although countries differ in the generosity of particular social programs, the safety net as a whole is much more tightly woven. It includes programs like those which provide, as percentage of the average industrial wage, 81 percent for unemployment benefits in Portugal, 100 percent for invalids in Germany and Luxembourg, and 107 percent in Greece for contributory pensions.[55]

Because of these programs, the average percentage of the gross domestic product spent on social protection in the European members of the OECD is, at 22 percent, 50 percent higher than the United States.[56] This spending pattern, however, has produced results. Poverty rates are typically 5 percent in France and the United Kingdom, and 4 percent or less in Sweden, Germany, and Netherlands, compared with 13 percent in the United States. The differential is even more striking for single mothers: while income transfers reduce their pre-transfer poverty by only 5 percent here, it reduces the number in poverty by 34 percent in Germany, 59 percent in France, and 89 percent in the Netherlands.[57]

In Europe, as in the United States, the global market tends to shy away from places with generous social protections. Although corporations have invested in countries such as England, with its reduced welfare state and comparatively low wages, they have underinvested in many other European countries. As a result, unemployment among OECD countries totaled 36 million people in 1996; among the European members of the OECD, it averaged over 10 percent, reaching 11.6 in Germany, 12.6 in France, and 23.8 percent in Spain.[58]

Unemployment in the United States is different than in Europe. In the United States, a worker has a greater likelihood of becoming unemployed, but an unemployed worker has a much greater chance of a quick rehiring. The European labor market is less fluid. Hence, while 11 percent of unemployed U.S. workers in 1992 had been out of work for more than one year, 40 percent of unemployed Europeans had been jobless for that long. Since American unemployment rates declined in the 1990s just as many European rates have gone up, the higher European rate often constitutes an integral part of the argument against any quest for higher wages and more generous social protection.[59]

This argument is wrong for several reasons. The most straightforward reason is that the United States and Europe do not use the same criteria to calculate their unemployment rate. In the United States, the rate excludes "discouraged workers" (those who have stopped looking for a job) as well as those who work as little as one hour a week. Most European countries include these workers in their unemployment rate. In addition, the United States has a rate of incarceration that is ten times the European. Since these inmates are often young, unskilled people of color, many would be unemployed if they were not in prison. If these factors alone were weighted properly, the American unemployment rate would double in size and approximate the OECD average.[60]

Besides, the real cause of high European unemployment is the austere economic regimen that many countries implemented in the aftermath of the 1992 Maastricht treaty. The treaty established a budget deficit of 3 percent of each country's GDP as a prerequisite for membership in the European Economic and Monetary Union. A tight monetary policy is recessionary; if people cannot borrow money, demand falls and unemployment rises. Although this austerity has produced double-digit unemployment, social supports such as children's allowances, long vacations, maternity leave, and day care still enable Europeans in the bottom half of the labor market to live better than their American counterparts.[61]

In Europe, the phenomenon of rising unemployment has generated two seemingly contradictory responses. Unlike the United States, many Europeans have been willing to raise their taxes. Some of these new taxes include a 1 percent tax on income to pay for the elderly and a doubling of the wealth tax in Germany; an increase in the highest tax rate from 51 percent to 56 percent and a 2 percent payroll tax to fund pension and health insurance in Sweden; and a rise in the value-added tax from 15 to 16 percent in Spain, along with other tax increases on transportation, electricity, gasoline, alcohol, and tobacco.[62] For others, however, rising taxes have fed rising doubts. Business people, especially, find it difficult to imagine how a policy of tax increases can be sustained over the longer term. This perspective is, of course, partly self-interested, but it is also based on a real truth: if corporations have always been tax-avoidant, the new mobility of capital truly gives them wings.

Germany occupies center stage in this debate. On a per hour basis, German productivity is still the best in Europe, and Germany remains strong in quality engineering of traditional exports. But since 1979, productivity has declined relative to the United States and Japan, so that Germany is no longer the world leader in sectors that it formerly dominated such as chemicals, machinery, and transport equipment. Germany has also been slower than other countries in its shift to a service sector. Finally, because its innovative capacity is relatively weak, it has lagged behind in some high-tech sectors of international trade like computers and advanced pharmaceuticals.[63]

These changing economic conditions have generated bewilderment abroad and self-reflection at home. The highest wages in the world—$25 an hour compared to $16.50 in Japan and $15.50 in the United States—combined with a guaranteed five weeks vacation and plentiful holidays astonishes some American commentators, who seem oddly incredulous that so many Germans prefer to spend time with their friends and family when they could be out working. For true believers in the new global economy, laboring longer for less pay and fewer benefits is the only plausible solution.[64]

Some German leaders share this view. Under pressure from both global competition and the costs of reunification with East Germany, they have moved to contract the wage and benefit system. Former Chancellor Helmut Kohl targeted Lufthansa and the phone company Deutsche Bundespost Telekom for privatization, cut welfare payments by 3 percent, and granted companies the option to reduce sick leave by 20 percent. Other possible changes include elimination of the legal obstacles to more flexible job schedules and a two-tier wage structure for new workers. IG Chemie, the chemical workers union, has made an unprecedented concession that permitted employers to hire young workers and the long-term unemployed at 90 percent of scale.[65]

The European countries value the social solidarity that benefits promote, and they have not acquiesced silently: if the United States is famous as a reluctant welfare state, the Europeans might well qualify as reluctant marketers. The 1995 French strikes sought to preserve their pension system; the German unions fought back when companies actually attempted to implement the new sick leave law.[66] Despite this resistance, it is clear that Germany has lost its exemption from the rules of the global marketplace, and that whatever protection it once provided, it will provide less now. Since the American welfare state never had the same generosity, ideology, or popular support as the European welfare states, any reduction in their system of social benefits represents a powerful indication of the pressure on ours. The global marketplace does not discriminate. Generous or reluctant, it takes a cut out of everybody.

Free Trade and Inequality

The crux of the new free trade is the price of labor. The new technologies make labor interchangeable; they permit goods to be produced virtually anywhere. If free trade depends even less on the exchange of resource-dependent materials—English textiles for Portuguese wine in Ricardo's classic example—then cheap labor emerges as the primary factor distinguishing one production site from another. It is this search for cheap labor that undermines the welfare state and depresses the wages of both industrial and white-collar workers.

The consequences of business mobility have crept steadily up the occupational ladder. When businesses first began to move, relocation only imperiled industrial workers. It does not take much skill to bolt the rear bumper on to an automobile: the simpler and more repetitive the work, the less the nationality of the worker mattered. Cheap foreign labor began to affect factory production in the early 1980s, cutting wages, reducing union membership, and turning the Midwest into a deindustrialized Rust Belt.[67] Technical workers in the United States initially believed they were immune from such competition. Once technology permitted the ready transfer of skill, however, their immunity also vanished.

The threat to skilled workers developed very quickly. Until 1990, U.S. computer makers produced motherboards for most personal computers in house. Then, suddenly, the technology dispersed, and within five years, 60 percent of motherboard construction was contracted out to 150,000 Taiwanese information-technology engineers. Texas Instruments is one of the many U.S. companies that have expanded its investment for computer-related technologies in India. Aided by a private satellite link, its computer-chip design operation in Bangalore expanded by 40 percent to 350 workers. India is a particularly popular site for computer outsourcing because its schools emphasize mathematical skill, and it has a tradition of English language education dating to colonial days. With experienced programmers getting one-third of the $50,000 annually that they would receive in the United States, Indian software exports grew from $225 million in 1992 to $1.15 billion in 1996, with $3.6 billion projected for the year 2000.[68]

Although some of the best programming jobs will undoubtedly continue to remain in the United States, powerful computers and the proliferation of high-capacity undersea cables will put many of the more routine white collar jobs at risk. The same dynamics hold, then, for both industrial and white-collar workers. It is not free trade alone that depresses wages. Rather, it is the convergence of technology and free trade together that commingles their labor with the larger reservoir of labor from other countries. This convergence injects new content into the meaning of free trade. Instead of primarily trading goods, the new free trade has established an international market for capital as well as, increasingly, an international market for labor. Success on the international capital market demands trading upward, for better stocks or a better currency. Success on the international labor market demands trading downward, for workers who will do the same job at a lesser wage. In the United States, trading upward for money and downward for labor threatens to dispose of a better paid labor force.

3

Disposable
Workers

It is essential that companies keep productivity ahead of wage increases. That is the only way to gain on your competitors, bring on new products, and increase the dividends to shareholders.

—Stanley Gault, CEO of Goodyear Tire

We did a lot of violence to the expectations of the American workforce.

—Frank Doyle, GE vice president, on GE's layoffs

Business power, technological change, and foreign competition have combined to transform the labor market. Few jobs are for life. Permanent employment with one company has also vanished, along with the likelihood of an employee getting internal promotions to ensure steady upward mobility. Instead, part-time and temporary work have spread through the labor force. Although many employees continue to have what are nominally permanent jobs, contract work has become the metaphor, if not the fact, for much of the labor market. Whether they sign up for a couple of weeks or a couple of years, more and more Americans know that their work at any particular job is time-limited, and their future probably includes a period of unemployment. Employees have always looked for jobs; employers have always done the hiring. Now, however, it is different. Search, hire, and fire; search, hire, and fire: not since the Great Depression has the constant churning of the U.S. labor market engendered such intense feelings of economic insecurity.

Of course, on the basis of unemployment rates alone, this comparison seems quite foolhardy. At 6 percent or less, unemployment rates in the 1990s have been one-third, or even at its height one-quarter, of what unemployment was during the 1930s. Yet even though this statistic was a favorite of both conservative analysts and Bill Clinton throughout his presidency, they largely missed the point. Workers in the United States do not merely fear unemployment. Layoffs, lower wages, loss of health benefits, and the suspicion that their skills do not quite measure up are certainly frightening, but what makes people most anxious is the end of a whole way of life. In the life that envelops them now, there is no permanence, and their labor is readily interchangeable with another worker's. The spectre of unemployment creates its own apprehensions, but what truly fuels economic insecurity is the premonition of insignificance: one worker or another—it does not really matter, except to workers themselves.

This economy is different, because in it, both the unemployed and the employed must be ever vigilant about looking for work. In 1996, Challenger, Gray and Christmas, the Chicago-based outplacement firm, noted that half of the callers to their job search hot line said they already *had* jobs, "a signal," they said, "of serious job insecurity." They called because, as another 1996 study underscored, 46 percent of American workers—up from 31 percent in 1992—acknowledged that they are "frequently concerned about being laid off."[1] These reports suggest that with the labor market turned into a free-for-all, many attachments have been turned into temporarily convenient associations. Workers suspect that even when they get a job, employers will use short-term economic criteria to fire them in an instant. Looking out for themselves, they then decide it would be wiser to search for the next job during their current employment.

This search is going to be particularly difficult if the job seeker also expects the next job to pay a living wage. In a study of the jobs available in Minnesota between 1990 and 1993, the Jobs Now Coalition found that although there were 260,200 job seekers, there were just 96,400 net job openings. Of these job openings, only 43,300 paid a livable wage, and just 8300 that paid a livable wage required one year or less of training. These numbers mean that there was an average of 2.7 new job seekers for every job; 6 new job seekers for every livable wage job; and 31 job seekers for every livable wage job that requires one year or less of training. These figures may seem fairly dismal, but they are actually better than New York's, where, with 50,000 jobs, 340,000 employable recipients of public assistance plus 200,000 officially unemployed people yield a jobless-to-jobs available ratio of more than ten to one.[2]

For some people, proportions like these are so troubling that they simply give up. In 1995, an average of 838,000 men between the ages of 25 and 54 left jobs and were not actively looking for work. With perhaps another several hundred thousand permanently withdrawn from the labor market, more than one million men are officially classified as "discouraged," the Department of Labor category that excludes them from the unemployment rate. In truth, these data merely accentuate a three-decade long trend. As technology rendered many skills obsolete, participation rates for men in this age group have been declining: if the 1971 participation rates held today, another 734,000 men would be in the labor force. Although the influx of women into the labor force offset men's disengagement in the 1970s and 1980s, women's participation has now stabilized at about 60 percent. In the meantime, men's participation in the labor force has continued to fall.[3]

Productivity

There are many reasons that economic insecurity has gone up, but among the most important has been the corporate drive for productivity. Productivity is supposed to be an indicator of what businesses can pay workers, on the assumption that businesses do not pay for what workers do not make. This principle assumes, however, that there is no substantial redistribution between capital and labor. When there is, as there has been in the private sector over the last twenty-five years, growth in productivity may slow down, but wage increases are even smaller.[4]

From 1959 to 1973, at the height of U.S. economic prosperity, wage increases slightly exceeded the growth in productivity—2.9 to 2.8 percent per year. Then this trend reversed. From 1973 to 1990, productivity dropped to .9 percent, but wages at .7 percent, began to lag behind. In the 1990s, this gap has widened still further, as a 1.2 percent annual increase in productivity far outdistanced the .5 percent annual drop in average private weekly earnings. From the President's Council of Economic Advisors on down, it is commonplace to speak of the decline in productivity as impeding a rise in wages.[5] Less frequently is it pointed out that business has kept wage increases below whatever was the rate of productivity growth.

Ultimately, though, this leverage boomerangs. As several economists have argued, while many factors entered into the decline in productivity, the single most convincing explanation is the social model. This model recognizes that although a lack of skill training, a shortfall of private investment, and an over-reliance on military spending have all contributed to the decline in productivity, the most fundamental cause of the decline is the resistance—subtle and not so subtle—that workers manifest toward their employers. In essence, this explanation contends that while employers can force employees to come to work, they cannot force them to care. If workers are treated badly on the job, if they come to work just to receive a paycheck, and the value of that check is itself declining, they are not going to commit to the enterprise. Productivity demands of workers resourcefulness and hard work, but the more the job wants a piece of them, the more it becomes necessary for them to withhold something of themselves.[6]

The best evidence that a social model explains a significant part of the decline in productivity comes from a summary of studies on the relationship between productivity and participation. Conducted by David Levine of the

University of California at Berkeley and Laura D'Andrea Tyson, formerly chair of the Council of Economic Advisors under President Clinton, the study stresses that participation generally has a positive effect on productivity. This is most likely when it is substantive rather than consultative and involves real decisions related to the shop floor. Together with a high degree of employer-employee trust and some financial incentive, the results can be significant and long-lasting.[7]

Workers' commitment, however, can still explain only a part of productivity growth, because so many other factors enter into it. These factors include quality of parts and raw materials; technology, plant, and equipment in use; scale of production; ease with which the product is manufactured; and the efficiency of the productive process. Naturally, studies of productivity by business experts tend to emphasize internal factors under management control. For these experts, the most efficient companies were those that ascribe great importance to productivity, innovate regularly, and seek to systematize contacts with customers at the same time that they are monitoring the competition.[8] Since public investment in the infrastructure is less subject to their control, it rarely appears in these discussions.

Yet lower public infrastructure spending is clearly another major factor in the decline of U.S. productivity growth over the past two decades. Among American economists, the bias against recognizing its role usually depresses estimates of its effects.[9] Imagine a factory that sits on a property one mile long. A fence divides this property from a public highway. If the company built a road just inside the fence, it would surely speed movement of employees and material on factory grounds and bring about a significant increase in the factory's efficiency. Now suppose the government improved the public highway just outside the fence at an equivalent cost. It, too, would facilitate movement of people and goods—this time, from both inside and outside the factory. Nevertheless, because the source of investment was public, its contribution to the productivity of the private sector would be much more grudgingly acknowledged.

The decline in the rate of productivity growth also raises a more general question about the organization of work in the United States. In part, productivity has declined because low wages and low capital investment may be cheaper for the individual firm, even though they are bad for the nation as a whole. The roots of this corporate strategy go far back in the history of the U.S. economic system, when it was organized in the early twentieth century around mass production and easy access to natural resources. The first time this system faltered in the Depression, Keynesian economic policy supplemented it. Eventually, however, changing technology and globalization of economic activity superseded conventional methods of mass production. Because the new global economy demands more attention to quality, productivity, and flexibility, it requires that companies, unions and countries wishing to be productive, world class players adopt very different models of work organization and human resource development. That the growth of productivity has slowed in the United States is the final legacy of this old mass production system.[10]

The United States is by no means the only country struggling to make this adjustment to a more productive workforce. There was a sharp spurt after World War II, but then, beginning in the 1970s, the rate of productivity growth in the already industrialized countries declined. The pressure on the United States stems from an increasing annual productivity rate in Japan and Germany during the period of its most rapid growth: between 1950 and 1987, growth averaged 5.9 percent in Japan and 3.8 percent in Germany, but only 1.4 percent in the United States. In metal working and steel production, labor productivity in Germany has caught up with the United States, though it still lags behind in seven other industries studied. In Japan, productivity is higher than the United States in steel (by 1.45 times), automotive parts, metal working, cars, and consumer electronics, but lower in computers, soap and detergent, beer, and food. Japan, in particular, exhibits the characteristics of a "dual economy," with state-of-the-art industries and craft processes side-by-side.[11]

Differences in corporate governance also drive productivity rates. In Germany, corporate governance consists of an insider system with a supervisory board that leaves management a good deal of autonomy and only intervenes in cases of clear failure. In Japan, most stock is cross-held by other corporations organized in industrial groups called *keiretsu*. Governance is more distributed through the business community, and while Japanese corporations have been well-positioned in the past for long-term investments such as challenging the United States in automobiles, the capital markets themselves do not monitor short-term changes in productivity the way that they do in the United States.[12] As capital investment globalizes, the German and Japanese systems of corporate governance have plainly lost some of their capacity to protect companies from high international standards of productivity growth. The crucial difference is that while German and Japanese companies tried to improve productivity by involving workers, the reflexive American response to declining productivity was to attack unions.

Unions and Productivity

Labor usually accounts for 70 percent of total production costs. With capital amounting to just 30 percent of total costs, a 10 percent increase in the nation's capital stock would raise productivity only 3 percent. By contrast, 10 percent greater efficiency in labor would yield another 7 percent more output per hour of work.[13] For this reason, when American corporate executives tried to boost productivity, they clearly had to turn their attention toward labor.

Unlike Germany or Japan, however, the U.S. management system is conflictual. Corporate executives could have tried to boost productivity by increasing participation and shifting decision-making downward to the shop floor. Since such a strategy conflicts with the organization of work in the United States, management instead launched a campaign against unions.

There were many components to this campaign. Corporations hired antiunion management consultants, sought to decertify existing unions, and fired union activists. They lobbied President Reagan to change the membership and policies of the National Labor Relations Board and threatened to move their businesses if workers misbehaved. The strategy worked. Trade unions lost power, and this loss of power weakened their capacity to establish a wage premium. It also dimmed their appeal to nonunion members.[14]

Of course, the campaign had a considerable tailwind. Changes in the economy—most especially, the process of deindustrialization—had already lowered union membership by one-third in the mid-1970s, from its high of 38 percent in 1954. Still another 10 percent decline occurred between 1978 and 1988, spurred, in part, by the 18 percent it fell among blue collar men age 25–34.[15] Its fall to 14 percent by the mid-1990s was costly for most working Americans. Instead of benefiting from what could have been a cooperative effort to reinvolve and reskill the U.S. workforce, they lost out to a crusade.

The drive by U.S. corporate management to weaken unions rests on a fundamental misconception. A low-trust, high-conflict environment, not unions themselves, is the source of reduced productivity. When roughly one-third of workplaces that vote for union representation obtain no collective bargaining contract, that is because the management of most American corporations follow a conflict model of labor relations which gives little ground. In another model based on high wages and high performance like Germany, unionization has been stable or even risen. To be sure, in Germany, as in the United States, businesses may complain about the inflexibility of union work rules, but these issues are negotiable. The real effect of unions on firm costs depends on the magnitude of wage premiums and productivity improvements. If these wage gains are translated into higher prices rather than lower profits, strong unions and the high-wage, high-performance strategy they represent will benefit most workers.[16]

A small number of U.S. companies are experimenting with changes in the workplace.[17] Yet whatever the strategy—redesigning the workplace, implementing total quality management, or the use of teams—the ethos of conflictual labor-management relations looms large. Workers obviously do not relish the prospect of participating in productivity improvements that might lead to their own downsizing. With the expanding possibilities of technology, robotics, and automation, this fear is particularly acute.

Naturally, whenever workers have expressed their concerns about the effects of technology and automation, employers and their allies have sought to reassure them. As William Lewis, director of McKinsey Global Institute, contended: "We've had arguments that automation will do away with employment since the turn of the century. It never turns out to be the case." In more unguarded moments, however, corporate management has begun to divide on this issue. Jack D. Rehm, CEO of Meredith Corporation, a $750 million a year media conglomerate in Des Moines, stated: "As businesses become more automated and productive, we need fewer bodies." Lawrence Siefert, AT&T vice president for manufacturing, offered a more specific rationale: manufacturing employment is primarily governed by technology, but new technology requires half the number of people in product assembly every six years.[18]

The relationship between the rates of technological change and of technological diffusion—between the development of technology and its spread—is not simple. A rapid rate of change may lead to a slow rate of diffusion, if buyers anticipate that change may continue at the same pace, and they would therefore be left with old or unstandardized technology. This is sometimes a consideration in the purchase of new computer equipment, when consumers hear that still newer technology will soon supersede what is currently on the market. If something is not going to be the state of the art for very long, there may be no point in owning it.

Another disincentive arises because the total social returns to innovation have historically exceeded the returns to a single company or sector by between 35 and 60 percent. The returns accrue in the form of a profitable new industry or the transformation of old industries. In the late nineteenth century, for example, the development of refrigerated steamships increased the available amount of perishable agricultural products throughout the world, but most of the benefits went to farmers and consumers, not the inventors of steamships. It is not, then, the mere existence of technology that prompts its introduction. Rather, companies invest in technology either in response to competition or because they believe it would help them undercut competitors.[19]

The steel industry represents a classic example of the effect of technology on employment. Two developments—continuous casting and minimills—have been particularly crucial. In traditional steel making, the molten metal was poured into molds and cooled. Then the mold was stripped off, and the steel was reheated so it could be processed. Continuous casting uses machines that turn molten metal into slabs that can be handled when they are still hot. Now 86 percent of steel is continuously cast, up from 20 percent in 1980. This technology has reduced the hours of work per metric ton to 4.42, better than Japan's 4.49, and down from 12.49 in 1976.[20]

Minimills have also had a powerful impact. Minimills employ scrap and electric furnaces to produce a lower-grade steel, and companies like Nucor have relied on them—and an increasingly nonunion workforce—to drive older firms like USX out of the steel business. Integrated systems for manufacturing steel need to produce as much as three million tons a year to remain efficient. Because minimills can get by on as little as 200,000 tons, they can survive periods of diminished demand that would bankrupt larger factories. In 1953, 650,000 U.S. workers worked in the steel industry. As a result of this technological restructuring, however, the number was down to 175,000 by the mid-1990s, prompting closure of steel plants like the one in Bethlehem, Pennsylvania that made the I beams for Rockefeller Center, the Supreme Court, and the George Washington Bridge.[21]

There have been some attempts to upgrade the skills of this smaller workforce. Of the 152 new hires in Allegheny-Ludlum Corporation in Pittsburgh, 15 have college degrees, and 86 have two-year degrees. The educational credentials at Gallatin Steel Company in Ghent, Kentucky are even better: 40 percent of the 200 workers have graduated from college. Some employees with college degrees work in factories because the pay is higher; others do so as a form of hands-on graduate work, to prepare them for a future in the industry. While this upgrading does represent an important trend, it is hardly enough to overcome the dominant fact that with every new technological advance, there is less human labor in steel making.[22]

Robots

If technology is usually labor-saving, robots are the form of technology that is most specifically intended to substitute for a worker. For industrial purposes, there are essentially three kinds of robots. One kind of robot is a fixed machine with manipulators that perform tasks automatically, such as spot welding or spray painting. A second type is a field robot with sensors that is designed to function in an unstructured environment, such as mining, firefighting, and undersea work. The third type represents the future of robotics, in which experimental computerized machines use artificial intelligence to solve problems as humans do. After many years of mixed results, robots have demonstrated their capacity to perform an increasing number of tasks at work. At General Motors, robots put a bead of urethane sealant around the windshield frame of vehicles before the glass is installed. In pursuit of more advanced functions, researchers at MIT and Purdue are jointly developing software for smart machine tools. In this concept, mobile robots would carry parts around the factory. When a robot came on to the floor, it would signal to machine tools what work its part required. The machine tools would then review their production schedules to determine when they would be available, and the computers would calculate what combination of machines could complete the job most quickly.[23]

Since the early 1980s, the cost of robots has dropped 50 percent, and reliability has increased four times. Today's robots can also be reprogrammed for new tasks. Nevertheless, despite their growing potential, most industrial robots are Japanese. The only major American company is Adept Technology, which makes robots for light assembly on circuit boards and electronic devices and is therefore not quite so dependent on the business cycles of the car industry.[24]

The most successful marketer of robots is Fanuc Robotics Corp., a Japanese company that now sells close to three-quarters of the world's robotics. Japan has a highly educated workforce. It also possesses a long-term commitment to key businesses, a dedication to top quality design and efficient production, and a government-encouraged leasing company (JAROL) that offers advice and machines at low cost. For all these reasons, Japan, more than the United States, has incorporated robotics into its economy. A shortage of labor and the tradition of lifetime employment by one company facilitate this process: Japanese workers were not going to be displaced by robots. Besides, unlike heterogeneous societies where guest workers or people of color do the unpleasant jobs, robots in Japan could do the unpleasant jobs and help industry increase its productivity.[25]

In Japan, the Fanuc factory near Mt. Fuji may foreshadow the factory of the future. Prior to 1982, a workforce of 108 people and 32 robots produced 6000 spindle and servo motors each month. After redesign, it employed 60 people and 101 robots to produce 10,000 servo motors a month, for a productivity increase of 300 percent. Still, the inclination to invest in robots, and the likely economic consequences of this investment, depend very much on political and economic factors like the organization of work. When automation rises in Japan, wages also rise, but in the United States, when automation increases, wages go down.[26] The United States has not yet turned to robotics as decisively as Japan, but the chances are that it eventually will. The question is: Will it do so as a conscious part of a high-wage, high performance strategy, or simply as still another method for keeping wages down?

Automation

Even if the trend toward robotics is slower in the United States, the trend toward automation is quite strong. Office automation, for example, which accounts for nearly 45 percent of real private investment in producers' durable equipment, has become the fastest growing demand component in the U.S. economy. Nor is it alone. At the GEO Fanuc automation plant in Charlottesville, Virginia, automation puts electronic components onto circuit boards in half the time of the older technology. Capacity has been doubled without a proportionate increase in headcount. Likewise, Solectron Corp, a Silicon Valley circuit board maker that won a 1991 Malcolm Baldrige National Quality Award, invested $80 million in similar equipment. Had it tried to produce a comparable number of circuit boards with the old machinery, it would have nearly had to double its workforce to 8000 people.[27]

Some businesses foresee agile manufacturing as the future of industry. The hope is that since it entails custom-made products delivered on time, customers will not have to maintain inventories. Eager to slash delivery time, some manufacturers might even return their production facilities to the United States, because the wage differential is no longer worth the extra shipping time. Developed at Lehigh University's Iacocca Institute, the concept gained further support from the National Science Foundation and the Pentagon's Advanced Research Projects agency. They helped to establish three agile manufacturing research institutes at the University of Illinois, the University of Texas, and Rensselaer Polytechnic Institute. In addition, more than 200 companies including Texas Instruments, Chrysler, and Westinghouse have joined the "Agile Manufacturing Enterprise Forum."[28]

These technological developments have cost some sectors of the economy a lot of jobs. Telephone operators are perhaps the prime example. Their number peaked at 250,000 in 1956. In the 1990s, however, voice-recognition technology drove their numbers sharply downward, passing 60,000 in 1995 as AT&T cut staffing by 55 percent in seven years. Similarly, Fleet Financial has replaced scores of credit officers with a software program that enables a clerk to approve or disapprove credit-card and home equity loans. At Pacific Gas & Electric Co., another software program that designs new electrical services and projects installation costs threatens hundreds of $50,000 a year technician jobs. In the near future, a 100-lot development will be designed in a half hour, instead of the one hundred hours a technician would have required. As a result, PG&E will slash the number of estimator positions by one-third from 500 over the next two years; moreover, since most have only a two-year degree, they will have to take a big pay cut. In 1995, Kansas City Power & Light became the first major electrical utility to place a small electronic device in each of its 420,000 meters, a device which broadcasts electric usage every few minutes and therefore dooms the $15 an hour jobs of the nation's 35,000 human meter readers. And, finally, there is the $25 billion vending machine industry, where route drivers used to open the machines, count the items remaining, collect money, and make sure the machines worked. Because hand-held computers costing five to six thousand dollars can now scan for these data, some companies that employ this system have been able to shrink the number of drivers by 30 percent. Soon, when the job can all be done from a central communication point, the reductions will be even larger.[29]

One of the biggest threats to job holders lies in retailing. Between 1990 and 1993, the move to bar codes contributed to the loss of 400,000 retailing jobs. Within another generation, the automated electronic marketplace might account for as much as 25 percent of all retail activity. From bank tellers to ticket agents, from librarians to sales clerks, any repetitive job drawing on a well-defined data base is therefore at risk.[30]

The best argument for the reality of the threat to jobs derives from the capacity of electronic technology to cut across many different sectors of the economy. When agriculture mechanized, and workers left the farm for the factory jobs in the cities, a rising industrial sector was available to absorb them. Now, however, no comparable sector can do that. The technological sector of the economy—the one part of the economy that is really growing—is itself so transformed by technical efficiency that even if the newly unemployed workers were sufficiently skilled, it could never absorb more than a fraction of those downsized by other industries. The renewed commitment to greater productivity would never allow it.

The experience of Compaq Computer illustrates the ambiguities of this trend. From 1991 to 1994, Compaq doubled the number of PCs produced per square foot of factory space and increased by 50 percent the number of machines produced per worker. Substituting three person production cells for assembly lines propelled much of this efficiency, because when an assembly line stops, it affects more people than when a cell does. On the other hand, an assembly line employs more people.[31]

This reorganization of work raises two problems. One is that in the absence of a widespread, labor-intensive industry, the fear of permanent technological unemployment has more basis now than at any previous time in modern economic history. Such a judgment does not imply that growing technological unemployment is an absolute certainty; it only suggests that circumstances are sufficiently different this time to temper the reassurances that history might otherwise provide.

The second and related confusion stems from a basic misconception about the nature of macroeconomic efficiency. The assumption is that if a commodity is produced with less, the economy is more efficient. This logic, however, leaps from the efficiency of the firm to efficiency of the whole economy. A firm's efficiency may increase, but the efficiency of the economy as a whole does not unless the unemployed proportion of the labor force gets alternative employment. In the worst case scenario, a company could completely automate production, downsize to a few employees who attended to the machines, and make the survival of its other workers a public responsibility. Yet because these improvements are strictly internal to the firm, its claims of greater efficiency would still ring hollow.[32]

It is, then, hardly surprising that workers view the reassurances about the effects of automation with some skepticism: if the reassurance is unjustified, it is they who will bear the costs of the transition. Sometimes, to ease the anxiety, managers make another promise; not only will there be jobs for workers, but automation will be used to give them greater initiative. For the most part, this is a rhetorical gesture, since managers usually end up investing more in the intelligence of the machines. Nevertheless, the gesture is revealing, because it suggests that managers, having recognized the liberating potential of automation for workers, must then repress it for the challenge it represents to their own authority.[33]

The Transformation of Work

While the drive for automation and heightened efficiency constitutes one part of the transformation of work, it alone does not suffice to describe the change that is taking place. Two other phenomena are equally important. They are the virtual office and the reorganization of work through reengineering, flexible specialization, and mass customization.

The move toward a virtual office takes several different forms. The more moderate form is evident at the new IBM sales office in Cranford, New Jersey, where there are 220 desks for 600 sales representatives. One day a week or less when sales representatives come in to pick up mail and see associates, the computer assigns them a spot with one chair, a telephone, and a jack for a laptop. Most of the time, employees do their administrative work by modem from home or in spare offices at customer sites. IBM was able to cut two layers of middle management by moving five sales offices to Cranford. It also halved the number of sales and service representatives.[34]

A similar upheaval occurred at Chiat-Day, the advertising agency in Venice, California whose commercial—one of the most famous of all time—introduced the MacIntosh computer during half-time at the 1984 Superbowl. Chiat-Day tried to depersonalize the office altogether. According to Jay Chiat, the office had become "an archaic space to store your stuff, very little of which had anything to do with what you did." Instead of arriving at a designated office, Chiat-Day employees check out portable phones and laptop computers from dispensaries known as the "Cage and Concierge," and then settle down at the first available workstation next to another colleague regardless of position. If you do not have to be in the office, you can work from home by computer. There is a high school style locker room to put your belongings, but otherwise no personal effects are allowed—not even family photographs.[35]

Virtual offices are profoundly contradictory places. In one sense, they are supposed to be liberating, freeing workers from constraints that might distract them from the tasks at hand. Yet the absence of personal belongings signals something else about the virtual office: it is also a "profoundly dehumanizing place with nowhere to put your feet up and snooze or sneak off for a conspiratorial powwow." In essence, when employees came to work, they were supposed to travel light, and the only item they must bring to work was their capacity to labor. Virtual offices are like that. Once you are connected electronically, you are always at work. With 7 A.M. to 11 P.M. work days becoming increasingly common, it was inevitable that rivals would eventually refer to the agency as Chiat/Day and Night.[36]

It is true that the virtual office can eliminate paper. In the United States, 600 million pages of printouts and 76 million letters are produced each business day. Altogether, U.S. business consumes nearly one trillion pages of paper every year. American corporations hope to get out from under this deluge by replacing written information with electronic reports. Nordstrom, the upscale department store chain, converted its written reports to computer-only information and saved $1 million a year. Likewise, when Aetna Insurance discovered that it had 435 manuals requiring constant updating, it placed all the manuals on computer. The change prevented 100 million pages of updates from being sent out and saved $6 million a year. By closing the warehouse facility that revised the manuals, Aetna could also lay off employees.[37]

In addition to the virtual office, another aspect of the drive to transform work involves the redesign or reengineering of a company's production process to achieve dramatic performance improvements. IBM Credit Corporation, a subsidiary of IBM, provides financing to IBM customers. Before the credit approval process was reengineered, four different specialists handled requests, which went through several different departments, taking an average of six days, but sometimes as much as two weeks. Two senior managers discovered that each request actually required just ninety minutes, and that the rest of the time was spent en route between departments. By substituting generalists for the specialists whose skills were needed only on a small number of credit applications, IBM reduced the seven-day turnaround to four hours. Without increasing staff size, it is handling one hundred times as many applications as before the reengineering process.[38]

Work redesign has even extended to agriculture. Many hogs, for example, are now raised on large finishing farms, under contract to big companies such as Murphy Family Farms, which recently became the country's largest pork producer. The hogs are bred in farrowing farms until weaning after seventeen to twenty days. Then they go to nurseries, and once they reach fifty pounds, to finishing farms, where mechanized delivery of food and removal of waste has meant that one farmer can do the work of many laborers. Thousands of hogs can be raised indoors, many times the number handled previously. This mechanization, however, reflects a different set of financial arrangements. The company, not the farm, owns the hogs, so farmers receive a flat fee. This makes them totally dependent on one company and subject to price squeezes.[39]

As part of reengineering, craft work has also returned to manufacturing. Clearly, craft methods are not efficient for gasoline and other nondiscrete products, nor are they useful for heavy complex manufactured goods such as final assembly of automobiles: Volvo has finally closed its craft lines at two auto plants in Sweden. On the other hand, a survey of 1042 American plants by Paul Swamidass of Auburn University for the National Association of Manufacturers found 34 percent saying they were using assembly cells with "moderate or extreme success." The assembly line produced uniform products, but now the one-size fits all era is gone, and companies need more kinds of products to secure a niche in a highly differentiated market. The NEC Corp. is typical. It makes nineteen different cordless phones, up from three ten years ago. Using a line shaped like a three-legged spider, thirty people in two spider lines make 1000 phones a day, the same number as seventy people used to produce on a conveyor system.[40]

The flight from mass production drives these changes, and that flight is nearly over. Mass production dominated from 1900 to 1970. It had 150 machine tools, produced ten to fifteen products, and reworked 25 percent due to poor quality. The traditional mass production company was bureaucratic and hierarchical, with workers repeating narrowly defined tasks under close supervision, but it had the advantage of yielding a plentiful supply of cheap standardized products. Flexible production, which superseded mass production, is expected to last from 1971 until 2000; it involves thirty to fifty machine tools and produces 100 to 1000 products, with a .02 error rate. Unlike its predecessor, flexible production relies on multipurpose equipment and seeks to innovate constantly. To its most enthusiastic advocates, it also represents an opportunity to return to craft forms of organization that are rooted in a genuine community of high-performance workers. Nevertheless, the era of flexible specialization is expected to be brief, with mass customization following close on its heels. Dominating industrial production in the first few decades of the twenty-first century, mass customization will utilize just twenty to twenty-five machine tools to produce unlimited products with error rates of only .0005 percent. By constantly reconfiguring people, processes, units, and technology, mass customization will give customers exactly what they want in the form of low-cost, high-quality customized goods and services.[41]

The first signs of mass customization have already begun to appear. In the clothing industry, for example, Levi is now able to sell made-to-order jeans. The customer's measurements are taken by computer, using software that allows 4224 possible combinations of four basic measurements—hips, waist, inseam, and rise. These data are then transmitted electronically to a Levi-Strauss factory in Mountain City, Tennessee, where a robotic tailor cuts denim for the precise fit. Arriving back at the store in three weeks, the pants costs about ten dollars more than mass-produced jeans. Mass customization will thrive on such just-in-time production, which will allow stores to cut down on inventory—and the jobs that go into maintaining it.[42]

In short, some remarkable technical changes have occurred over the last twenty years. The changes, which have brought about growing product complexity, are themselves the result of the diffusion of data processing, software, and improved machine tools, as well as a preference for modular techniques. Modular techniques are important because they let managers oversee a manufacturing process whose intermediate technical steps all converge at the end. The key to the smooth operation of this process is avoiding congestion through decentralized production. Managers have also sought to conserve physical space through integrated circuits, sensors, micromotors, minirobots, and microtunnelling equipment. These technical achievements have combined with the rapid improvements in information management to effect a major transformation in the world of work.[43]

Downsizing

Once technology, like foreign labor, could substitute for American workers, more could be made with less. These new possibilities intensified the demand for greater efficiency; they established the conditions necessary for a period of corporate downsizing. And downsize business did, starting in industry during the 1980s, but soon spreading rapidly to other sectors. By the late 1990s, corporate downsizing had become an established feature of American economic life, in good economic times as well as in bad.

In the first phase of corporate downsizing, from 1981 to 1990, about two million workers a year lost their jobs. These layoffs followed a distinct pattern: the largest layoffs occurred at both the top and bottom of the plant-wage distribution.[44] This trend suggests that goods from high-wage plants could be produced more cheaply overseas, while the labor of many low-wage, low-skill workers became superfluous. The resulting economic dislocation was severe. Those fired were predominantly industrial workers, who spent an average of thirty weeks unemployed. Among those who subsequently got jobs, one-third suffered earnings losses of at least 20 percent. Wage losses were sharpest for those who had been with their employer the longest. Indeed, for those with ten years of tenure, a 20 percent loss was nearly four times as likely as a 20 percent gain.[45]

In the second phase of corporate downsizing, layoffs began to creep up the economic ladder. Now white-collar workers were at risk: they constituted 40 percent of the unemployed in the recession of the early 1990s, compared with just 22 percent ten years earlier. The *Fortune* 1000 led this purge of white-collar workers when, between 1987 and 1991, 65 percent of these firms laid off white-collar workers. And white-collar executives were not only fired; they were fired fast. Instead of the typical one-year trial period granted to new hires, 22 percent of firms in an American Management Association poll fired an executive after less than three months. Corporate downsizing cut such a wide swathe that it even affected Harvard's graduating class of 1958, which despite an average income of $170,000, nonetheless had job losses of 10 to 20 percent. Overall, during the period from 1988 to 1993, 1.4 million managers and executives lost their jobs, compared with just 782,000 between 1981 and 1986.[46]

By the mid-1990s, corporate downsizing had become frenzied. Spurred by an immediate spike in the stock price of most corporations that announced layoffs, companies laid off 108,946 workers in January 1994—a one-month record. Downsizing quickly became the mainstay of all management strategies, the consistent response to whatever ailed a corporation. Whether it was overseas competition, an insufficiently "flexible" union, or hypervigilant institutional investors, downsizing sent a message that management had taken charge. An extraordinary number of companies found this message so compelling that they sought to send it themselves. Within a comparatively short period, businesses laying off more than five thousand workers included General Motors, 69,550; Sears Roebuck, 50,000; IBM, 38,500; Boeing, 31,000; and Philip Morris, 14,000.[47]

Remarkably, downsizing on a large scale continued even as economic conditions improved. In the late 1990s, unemployment declined to 5 percent, but the list of downsizers dwindled only slightly. In 1997, Kodak cut 10,000 employees or 10 percent of its workforce. At the same time, Levi-Strauss paid its retiring CEO $126 million and laid off 6395 workers. In 1998, both AT&T and Motorola announced the elimination of 15,000 employees.[48] Although these layoffs were somewhat more whispered and apologetic in tone, the persistence of downsizing in better economic times kept the labor market churning. As the latest method for managing the workforce, downsizing was the one tool that did not require the workforce to be employed.

To evaluate the phenomenon of downsizing, we must distinguish clearly between its effects on workers and its effects on the company. Downsizing plainly has a negative effect on workers. That downsizing should have such mixed effects on companies, however, is neither quite so apparent nor quite so well known.[49]

The effects of downsizing on workers have been amply documented. In addition to typical—and often sharp—declines in salary, there are social ramifications of downsizing: a shame so severe that suburban executives will not even step outside their house during the day, lest the neighbors surmise the real reason why they stayed home; an increase in violence, like the 100 percent leap in the caseload of abused wives and other crime victims at counseling centers near Poughkeepsie, New York, after a flood of IBM layoffs; and the disintegration of communities like Lower Northeast, a Philadelphia neighborhood where real estate values plummeted 80 percent when unemployment rose as layoffs at Canada Dry, Mrs. Paul's Kitchen, and Sears totaled 3200 workers.[50]

Such large social consequences would seem to demand a cogent, unequivocal business rationale. Yet even within the business community, evaluations of downsizing are quite ambiguous. There are those who say it does what it is supposed to do—cut labor costs, eliminate unnecessary management, and sharpen organizational competitiveness. For them, the social consequences either fall within acceptable bounds or are totally irrelevant to a purely business decision. On the other side are those who, after adding up all the negative fallout from downsizing, assert that it does not even achieve its own stated ends. This fallout includes failure to improve corporate performance; decline in product quality and productivity because employees feel anxious and betrayed; greater employee stress leading to bigger health care costs; and higher rates of tardiness, absenteeism, and turnover. In one American Management Association study, for example, only 43.5 percent of 547 organizations that had downsized in the past six years experienced an improvement in operating profits, and 67 percent of managers observed no growth in productivity.[51] Similarly, the Wyatt Company's 1991 study of restructuring in one thousand large firms found that less than half achieved their expense reduction goals; less than one-third increased profitability; and less than one-quarter increased productivity or achieved other restructuring goals.[52] The major reason for these unexpected results was the effect of downsizing on the survivors. Having imagined downsizing as a simple matter of reducing the cost of labor inputs, management discovered that the remaining labor inputs turned out, in fact, to be some very angry people.

Downsizing has severed the psychological bond between management and employees and drastically altered the way U.S. workers see business. By a 75 to 6 percent margin, workers now think that companies are less loyal today than they were ten years ago. The atmosphere at work has changed, too. By a 70 to 20 percent margin, employees believe that they are more likely to compete, rather than cooperate with, their coworkers, and by a 53 to 8 percent margin, they see their worksite as an angrier place.[53] Despite management's intentions, the likelihood of making significant productivity gains in an environment like this seems very questionable.

Obviously, the simple, reflexive strategy that prompts corporate managers to downsize will not work. They assume that it will be easier to make a profit because a company with 5000 fewer employees will have lower expenses. This assumption rides roughshod over the complex set of human relationships that make up any large institution, and it overlooks the organic nature of the business enterprise. The social consequences of downsizing are immeasurable. But viewed just as business strategy, downsizing only succeeds when it combines staff reduction with a wholesale restructuring of the organization. Simply chopping away at the headcount does not work.[54]

The Growth of Part-Time and Temporary Jobs

Downsizing mirrors the growth of contingent labor. At the same time many corporations laid off large numbers of permanent workers, they expanded their use of part-time and temporary employees. Of course, corporations have always limited hiring to the people whom they needed. With contingent workers, however, corporations are increasingly committed to hiring the labor *without* hiring the people. This attempt to purchase units of labor disembodied from the laborer fundamentally shifts the relationship of businesses and their employees. It suggests that part-time and temporary workers have become "the human equivalent of just-in-time production, where parts arrive in a factory only as they are needed."[55]

Part-time or temporary work may be a good option for workers with hi-tech skills, or those such as working mothers who wish to retain some flexibility over their work schedules. Hi-tech workers, in particular, are the elite of the temp workforce, with technical editors at Microsoft earning $30 an hour, three to four times the rate for other temporary workers. In both wages and freedom to choose their work, however, they are the exception. The majority of temporary workers are not involuntary. In fact, after rising sharply to 4.3 percent in 1989, the overall rate of involuntary unemployment dropped to 3.2 percent in 1997, just one-tenth of one percent above its 1973 level.[56]

Yet the total number of part-time and temporary workers remains a subject of some controversy. The debate has intensified ever since 1989, when a study by Richard Belous asserted that between 29.9 million and 36.6 million people were contingent workers. While virtually everyone acknowledges that the numbers have grown—perhaps, since 1982, at three times the rate of permanent employment, there has been a considerable effort to minimize the total number. The President's Council of Economic Advisors, for example, has contended that the total number of contingent workers is less than 3 percent, and the Department of Labor conducted a study that found contingent labor to constitute just 2.2 to 4.9 percent of the labor force. The study constricted the definition of contingent work to arrive at this number. It excluded part-time workers who wanted full-time work, people who consider themselves independent contractors, those working for temporary help agencies, and those "on call." Had they included these categories, their own numbers would have pointed to a contingent labor force of between 16 and 18 percent.[57]

The debate about part-time work is so keen because its growth points to the likelihood of further downward mobility. Part-time workers received lower wages—80 percent of full-time wages for women and about 75 percent for men. They rarely get health care benefits, and their employment benefits such as unemployment, sickness, disability, and maternity or retirement pay are usually prorated. Lower salaries and less social protection means that one in six part-time workers and one in five involuntary part-time workers has a family income below the poverty level.[58]

The spread of temporary work has triggered an explosive period of growth among agencies that provide temporary workers to American companies. Between 1983 and 1997, the number of temporary workers placed by these agencies increased from 500,000 to almost 2.5 million or 2 percent of the workforce. Increasingly, big companies designate one agency to supply all their temporary workers. Manpower and Volt Information Group does it for Hewlett-Packard in the United States, with Manpower providing 50 percent of their temporary workers, up from less than 40 percent, but projected to reach 80 percent in two years. Similarly, Kelly has contracts with Kraft General Foods and Johnson & Johnson; the Olsten Corporation serves AT&T, Bristol-Myers Squibb, and the computer services unit of General Electric; and Adia

Services serves the Bank of America. Partly as a result of these major contracts, Manpower, Inc., with 767,000 employees, had by 1996 replaced Wal-Mart as the second leading employer in the country.[59]

The trend to part-time and contingent work is likely to continue, simply because the incentive is too great. To diminish that incentive, some significant reforms would be necessary. Certainly, health benefits would have to be national, rather than dependent on a particular job. All workers would also require representation in decisions affecting hours of work, and pay would have to be equalized at a minimum of 50 percent of the median hourly wage, regardless of whether it is full or part time. Without these reforms, many employers will continue to indulge their preference for hiring labor in the smallest possible units.[60]

Race and the Job Shortage

The obvious consequence of hiring in the smallest possible units is that some people do not get hired at all. This is true for factory workers, who lost almost six million jobs between 1979 and the early 1990s. It is also true for white-collar workers, who are increasingly vulnerable to downsizing and the vagaries of the job market. And it is especially true for people in the lowest wage decile, whose time as jobless increased by 16 percent, or eight weeks, between the late 1960s and the late 1980s.[61] While all these groups now have a more tenuous relationship to the job market, none specifically reflects the racial dimension of this shortage, which is, in some respects, the most wrenching of all.

A study of the Milwaukee job market illuminates this racial dimension. It shows that during one week in May 1993, 11,870 full-time and 9277 part-time jobs were available for immediate hire in the four-county Milwaukee metropolitan area. These jobs represented about 20 percent of the full-time, and 35 percent of the full-time and/or part-time jobs, needed for the more than 61,000 persons seeking work in that month. Although these proportions were bad enough, the racial differential made it even more severe: only 1248 of the full-time job openings were located in central city neighborhoods, where some 17,000 people were unemployed, and just 48 percent of these jobs offered health insurance and wages above the poverty line for a family of four.[62]

The shrinking supply of jobs has had particularly dire consequences for African-American men. In 1996, for example, 4.7 percent of white men, but 9.4 percent of working age black men, were unemployed. As William Julius Wilson has argued, the decline in manufacturing explains a large part of this discrepancy, because a prime source of employment for young African-American males simply disappeared. Between 1973 and 1987, for example, the percentage of African-American males ages 20–29 employed in the manufacturing sector dropped from 37 to 20 percent. Equally important, this decline in manufacturing not only cost jobs, but also cost the comparatively good wages that went with those jobs. Between 1973 and 1989, the mean earnings of African-American male high school dropouts fell by nearly half, compared with only one-third for white male dropouts; for African-American male high school graduates, the decline was one-third, in contrast to one-fifth for white male high school graduates.[63]

In addition to the decline of manufacturing, a multitude of other factors has combined to disadvantage African-Americans in the job market. The most rapid job growth has shifted from the northeast to the southwest, where African-Americans are not the dominant minority. Within this shift lies still another spatial mismatch, in which suburban, service-sector jobs have replaced manufacturing positions in the inner city. Since employers with these jobs are often reluctant to hire black men, women and immigrants are able to compete more successfully. Between the decline of manufacturing, regional shifts in the job market, racism on the part of some employers, and the increasingly stiff competition for service jobs, the transformation of the labor market has had an especially destructive impact on the African-American community.[64]

African-American female college graduates constitute one of the few exceptions to this trend. Those with one to five years experience on the job now make slightly more than college-educated, African-American men, $11.41 an hour compared to $11.26 per hour. This advantage not only contrasts with the familiar differential between white women and white men ($11.38 and $12.85), but also represents a reversal from the late 1970s, when African-American males, like white males, earned more than women of the same race. African-American women have gained this lead, in part, because even comparatively middle-class black males are still threatening to some people, and employers can easily hire women in service-sector jobs to satisfy demands for diversity.[65]

Since, to a large extent, African-Americans are still the last hired and the first fired, it would require a sustained period of full employment to make much of a dent in their unemployment rate. In fact, a study of the minibooms in Anaheim, California and Boston, Massachusetts during the mid-1980s suggests that to provide sufficient opportunity to poor youths, unemployment would have to drop to as low as 3 or 4 percent.[66] When unemployment reached 5.5 percent in the mid-1990s, the rate for African-Americans did dip below 11 percent (10.4 percent in 1995) for the first time in more than two decades. Yet even at this level, unemployment among African-American youth remained well above 30 percent (37.1 percent for males, 34.3 percent for females), about two and a half times the rate for whites. Moreover, because these rates exclude discouraged workers, they reinforce the notion that the real unemployment rate would have to go much lower.[67] In the absence of political pressures that would compel the financial markets to tolerate such a boom, the job shortage is likely to persist, leaving Americans of all races either insecure in their jobs or searching for work.

4

The Low-Wage, Low-Skill Strategy

It is not that there are too many low-wage jobs, but that there are not enough jobs for low-wage workers.

—Donald Deere, Kevin Murphy, and Finis Welch

It's so easy to pay low wages in the United States that corporate eyes gleam like kids in a carnival when they enter the labor market. . . . In order to push U.S. employers toward the high road, their labor costs need to rise. They need to begin modernizing or get out of the kitchen.

—David Gordon

Downsizing is a powerful tool for disempowering and enfeebling labor. So are threats to move, the expressed willingness to automate, and the proliferation of part-time work. The top fifth of the labor market is increasingly hi-tech and competes globally: it benefits from, or else is comparatively immune to, these phenomena. Within the specifically American labor market, however, the impact of these changes is not nearly so benign. Competition in the international labor market demands workers of high wage and high skill. For the remaining U.S. workers, however, all that is left is a low-wage, low-skill strategy, one that is often played out with special force on women and people of color.

This strategy takes many forms. Despite shortages in their local labor markets, some companies resist raising wages. Their tactics include turning away business as well as hiring low-skill workers and training them. If the training is sufficiently job-specific, then employees are less likely to leave, and despite a modest increase for the trained worker, there will not be much of a ripple effect on other salaries. The company's overall wage structure can then remain intact.

In some labor markets, however, businesses do not even want to take this risk. The jewelry industry in Providence, Rhode Island represents a significant part of the local labor market, but employers there are even more deeply committed to low wages and skills. When government researchers tried to analyze the operation of this market, one employer said that he could not participate in the project because the research might lower the high school dropout rate, on which he depended for an ample supply of low-wage labor.[1]

Sometimes calculations like these pervade the economies of whole cities. Cedar Rapids, Iowa; Sioux City, South Dakota; and Jacksonville, North Carolina are three locales where low wages predominate. In Cedar Rapids, the typical wage is $6.50 an hour, and 17 percent of families during the 1990 census had incomes less than half the median wage. Wages in Sioux City, South Dakota are similar, with many jobs paying $6 to $7 an hour. Jacksonville, North Carolina, however, is the flagship city of the low-wage, low-skill strategy. For four consecutive years, Jacksonville, a city of 80,000 people, has had the lowest annual pay of the nation's 310 urban areas. While more run-of-the-mill houses sell for fifty to seventy thousand dollars, one-quarter of Jacksonville's population lives in mobile homes. The average pay for all jobs is, at $7.50 an hour, $4 less than the national mean. Although the poverty rate and the unemployment rate are both below average, factories employing 800 workers have closed in Jacksonville and the surrounding Onslow area, and those that remain employ just 6 percent of the workforce, compared to 21 percent nationally. In addition, only 13 percent of Onslow has more than two years of college. A fading manufacturing sector and an undereducated labor force have therefore combined to foster a drift toward a restaurant-level minimum wage, and it is this combination that makes Onslow the prototypical low-wage, low-skill county.[2]

Besides low-wage counties, there are also low-wage jobs, not tied to any specific locality. They demand routine or dirty work, have no prestige, offer little chance of promotion, and pay wages at, or not much over, the minimum. At Electronic Banking System, in Hagerstown, Maryland, Ron Eden, former financial controller for the National Rifle Association, monitors his mostly female workers as they open envelopes for charitable donations. Eden has covered the office windows and banned coffee mugs, religious pictures, and other paraphernalia from his workers' desks. In his company, repetitive tasks predominate. Monitoring key strokes and mistakes by zooming in with his camera, Eden watches workers in the cage open envelopes, while those in the audit department compute figures, and data entry clerks enter the information. "We don't ask these people to think—the machines think for them." Eden says. "They don't have to make any decisions."

Other common dead-end jobs include environmental workers who extract metal, glass, and paper from household trash that sometimes contains dead animals and used hypodermic needles, and poultry workers subjected to speed-up on the line and an unending parade of dead chickens. There are now 400 material recovery facilities (Surfs) nationwide. They pay about one dollar above minimum wage, and it is not a pleasant job. "We've had a lot of trouble convincing people that disposable diapers are not recyclable," says Robert Sink, manager of the Omaha, Nebraska facility. Poultry processing is equally unpleasant and much more dangerous. Heavily dominated by women and people of color, it is, since 1980, the fastest growing factory job in America, employing 221,000 people, or about as many as steel. Poultry processing also ranks as the eleventh most dangerous industry, with an injury rate of 23.2 per 100 full-time workers. Part of this danger derives from speed-up on the line, where the rate of processing chickens has risen from the high 50s to 91 chickens a minute over the past fifteen years. Common in the Broiler Belt stretching from Delaware to east Texas, processing chickens is the second lowest paid manufacturing industry after apparel.[3]

At least three clear economic consequences emerge from this reliance on low-wage labor. The first is lagging productivity growth. Since machines are faster than people, the reliance on low-wage labor limits the productivity gains that can be made—even if, with speed-up, low-wage employees are compelled to work more quickly. Machinery, especially machinery introduced into a participatory workplace that gave employees a considerable measure of autonomy and control, would spur much greater productivity growth.

A dependence on low-wage labor also tends to create an environment in which employers import labor. As workers acclimate to their new country and become more confident, they begin to demand better pay and safer working conditions. A constant supply of cheap immigrant labor represents one of the best methods of undercutting these demands and also helps to forestall the growth of any wider militancy. Employers who rely on this strategy strongly oppose collective bargaining and other cooperative methods of mediating economic conflict. They have also been enthusiastic supporters of U.S. immigration policy over the last twenty years.[4]

Finally, and most fundamentally, dependence on low-wage labor is addictive. By comparison, investment in machinery is expensive, and it is risky to create a more participatory environment. Since any payoff from these strategies will most likely be realized over the longer term, an employer of good will who considers the longer term is invariably vulnerable to a competitor's current low-wage, low-skill strategy. To be sure, some far-seeing employers may take this risk, and a few especially resourceful ones, who completely upgrade and restructure their workplace, may even succeed. For most, however, the economic advantages of a low-wage, low-skill strategy are simply too seductive. Unless government prods companies to develop industrywide incentives, they will find it very difficult to upgrade their labor force's wages and skills.

Wage Differentials

The evident difficulty of breaking the dependence on low wages and low skills obscures a larger and still more basic issue. That issue is whether low wages inhere in the worker or in the job. Most mainstream economists contend that workers' skills determine what they get paid. Their argument follows from a conception of production that makes implicit analogies to a machine: a fixed level of skill—as one "factor of production"—combines with a fixed level of technology to yield a product or service. In this model, the market—an aggregate set of wages and prices that a single employer cannot modify—determines the compensation of workers.[5]

Others do not share this model's assumption. For them, the problem is not low-wage workers, but low-wage jobs, and wages, rather than being objectively determined by the market and simply passed on as received by the employer, are in fact subject to a variety of other influences. These influences are largely political, encompassing a range of factors from the militancy of the labor movement to the government's support for wage-setting policies like a high minimum wage and comparable worth. Because of the disproportionate power that employers have over workers, employees must accept the jobs that are available to them in order to survive. In essence, this means that it is the jobs, not the workers, whose characteristics are assumed to be fixed. Changing these jobs into positions with high wages and productivity requires a number of important policy measures, including a substantial increase in the value of the minimum wage, active anti-discrimination policies, unionization in low-wage sectors, and other strategies to equalize pay by pushing from the bottom up. In keeping with the basic premise of this view that there are no inherently low-wage workers, you modernize, pay high wages, or get out of business.[6]

As wage differentials in the United States have widened, economists have searched energetically for causes. They have focused on issues such as the returns to skill, the skills mismatch thesis, and the expanding gap between the pay of high school and college graduates. The concept of a return to skill simply refers to the belief that employers both prefer, and pay higher wages to, more skilled workers. Taking this premise one step further, partisans of the skills mismatch thesis insist such workers are actually in short supply. Together, both of these theories have been used to explain why workers with less education have been losing so much ground to their better educated counterparts.

In truth, all these theories are really another version of the debate: Is it the worker, or is it the job? The short answer is that the structure of the job market both fosters low pay and places the burden for that pay on the deficiencies of the individual worker. From this perspective, the skills of the individual worker do indeed seem to matter. Viewed more systemically, however, the expanding wage differential can be reversed if policy makers focus on the structure of the entire labor market. Then debates about the returns to skill, the skills mismatch thesis, and the gap between the pay of high school and college graduates can be seen for what they are, as reflections rather than causes of the wage differential.

Once again, international comparisons reinforce the value of this distinction. Wage differentials narrowed in the 1970s in France, Great Britain, Japan, and the United States, but then wage inequality expanded dramatically in Great Britain and the United States, and more moderately in Japan. In France, however, sharp increases in the minimum wage and the ability of French unions to extend contracts, even in the face of declining membership, helped to prevent wage differentials from expanding in the 1980s. While one might argue that "simple supply and demand measures go a reasonable distance toward explaining the differences and similarities among these countries in patterns of relative wage movements," it hardly seems coincidental that during this period, the United States and Great Britain—the countries with the most rapid expansion of wage inequality—had conservative governments that were reluctant to intervene in the labor market. Obviously, a structural approach to the labor market cannot completely override the laws of supply and demand. A glance at what other countries have done, however, does demonstrate that an activist government can significantly modify these laws.[7]

The whole debate about the causes of the wage differential revolves, then, around what are frequently perceived as two distinct sets of questions. One set of questions involves issues like the relative demand for skills, the supply of skilled workers, and the effects of technological change. Such depoliticized questions are easily treated as internal to the market. Mining them for clues, economists tend to highlight the impact of technology and observe that workers who used computers on the job had bigger wage increases in the 1980s than those who did not. Yet the market does not so readily contain the other set of questions. These questions include more political factors such as trade, globalization of the economy, the decline in the minimum wage, and decreased union membership. Insistence on the importance of these factors suggests that wage differentials are rising for reasons largely unrelated to the relative demand for skills. Inevitably, they lead to troublesome facts like the study from the Bureau of Labor Statistics reporting that while 12 percent of college graduates worked at jobs that did not require a college education in 1980, the proportion was almost 20 percent ten years later. In the end, it is plain that something else is going on.[8]

Returns to Skill

The usual explanation for wage inequality is comparatively straightforward: a shift in the relative demand for labor has prompted employers to prefer more educated and skilled workers over the less educated and less skilled. The introduction of computers is part of a technological revolution that has heightened the demand for skilled labor. Those who advance this perspective often assert that returns to skill are mostly associated with changes within industries and not merely in the shift from industry to service. Although some economists do mention the role of other institutions such as the decline of unions, this explanation customarily focuses on the kinds of market factors that mainstream American economists have always favored.[9]

The pattern they analyze is unmistakable. While the average weekly wage of working men decreased 5 percent between 1970 and 1989, wages for those at the tenth percentile of the wage distribution fell 25 percent. At the ninetieth percentile, by contrast, wages increased 25 percent during the same period. In fact, for the lowest 40 percent of workers, real wages were lower in 1988 than in 1964, indicating that this group's standard of living had stagnated for almost a quarter century. The education differential parallels the wage differential: workers with a college education who earned 45 percent more than high school graduates in 1973 earned an additional 65 percent by 1995. More education makes an even bigger difference: those with advanced degrees saw their income increase 12 percent between 1979 and 1997, while those with a high school education saw their income fall about the same amount.[10]

These data appear to offer powerful support for an analysis based primarily on supply and demand factors. After all, changes in the workplace over the last quarter century have been substantial, and the benefits from these changes do often seem to accrue to those with better skills. There are reasons, however, to doubt the adequacy of this explanation, and these reasons are most clearly apparent in analyses of the skills mismatch thesis.

Skills Mismatch

The skills mismatch thesis refines and elaborates supply-and-demand interpretations of the wage differential. While debates about the returns to skill emphasize extra compensation paid to more skilled workers, the skills mismatch thesis posits an actual discrepancy between the supply of skilled workers and the number of such workers that employers need. Supposedly, this discrepancy has led to steady upward bidding in the price of skilled labor. It is also the most common explanation for the economic problems of the lower half of the skill distribution.[11]

Because advocates of this thesis tend to place a high value on differences in skill, they often stress the importance of technology in fostering large wage differentials. In addition, some follow the logic that if there is a deficiency of skill, training to remedy that deficiency is the natural remedy. Although these positions seem commonsensical, both contain unwarranted assumptions that have been the subject of considerable debate. It is very difficult, for example, to measure the effect of technology or gauge the real extent of its contribution to the wage spread. Nor is training of much value in the absence of real jobs. Common sense always has its appeal, but no approach to the increasing disparity of wages should display so many obvious vulnerabilities.[12]

A full critique of the skills mismatch thesis begins with the fact that it refers to three-quarters of the workforce without a college degree, including a number of less educated but highly skilled people such as technicians and electricians. These workers possess distinct skills, but have been downwardly mobile anyway. Then again, there is the trajectory of wages among college graduates. In the almost two decades from 1979 to 1997, they rose just 5.6 percent.[13] So modest an increase cannot explain the growing wage premium. The clear implication is that the premium derives not so much from a rapid upward trend of wages among the college-educated as from a sharp drop in the wages of those without a college education.

In addition, half the growth of wage inequality was due to the growth of wage inequality among workers with similar levels of education. Since there is no evidence that this is related to any skills mismatch, it suggests that some workers may have simply been more vulnerable to pressure from employers. This argument makes particular sense in the United States, because except for an increasingly laissez-faire Great Britain, the phenomena of technologically driven skills mismatch does not appear to be occurring in other countries.

There are also a host of measurement problems. Since it is difficult to calculate the effect of technology on wages, advocates of the skills mismatch thesis have tended to proceed by assumption. If all the usual supply-and-demand factors are not very helpful in explaining the wage premium, technology becomes the only possible remaining explanation. Not only is this reasoning by adduction, but it suffers from a further weakness. Although the technical requirements of many jobs may have grown over the last thirty years, there is no evidence that they grew both especially quickly and at the very same time as the spurt in the wage gap. In fact, as we have already noted, wages of college graduates began to decline in 1987, soon after the introduction of computers in the mid-1980s. The skills mismatch thesis seems like a very unlikely explanation for these trends.

The difficulty of estimating skill requirements is still another measurement problem. Lacking a more precise method, the skills mismatch thesis usually takes educational level as a shorthand index of skill. Yet, as virtually every study has shown, and many of us have personally experienced on the job, little relationship exists between job skill and educational level. This difficulty casts the whole premise of a sharp rise in skill requirements into still further doubt.[14]

All these questions about the skills mismatch thesis inevitably lead to one other. If the thesis is so weak, why is it so popular? The best answer: it represents a market-based explanation that implicitly blames the individual worker for any deficits of skill. This rationale shifts the burden of proof. No, wages have not declined because corporations have downsized, resisted unions, or threatened to move elsewhere. No, wages have declined because workers in a changing economy failed to master additional skills. With this argument in hand, corporate executives like Frank Doyle, General Electric's vice president for external relations, have an alternative explanation for declining wages. When General Electric closes fifty plants in the United States and lays off 46,000 workers, those laid off are not unskilled: they are, instead, electricians, machinists, engineers, and white-collar managers. Hence, while the assertion that skill is the issue may have the considerable merit of sounding plausible, we must look elsewhere for an explanation that is both plausible *and* true. A true explanation looks instead to a different set of causes—to deunionization, wage concessions, the downskilling of work for the less educated, and the increased use of contingent workers—indeed, to all the components of a low-wage strategy.[15]

The College–High School Differential

Another prominent symptom of the wage gap is the growing college–high school differential. The pattern is clear: in 1980, the median male worker with a college degree earned about one-third more than the median male high school graduate without a college degree, but by 1993, this gap had reached 70 percent. Although the trend has slowed—it even declined slightly in 1995—its broad outlines are hardly unique to the United States. The United States is, however, the country where the college premium grew the fastest.[16]

Once again, however, the key factor propelling this differential is not a sharp rise in the real income of the college-educated, but rather a decline in the wages of those who are not. Between 1979 and 1997, college-educated males gained a modest 1.8 percent in real hourly wages, while the wages of those with less than four years of college dropped 16.8 percent. Among women, the pattern was somewhat different, but the outcome was the same: as wages stagnated among the less educated, and grew for those with college degrees, the differential increased from 30.8 percent in 1979 to 51.1 percent in 1997.[17]

Education does help, of course. Even if wages have stagnated, unemployment rates are much lower among the well educated. By educational attainment, unemployment rates in March 1993 ran from 12.6 percent for those with no diploma and 7.2 percent for high school graduates down to 2.8 percent for those with a bachelor's or master's degree and 1.1 percent for holders of a professional degree. These numbers provide some comfort. The credentialed may not be earning much more than they used to, but at least they are more likely to have a job.[18]

Still, it would be wrong to overreach and make too many assumptions about the rate of return to education. Such assumptions skim over issues of school quality, downplay the question of ability—even skewed as it is by issues of race and class—and ignore the issue of selection bias. If the people who get an education are different in both observable and not so observable ways, then more education is not necessarily the remedy for most people's declining income.[19]

This is particularly true, now that continued growth in the income of the college-educated—especially college-educated males—is no longer assured. Indeed, it is even more pertinent because with an abundant supply of college graduates, supply-and-demand is likely to reinforce the trend toward stagnant wages for the foreseeable future. According to the U.S. Bureau of Labor Statistics, almost 20 million college graduates will join the workforce between 1996 and 2006, but only 7.3 million jobs will require a bachelor's degree. As a result, nearly two-thirds of college graduates may have to take jobs for which they are overeducated. Since about 20 percent of college graduates earn less than the median salary for all high school graduates, the existence of a college premium can only be interpreted to mean that they are doing better than those with a high school education, but not necessarily that they are doing well.[20]

Minimum Wage

A low minimum wage is the cornerstone of any low-wage strategy. Set above the public assistance level but below every other wage in the labor market, the minimum wage represents the dividing line between those who do not work and those who do. For those who do not work, the wage represents a minimum to which they can aspire. For those who do work, the wage establishes a floor under the level of compensation for their own labor.

The Clinton administration raised the minimum wage from $4.25 an hour to $5.15 an hour in 1997. Raising the minimum wage was politically popular, since 84 percent of Americans favored such an increase. The increase was much less popular among professional economists, however, with 77 percent of the members of the American Economics Association believing it would cost jobs. Although this clash of opinion is fairly common, it was especially intense this time because some new research has suggested that textbook explanations about the effect of an increase did not carry over into the real world.[21]

It is easy to see why raising the minimum wage is politically popular: most Americans work for somebody else and want to be paid more. Minimum wage workers are not receiving welfare: they work, and because they work, they elicit the ready sympathy of other, better paid workers who sense that supporting any increase in the minimum wage may also help themselves. About 4.2 million workers paid by the hour had earnings at or below the minimum wage. This figure included 2.5 million people at the minimum wage, and another 1.7 million at less than the minimum wage, either because they were exempt from it or because they were illegally paid less than the minimum. In addition, there was another substantial bloc of ten million workers whose wages were pegged between $4.25 and $5.15, the old and new minimums. Consistent with the other dimensions of the low-wage strategy, women make up 62 percent of all minimum wage workers.[22]

The political dynamics of the minimum wage frighten many American economists, because they fear that when the electorate holds sway, politics might displace what they consider sound economic reasoning. Such reasoning opposes increases in the minimum wage on the principle that workers cannot be paid more than the value of their contribution to the firm. If government responds to popular opinion by pushing the minimum wage above this level, then businesses will fire those employees whose new wages now exceed their contribution to the firm's output. Beyond the clear statement that the market determines wages, this analysis contains a larger ideological message: breach the wall between politics and economics, and it will always backfire on you.

Although this reasoning appeals instinctively to the notion that people can only be paid what they are worth, its origins in the neoclassical economics rule out a number of assumptions. The neoclassical school of economics retains traces of the model derived from smaller, more competitive enterprises. In a small firm of ten or twenty people, it was relatively easy to determine what one worker's contribution might be. As firms grew bigger, however, the contribution of the five hundredth or one thousandth employee can no longer be determined with mathematical precision, and companies can begin to shape the market—its prices and its wages—just as the market shapes them. When neoclassical economists assume that an increase in the minimum wage will cost jobs, they fail to consider the possibility of higher wages improving worker productivity and reducing shirking. They also assume interpersonal comparisons do not affect employees' productivity and turnover rates, so employers need not worry about the perceived fairness of their wages. By implication, too, businesses already operate at peak efficiency, so they cannot negotiate lower prices from their suppliers if an increase in wages begins to shrink their profits. Lastly, the neoclassical model presupposes that even quite profitable firms do not share some of their profits with workers by offering higher wages or bonuses.[23]

All these criticisms have emerged from some recent analyses that cast doubt on the prevailing orthodoxy about the economics of the minimum wage. The most influential of these studies is David Card and Alan Krueger's *Myth and Measurement,* which examined several different increases in the minimum wage at both the state and federal level. By comparing job gains and losses in these cases with the results in states that did not raise the minimum, Card and Krueger were able to conduct what is in effect a natural experiment complete with treatment and control groups. The results of these studies show that the minimum wage produced higher wages, but did not cause any job loss. In what was perhaps their tidiest piece of research, Card and Krueger compared the effects of New Jersey's 1992 increase in the minimum wage to $5.05 with Pennsylvania, which adhered to the $4.25 federal minimum. Their analysis, which focused on workers in low-wage restaurants like Burger King and Kentucky Fried Chicken, found that contrary to all conventional expectation, employment actually increased in New Jersey.[24]

Not surprisingly, a "natural experiment" with these results provoked some fierce debate. Determined to defend the old thesis that 1 percent of minimum wage workers lose their jobs for every 10 percent increase in the minimum wage, a number of economists have tried with little success to rebut their arguments. One study found some job loss, but did not give very much weight to the fact that the job loss occurred during a recession. Another used a nonrandom sample of restaurants provided by the business-financed Employment Policies Institute. And insisting that dog still bites man, a third—the director of the Institute who has served as a lobbyist for restaurants—stated wrongly that the authors did not factor part-time employment into their conclusions. Although all these critiques suggest that some cautions may be warranted, no one has yet been able to discount the study's main conclusions.[25]

Obviously, the implications of this thesis are not limitless. The lack of observable job losses when New Jersey raised the minimum wage does not mean that an increase of any size in the minimum wage would never have an effect: increases in wages have consequences, just the way reductions do. It does suggest, however, that a model based simply on the "marginal utility" of each additional worker may not adequately explain the economics of the minimum wage. A low minimum wage is likely to reduce loyalty to the firm and undermine the willingness of employees to work together. When employers weigh these factors, they find that even with higher labor costs, minimum wage workers still are a bargain.

Exactly how much of a bargain is evident from a historical perspective on the declining value of the minimum wage. The minimum wage lost 8 percent of its value from 1968 to 1979, falling from 53 percent to 43 percent of the average production worker's wages. Although Congress raised the wage to $3.35 in 1981, to $4.25 in 1991, and finally to $5.15 in 1997, these increases have only partly offset its downward drift: to equal the value of the minimum wage in 1968, it would have to be increased to $7.33. An increase of this magnitude would affect three different subgroups. The first of the these groups consists of those who now receive the minimum wage; the second, those who fall below the current equivalent to the old minimum; and the third, those above the new minimum whose salary would be pushed upward through a ripple effect. Even if just 4.2 million workers were receiving the minimum wage in 1995, a true estimate of the impact of the minimum wage on all these subgroups would show that its decline actually brought lower wages to almost one-quarter of all private nonfarm wage and salary employees, or 21 million people.[26]

That the wage floor has dropped for so many explains a significant portion of the growing disparity in income. Less than one-third of minimum wage workers are teenagers. Although just 22 percent of hourly wage workers paid at or below the minimum were poor, the minimum wage does contribute to poverty among families: by comparison, poverty rates among workers earning more than the minimum wage remained at 6 percent. Complaints about "target inefficiency" clearly miss the point. Whether workers receive the wage as unrelated individuals or as supporters of families, a low minimum contributes to a shortfall in their income.[27]

In fact, early returns on the 1997 increase firmly demonstrate its benefits. Consistent with the newer research, the first phase of the increase showed no significant job losses. It also confirmed that almost ten million people derived immediate benefit from the full raise, with 57 percent of these gains going to working families in the bottom 40 percent of the income scale. In eighteen states—predominantly those in the South and Southwest—wages were so low that the 1997 hike in the minimum wage increased the income of 10 percent of the workforce.[28]

To be sure, if the minimum wage were pegged to 50 percent of the average industrial wage and indexed to inflation, there would be consequences. Although the new research casts doubt on the notion that there would necessarily be a reflexive laying off of workers, an increase of this size would certainly stimulate the economy and promote modernization. In the past, modernization has erased small firms who lacked the financial capacity to remain competitive. The overall number of jobs, however, has continued to grow. To defer modernization out of a fear of its effect on small businesses, then, is to shackle the economy to a low-wage, low-skill strategy. In the end, this strategy is perhaps the ultimate price we pay for maintenance of a low minimum wage.

Still, while all modernizations tend to eliminate small businesses, not every modernization promotes the development of a high-wage, high-skill workforce. Some who modernize may instead prefer automation and worker displacement—a labor force with few workers, rather than one which is merely well or poorly paid. Modernization is therefore too important to proceed on its own. Whether it is as a result of an increase in the minimum wage or any other mechanism, the right kind of modernization can only be achieved by conscious effort, through jobs, training, and government policies that steer the marketplace to this specific goal.

The Split in the Workforce

With the minimum wage anchoring the bottom of the workforce and high-tech professionals enjoying rapid upward mobility at the top, the middle of the labor market has ruptured. The service sector has developed both a high and a low end, and this trend has spread so far that nowadays it even encompasses Wall

Street. Uniformly high salaries could be overlooked in many securities firms when the return on equity was 30 percent. But, as one managing partner put it, "increasingly, there's been greater differentiation between the real impact players and everyone else." In the late 1980s, junior analysts in their twenties were getting six figure bonuses, and computer technicians and accountants were getting several times what they would have been paid in other large, successful businesses. After crackdowns of 20 to 30 percent and the substitution of equity for cash in bonuses, this compensation policy has been abandoned.[29]

What has happened to secretaries best illustrates the effect of this trend on a single profession. Between 1983 and 1993, the total number of secretaries declined by 8 percent, falling from 3.9 to 3.0 percent of the civilian labor force; another 3 percent are projected to lose their jobs between 1996 and 2006. Technology has eliminated some previously vital secretarial skills. Voice mail takes messages, and middle managers often use a computer at work to do their own writing. The secretarial ranks declined even further when middle managers were laid off, and many secretaries were laid off with them. The remaining pool of secretaries has been splitting into two distinct groups. Those women who have been upskilled work with spreadsheet software or organize data and systems for an entire office. This process of professionalization has enabled some secretaries to improve their standing: for example, Professional Secretaries International in Kansas City says that $27,000 is the average salary of its 40,000 members, but that 6 percent earn more than $41,000. On the downside, however, for the nation as a whole, the average hourly wage for female administrative and clerical workers in 1997 was only $10.44, a wage that has slipped behind inflation in recent years.[30]

Pulled apart by this growing split in wages, the middle of the labor market has begun to vaporize. In the mid-1950s, almost half of all Americans—including many factory workers—received a modest but comfortable income. That core expanded for the next fifteen years, until by 1969, it encompassed more than 62 percent of all families. By 1996, however, this figure had dropped to only 52 percent. Defining the middle class in another way, the same pattern emerges: those who earn between half and twice the median income fell from about 71 percent in 1969 to less than 62 percent by 1996.[31] With all the concern about multiculturalism, with all the fears that American society cannot hold together amid a proliferation of cultures, few people raise the key analogous question: What will hold American society together if its economic center is hollowed out?

The Low-Wage, Low-Skill Strategy and the Fragmentation of the Middle Class

The American middle class defined the popular vision of the postwar era. It was largely white. It became increasingly suburban. It produced a vast array of products, many of which it was paid well enough to consume. Criticized for its conformity in the 1950s, it bred the children who spearheaded the political and social changes of the 1960s. Yet whatever feelings the existence of this class aroused—criticism, contempt, or nostaglia—there is no doubt that its fragmentation substituted the development of a set of polarities for what was once a fairly encompassing middle. Admittedly, this middle pushed racial minorities to the margins, but then, for a brief time at the height of the post-World War II boom, the polarities themselves did not seem quite so fixed. Now we have white and black, rich and poor, suburban and inner city: the polarities are entrenched, and people expend a good deal of energy in defining themselves as not-their-opposites. A sense of stability and comfort has been lost, and with it, the sense that this stability and comfort might gradually be extended to include an ever larger number of people.

The diminished likelihood of upward mobility compounds this feeling of loss. Until the last quarter of the twentieth century, most Americans were supposed to experience a discernible improvement in their standard of living. If it did not happen to them, then, with luck, they would live long enough to see it happen to their children. For many years, the existence of a frontier contributed to this sense of possibility: one could travel to California and measure, with a quick glance back East, the person you had become. Now an easterner going West is just as likely to encounter a Californian heading the other way, and for the first time, the possibilities seem not so unbounded.[32]

The data confirm this sense of closure. Using information about five thousand households from the Panel Survey of Income Dynamics at the University of Michigan, researchers compared the movement among low, middle, and high income groups from 1967 to 1979 and 1980 to 1991. The researchers defined $24,000 or less as poor and set $72,000, in 1994 dollars, as the threshold of affluence. During the first period, slightly less than one-third of the top 10 percent of the population became middle class, while slightly more than one-third of the poor rose into the middle grouping. From 1980 to 1991, however, the income pattern petrified, with fewer of both the wealthy and the poor becoming middle class. In short, despite all the powerful American myths about upward mobility, the affluent in the United States today are more likely to stay affluent, and the poor are more likely to stay poor.[33]

A petrification of classes in the United States might be acceptable if it occurred during a time when the distribution of income was at record levels of equality. When classes become more stratified now, however, it is record levels of inequality that are being frozen. These inequalities reflect the cost of the low-wage, low-skill strategy and manifest themselves in a multitude of economic, political, and social tensions that have methodically eroded the quality of life in the United States. An economy that confers its benefits on an ever-decreasing minority; a political system seriously deficient in giving voice to—much less responding to—most people's needs; and an intensification of racial disharmony: when the pie is both inequitably divided and not growing very fast, conflict sweeps through the land.

Despite the corrosive effects of these phenomena, proponents of the low-wage, low-skill strategy say that we really do not have any choice. They contend that their strategy is an effective response to the new era of international competition, because only low benefits, low wages, and reliance on an under-skilled workforce can successfully counter the high-wage, high-skill policies of most other industrial nations. They are wrong. A quarter century of this strategy has already shred the fabric of life in our workplaces, homes, and communities. Even if this strategy "succeeded," the terms of the victory would represent a significant defeat.

A low-wage economy implies significant inequality. A low-skill workforce implies a rearguard economic strategy in which poorly paid American workers assemble hi-tech products that others have conceived and designed. Together, a low-wage and low-skill economy ensure a society in which everyone is so self-seeking that the capacity for empathy has vanished, and competitiveness becomes a caricature of Social Darwinism. Although some may promote the ethic of "personal responsibility" to explain why so many have fallen behind, such a sharp rise in the incidence of "personal irresponsibility" seems to lend itself better to structural rather than individual explanations. Yet that possibility gets little attention amid America's rush to the market.

Nevertheless, what is at issue in this debate is not markets themselves, but the distinctive American policy toward them. The United States has a scatter-shot employment policy, no national health care, no universal family allowance, little publicly funded day care, and an *unpaid* family leave policy: in short, because government intervention here has generally been partial, fragmented, and incomplete, it has never gone as far as government intervention in most other countries. Now, however, the traditionally reflexive American posture of laissez-faire serves a low-wage, low-skill strategy. The results—stagnation or downward mobility and a deteriorating quality of life for fourth-fifths of the American population—suggest that the presumption of laissez-faire and the low-wage, low-skill strategy both need to be reexamined.

In the United States, education, job training, and income programs such as welfare have been the three primary methods of providing help to people and giving them an opportunity to improve their standard of living. Although the debates about these issues were always intense, the hope and expectation of upward mobility prevented most Americans from questioning their basic premises. Now that we have become apprehensive about our economic future and sense that forces we cannot control may be working against us, these premises are no longer sacrosanct, and we can rethink the values and functioning of all three programs. At the same time, however, the notion that reforming them alone will reawaken the possibilities of the post-World War II era is too heavy a burden for them to bear. They exist, after all, in a context defined by the government, civil society, and the developing global marketplace. To have any chance of success, their role, too, needs to be reconceptualized.

Part 2

The Path Upward?

5

Education: Choice, Profit, and Democracy

> There is endless talk about education, but between the hysteria and the cynicism there seems to be little room for civic learning, hardly any for democracy.
>
> —*Benjamin Barber*

> The notion that choice would create a nation of small, effective schools is a construction as mythical as the notion that the market can maintain a nation of shopkeepers.
>
> —*Robert Lowe*

Wages are stagnant or falling, and the job market is full of uncertainty. No wonder Americans have turned with unusual fierceness to the issue of education. In the past, when wages rose, and the job market was more stable, those with educational credentials could claim their right to upward mobility. Now employers complain about students' inadequate preparation, and parents indict the schools for failing their historic role.

Some of this concern about education reflects anxiety about the economy, displaced onto the schools. The schools, after all, do not determine the level of corporate investment, the amount of business profit, the unemployment rate, or any other indicator of economic well-being. Nevertheless, they have become an indicator of the prospects of future workers in this business environment. That alone is sufficient to fuel considerable anxiety.

This anxiety fixes quickly on signs of faltering performance, and the schools have certainly given plenty of that. In the Chicago public schools, for example, one-quarter of high school graduates read at or below the sixth grade level, and the average school scores on the American College Test (ACT) place half of the city schools in the bottom 1 percent of all U.S. schools. Likewise, the National Assessment of Educational Progress reports that among high school seniors, only 34 percent met the performance standard in reading, and just 16 percent attained the performance standard in math.[1] Although other test scores have shown some modest progress in recent years, these are not propitious results if success in the coming job market really does depend on the ability to conceptualize and manipulate symbols.[2]

International comparisons are no more reassuring. The Third International Mathematics and Science Study compared the proficiency of high school seniors from twenty-three different countries. The United States outperformed just two countries—Cyprus and South Africa—in general math, and finished last in both advanced math and in physics. In another comparison, the top 1 percent of American math students ranked thirteenth out of thirteen in algebra and twelfth out of thirteen in geometry and calculus. The gap in math is, in fact, so large that a comparison of high school seniors enrolled in college preparatory math classes found Japanese students at the fiftieth percentile to be performing slightly better than the top 5 percent of U.S. students.[3]

Many American parents do not need to research the data on comparative performance to know something is wrong with their schools. For a lot of them, a walk through a hallway will suffice. In a study conducted by the U.S. General Accounting Office, the monitoring agency for the federal government, the GAO reported that the nation's elementary and secondary schools need $112 billion in repairs and upgrades to bring them up to satisfactory condition. To be sure, two-thirds of the schools were in reasonably good condition, but 14 million students do attend schools that need significant renovation, and nearly 60 percent of America's schools had at least one major building component in serious disrepair.[4] Although Americans have long had an ambiguous attitude toward education, the extent of this disrepair puts these ambiguities on full display.

The Ambiguous American Attitude Toward Education

Most Americans say that they value education. Yet the real meaning of this statement is probably less open ended and inclusive than it sounds. Americans value education as a ticket to upward mobility. From high school on through graduate school, they see it as an elaborate mechanism for classifying and credentialing people. Except for those with great inherited wealth, where you went to school, and how far you went in school, are seen as short-hand indicators of both your family's background and your future economic prospects. Americans are not wrong in these perceptions either. In fact, a study by the National Center on the Educational Quality of the Work Force showed that each year of education adds 8 percent to a worker's salary.[5]

Employers have had a somewhat different perspective on the value of education. Long before education was necessary in the factory for the development of specific skills, employers thought it was useful to inculcate morals and ethics. As Homer Bartlett, agent of the Massachusetts Cotton Mills, said in 1841:

> From my observations and experience, I am perfectly satisfied that the owners of manufacturing property have a deep pecuniary interest in the education and morals of their help: and I believe the time is not distant when the truth of this will appear more and more clear. As competition becomes more close, and small circumstances of more importance in turning the scale in favor of one establishment over another, I believe it will be seen that the establishment, other things being equal, which has the best educated and most moral help will give the greatest production at the least cost per pound.[6]

Industriousness, obedience, and loyalty were the primary ethics that employers valued in a good worker, and the schools certainly did everything they possibly could to impart these values. As one teacher recalled, "[t]he proper way to read in the public school in 1899 was to say 'page 35, chapter 4 and holding the book in the right hand, with the toes pointing at an angle of forty-five degrees, the head held straight and high, the eyes looking directly ahead, the pupil would lift up his voice and struggle in loud unnatural tones.' "[7] Such ritualized theatrics had little to do with the content and nothing to do with any real learning. It was, instead, a method of inflating what constituted learning at the same time that it instilled the deference that was the hallmark of good behavior. Students who learned this lesson well were far more likely to make compliant workers.

Most Americans, then, took a utilitarian attitude toward education. For prospective employees, education was useful as a vehicle for upward mobility; for employers, education identified which workers were entitled to be upwardly mobile. The whole enterprise was therefore imbued with a quintessentially American spirit: hopeful, practical, and concerned with education but fundamentally wary of "book" learning. Despite the tension between these viewpoints, they coexisted uneasily as the ideology underlying the U.S. educational system until the explosion of mass education in the 1960s.

Now that uneasy coexistence is gone, pulled apart by several centrifugal forces. For most students, the rise of mass education and the growth in the number of junior colleges has infused the educational experience with a decidedly vocational purpose. Colleges teach, but the real question about what they teach is how useful it will be for work. Students' attitudes about this issue have changed dramatically. Between 1968 and 1997, the number of freshmen who said that the main purpose of college was to "be very well off financially" rose from 41 percent to almost 75 percent, while those who said they wanted to "develop a meaningful philosophy of life" dropped from 82 percent in 1968 to 41 percent in 1997.[8] The idea of college as a place to think has been replaced by the idea of college as a place to develop a better resumé.

Nor is this vocational purpose restricted to the less prestigious schools. At a time when the notion of majoring in English is inevitably followed by the question, "But what are you going to do with it?", the classic conception of a liberal arts education has vanished completely. Of course, for many in the better schools, a liberal arts education was only supposed to provide the cultural veneer that a gentleman required before he entered the world of investment banking. The veneer might be a flimsy one, but at least a liberal arts education tried to preserve a thin wall of separation between the world of the university and the world of commerce. That wall exists no longer.

The presumption of education as training for the labor market has trickled steadily downward. High schools train for the labor market the 75 percent of Americans who do not graduate from college, and grammar school prepares students for high school. One might argue that this was always what high schools did, though the function was only evident in all its explicitness with those who took shop and auto repair. Now, however, as computer training replaces auto repair, the last fig leaf has fallen away, and high school has become everybody's job prep, with those attending college just needing a little more training. Plainly, the vocational model has triumphed, and this triumph has simplified education's role by eliminating any ambiguity about its current purpose. Yet so complete is this victory that we tend to miss its greatest irony: at the very moment when a consensus has developed about the goals of education, a fierce debate has arisen about the means.

This debate has three main causes. The first cause stems from the increasingly competitive job market. As the gap between winners and losers becomes more stark, parents besiege schools in the hope that their child will somehow gain a competitive edge. Poor reading scores were never a sign of good economic prospects, but at least in the past, a poor male reader could support himself and his family through physical labor, perhaps even in an assembly line job with benefits won by his union. Now such reading scores mean that a student is going to do as poorly in life as in school. Do students fail because the bureaucracy is unwieldy, the teacher aloof, and the school crowded? Or are some just innately slow readers? In a era when a lack of scholastic success may well point the way to a lifetime of low-wage jobs, it is understandable that parents first look for deficiencies in the school as an institution before they are willing to accept the notion that anything could be the matter with their children.

The debate finds its second cause in the effort to teach the poor. Since this effort is accepted in principle, yet bitterly contested in practice, it helps to see the attempt to educate the poor as the third phase in the history of literacy. In the initial two phases, education first served the wealthy, and then the middle class. Subsequently, in the beginning of the third phase, poor people were expected to attend school, but by now, they are supposed to graduate. Often, when the functioning of our educational institutions and the needs of the poor do not mesh, this expectation is what arouses the sharpest controversy.[9]

In order for schools to motivate, students have to see in them some part of who they would like to be. In the most affluent suburbs, where the fit is closest, many schools embody a student's aspiring self, and students work hard to bring that self into being. In the poorest neighborhoods, however, schools often seem alien. With rigid bureaucracies, low teacher expectations, and irrelevant, fragmented curricula, there is little reflection of who students are or might become. Without this reflection, it is difficult for students to find their own voice. Then, when they fail, their poor performance has its own consequences. Foremost among these are teachers who further disengage and taxpayers who resent funding what seems to them like an ever more hopeless enterprise.

Race, the third component of this debate, permeates the issue of educating the poor and makes it especially explosive. If some people have doubts about the wisdom of investing too much effort in educating the poor, even more truly dislike the idea of paying for, or having their children go to school with, children of color. Residential segregation enables them to act on their feeling. African-Americans migrated from the South to cities in the North and West—some 1.6 million in the 1940s, and another 1.5 million in the 1950s. By 1970, 47 percent of African-Americans lived outside the South, and three-quarters lived in metropolitan areas. By then, in another massive emigration, whites had withdrawn to the suburbs.[10]

Although the civil rights movement of the 1960s tried to implement the desegregation ruling of *Brown v. The Board of Education,* it was mostly successful in the South and in some northern cities. Efforts to enforce it in the suburbs resulted in a decision that limited the applicability of the law. The key legal case was *Milliken v. Bradley* (1974), where the Supreme Court overturned the ruling of a lower court that "local autonomy" must take precedence over the effort to desegregate the children of Detroit and its surrounding suburbs. Under the new standard, civil rights advocates had to prove that violations had occurred in suburban districts, most of which had few minority students, or that suburban district lines had specifically been drawn with a racial intent. As Justice Thurgood Marshall pointed out in a prescient dissent, this decision could only worsen their racial and economic segregation of American cities.[11] It has, but with the new twist that nationwide, it is now Latino students who are the most segregated.[12]

Race is a stubborn issue. Since suburbanization reconfigured geographical space and created whole new governmental units, it fit all too well an American federalism predicated on decentralization and devolution of power. There is certainly no guarantee that larger units of government could have orchestrated a political dialogue to resolve the interplay of race and education. Nevertheless, under the aegis of an American federalism, the withdrawal to separate communities ensured it would be difficult to make much progress.[13]

The federal government is itself deeply implicated in this deadlock. Property taxes are the primary method of funding schools. Yet because differences of several thousand dollars per student are common between the city and the suburbs, one classroom of thirty students can be shortchanged as much as $60,000. Along with the interest on mortgages, property taxes are deductible on the federal income tax. In effect, this tax policy means that the federal government continues to subsidize unequal education.[14]

Ultimately, in an endless cycle, unequal education provides continual fodder for the debate about race and education. In a 1994 test, the National Assessment of Educational Progress found that among twelfth grade students, 30 percent fewer African-Americans, and 23 percent fewer Latinos, could meet the performance standard in reading.[15] For some parents worried about the economic future of their children, it does not matter whether the poor performance of students of color is a cause or a consequence of their inequality. All many white parents know is that they do not want their children to go to school with them.

With economic insecurity, the issue of educating the poor, and the impact of race, the debate about education has intensified. This debate has primarily focused on matters such as choice, charter schools, and the role of multiculturalism in the classroom. Although all these issues are important determinants of educational quality, what lurks behind them may be even more decisive, and that is the issue of school financing.

Financing

The modern system of using property taxes to finance the educational system dates from the 1920s. In the wealthiest district, property taxes are generally sufficient to fund the school system at adequate levels, but where they do not, the state is supposed to provide aid. Since, however, the basic level is set very low, state legislative politics usually requires that funds be distributed to every district in order to get some money to the poorest. As a consequence, remedial financing programs that are designed to reduce the gap between the poorer and more affluent districts merely succeed in replicating the same gap at a slightly higher level.[16]

Angry at the slow pace of change, advocates of more equitable spending tried to circumvent the state legislatures by turning to the courts. Beginning in the late 1960s, they filed a battery of law suits about educational financing. The initial forays in the federal courts culminated in 1973, where the Supreme Court ruled in *San Antonio v. Rodriguez* that despite glaring inequalities in the Texas system, education was not a fundamental right under the U.S. constitution. The court also declared that the Texas system bore some reasonable relationship to the state's concern for local control.

Two successive waves of state lawsuits followed after the failure of the federal initiative. The first, in the 1970s and early 1980s, included lawsuits in eighteen states, with the highest courts in these states declaring eight financing systems to be unconstitutional. The most famous of these cases are *Serrano v. Priest* in California and *Robinson v. Cahill* in New Jersey. In the California case, the court ruled that because a child's education was based on the wealth of an individual district rather than the state as a whole, the system was illegal. Soon, however, the passage of Proposition 13 sharply curtailed local spending for education, resulting in a considerable leveling down of funding for all schools. Although this outcome was hardly the objective that educational advocates desired, it produced sufficient convergence to elicit a 1986 ruling from the California Supreme Court that the state was acting lawfully.

The New Jersey legal battle dragged on for twenty-eight years. Despite the state court's initial ruling, the court had to close down New Jersey's school system during the summer months in the mid-1970s before the state legislature complied. The suit subsequently appeared before the court a dozen times in as many years. When, finally, the successor case of *Abbott v. Burke* resulted in a firm insistence on equity, Governor James Florio developed a viable plan. The tax increases that this plan required provoked such public outrage that the Republicans rescinded them when they swept into office in 1994. Then, in 1998, one year after declaring that the Republican plan—a statewide curriculum standard—was no substitute for a more equitable division of money, the New Jersey Supreme Court changed its mind and decided that no new money was needed. Even more pointedly, it renounced any future intention to oversee the education of poor children in the state's schools.

The second wave of lawsuits began in the mid-1980s. The outcome of these suits has nominally been more favorable: seven of eleven systems have been found unconstitutional. The most dramatic of these cases is probably *Rose v. Council for Better Schools,* a 1989 Kentucky case where the high court broadened its verdict to insist on reconstruction of the whole educational system. Although a 60 percent increase in the state education budget has equalized the performance of elementary school children in affluent and poor districts, high school dropout rates have not improved, and college admission test scores remain unchanged. The addition of $2300 bonuses also raises concerns about whether test scores are rising because teachers are teaching to the test.[17]

Other states have also reformed their system of school financing. In Texas, the State Supreme Court three times declared variations of the old system to be unconstitutional. Texas, which has 36.2 percent minority students, has an expenditure ratio of 2.8 to 1 for areas with small minority populations compared to areas with large minority populations. It is also divided into 1045 school districts—among the most of any state. Partly, this large number results from Texas' size, but it is also true that many have very small enrollments: 700 districts have fewer than 1600 students. While Texas gives these districts special financial assistance to compensate for diseconomies of scale, small districts tend to accentuate differences in wealth, and school finance experts generally agree that consolidation leads to greater equalization. In the mid-1980s, the ratio of assessed valuation per child in the wealthiest district was seven hundred times that of the poorest district. The 1993 legislation seeking to remedy this inequity relies on state aid and local property taxes. Intended to raise $16.5 billion with 45 percent coming from the state, the law sets a ceiling on school spending from property taxes and compels 96 affluent districts either to send some money for redistribution by the state or partner with a poorer district.[18]

Since a majority of funds still come from property taxes, the Texas law is vulnerable to criticism. Michigan, by contrast, represents an example of a state financing initiative that looks to other sources of income. In Michigan, the state boosted the cigarette tax from $.75 to $2.55 and raised the sales tax from 4 percent to 6 percent, giving property owners a $1.9 billion rebate. The state guaranteed each of its 570 school districts $4200 a pupil. Although the plan requires school districts to take on new expenses such as the costs of employees' Social Security and retirement plans, it also limits those that spent much more than the average to a 1.5 percent annual increase in spending. Most important, by pooling funding within state government, it boosted the state's share of total public school costs from 33 percent to 79 percent.[19]

Vermont has gone even farther. After its Supreme Court ruled against the old system in *Brigham v. Vermont,* the state government passed Act 60, the first property tax to be income-based. The 89 percent of Vermonters with incomes less than $75,000 will pay school taxes based on their income, and no Vermont taxpayer with a household income of under $47,000 will be required to pay more than 5 percent of this income on school and municipal taxes. If wealthier districts wish to compensate for the loss of revenue that now goes to the state, they can supplement their local budget, but the state will collect some of the new money they raise. This combination of an income-based property tax and the statewide pooling of education revenues make Vermont the unquestioned leader in the movement for school financing reform.[20]

Nationally, then, the methods of school financing are in transition. Under siege from state courts or political pressure from a public indignant about rising property taxes, some states have indeed tried to alter their method of financing the public schools. With the exception of Vermont, however, these steps toward equality have generally been tentative and halting—changing the state formula like Texas, or substituting one form of regressive financing for another—the sales tax for the property tax—as in Michigan. Both the structure of government and the power of an affluent minority slow the pace of reform. While the courts have been more willing in recent years to do something about blatant inequities in school financing, they usually flinch at any ruling that goes too far, either by violating the legal principle of separation of powers or turning the judiciary into administrators of the state public schools. Their self-restraint has left most advocates of genuine financing reform without the support of a powerful governmental institution. And, without such political advocates, affluent districts may bend a little, but what they have preserved is still instantly recognizable as the maintenance of privilege in their schools.

Overall, it is true that the generous amount of money spent on wealthy districts helps to push the United States into the higher ranks in international comparisons of aggregate spending. In 1996, for example, the United States was fifth (behind Canada, Denmark, Finland, and Sweden) among nineteen OECD countries for total spending on all levels as a percent of the GDP. Because of its effort to open colleges to a broad spectrum of the population, the United States does better in its comparative spending on universities than with kindergarten through twelfth grade. These statistics, however, are somewhat deceptive: like the data on per capita income, their aggregation of money obscures some real differences in expenditures on education. Other data tell a less flattering story. If one lists dollars spent on education per student per year among sixteen nations, the United States finishes ninth. If the same list is used as spending as a percent of per capita income, the United States finishes fourteenth out of sixteen. The same is true if the calculation is the amount per capita GDP: the United States finishes right at the median of nineteen OECD countries. Plainly, Americans value education, but as a country with wide disparities between rich and poor, we value education as we value any other esteemed good or service, more for the prosperous than for the poor.[21]

Remedies for the State of American Education

Between the real problems with the U.S. educational system and the anxiety about the economy displaced onto it, the question of how we educate our children has become one of our most compelling public issues. New strategies for improving the system proliferate. Dissenting from the long tradition of local control in education, some believe that the federal government should take a larger role. By smoothing the transition from school to work, others want to refocus on the majority of the population that do not go to college. And finally, in the most controversial cluster of proposals, there are those who insist that only the introduction of market principles into the field of education will effect a dramatic improvement. Choice, vouchers, for-profit, and charter schools are their remedies to transform the state of American education.

Given the historic antipathy to federal involvement in the schools, it is a measure of the level of public apprehension that the federal government under a Republican president, George Bush, should have established a National Education Goals Panel. This panel of governors, members of Congress, and administration officials grants a new role to the federal government. Not quite the arbiter of national standards, it is, nonetheless, for the first time allowed to explore the question of what those standards might be. Created at the president's 1989 Education Summit to report on progress in education, the panel set some benchmark goals for the year 2000. By then, all children will start school ready to learn; the high school graduation rate will exceed 90 percent; students will demonstrate competence in English, math, science, history, and geography; U.S. students will be first in the world in science and math achievement; every adult will be literate and able to compete in a global economy; and every school will be free of drugs and violence.[22]

In 1991, in response to the efforts of the National Goals Panel, Congress established a National Council on Education Standards and Testing. NCEST was mandated to develop a voluntary system of assessments measuring the performance of students. As an attempt to catalyze not one but fifty reform plans, it seeks to move toward a loose agreement on an essential academic core, rather than an explicitly national curriculum. Like the National Goals Panel, the National Council must proceed gingerly. Yet the very fact that both have been granted powers previously denied to any federal agency establishes a new policy precedent.[23]

Half-way through its decade-long mission, the National Goals Panel published a report on the nation's progress toward achieving its goals. The news was not good. Tests did show some improvement in math scores: the percentage of students meeting national standards in math climbed from 13 to 18 percent for fourth graders, from 20 to 25 percent for eighth graders, and from 13 to 16 percent for twelfth graders. But the graduation rate, which remained about the same at 86 percent, showed no sign of reaching its goal of 90 percent, and the proportion of twelfth graders attaining the required performance standard in reading dropped three points, from 37 to 34 percent. These preliminary results suggest that while a national standard-setting body might be better able to monitor whatever ails American education, the local orientation of education policy continues to deny the federal government the power to do very much about it.[24]

Although the hurdles for federal government's involvement in overall education policy remain high, they are somewhat lower in programs that seek to ensure equal opportunity. About 70 percent of federal education funds address this issue, including the best-known education program, Title 1 of the 1965 Elementary and Secondary Education Act. Reflecting widespread concern that this thirty-year-old law needed to be updated, Congress enacted some changes in 1994 designed to prepare students for a more demanding labor market. The old law created a two-tier system where economically disadvantaged students were only supposed to master basic skills; the new law calls on the state to produce content standards, specifying the skills in each subject that children must master. In addition, all states now must devise new forms of assessment, aligned with the content and curriculum, to measure what children actually know and can do, and schools must make steady "adequate progress" in moving students toward proficient and advanced levels of achievement. Lastly, there is a greater emphasis on the whole school approach: instead of taking disadvantaged children out of school for a brief period each day, a school will be able to initiate schoolwide programs if half of its students are economically disadvantaged.[25]

The Head Start program is probably even more popular than Title 1. Unlike Title 1, which is merely a source of funding, Head Start is a program whose outcomes can be clearly evaluated. Those evaluations have now been conducted for over twenty-five years, with fairly consistent results. Designed to help young, poor children develop the skills they will need in school, Head Start has consistently demonstrated effectiveness over the short and middle term. These are the outcomes that make Head Start popular. As the effects fade over time, however, it soon becomes impossible to distinguish those who participated in Head Start from those who did not.[26] While this convergence is most dramatic in I.Q. scores that have long been criticized for their cultural biases, it does illustrate both the burdens and the limits placed on federal educational policy. In a policy arena dominated by local control, the federal government is supposed to intervene, overcome problems that have deep structural roots, and get out quickly. The children on whose behalf they intervene are supposed to be an exception to the norm: were they not, it is unlikely that the federal government would be allowed to intervene at all. Yet because the intervention is presumed to be short and quick, its long-term effects are both feeble and foregone.

In a broader sense, what is at issue here is the way the interplay between class and education expresses itself in formal and informal methods of tracking. Head Start intervenes to help children. But after its effects dim, the correlation between class background and educational achievement arises anew, and the schools face the problem of what to do with the bottom three-quarters of the population who do not graduate from college. In the past, this was quite clear: white students from comfortable backgrounds went to college, and with a few spectacular exceptions, almost everyone else was tracked into vocational education. Subtler forms of this kind of tracking still go on. In 1990, for example, Jomills Henry Braddock of Johns Hopkins found that two-thirds of the principals of middle schools reported tracking in some subjects, and one-fifth reported tracking in all subjects.[27] Still, amid the recognition that the skills of the twenty-fifth to the seventy-fifth percentile are vital to the nation's economic success, the issues of who is tracked and what they learn become ever more pressing.

A sense of arbitrariness has long bedeviled the question of who is tracked into vocational education. Students on the vocational track were supposed to be less intelligent, but what is intelligence, and how does one measure it? For much of the twentieth century, the answer to this question was circular and unquestioning: "intelligent" meant you tested well on a short list of cognitive measures. When critics assailed the cultural narrowness and parochialism of these measures, their proponents retreated to a second line of defense. Perhaps these measures did not actually test for something called "intelligence"; perhaps, in an economy where it mattered whether a student possessed certain cognitive skills, they were just reliable predictors of one's future success. Since whites from comfortable family backgrounds were fairly confident of future success, they were most likely to be classified as intelligent. Others had to prove themselves.

Although such explicit forms of tracking are becoming less common, the recent effort to develop youth apprentice and school-to-work programs risks becoming a new version of tracking for the twenty-first century. As always, the tension is between a blend of class and race on the one hand, and social mobility on the other. Some degree of class stratification will surely persist. If, however, stratification hardens into a petrified system or only college-bound youth are exposed to critical thinking, then these programs will simply be tracking by another name. Such an outcome will not only be constricting for students, but will also shackle the competitiveness of the U.S. economy. After all, the purpose of these programs is to upgrade the skills of employees who actually work on the shop floor. Should instruction in critical thinking be withheld from them out of fear that some workers might focus on some broader social issues or even more frighteningly, direct it at their employers, then the benefits of these programs will be lost.

These concerns have by and large been cast aside in the rush to do something about the job futures of mid-level students and make the United States more competitive. Enticed by the example of Germany, where the noncollege bound enter a dual school-industry apprenticeship system at sixteen and graduate from journeyman to master after six years of extensive work and study, a number of educators have expressed interest in youth apprenticeship programs. In these programs, employers would offer participants a learning experience within a particular industry or occupational cluster. The program would require at least two years. Collaboration between schools, employers, relevant unions, and other key institutions would foster an innovative curriculum in the classroom and at work. Ideally, the secondary and postsecondary components of the program would also be closely linked, leading to a high school diploma, postsecondary credential, and certification of occupational skills.[28]

In some states, the whole question of a youth apprenticeship program has broadened out to encompass the more general issue of preparing students for work. Indeed, four states have enacted statutory provisions to prepare high school students for workplace requirements. The laws in these four states—Florida, Oregon, Tennessee, and Wisconsin—have stressed processes for developing academic and occupational competencies; career education and development; extensive links between schools systems and employers; and meaningful workplace experiences. Oregon, for example, which was the first state to implement a school-to-work program, mixes career academies, where a high school with a single professional orientation has ties to businesses in that industry, with a technical preparation school, which combines training and attending school, and cooperative education, which puts students into jobs while they are in school. Similarly, in 1991, the Wisconsin legislature enacted Tech-Prep, a new vocational program that uses a "Gateway Assessment Test" given at the end of the tenth grade to guide average students into an applied curriculum of math, science, and communication skills.[29]

These state initiatives have their federal counterparts. The Carl D. Perkins Vocational and Applied Technology Education Act of 1990 focuses not only on vocational and academic education, but also on giving students experience and understanding of "all aspects of industry"—planning, finance, management, labor, and the community, as well as underlying principles of technology, health safety, and environment. Such a broad mandate has inevitably elicited criticism in some states, on the grounds that these states have simply rephrased the act's provisions without plans for implementing any fundamental changes. This is a fairly common practice in federal-state relations: states pocket federal money by writing up their existing programs as if they already conformed to the requirements of a new act. Hence, whatever real hopes the Perkins Act aroused, the federal-state conflict reflected in its drafting hindered another opportunity for reform.[30]

Clinton's School-to-Work Opportunities Act of 1994 builds on the Perkins Act. Using about $300 million in federal funds as venture capital in order to create a universal, high-quality school-to-work transition system, it asks that states review all aspects of the industry, tech-prep, youth apprenticeship, and school-based enterprise initiatives to see how well they are functioning. Although this figure may not seem like very much for a nation with 16 million high school students, spending money directly on students is not the act's main purpose. The purpose is, rather, to use partnerships and development funds to establish some national standards in school-to-work programs. Some of these standards include the integration of school and work-based learning, the establishment of effective linkages between secondary and post-secondary education, and the provision of a full range of program components to all students through a coherent sequence of courses or experience in their chosen career.[31]

On both the state and federal level, then, public officials have tried to revamp our educational system for the three-quarters of the students who do not have a college-degree. In this effort, they bear more than a passing resemblance to the advocates of vocational education at the turn of the century. Just as those advocates tried to prepare average students for their work in an industrial system, the modern proponents of school-to-work programs seek to prepare great masses of average students for their work in a postindustrial economy. Still, most evaluations conducted over the last fifty years show that vocational education has had few positive effects.[32] Although contemporary proponents of school-to-work programs try very hard to get out from underneath this shadow, it is difficult to imagine that their recent initiatives will have much more satisfactory results.

School-to-work programs do have inherent appeal. Many students do not learn from theory alone; many others will do, but not design, work. Clearly, a school system that fails these students is not doing its job. At the same time, however, school-to-work programs are based on several premises that do not stand up under critical scrutiny. It is true that some young adults have difficulty choosing a career and making the transition from school to work. Yet there is little evidence that this period of adjustment damages the worker's long-term prospects of employment. Besides, as we saw in the preceding chapter, many employers are reluctant to offer good jobs with decent benefits to young workers, and despite allegations to the contrary, tend to hire for reliability and attitude rather than for pure technical skill.

A second premise is equally questionable. It is the idea that a school-to-work program would help workers search for jobs. Most research on job searches suggest that workers find work through an informal network of friends and family. If, as in the inner city, this network is not tied to the labor market, then efforts to look for a regular job are less likely to be successful. School-to-work programs may be helpful in creating an alternative route into the job market. But they cannot compensate for the racial discrimination that many people of color face when they look for work, or the scarcity of jobs themselves in the absence of a full-employment policy.[33]

School-to-work programs, then, are another example of our tendency to overburden the schools with responsibilities that properly belong in other political and economic arenas. Born out of a concern for the declining wages of the average worker, advocates tinker with the schools when the real, larger problems lie elsewhere. School-to-work programs are at best a very partial answer to what ails the average student. If, however, there is no significant attempt to address these problems over a sustained period of time, it is going to be harder and harder to distinguish between the very partial answer that they provide and the old system of tracking.

Market Answers: Choice, Vouchers, and Schools for Profit

While school-to-work programs prepare students for the job market, they are not an explicitly market-based strategy for reforming the schools. Yet, with education as in so many other policy arenas, market-based strategies have dominated the debate about reform in recent years. The principal market strategies for reform in education are choice, vouchers, charter schools, and schools for profit. The theory is that with choices to empower parents and profits that enrich entrepreneurs, the market's dynamism and competitiveness will invigorate a stale public bureaucracy.[34]

Choice is a vague concept. As a strategy for improving education, it actually covers many options. When we talk about choice, it makes a big difference whether we refer to choosing among public schools or among both public and private schools. The amount of public subsidy and the geographic locale introduce further complications. At opposite ends of contemporary usage, choice can mean anything from selecting among several different schools in the same public school district without any public subsidy to a public subsidy for attendance at a private school many miles away. While the idea of choice may be appealing, part of the appeal derives from its imprecision.

Choice is also an abstraction. As long as it remains abstract, everyone favors it. It turns education into a consumer good, obtainable in the marketplace, with all the advantages of the marketplace ensuring that the best quality consumer good gets the most customers. If this was all that choice involved, few could object to it. Unfortunately, people have different amounts of money with which to choose, and this discordant fact injects a crucial inequity into the equation, one that transforms "choice" from an appealing to an empty abstraction.

Left to its devices, then, choice will mimic the natural operation of the marketplace and replicate its inequalities. But choice is not absolutely and always doomed. In some places like East Harlem, choice has invigorated a local school system.[35] These have usually been places where the concept of choice in the schools emerged out of the vision of an activist group for a small, vital, democratic community of learners. By conscientiously addressing every likely manifestation of inequality, these activists have tried to offer students from many different backgrounds a wider range of options. The results have hardly been miraculous; on the basis of tests alone, performance has merely improved from poor to middling. Still, energy, activism, and commitment have brought a feeling of excitement to these schools.[36]

Since, however, few districts have this kind of political commitment, choice usually runs up against inequality, and inequality usually wins. In the Carnegie Foundation's study of choice, for example, just 2 percent of students nationally actually took advantage of the program, and no school met the Carnegie Foundation's minimum criteria of providing parents with enough information, compensating for the spending gaps between rich and poor schools, and paying for transportation. The issue of transportation is especially jarring, because the pattern of residential segregation in this country quickly shatters the premise that parents who are liberated by school choice will indeed become free to choose. For the typical family in the United States, the three nearest schools are, on average, two, four and a half, and between ten and eighty miles away. In Arkansas, students must pay their own transportation costs for interdistrict transfers. In both Minnesota and Ohio, students must provide their own transportation to the borders of the new school district. Full transportation reimbursement would therefore add millions to the cost of school choice.[37]

Essentially, advocates of choice are setting forth on an enterprise in which the methods and goals are completely mismatched. Disregarding differences in income whose value they otherwise justify, they expect a market-oriented system to transcend the principles on which it is based. The San Antonio experiment typifies the resulting bias. When parents in San Antonio chose a multicultural public school program, 32 percent of those who participated had some college education, compared to 12 percent who did not, and the children of the better-educated parents outperformed the children of the less educated by scores of 57 to 27 on district reading tests. Not surprisingly, 20 percent of participating parents, as opposed to 34 percent of the nonparticipating parents, had incomes of under $10,000.[38] If school choice is a useful strategy, the market that produced this differential is not the mechanism for remedying it.

Then there is the question of the effect of competition on schools. Promoters of school choice believe in the market analogy where the best automotive supply store prospers, and the one with the reputation for the shoddiest service closes its doors. As Tommy Thompson, the Republican governor of Wisconsin, argues:

> Competition breeds accountability. Under the concept of parental choice, schools will be held accountable for their students' performance. Schools providing a high quality education would flourish, the same way that a business improves its quality for consumers. Schools failing to meet the needs of their students would not be able to compete, and in effect would go out of business.[39]

Schools, however, are public necessities, not businesses, and the blithe notion that the bad ones will not be missed seems certain to narrow, rather than expand, the range of options that students have. One can try to address this issue, as David Osborne and Ted Gaebler do in their popular book *Reinventing Government,* by insisting that choice will increase equity, so that a poor student with other options would presumably remain unaffected by a closed school. But this is to square the circle. When the most desirable schools have already been filled, where would the other students go? Without a commitment to improve educational quality in all schools, choice might, at best, marginally improve the performance of students in some schools—most probably, those students who are already better off. It seems quite unlikely, however, to produce a general increase in the quality of education across the board.[40]

Fortunately, we do not need to accept the claims of advocates for school choice on faith alone. The concept of choice is tested daily throughout the economy, but its consequences are especially visible in the poorer neighborhoods, where advocates say it would be most beneficial. Residents in the inner city have a choice of housing, and get slums; they have a choice of medical care, and they get uniformly poorer indices of health; and they have a choice of banks, or at least a choice of those few banks who have not fled from the limited potential for profit in the inner city. Advocates contend that school choice would be different, but it is very difficult to reconcile the visible evidence of how markets operate with their belief that choice would benefit the schools.

Since choice alone seems destined to produce a two-tier system, vouchers have the political task of making choice appealing. The premise is certainly seductive: declare each family an entrepreneurial unit, empower them with a little extra cash, and let them loose in the educational marketplace. Everyone should benefit under this theory: consumers, because they have more options, and the educational system, because once again, competition has spurred improvement in the product. Together, these benefits should provide school choice with sufficient political cover. Over time, however, experience has badly tarnished this political cover: vouchers cost too much, supplement family income too little, and exhibit no clear performance gains over conventional education. Moreover, since those who advocate vouchers for poor and minority kids are frequently the same people who have long opposed equal funding for the schools, vouchers also warrant scrutiny as, in fact, just the latest strategy to undermine public education.[41]

Although cost comparisons initially seem to favor vouchers, the advantage vanishes upon closer examination. To be sure, private schools do seem to cost about one-third less than public schools. But that is before we factor in the hidden subsidies. Churches, wealthy alumni, and the public (through aid for transportation and textbook costs) heavily subsidize private schools. These school can also pick and choose their students, excluding those that public schools would refer for remedial work or track into expensive special-ed classes. And they pay teachers less, a practice appealing to some taxpayers, but which does not reflect much respect for the profession and produces a turnover rate that is one-third higher. Finally, no comparison can be complete without including the cost of the bureaucracy that would be necessary to ensure the accountability of public monies. For all these reasons, there is little basis to fund vouchers on the grounds that they steer students toward a cheaper, more efficient private education.[42]

While vouchers do promise choice, they rarely offer enough money to make that choice a reality. The typical voucher offers several thousand dollars a year. Although this figure is enough to sound like a real voucher program, it leaves many poor parents with a tantalizing shortfall. In Milwaukee, Wisconsin, the nation's longest running experiment with vouchers, officials tried to address this problem by requiring that private schools accept the voucher amount as the full tuition. The law soon prompted its own abuses, with some schools demanding "fees" as high as $475 or insisting that parents fund-raise hundreds of additional dollars. Proposals to set the voucher at higher amounts, like the 1993 California referendum, quickly become too expensive, while proposals to set the vouchers at lower amounts, like New Jersey Governor Whitman's recommendation for $900 to $1300 of assistance, do not provide enough aid. Vouchers either do not help enough or are too costly. They arouse the fears of taxpayers that their money might subsidize parochial schools, and they worry religious groups who believe such assistance might come at the price of tighter government regulation. So far, these objections have combined to bring about defeat for voucher initiatives in California, Texas, and Washington, D.C.[43]

Of course, if there was convincing evidence that voucher programs worked, many of these objections would disappear. Although proponents have labored mightily, that evidence is not yet forthcoming. Milwaukee has the largest experiment and has been the site of the biggest controversy. There, two evaluators, John Witte of the University of Wisconsin and Paul Peterson of Harvard University, have conducted an acrimonious debate about the results of the local program. While Witte has found no difference between pupils in voucher and nonvoucher schools, Peterson argues that differences emerge in the third year. These contentions hardly settle the matter, however. Peterson maintains that the reason Witte found no differences was because he compared the performance of low-income blacks in the program with middle-income whites who attend better quality Milwaukee public schools. Witte responds that Peterson's claim of improved performance in the third year omits the scores of those students who dropped out because they were doing poorly. Amid all these charges and countercharges, there is the statement of Peterson's own coauthor, Jay Greene of the University of Houston, who admits that the substitution of the term "substantively significant" for the usual test of "statistical significance" may have lowered the threshold for proving that the results were not produced by chance. In sum, Witte and Peterson have fought the battle of Milwaukee to a standstill, and the voucher movement has been denied a victory that many thought should have easily been within its grasp.[44]

The final criticism of vouchers is perhaps the most fundamental. It is based on the premise that education represents a collective public good. Taxpayers fund this collective public good. They do so because they believe that when children share the experience of learning with other children in a public school, it enhances their capacity for toleration and prepares them to function in a democracy. Although, initially, the voucher movement may only desire to chip away at funding for this collective public good, its long-range objective is to reduce sharply the total number of collective public goods and expunge from popular consciousness the belief that a democracy might require their existence. With every dollar that is withdrawn from the funds for public education and redirected elsewhere, the movement is one step closer to this goal.

Schools for Profit

While both the choice and voucher movements wish to contract out education to the private sector, the schools-for-profit movement wants to assume full responsibility. One method of acquiring full responsibility is to establish a charter school. A charter school is a public school that is independent of the rest of the educational bureaucracy. Since St. Paul, Minnesota opened the first charter school in 1992, 780 such schools have been established, and another 69 have been approved. In sixteen states and the District of Columbia, 105,000 children attend these schools.[45]

Of course, not all charter schools are profit-oriented. Some nonprofit other groups—teachers, parents, and community members—have started charter schools within a public school system. Under the auspices of the National Education Association and the American Federation of Teachers, unions have, too. Union-sponsored schools already exist in Houston and Lanikai, Hawaii; more are being developed in San Diego, Phoenix, Colorado Springs, and Connecticut. Seeking to prove that their contracts do not interfere with a quality education, unions have usually focused on establishing charter schools with a distinctive educational mission. In Phoenix, for example, a charter school for seventh to ninth graders is planned to smooth the transition to high school and lower the 20 percent dropout rate.[46]

For conservatives, however, union control of a charter school nullifies its entire purpose. As Chester Finn of the conservative Hudson Institute stated, "The single most important form of freedom for charter schools is to hire and fire employees as they like and pay them as they see fit." This seems like a questionable first principle for a charter school. It is, after all, difficult to envision how shifting all the power to the school administration and paying teachers less is likely to attract more qualified people to the profession. And although it is undoubtedly true that some regulations protect incompetent teachers, protection of teachers as employees seems necessary, on balance, to ensure that they do not serve at whim, a condition which is unlikely to promote continuity in their relationship with their students or get them to commit wholeheartedly to the classroom. Charter schools reflect the wish to deregulate education. This wish may be appealing, but children suffer the consequences: the two most common reasons for the failure of charter schools have been administrative inexperience and lack of accountability.[47]

Instead of the right to hire and fire as administrators see fit, the evaluation of charter schools demands another set of standards. These standards require that each charter school strengthen the local educational system, be innovative in addressing a need that no existing public school currently meets, and remain explicitly accountable to the public and the local school board. In addition, charters should receive the same amount of money as other schools, no more and no less, and their teachers should have the right to bargain collectively. The purpose of these stipulations is to resolve the issue of account-ability, so that the successes of charter schools will accrue to public education, and the failures will demonstrate what is illusory about their potential.[48]

While charter schools by themselves have no definable orientation, the perspective of for-profit schools is notably unambiguous. The proponents of for-profit schools want them to educate children better and make money, and they do not see any inconsistency between these goals. For-profit companies already take in $30 billion of the $340 billion that the United States spends each year on nursery to twelfth grade education, a figure that includes the sale of textbooks, the design of curricula and some classroom instruction, as well as for-profit schools. In a recent study for the National School Boards Association, more than 60 percent of all school boards had considered employing a private company to manage all or part of their district. The reliance on the market in education lags behind the reliance on the market in health care, but the trend for both points in the same direction.[49]

The prime impediment to the expansion of for-profit education has been the actual experience. In both the Baltimore and Hartford school systems under the auspices of Education Alternatives Inc. (EAI), and through the initiatives of the Whittle Communications Company, especially the Edison Project and Channel One, the outcomes have fallen short of expectations. Although the outcomes have not silenced the advocates of privatization, it has left them with some results to explain.[50]

EAI's experiment in Baltimore occurred first. The 183 schools in the Baltimore school system serve about 130,000 students, and their test scores have usually ranked lowest in the state. A 1991 state study reported that another $26,250 per classroom would be required to raise per pupil expenditures in Baltimore to the average prevailing in the rest of Maryland. The problems in the school system seemed systemic and intractable. When a new superintendent, Walter G. Amprey, was hired in 1991, the city decided it was worth the risk to contract with EAI in order to see whether private, for-profit management could significantly improve school performance. Nine schools were part of the original experiment: one primary, seven elementary, and one middle school. EAI received a five-year contract beginning in 1992 and was to be paid $27 million a year.[51]

The experience was not a happy one. At first, EAI secured a measure of good will by spending $7.5 million of its own money to spruce up the appearance of its schools, but it soon dissipated this good will through cutbacks and a pattern of deception. EAI reduced the number of teaching positions by 20 percent, replaced neighborhood-based paraprofessionals earning $13 an hour with $7 an hour college students, and substituted cheaper custodians for better paid union members. Public schools are one of the last sources of stable employment in the inner city, and while the reduction of salaries to save taxpayer money might be arguable, the reduction of salaries for private enrichment was not.

Next, EAI repeatedly manipulated the evaluation data. It touted an August 1993 improvement in student test scores, but when it turned out that the scores came from an unrepresentative sample, the company claimed the report was a mistake. The following year, local school officials initially reported improved reading and math performance in EAI schools. Then EAI blamed a clerical error after the actual data showed a decline in reading scores and gains in math half of what had originally been publicized. EAI also dropped the lowest scoring students from its analysis of the 1993–94 test scores and benefited when the school district modified the control group by substituting low-scoring for high-scoring schools. Although the company received 11.2 percent more per student in funding, and an independent evaluator from the University of Maryland at Baltimore noted that it was teaching more to the test, the results after three years nonetheless showed little significant difference between EAI and non-EAI schools. As a result, after much controversy, Baltimore terminated its contract with the company in 1995. EAI's stock, which had reached 48 and 3/4 in 1993, immediately plummeted to a new low of 4 and 3/8ths.[52]

Hartford's experiment with EAI lasted just 16 months. In 1994, EAI took over responsibility for the entire Hartford school district. Two-thirds of the 24,000 children in this school district lived in poverty, and as in Baltimore, the district's standardized scores were the state's worst. Still, in many respects, Hartford seemed easier to reform. Hartford spent $10,000 per student—80 percent more money than Baltimore. In addition, some components of this sum, like $510 per student on pensions but only $13 per student on textbooks, begged for modification. After four years of a fiscal crisis, some members of the Hartford school board were getting desperate. Stalemated in their own city, they looked to EAI as the outsider who could give the district the boost it needed.[53]

The contract the Hartford school board signed with EAI contained several essential ingredients. For starters, EAI agreed to invest $20 million of its own money in repairs and computer labs for the schools. It also stipulated that it would be paid out of savings at the end of the year from the $170 million school budget. Although the latter clause might seem risky for EAI, it did permit the company to list the entire Hartford budget as part of its total revenue. Profits might not be mounting as rapidly as it had once hoped, but when EAI went prospecting for new investors, the Hartford budget made it appear as if there had been a dramatic upturn in "sales."[54]

Conflict quickly broke out over this contract. While EAI believed that the money it spent was a reimbursable operating expense, the board thought that the company was making a speculative capital investment. The crunch came in the summer of 1995, when EAI proposed elimination of 320 jobs in order to fund its strategy of relying on computers for the classroom. The board rejected this proposal; soon thereafter, it cut EAI's responsibilities from thirty-two to five schools. With EAI blaming its $7.5 million loss for the 1994–95 fiscal year on its problems in Hartford, EAI and the board spent the last months of the denouement quarreling about paying the company for its expenses. Early in 1996, the board finally terminated the contract.[55] Ironically, it was the *Hartford Business Journal* which best anticipated what might happen to EAI in Hartford. In a 1994 editorial, it warned:

> State and local governments have been running these [school] systems around the world for years. They end up running them because there is no money in it, just like there's no money in running a police department, fire department, and so on. You can't turn an inherently unprofitable business into a profitable one just by turning it over to the private sector.[56]

The performance of Whittle Communications, the other celebrated player in the education marketplace, has been equally shaky. Whittle Communications originally consisted of two main projects. In the first project, Whittle sought to install Channel One, a television program with ten minutes of news and two minutes of commercial advertising, in every public school classroom. In the second, Whittle created a line of for-profit schools called the Edison Project, which Chris Whittle, owner of Whittle Communications, described as the "educational version of Home Depot, McDonald's, or Wal-Mart."[57] Neither product lived up to its expectations.

In the case of Channel One, the basic agreement provided for the schools to receive "free equipment"—a satellite dish, two central VCRs, and one color monitor for each classroom. In exchange, schools were supposed to guarantee that for the length of the contract, 90 percent of the pupils in the classroom watched 90 percent of the time. Although New York, California, Rhode Island, and North Carolina barred Whittle, by 1997, Channel One had signed up more than 12,000 schools, reaching an estimated 40 percent of the nation's teenagers. The states' receptivity to Channel One plainly reflects the dismay about functional illiteracy and the perceived decline in the quality of our public schools. Yet what Channel One really signified was "the officially sponsored opening up of school content to commercial sponsorship and organization." Teachers cannot use the equipment to get anything but Channel One. The most pertinent fact of this sponsorship is, then, that at the same time businesses strive mightily to reduce their tax burden, they will only help to finance schools if they can advertise in classrooms.[58]

This advertising tended to color the news. In 1992, Time Warner owned 37 percent of Whittle. Phillips Electronics owned another 17 percent. On the day of the 1992 California primary, the Department of Defense came out with a serious criticism of Star Wars. President Bush announced an ambitious forest conservation plan. Yet the lead story on Channel 1 was a super light bulb made by Phillips. In two weeks of viewing by media critic Mark Crispin Miller, there was also a long, soft focus interview with film director Oliver Stone, a story on ticket sales for *Lethal Weapon 3* and *Batman Returns,* and soundbites from both the publisher of *Time* and the editor of *Premiere* magazines. All of these properties were owned by Time Warner. As Miller put it delicately, "This seems to me to represent a disproportionate reflection of certain corporate interests."[59]

After several years of financial difficulty, Whittle Communications sold Channel One to K-III Communications, a subsidiary of Kohlberg, Kravis, and Roberts, the leveraged buyout firm famous for engineering the 1988 takeover of RJR Nabisco. Time Warner had to write off its entire $185 million investment in the company. At first, K-III Communications agreed to purchase Channel One for $300 million. It reduced the sale price to $240 million, however, when it discovered that Whittle had failed to pay state personal property taxes on the hundred of thousands of videocassette recorders used for Channel One and had inflated current revenue some 20 percent by running extra spots when it could not sell the advertising time.[60]

The Edison Project started boldly in 1991 with a long-term goal of 1000 schools, including 200 by 1996. Instead of EAI's strategy of large-scale capital investments, Edison planned to form partnerships that would bring its schools up to standard. Operating efficiently within the systems it inherited, the project hoped to streamline the educational process. Their facilities would have longer days, no educational tracking, and computers that linked home to school. It sounded appealing, but by 1994, Edison had already invested $40 million without opening a single site. Only a last-minute infusion of $30 million in venture capital saved it from bankruptcy long enough for it to get a small piece of the education business.[61]

This small piece consisted of four experimental schools in Boston; Mount Clemens, Michigan; Sherman, Texas; and Wichita, Kansas. Many critics applauded the results from the school's first year. In Wichita, for example, students at the Dodge-Edison Elementary School spend an hour and a half on reading each day, attendance is up, and parents can use the computers in their homes to e-mail messages directly to Chris Whittle. Larrie Reynolds, the principal of the Wichita school, contends that even as it invests additional money in resources for instruction, Edison can eliminate some administrative inefficiencies and still make money. Indeed, except for the capital investment, all four schools operated at a profit during their first year.[62]

Edison's first year was more successful than anything that EAI ever managed, enabling it to expand to twenty-five schools in eight states with about $70 million in revenues. Still, its long-term prospects remain doubtful. In many respects, Dodge-Edison is a showcase school, the kind of loss leader whose customer appeal far exceeds its capacity for regular and consistent profit. Admittedly, the school did achieve some administrative savings, but some of these savings, like getting the parents to paint the school for $500 when a contractor had estimated $43,000, are probably not sustainable. This makes the clash between the delivery of a quality education and Edison's need to show a profit all the more inevitable. Parents already complain when the salaries of public school administrators begin to rise out of sight. Whittle hired Benno C. Schmidt, Jr., the former president of Yale University, as the president of Edison, at a salary of $800,000. Although most Americans take a more indulgent view toward high salaries in the private sector than they do in the public, it is an open question how long they will be willing to paint the school themselves in order to pay salaries like Benno Schmidt's.[63]

All investors in for-profit schools are therefore caught in an irresolvable dilemma: they can forgo their profit, opt for quality, and run themselves out of business, or they can insist on their profit, give short shrift to quality, and wait for public indignation to mount. Believing that its capital spending simply represents start-up costs like those of any other business, Edison, with its loss leader schools, seems to have chosen the former strategy. This strategy may be wiser in the short term, but it is ultimately a temporary one. After all, like any other for-profit company, Edison must eventually make money. In the end, it is both Edison's misfortune and ours that it has decided to make this money by turning the business of education into the education business.

Choice, vouchers, or for-profit schools: whatever the initiative, any realistic evaluation of market-based strategies for improving education must give rise to serious doubts about their viability. Many parents may still warm to them; given some school systems' dire straits, many officials will still want private executives to take the responsibility for schooling out of their hands. As a method of renewing education, however, market mechanisms are a mirage. Speculating in them may briefly yield some a quick profit, but they certainly cannot improve the educational or economic prospects for the vast majority of Americans.

The Purpose of Education

Despite the defects of their proposals, proponents of market-based educational reform have brought some important considerations into the debate. They want a system of education that mirrors the market's dynamism and energy. In the United States, we usually associate this dynamism and energy with the competitive spirit and profit orientation of the business sector. The evidence strongly suggests, however, that these business principles cannot help the educational system and might lead it seriously astray. The task, then, is to give the educational system dynamism and energy without the inequities that a for-profit orientation brings. This is not an easy task, for it requires defining an overarching educational goal that is large enough to warrant and nurture such qualities. Learning as preparation for democracy and participation in civic life is the most likely candidate to meet this standard.

This goal is, simultaneously, both self-evident and obscure. It is self-evident because public education seems so naturally generative of a public life. From this perspective, public education is not just something for which the public pays; in its curriculum, the composition of its student body, and its roots in the community, it is designed to engender and enhance active civic participation.[64] Yet despite the natural linkage of a high quality public education and a high quality public life, this conception has faded, as both the quality of public education and the quality of public life have themselves declined. In their place, two other perspectives have arisen about the role of higher education. These perspectives are, alternatively, either not of this world or too much a preparation for the work in it.

The first of these visions is fundamentally purist. Positioning the university as a society apart, this vision is aware of the social context, but seeks a refuge from it. In this perspective, learning reflects knowledge of eternal truths and is prized, at least in part, because it does not possess immediate material value. By implication, of course, people who hold this perspective have sufficient confidence in their socioeconomic status that they do not need to be concerned with the issue of whether their education has practical economic consequences.

The second vision is the opposite of the first. In this, the vocational model of education is merely preparation for the labor market, and the university is simply another corporation. From the earliest grades on, this model dilutes learning to those skills that will be useful on the job. If something does not have immediate practical value, it has, as mere book learning, little possible utility. Universities adhering to this model serve the marketplace. They follow the research parameters that corporations proffer to them, and they train professionals for the uncritical practice of their profession. This is not a criticism of all major universities, which nowadays need research funding to survive. It is, however, a criticism of those who, in their eagerness to obtain funding, lose the capacity to distinguish between a corporation in the marketplace and an institution of higher learning.[65]

Neither conception of the goals of education is satisfactory. The first hearkens back to the classical ideal of a liberal arts education, while the second fast-forwards to the dreary hi-tech vocationalism of the post-industrial era. The goal of education as democratic participation requires some careful navigation between them. Above all, it demands that, from what happens inside the classroom to issues of school governance, every aspect of the educational system works toward this end.[66]

Reforming the Schools

Much of the debate about reforming the schools is really an argument about how children learn. Learning takes place between a subject and an object, between a student and a body of knowledge: the appropriate relationship between subject and object is therefore the issue around which this debate swirls. In theory, of course, everyone wants students to achieve academic mastery, but in practice, there are major differences in their judgment about how this mastery should be achieved. Some educators see knowledge as true, fixed, and indispensable to future advancement. For them, the best way of validating the student is simply for the student to master the material. Because any emphasis on students detracts from time and energy spent on what they should be learning, this perspective usually avoids educational practices in which students themselves become the objects of study. As a result, it rarely allows much room for discussion of the student's feelings, values, and cultural background.[67]

To some other educators, however, it is unlikely that children will ever master a body of knowledge unless teachers first validate them as valuable in their own right. They reason that a body of knowledge may be significant; it may even be essential to the student's future success. Yet if the teacher venerates the knowledge without valuing the learner, little learning will take place. In a typical passage, educator Judith Rényi anticipates the obvious objections to this strategy and explains why it is vital for children to construct their own story:

> Are there no facts to learn, no verities to transmit, no absolutes in our society, you wonder? Does every child make her own curriculum? Aren't the *Federalist Papers* of greater value, more worthwhile as the subject of school time, than grandmother's sweet-grass baskets? Shouldn't children at least spend most of their school work on the things (like the *Federalist Papers*) that we all share, rather than on baskets that only a handful of us will ever see? I want both the baskets and the *Federalist Papers*. But I doubt that the student will ever get to the *Federalist Papers* unless he's given a chance to start with something he can do, and use that to find his way into the school and the society.[68]

Although Rényi's perspective is probably more on target than the traditional approach, she does underestimate the ease with which her perspective can quickly degenerate into a caricature of itself. That, at least, is part of what happened with outcome-based education (OBE).

The Bush administration embraced OBE because it shifted the focus from inputs—hours spent in class, years of school completed, courses taken, dollars spent—to the definition and measurement of academic outcomes. The idea was that the state would set guidelines for what the student should know and do; the local school would determine how to reach those goals. In effect, OBE reopened the question of what should be taught, leading conservatives to complain that it undermined religious faith and destroyed the family. Some of its vulnerability to this accusation undoubtedly derived from its tendency to use phrases such as "positive self-image" and "interpersonal competencies," while holding students to unmeasurable standards such as those featured in a draft of the OBE guidelines for Pennsylvania: "All students [will] understand and appreciate their worth as unique and capable individuals and exhibit self-esteem." It was statements like these that caused OBE to be sharply modified in Pennsylvania and completely withdrawn or blocked in Virginia, Ohio, and Oklahoma.[69]

This distortion of OBE contains a lesson, and the lesson is that a primary focus on the student to the point of obscuring the subject matter is just as bad as a primary focus on the subject matter to the point of excluding the student. This lesson then leads to the first principle of good educational practice: for real learning to occur, both the student and the subject matter need to be continually validated. This principle is plainly a question of balance. If the subject matter is so revered that the student feels invisible, then the student will act invisible and disengage from the subject matter. At the same time, however, the opposite mistake is equally misguided. A demonstrated respect for the values and feelings of some students may be the only way to ensure their involvement in the classroom, but expansion of the capacity for critical analysis and learning should never stop there. It should instead extend far beyond, to all that it may be necessary to apprehend in order to participate in the world outside.

Several collateral principles accompany this learning process. They are small classes, improved pay and training for teachers, a curriculum based on vital learning, and a sane approach to multiculturalism. Small classes are necessary if we are to leave behind the undifferentiated factory model of education. They are also crucial to a learning process that is respectful of both the student and the subject matter. The New York School for the Physical City nicely models this approach. Instead of one teacher seeing 180 students a day in classes of 36, this junior high has a total of 180 students, with no class having more than twenty. Because such small classes enable teachers to squeeze every possible drop of educational content from activities like making and flying kites in science classes, students can learn about the molecular content of the atmosphere, the basic principles of aerodynamics, and the preparation of a formal laboratory report. By contrast, a class of thirty-six involved in making and flying kites could quickly degenerate into one of those school field trips that gets a little bit out of control.[70]

Better pay and training for teachers is the second component of any plan for educational reform. Women used to dominate the teaching profession, but now that the ablest have other, better-paying options, the test scores of education majors are lower today than they were in 1970. The consequences of this decline are apparent. For instance, it is now estimated that one-quarter to one-third of all math and science teachers in the United States are unqualified, a fact that correlates all too closely with the mediocre test scores of U.S. students in most international comparisons. In one of these comparisons, evaluators first videotaped math teachers from Germany, Japan, and the United

States and then transcribed the lessons to eliminate any cultural bias. Eighty-seven percent of the American teachers received low marks for the content of their lessons, while 13 percent were assigned medium grades. By comparison, in Japan, 13 percent got low grades, 57 percent received medium grades, and 30 percent were rated highly.[71]

There are two primary reasons for these ratings, and both relate to our fundamental devaluation of teaching. Devaluing teaching as a skill, we deposit many U.S. teachers in the classroom without either the training or the mentoring that they receive in other countries. Devaluing teaching as a profession, we pay teachers less relative to other jobs than do other industrial societies.[72] It is true that many Americans believe in the market and resist compensating people well for work in the public sector. For all their faith in the market, however, it is odd that in this one instance, they do not see any connection between the pool of available talent and what the market pays.

A curriculum based on vital learning represents another link in the learning process. The objective of vital learning is to weave a thematic, interdisciplinary course of study that is experiential, hands-on, and project-oriented. It should take place as often as possible in heterogeneous groups and encourage the exercise of each student's citizenship through meaningful community activities.[73] From her experience as founder and director of Central Park East, a group of alternative schools in East Harlem, Deborah Meier outlines the skills that she sees such a curriculum developing.

> Can one become intellectually competent and nonacademic? And curious—someone who asks, "How come?" and "Is It Truly So?" Someone who is closely observant, open to patterns and details? Playful and imaginative? In the habits of imagining how others think, feel, and see the world; in the habit of stepping comfortably—even uncomfortably—into the shoes of others. Skeptical—with an open mind to other possibilities? Respectful of evidence and open to reason and discourse? Able to communicate carefully, persuasively, in a variety of media?[74]

The goal of such a curriculum, Meier says, is not to be learned, but a learner, something you do for the rest of your life, rather than something you are.

Multiculturalism represents the final component of this package for classroom reform. The acrimonious debate that it has sparked must be viewed in historical perspective: the demographics of the U.S. population are changing dramatically. Between 1980 and 1989, for example, nearly three times as many immigrants entered the United States as during the 1950s. The numbers, however, are only part of the story. Forty-eight percent of the immigrants during the 1950s were from Europe, compared to just 10 percent three decades later, with the rest coming from Latin America, Central America, and Asia.[75] As a result of this trend, the United States will no longer have a majority white population some time in the middle of the twenty-first century. Since we are in the midst of a demographic transition from numerical dominance by one part of the population to numerical dominance by another, it is hardly surprising that we should be engaged in a long parallel debate about what this changing population should be taught.

The demographic explanation of multiculturalism is nonetheless far too sober-minded to comfort those who feel that our national heritage has been lost. They feel angry and betrayed. Lynne Cheney, for example, who headed the National Endowment for the Arts in the Bush Administration, denounced the history standards developed for the federal Goals 2000 project as a document whose "authors save their unqualified admiration for people, places, and events that are politically correct."[76] Even moderate liberals such as Arthur Schlesinger have taken offense at the changes in curriculum. In his *The Disuniting of America: Reflections on a Multicultural Society,* Schlesinger argues strongly against multiculturalism and in defense of the neutrality and sanctity of the classroom. There is, however, one small discomfiting fact: Whittle Communications published the book. This puts Schlesinger in the awkward position of pleading for the neutrality of the classroom by relying on the leading marketer of classroom advertising.[77]

Clearly, there are serious dangers in hyperpluralism, in an America constituted merely as an endless string of hyphenated ethnic groups. Clearly, too, "political correctness" that veers into a prohibition on speech is dubious in any educational setting. Yet neither of these propositions negates the principle that some validation of students, some opportunity for everyone to tell his or her own story, is essential if both culture and education in the United States are to rise anew. The essence of this renewal is not for new hyphenated-Americans to append their culture to some ideal, fixed—and spurious—concept of the old, but rather that people from many different cultures contribute to the creation of a common one.[78] And ultimately, it is this evolving, common culture that should be taught in the classroom.

Reforming the Structures of Governance

Changes in school governance are necessary to complement the changes in the classroom. The modern system of school governance dates to the Progressive Era, where, like the system of city managers, it was designed to insulate the administration of the schools from the white ethnic and working class community. Affirming the expertise of educators, it assumed that this expertise functioned most successfully in a political vacuum. In the wake of suburbanization, however, this system broke down. School bureaucracies could maintain their expertise over a largely white population, but when whites left for the suburbs, the combination of racial and economic inequities severely tarnished their legitimacy. The decline of the inner city economy in subsequent years further dimmed the prospects of neighborhood children and greatly intensified the feeling that changes in school governance were necessary to improve their schooling.[79]

But what, exactly, should these changes entail? Changing the governance of a school system involves balancing the interests of four major stakeholders: the administration, teachers, parents, and the community. Yet since the call for reform comes most powerfully from teachers and parents, the main proposals present somewhat different plans. Teacher groupings tend to urge child-centered school reform, which would minimize tracking, reduce the number of students in a class, and downsize the educational bureaucracy. Activist parent groupings share these goals, but are more likely to gravitate to an empowerment model that emphasizes testing, accountability, and a larger role in decision making.[80] After many years of experimentation, some gains have been made with both plans, but neither has demonstrated sufficient superiority to furnish a broadly applicable precedent.

The most successful implementations of these plans have occurred where activists forged coalitions between school systems and communities. By consciously tying education of the community's children to the political project of enhancing democracy, they have changed the perception of schools from an alien institution to something linked to the daily lives of local people.[81] In poor communities, especially, economic conditions have impelled the creation of these coalitions and also set strict limits on their success. But therein lies the crucial problem. Although better schools would undoubtedly help, and a campaign to improve the schools can foster a sense of community, the possibilities for democracy and a good education both suffer when the community is in economic disarray.

Accountability and National Standards

In addition to the debate about educational governance, another major controversy revolves around national standards. Concerns about the wisdom of establishing national standards are powerful and real. It might lead to a national curriculum, stifling reform and experimentation among the states. Comparing scores from a national test, some critics might be inclined to discount inadequate funding or deteriorating social conditions as factors in a district's performance. Furthermore, tests based on these standards could be of limited utility, since when overall scores improve, we never know whether the improvement reflects weaker students dropping out or an actual change in classroom practice. Finally, there is the risk that the establishment of a national curriculum will only trivialize learning by inducing teachers to teach to the test.[82]

These concerns have merit, but each should be addressed in the process of developing national standards. National standards would increase educational accountability and provide an incentive for students to work hard in order to master challenging material. They would also bring the weight of the federal government to bear on the need to raise educational achievement. The issue is a very delicate one in the United States, where many romanticize a tradition of local, neighborhood government in which nothing is more local than education. Nevertheless, in international comparisons, in every one of the best-performing countries, the national government has a larger role that includes national standards. Over 14,000 separate school districts exist in the United States. With such a large number, we can encourage experimentation, give local autonomy its due, and still grant the federal government sufficient political authority to develop national standards. President Clinton's proposal for voluntary participation in testing of fourth grade reading skills and eighth grade math abilities represents one very small step toward this goal.[83]

To sidestep some of the difficulties associated with national standards, the American version should rely on portfolios that stress critical thinking, rather than on multiple-choice tests. Patterned after the English national testing system, these compilations of schoolwork offer a more discriminating picture of each student's progress. They also have another advantage: if they are graded on the evidence of analytical thinking, it is no longer problematic if the teacher teaches to the test. While one component of the grade on these tests would use a national standard to measure student performance, the tests would also include a "value-added" index. In this way, grades would capture improvement over time—what the school actually did, rather than the advantages that the children of some affluent parents bring to the classroom.

Education, Democracy, and the Public Sector

These reforms will cost money. And they are not magical: despite their expense, it would be ill-advised to oversell what they might do. Even if all were implemented, they would, at best, only begin to restore a rising standard of living. There is a simple explanation why our expectations about the economic benefits of education need to be deflated at the outset: education represents the supply-side answer to the reskilling of the labor force. After all, business still makes decisions about investment and hiring. It may be seductive to think otherwise, but as long as business retains this role, a better educational system will not provide most Americans with that much economic traction.

Other benefits, however, make these reforms worthwhile. Because these proposals reject for-profit education and focus on the public sector, they avoid the prescriptions that have recently misdirected American education. If for-profit schools are no better than comparable public schools and in fact succeed mostly in enriching private entrepreneurs, then the experiment with them expends resources that could be better invested in public education. And since private entrepreneurship in education is likely to foster a two-tier educational system that is inimicable to the possibilities for active civic participation and fuller democracy, speculating on the capacity of private enterprise to reinvigorate the educational system undercuts that democratic potential. Investing in public education is a risky enterprise, but it is a risk that is worthwhile because it is undertaken not for the benefit of wealthy private individuals but rather on behalf of a broad civic purpose.

6

Jobs and Job Training: The Field of Dreams

They cut people's throats in this country and then they argue about what size band-aid to apply.

—*Rudy Kuzel, president of the United Auto Workers*
Local 72, Kenosha, Wisconsin

Reform of the educational system is one imagined remedy for declining income. Jobs and job training are the other. Here too, however, the prospects are limited, because neither a trained nor an educated workforce is, by itself, a guarantee of future employment. Employment programs confront just too many barriers to success. A trained worker may be hired over an untrained worker, but without a specific government commitment to job creation, businesses still determine the total number of workers they are going to employ. And if together, all their individual judgments threaten to create too many jobs, the Federal Reserve can be counted on to raise interest rates before unemployment gets too low.

The haphazard design and merely palliative intent of many employment programs compound these macroeconomics obstacles. To defuse opposition to free trade, Congress enacts a special program for the workers NAFTA displaced; to calm the inner city, it enacts a job program in the wake of riots. The programs keep multiplying, but they are generally small, underfunded, and embody no coherent federal policy. For these reasons, the political and economic forces producing unemployment overwhelm them every time.

Looking back over the twentieth century, a 2 percent unemployment rate has been achieved just seven times—in 1906, 1918–19, 1926, and 1943–1945. War drove the rate down to this level in four of the seven years. It also played a significant role in the nine years unemployment dipped under 3 percent and the twenty-four times it sunk below 4 percent. Although the unemployment rate in the twentieth century has averaged almost 7 percent, this average disguises what are really three distinct periods.[1]

The first period ran from the beginning of the century to the end of World War II. Reflecting wild swings in the unemployment rate from 1.8 percent in 1926 and 1.2 percent in 1944 to as high as 24.9 percent in 1933, it encompasses both the laissez-faire policies before the New Deal and the total mobilization for war. The total mobilization is particularly important, because it suggests the limits of the New Deal. Although the New Deal had gradually brought the unemployment rate down to about 14 percent in 1937, it went back up to 19 percent the very next year. When it began to decline again, it was plainly the mobilization and not the New Deal that eliminated Depression-era levels of unemployment.

The United States never really demobilized again. Instead, in the second period over the next thirty years, it combined military spending with spending on social welfare to keep unemployment within more tolerable limits. Operating within the political and economic context of the Cold War, Keynesian policies of deficit spending and demand management never permitted the unemployment rate to exceed the 6.8 percent it reached in 1958. With a tailwind from real wars like Korea and Vietnam, it was even able to push the unemployment rate down to 2.9 percent in 1953 and 3.6 percent in 1969.

When unemployment rose to 8.5 percent in 1975, however, it marked the beginning of the third era. Admittedly, Keynesian economic policy had been losing effectiveness. Between 1946 and 1959, the median unemployment was 4.2 percent. It rose to 4.9 percent in the 1960s and 5.9 percent in the 1970s.[2] Since the federal deficit seemed to rise along with the median level of unemployment, federal economic policy virtually invited a reorientation. Ever since then, the federal government has increasingly relied on monetary policy to manage the unemployment rate.

Fiscal and monetary policy are supposed to work together to sustain moderate growth with low unemployment. Yet unlike the Keynesian approach, which viewed a low unemployment rate as one of its primary goals, monetary policy has other uses—most particularly, as a method of throttling inflation. A heavy reliance on monetary policy precipitated the most severe of the post-World War II recessions, when Federal Reserve Bank Chairman Paul Volcker choked the money supply, "zapped labor," and drove the 1982 unemployment rate to 9.7 percent.[3] With more leverage over labor during the Clinton presidency, fiscal and monetary policy could control the effects of a declining unemployment rate, so that even when the rate dropped below 5 percent, very little inflation occurred.

Actually, in current circumstances, the official unemployment rate is a very misleading indicator of the economy's health. The official unemployment rate omits the 1.7 million Americans in prison and excludes both discouraged workers who have stopped looking for work and part-time workers who would prefer full-time jobs. As a result, the real level of unemployment is probably at least twice as high. From cuts in social welfare to reductions in wages and campaigns against unions, conservatives have joined with business over the last twenty-five years to support policies that foster development of a cheap, plentiful labor force. In these economic conditions, a low unemployment rate is hardly cause for celebration. As *The Economist* put it:

> America's labor market delivers more employment than Europe's . . . but the price is worse poverty in and out of work and greater economic insecurity. This is not an accidental conjunction. America's harsh benefits system, which threatens the unemployed with poverty, and then delivers on the threat, is a crucial reason why America suffers less from unemployment in general, and from less long-term unemployment in particular. In a labor market in which wages can fall to whatever level is needed to match supply and demand, an impressive rate of job creation is to be expected.[4]

Unlike Europe, employment policy in the United States was never a grand corporatist arrangement with government presiding over negotiations between business and labor. Instead, employment was mostly a category of macroeconomic policy, with job training programs targeted to displaced workers and minorities taking up the slack. In the midst of a transformed labor market, this policy has resulted in a workforce which is underpaid, underskilled, and, despite the official statistics, underemployed. These are all the classic indicators characteristic of the low-road strategy. They also raise the question: Why has the federal government historically put forth such a limited response?

The Inadequacy of the Federal Response

In the United States, employment policy has never addressed broader questions about the labor market. Policy has never conceptualized the issue as a matter of matching the workers' needs for well-paying jobs with business's needs for a skilled labor force. Instead, labor market policy has focused on the narrow question of unemployment. Most Americans think of the federal government as an enormously powerful institution. They therefore believe that if the federal government is charged with the responsibility of dealing with the issue of employment policy, it actually has the capacity to do so. They are mistaken. The federal government is large but decentralized, commanding but enfeebled, and nowhere are its fragmentation and institutional incapacities more evident than when it tries to address a serious social problem such as employment.[5]

The first major obstacle is separation of powers. The United States does not have a parliamentary system, where the leader of the victorious party becomes prime minister, thereby effectively unifying the legislative and executive branches. It does, however, have a judicial branch that can declare actions by either the legislative or the executive branches to be unconstitutional. As a result, while other countries usually have a strong legislative branch and two distinctly weaker branches, the United States has three equally powerful parts of government. Besides this horizontal system of checks and balances, the battle by states to preserve their rights acts as vertical constraint upon the federal government. In short, this constitutional system is large, sprawling, and ungainly. Designed in the eighteenth century to prevent governmental power from being exercised too freely, it can easily prevent power from being exercised at all.[6]

Separation of powers became a crucial obstacle to the development of an employment policy because it defined a narrow sphere of political activity for the executive branch. This constraint first became evident during the New Deal. In an attempt to improve the management of economic policy, Roosevelt proposed his 1937 plan for executive reorganization. The plan created three new cabinet-level departments—Conservation, Social Welfare, and Public Works—and placed both a strengthened Bureau of the Budget and a National Resources Planning Board under the direct control of the president. The reorganization would have bolstered the power of the executive branch and enhanced its administrative capacity enough to manage an ongoing program of public works spending. When Congress enacted the proposal, however, it was significantly watered down. Instead of a reorganization of the federal government and a major expansion of executive power, the legislation merely established an Executive Office of the President. The original plan had failed because it was tainted by its association with Roosevelt's effort to pack the Supreme Court, as well as by the antipathy, even among more liberal congressmen, to such a significant expansion of executive power.[7]

Business opposition and the absence of a strong executive branch with hierarchical lines of authority meant that the original version of the 1946 Full Employment Act, which guaranteed everyone a job, could not be passed. Once again, instead of authorizing broad economic powers, Congress created another agency—the Council of Economic Advisors—under the president's control. The Council of Economic Advisors is a small office with limited resources. After it, rather than the Department of Labor, was charged with primary responsibility for employment, policy development fragmented among a host of other federal agencies.[8] In effect, separation of powers had blocked the accumulation of too much power by any one agency within the executive branch.

The legacy of this fragmentation persists today. Within the federal government, responsibility for the larger issues of economic and tax policy falls to the House Ways and Means Committee, the Joint Economic Committee, and the Treasury, while the Labor and Human Resource Committee oversees human resources development policy in the Senate at the same time that the Committee on Education and the Workforce oversees it in the House. Oversight for programs is similarly dispersed. In the House of Representatives, the Committee on Education and the Workforce monitors the Economic Dislocation and Worker Adjustment Act, but in the Senate, the Labor and Human Resources Committee is responsible for on-the-job training and education funds.[9] With power so dispersed, it is hardly surprising that no coherent employment policy can emerge.

Separation and fragmentation of power handicap the institutional capacity of the federal government. Development of this capacity trailed behind most of the European monarchies, which centralized administrative authority under the king long before democratic representation arose. By contrast, political reformers in the United States had to bypass entrenched systems of political patronage. The few agencies with the capacity for administering social programs were often isolated islands of expertise within the government bureaucracy. There were exceptions to this general rule—for example, both the Social Security System and the Department of Agriculture enjoyed unusual jurisdictional autonomy and close ties with the relevant congressional committees—but no federal agency concerned with employment policy has ever been among these exceptions.[10]

In other countries, some national department—perhaps of Labor or Human Resources—has usually acquired the portfolio for employment policy. Its bureaucracy thick with expertise, it conducts the analytic and administrative work necessary for the planning, operation, and evaluation of employment programs. Moreover, this work does not go on in some dark recess of the national government, but, rather, has close ties with, and the blessings of, the national political authority. Of course, none of these institutional arrangements ensure success: a country can have all of them in place and still fail to implement a satisfactory employment policy. Without them, however, the likelihood of succeeding is fainter still.

Who benefits, then, from a national government that is so fragmented and ineffective it cannot develop a successful employment policy? In the end, business is the ultimate beneficiary. Business has consistently opposed expansion of federal government into this policy arena, fearing it would usurp the private sector's right to manage the workforce. This is perhaps the final and decisive reason why employment policy in the United States is so underdeveloped. Comprehensive labor market policies naturally incline toward comprehensive employment, and comprehensive employment makes labor scarce and drives up wages.

Admittedly, business opposition to a sound jobs policy is not a single, all-encompassing cause: it is shaped by, and also shapes, the institutional arrangements of the United States as a federal democracy with a decentralized administrative structure. Yet this opposition is crucial. Without it, any analysis of national employment policy is seriously incomplete.[11]

Altogether, over the long term, these constraints gradually shrank the area in which employment policy operated. They have replaced the potential of policies for the whole labor market with an occasional mandate to use macro-economic policy to address the issue of unemployment. For the kind of ongoing training necessary for a high-skill workforce, they have substituted a multitude of small, underfunded programs serving categories of workers such as youth or the "economically disadvantaged." And finally, in a disproportionate number of instances, the programs target racial minorities when, in a more comprehensive model, employment policy would have been race-neutral. The cumulative effect of these decisions has been to chip away at the scope of employment policy, stigmatize the participants in job training programs, and ultimately, to persuade the public that most of the programs are wasteful.[12]

Such cynicism about employment programs dates to the 1930s and has grown ever since. During the New Deal, the Federal Emergency Relief Administration (FERA), the Civil Works Administration (CWA), and the Works Progress Administration (WPA) provided work for between 1.4 million and 4.4 million people. Participants in these programs taught classes, repaired roads, constructed buildings, built recreational facilities, and staged all kinds of theatrical performances. Three oft-repeated accusations, however, dogged most of the projects: the jobs consisted of make-work; the payments were too high; and the projects competed unfairly with private enterprise. As a result, between the underdevelopment of the federal government and the opposition of the business community, these programs left a very small institutional legacy.[13]

Operating from this limited institutional base, the next major package of job training programs had to wait until the 1960s. Although a few of these programs such as the Manpower Development Training Act of 1962 focused on the effects of automation, issues of poverty and race were usually the primary concern and soon gave the programs a distinct racial cast. By 1968, African-Americans made up 47 percent of the Neighborhood Youth Corps, 59 percent of the Job Corps, and 81 percent of the Concentrated Employment Program. In addition, the programs were also lodged in several different federal agencies: the Department of Labor administered the Neighborhood Youth Corps, but the Office of Economic Opportunity (OEO) operated the Job Corps. Admittedly, between 1964 and 1970, total federal expenditures on job training did increase from $200 million to $1.4 billion. Nevertheless, between the perception that the programs rewarded rioting and the jurisdictional disputes within the federal government, the potential for a systematic enhancement of the government's capacity to administer these programs was never very real. In these political circumstances, the expansion played into latent racial prejudices and stigmatized programs even as they grew.[14]

The Comprehensive Employment Training Act (CETA) further amplified these themes during the 1970s. After an initial emphasis on job training, the focus of CETA shifted under the Carter administration toward combating unemployment through the provision of public service slots. During the Nixon administration, however, Secretary of Labor George Shultz had crafted a Republican employment policy that would reduce federal administrative responsibility and devolve responsibility to the states. Overt patronage and corruption was much more prevalent at the state level, so the local provision of public service jobs quickly drew charges of careless management and enrollment of ineligible applicants. In 1981, when Reagan became president, these charges prompted the elimination of funding for these jobs, and the following year, of CETA itself.[15]

In 1983, the Job Training Partnership Act (JTPA) replaced CETA. The headliner among a raft of job training programs, it substituted a commitment to the private sector for a commitment to the public. Yet even this policy shift could not overcome the joint stigmas of race, government assistance, and the considerable burden of job training as a policy issue. JTPA has its own substantial flaws: it does not provide supportive stipends, it creams the instantly employable candidates to the disadvantage of some women and people of color, and its private industry councils are often tainted with patronage and corruption. It suffers from something larger, however, merely from being an employment program in a country that has little patience for them.

This is not to suggest we do not have any employment programs. Quite to the contrary, the federal government funds a total of 125. Sixty-five of these programs serve the economically disadvantaged, and forty-eight target out-of-school youth under twenty-two years of age. Eighteen programs serve veterans, ten programs serve Native Americans, and four programs serve homeless people. Furthermore, since ninety of the 125 programs offer career counseling and seventy-five offer occupational training, the programs are not distinguishable by the services they provide.[16] Instead, for most, their only distinguishing features are the special circumstances—racial unrest, unemployment among youth, or a trade agreement whose political prospects are uncertain—that prompt overriding the presumption against them. Participants in these limited circumstances will get a little help, but few get enough to obtain a decent job.

Unemployment Insurance

Americans believe in the work ethic. Yet 80 percent of the U.S. expenditures on the labor market are funneled through a system of insurance that pays people for their unemployment. Admittedly, unemployment insurance provides support during a difficult time. Still, since we have no coherent approach to employment policy, unemployment insurance also reflects the assumption that workers themselves are personally responsible for their own upgrading. Because many workers do not command the resources necessary for this upgrading, they cannot compensate for the perennial federal reluctance to invest in the workforce.[17]

Although more money was spent on unemployment insurance than on investment in the workforce, these expenditures at least had the virtue of offering a minimum of coverage. Like other cutbacks in social welfare, this has changed in recent years. During the recessions of the 1950s through the 1970s, the percentage of workers receiving unemployment benefits held fairly steady at about 50 percent. Ever since then, however, it has headed steadily downward to 43 percent in 1980, 37 percent in 1981–82, and 36 percent in 1996.

The transformation of the labor market is part of the reason for this decline. Unemployment insurance benefits (UIB) used to tide workers over between manufacturing jobs, or often, between temporary layoffs in the same factory. In the four recessions prior to the downturn of the early 1990s, 44 percent of the workers returned to their old job; in the recession of the 1990s, this proportion dropped to 15 percent. With their old manufacturing job gone forever and no new jobs readily forthcoming, more than half of the displaced workers who received unemployment benefits eventually exhausted them.[18]

In part, unemployment insurance is less available because state trust funds tightened the eligibility requirements. These steps improved the financial solvency of state trust funds and made the states more attractive to business, but they also resulted in distribution of $20 billion less benefits during the 1990–91 recession. As a consequence, between 1980 and 1990, the portion of lost wages replaced by unemployment benefits decreased by 18 percent, and 260,000 people were added to the poverty rolls.[19]

In a stable labor market, unemployment benefits used to act as a bridge between jobs. Originally designed to substitute insurance as an earned right for the social stigma of needs-tested relief, it now constitutes a necessary but insufficient support for those who have been laid off.[20] It is necessary because in an unstable labor market, workers need more, rather than less income. At the same time, however, money that is merely spent to offset the loss of wages is not being spent wisely.

To rationalize the unemployment benefits program, two significant improvements are necessary. The first would provide short-term compensation in slack periods. As a result of the 1992 amendments to the unemployment compensation law, there is a firm basis for this modification, which has already been adopted in seventeen states. Eligibility for UIB usually demands either that claimants be completely unemployed during a given week, or that they work part-time and receive limited earnings, enabling some benefit to be paid. Under short-term compensation, employees retain their eligibility for unemployment benefits, even though the employer has reduced the number of hours that they work. This means that if workers are employed for four days a week, they get 80 percent of their old salary plus 20 percent of what would otherwise be the value of their unemployment insurance. The German variant of this program has existed since 1927 and replaces about 68 percent of previous net pay. Although the American version would replace a lower percentage of lost wages, it is still preferable to an irrevocable layoff and the loss of continuity with the same employer.[21]

Nevertheless, since dangling by a thread at your old place of employment does not bode well for your future job prospects, the whole system of unemployment insurance needs a tight link to a more comprehensive system of job training and job creation. Successful job training requires the systematic reintegration of education and job training at every stage of the process from high school through both two year and four year colleges. It will also require better pedagogical techniques and the expenditure of much more money.[22] This prescription does not obviate education as a fundamentally civic enterprise; it just means to the extent schools do prepare students for work, they should do it well. In short, job preparation and critical thought, like work and citizenship, should be complementary rather than oppositional.

There is also one more stipulation. Even as we redesign job training, we must not forget that the low-road, supply-side strategy is itself fatally flawed. The simple fact that workers are highly skilled does not necessarily mean that anyone will hire them. After all, the discussion about a more comprehensive system of employment training, greater attention must be paid to that fact, too.

Skill or Attitude?

The obstacles to the success of job training do not end with the likely insufficiency in the number of jobs. There is also another problem. Employers say they value skill, but in actuality do not. The contention that they value skill usually comes from a multitude of official corporate pronouncements— speeches by senior executives or press releases to the local media. Yet a study by the Towers Perrin consulting firm found these pronouncements starkly at odds with what executives actually think. While nine out of ten executives told researchers that people are a company's most important resource, and 98 percent said improved employee performance would enhance the bottom line, an actual ranking of strategies to bring success showed that executives ranked customer satisfaction, financial performance, and product/service quality as their three top business priorities. Performance and investment in the workforce ranked near the bottom. Moreover, among the executives who claimed that customer satisfaction was their first priority, only the line managers connected it to training employees.[23]

The Bureau of the Census and the National Center on the Educational Quality of the Workforce found a similar devaluation of skill and training. In their joint project, researchers questioned plant or site managers at three thousand locations with more than twenty workers. Fifty-seven percent said that skill requirements in their workplace had increased in the last three years, and only 5 percent said they had declined. They also estimated that fully one-fifth of their employees could not perform their jobs competently. Despite these assessments, employers ranked attitude, communication skills, and work experience as the top criteria for making hiring decisions. At the bottom, they put academic performance, experience or reputation of an applicant's school, and teacher recommendations. Having little faith in the capabilities of schools to train the workforce, they preferred to rely on buyers or equipment suppliers.[24]

There is also another disincentive. Workers who come to a company already trained are likely to demand higher wages. Since companies that train their own workers retain greater control over their entire wage scale, they often prefer to hire low-skilled workers and train them. Jasco Tools Inc. in Rochester, New York pays its machinists $10 to $15 an hour and needs twenty more machinists to keep up with production for auto and aircraft parts, cutting tools, and other metal products. But the company president Gary Rogers fears that if he raises wages for machinists, the base wage for everybody else will go up. So he turns away business. Then, drawing on a pool of people laid off by Eastman Kodak and Xerox, he employs a full-time instructor to train high school graduates. This strategy enables him to hire workers at $7 an hour and pay his most qualified employees only $10 an hour after four years.[25]

The existing context for training, then, is not necessarily propitious. Employers say they want trained workers, but trained workers cost more money, and some employers are simply unwilling to pay the additional premium. Besides, what many employers desire most in their workers is not so much a skill as a good attitude. They want workers who will be cooperative and obedient, who will be agreeable to them and to their customers while they are doing their job. Furthermore, in a labor market where workers are usually cheap and plentiful, there is a considerable incentive to downskill jobs, because if a job is less skilled, then more intense competition is likely to restrain wages. These factors suggest that despite calls for training to upgrade the U.S. labor force, a low-wage, low-skill environment may not be the most hospitable context for that training to take root.

Compensating for Large Deficits: Too Little, Too Late?

Job training in the United States reflects the fundamental American tendency to try to fix large problems on the quick. The United States is a country where major disparities exist, where some people have every possible advantage of wealth and education while others encounter enormous obstacles to meeting their most basic needs. The labor market not only mirrors these disparities, but also is often their point of origin. At the lower end of this market are people who have no independent source of wealth, are poorly educated, and are either unemployed or work in unskilled or unstable jobs. Their deficits of resources and skill accumulate over the years, until some crisis simply leaves them too short. Unemployed, downsized, laid off, or underskilled, they then get sent off to a training program. Four years of college at the best schools can cost $120,000. By contrast, the typical training program lasts twenty weeks and might cost $2500. It cannot easily compensate for long-term deficits.

The size of the gap between problem and solution explains why the word "modest" is so often used to describe the success of job training programs. The American model of training mimics the American model of crisis intervention: occurring at a time when the participant is most vulnerable, it repairs just a small part of the damage and lasts only until the crisis has passed. In one study of displaced Pennsylvania employees, workers were still experiencing annual losses of 25 percent a year, or $6500, five years after layoff. Including discounted earnings, their total costs stemming from the layoff reached $80,000. Since estimates of the income gain from job training tend to run between $500 and $1500 annually, the damage far exceeds the remedy.[26]

Some distinctive characteristics of the American approach to training go a long way toward explaining the size of this gap. In a fiscal environment where constraints are presumed, public officials tend to oppose depth to breadth: intensive job training for a few people, or cheap job search assistance for the many. This conflict has sharpened in recent years, where despite all the talk about the value of job training programs, expenditures on them actually declined 35 percent between 1986 and 1997. And finally, since most public officials see training rather than job creation as the solution to unemployment and underemployment, they have generally designed programs that are job-specific. Job-specific training programs carry on the educational system's tradition of tracking. Unlike formal educational institutions, they are not charged with instructing students as future workers in the development of broad general skills.[27]

It is different elsewhere. In most other countries, job training consists of both general and firm-specific skills. Confident that they will be able to capture the returns from any investment in training, foreign companies are more willing to teach generic skills. Their confidence stems, however, from specific organizational arrangements that do not exist in the United States. In Japan, for example, companies have much greater loyalty to their workers, and poaching has a high social cost. Similarly, in Germany, the entire tripartite structure—government, business and trade unions—shares the cost of training and enforces policies to protect firms with the greatest training investment. Hence, training in these countries is not merely a technical issue—a matter of borrowing this or that feature of their training program. Rather, their training programs have emerged from a whole complex of relationships between institutions, many of which do not currently exist in the United States.[28]

This stipulation aside, some of the comparative data on training puts the United States in a very poor light. On average, new hires in Japan receive 300 hours of training, compared to just 48 hours in the United States. Only 4 percent of noncollege youth here get any formal training at work. The overall proportion of workers receiving training in Germany and the United States does appear similar—11.8 percent of U.S. workers versus 12.7 percent of the German. The nonprofit National Center on Education and the Economy reports, however, that one-half of 1 percent of companies account for 90 percent of all private sector training expenditures in the United States, with two-thirds of these expenditures going to college-educated employees who arguably need it the least. These participants are therefore quite different from those in Germany, where line workers represent the majority of participants. Many of these line workers have already graduated from an apprenticeship program with an official certificate testifying to their skill. Their higher initial level of skill helps to explain why despite a comparable investment in training, U.S. workers tend to lag behind.[29]

Employment Training in the United States

Employment training in the United States is a grab bag of programs serving a variety of groups including displaced workers, older workers, youth, and the disadvantaged. Over time, some pieces of legislation such as the Job Training Partnership Act have diversified enough to distribute funds to each group. Nevertheless, this distribution has not enabled JTPA to become much more than a funding stream. Passing through, the money may acquire a slight JTPA imprint—its eligibility requirements or its preference for the private sector. Yet even when it acts as omnibus legislation, JTPA has not succeeded in imposing greater coherence on the multitude of employment programs.

Most of these programs schedule similar activities. They provide on-the-job training, classroom training, or job search assistance. The usual prescription says that on-the-job training is most appropriate for firm-specific skills, classroom training is best for workers whose skills are obsolete, and job search assistance is basically designed to assist job-ready workers to become more effective job seekers. For a long time, however, a debate has raged within the policy community about the comparative merits of these practices. Job search is generally the cheapest, but then that may not say very much, since its participants are the most job-ready. The benefits of on-the-job training tend to derive more from getting the employee into the workplace and increasing the amount of time worked than by raising wages. And while classroom training requires more time and is the most expensive, poor pedagogy and a disengagement from the labor market has often diminished the results. The issue is clouded still further, because what works best for one group—on-the-job training for adult males—may not be very successful with another—for example, young females, who benefit more from classroom instruction.[30]

Amazingly, only half of the employment programs the federal government operates actually collect data about what happened to participants after they graduate. This omission makes it difficult to take all these issues into consideration and render a firm judgment. Nonetheless, past experience seems to demonstrate that two different approaches are most likely to attain the "modest success" associated with the best U.S. employment programs. The first approach involves activities like on-the-job training. It is relatively inexpensive and shows positive results by getting people jobs and socializing them into the workplace. A second strategy is more comprehensive. Designed to enhance individual competence, it involves remedial education, skill development, and supportive services. If the first requires a small investment, and the second demands one that is somewhat larger, at least both yield returns that exceed their costs.[31] The real challenge is, then, to build on these strategies and expand the returns into something that is more than just modestly successful.

Displaced Workers

To improve their success rate, displaced workers are one group with whom employment programs must deal more effectively. Although the absence of advanced notice used to constitute one of the major obstacles to helping displaced workers, this obstacle receded somewhat when in 1988, the United States enacted the Worker Adjustment and Retraining Notification Act (WARN). WARN requires notification where employers with one hundred or more workers lay off at least one-third of their labor force. This loophole has proven quite large. In one study of WARN's effects, workers were more likely to receive notice after the enactment of WARN, but about one-half of employers with one hundred or more workers that closed or had a layoff were exempt because they laid off less than one-third of their workers. Unlike advanced notification in most European countries, WARN does not demand that employers offer their workers any financial compensation. For this reason, 61 percent of employers could report that the notices cost them under $500. Doubtlessly, the true cost of compliance is somewhat larger, because 29 percent of employers observed a drop in productivity after their WARN notices were filed. Yet compared to the workers who sustained many years of significant losses, employers still got off very cheaply.[32]

Displaced workers are usually perceived as older, less educated men. This description, however, is a more accurate characterization of the types of workers who experience the highest cost of displacement—those who are most likely to encounter difficulty in finding reemployment—than it is of the characteristics of all displaced workers. Older workers with seniority do not manage as well as younger workers in joblessness and subsequent earnings, but since older workers are less likely to lose their jobs, they constitute a relatively small share of total displacement.[33]

The figures for total displacement suggest the magnitude of the upheaval. Each year during the 1980s, roughly two million people lost their full-time jobs and were not recalled by their former employers. Although 55 percent had weekly earnings at 95 percent or more of their previous wages, the earnings of one-third were at least 20 percent below their old jobs. Surveyed some thirteen to thirty-six months later, almost three-quarters of these displaced workers had returned to work. In the meantime, however, more than half who received unemployment benefits had exhausted them.[34] Their predicament did not improve in the 1990s, either. Of the 4.2 million workers displaced between 1993 and 1995, about the same percentage had returned to work by 1996.[35]

Eliminated in the 1995–96 budget cuts, the Trade Adjustment Assistance (TAA) program illustrates some of the problems associated with programs for displaced workers.[36] Originally, under the Trade Expansion Act of 1962, trade adjustment assistance recipients had to show that their job loss resulted from the lifting of import restrictions, but they did not have to show the loss was permanent. The Trade Act of 1974 relaxed those eligibility requirements. Now workers only had to demonstrate that imports contributed to their layoffs. The act also increased the maximum potential duration of unemployment benefits and the level of those payments. Then, in 1988, the Omnibus Trade and Competitiveness Act of 1988 reoriented trade adjustment assistance to emphasize the importance of training rather than unemployment compensation.[37] In subsequent years, however, both the Department of Labor's own inspector general and the independent policy consultant Mathematica reported unfavorably on TAA's training program. The DOL's inspector general found that TAA more clearly resembled an entitlement-compensation than a genuine training program, and Mathematica reported that three years after receiving their initial unemployment benefit claim, three-quarters receiving trade readjustment allowances earned less in their new job than they did before layoff.[38]

The case of the workers at the Zenith Electronics Corporation typifies TAA's effects. Between the 1970s and 1993, Zenith rapidly expanded its workforce in Mexico and reduced the number of its employees in Springfield, Missouri by 90 percent. Of the former Zenith workers who registered for retraining, less than 40 percent reported that they had found jobs one and a half years later. Their average wage was $7.15 to $7.25 an hour, and more than one-quarter of the employed were receiving less than $6.00 an hour. Even more distressing, with training requiring two years while benefits lasted only one and a half, some of the workers were left completely without support.[39] In short, TAA constituted a political quick fix. Since the federal government never invested enough in the program to reskill workers displaced by trade, it was comparatively easy to eliminate TAA when evidence of its failures mounted.

The Economic Dislocation and Worker Adjustment Act (EDWAA) offers more diverse kinds of assistance, but outcomes so far have proven equally disappointing. Enacted in 1988 as an amendment to Title III of the Job Training Partnership Act, EDWAA sharply increased the federal funding available to the states for programs designed to meet the adjustment needs of displaced workers. Training is shorter-term than with TAA, but the list of services is more extensive: along with classroom and on-the-job training, there is career counseling, testing and assessment, as well as job search, commuting, and child care assistance. Consistent with the conservative view of employment programs, no public service employment is allowed. While eligibility for EDWAA is supposed to extend to millions of workers, funding constraints have generally limited participation to 120,000 a year. And, though no formal evaluation of EDWAA has been conducted, results from the kind of job search program that it features suggest that the loss in long-term earnings will still average about 15 to 20 percent.[40]

None of these programs are likely to provide any genuine relief for displaced workers. Unfortunately, as we shall see in reviewing programs for other groups, their ineffectiveness is hardly unique.

Programs for Youth:
Job Corps and the Job Training Partnership Act

The most important job programs for youths are the apprenticeship program and the Job Corps. School-to-work programs have already been discussed in the preceding chapter. Either as educational curricula in the schools, or as training experience administered in the workplace, the modesty of their success puts them squarely in the tradition of employment programs. Job Corps targets an even more difficult population. Its participants are severely disadvantaged young people, ages 14–21, mostly from the inner city, who have dropped out of school without acquiring any marketable skill.

Established in 1964, the Job Corps program offers this population a broad array of services. For about $1 billion a year, the Department of Labor serves 66,000 participants in 112 residential settings nationally. Because it is residential, and the people it serves usually have more problems than participants in other programs, it has always been, at about $15,000 a person, the most expensive training program. For a long time, however, favorable evaluations immunized the Job Corps against criticism about its costs: one 1980 evaluation even concluded that benefits exceeded costs by some 40 percent. Yet more recent evaluations have not been so favorable. In a 1995 study by the General Accounting Office, only 36 percent of participants completed training, and just half of those found low-skill, training-related jobs. Within two months, 50 percent of these workers had left this job; within two years, a mere

12 percent remained with their first employer.[41] The difference between these evaluations may be attributable to the greater methodological sophistication of the latter study—unlike the 1980 evaluation, it included a control group— or it may simply reflect the growing difficulty the least skilled workers encounter in the labor market. Either way, $15,000 a person is both too much and apparently, too little. It is too much because it is a lot of money to spend to get such poor results. But it is also too little because despite the expenditure, participants still do not have a decent paying, reasonably secure job in the labor market.

Job Corps is now actually part of the Job Training Partnership Act, the 1982 omnibus training program enacted under President Reagan. In addition, as part of the Job Training Reform Amendments of 1992, some JTPA titles were split into separate youth and adult components. The youth component (JTPA Title IIC) serves young people ages 16–21. It seeks to improve their long-term employability, increase earnings, and address problems in the transition from school to work. Another JTPA title, IIB, offers summer employment to youth. It is one of the programs that local mayors rely on to occupy young people in the midst of a hot summer. Young people are often resistant to authority and dubious about the connection between a poorly paid entry level job and a satisfactory long-term method of supporting themselves. Most assessments of their performance in job training programs are negative, and the JTPA youth programs are no different. In one recent evaluation by Abt Associates, the policy consultant firm, young female participants earned only $135 or 1.3 percent more than nonparticipants, and young males without a criminal record nevertheless dropped out of the program at such a high rate that they actually earned 3.6 percent less.[42] Although employment programs for youth can achieve outcomes like these on their own, the design of JTPA as an omnibus employment program makes its own contribution to obtaining such disappointing results.

The Design of the Job Training Partnership Act

Designed in response to perceived problems with the operation of the Comprehensive Employment Training Act (CETA) in the public sector, JTPA suffers not from accusations of boondoggle and make-work, but from the lack of accountability. This is the private sector's failing. In managing publicly funded programs, it reconfigures public goals for private purposes. The consequences are not the stereotypical public sector job of raking leaves. Instead, private firms with connections to the local JTPA network (called a PIC, or private industry council) get a supply of cheap labor to conduct activities that do not necessarily warrant the designation of training. Participants may get some work experience, but by and large, JTPA is a program organized around the needs of employers. Sometimes, private industry councils are even quite open about this purpose. As the Houston's PIC wrote in its annual report, the JTPA program is intended for "businesses that want to reduce labor costs and increase profits."[43]

JTPA's deference to the private sector means that suppliers are able to meet the performance standards without producing real, long-term changes in trainees' productivity or employment prospects. There are several reasons for this outcome. Under JTPA, training is driven more by the need of employers to fill a job quickly, rather than by much concern for any long-term payoff. As a result, job-readiness, and not an actual need for training, tends to determine who gets into the program. Since participants' wages are usually public subsidies originally intended for on-the-job training, JTPA actually buys little or no skill development.[44]

The experience of JTPA in Chicago illustrates these tendencies. Soon after its implementation, the percentage of high school dropouts in job training programs declined by half. Because JTPA provided a greater number of placements at lower cost, contractors could offer shorter training to more carefully screened candidates. There were also significant racial disparities in placement rates and wages for those completing the program, and virtually no machinery for civil rights enforcement. In short, the JTPA program "provided limited opportunities for relatively well prepared workers to upgrade skills, and almost no opportunity for the large numbers of workers without basic skills to acquire them."[45]

Better monitoring might have prevented some of these problems. At least it would have highlighted the patterns so characteristic of JTPA training and prompted some corrective action. In fact, in the year between the passage of JTPA and its implementation, the Department of Labor did design an information system requiring local programs to record detailed information about all trainees and report their experience before training, at the end of training, and thirteen weeks later. A sample of participants was also supposed to be examined at greater length before and after participation and compared with a control group. Nevertheless, the Reagan administration was determined to grant the private sector unusual autonomy in managing the program, and it bridled at any demands for monitoring. Vetoing this information system as an unduly expensive burden on the policy of federalism, it only allowed a few broad pretraining characteristics to be collected.[46]

Although more elaborate analyses have since been conducted, JTPA retains a large measure of protection from prying eyes. This protection is built into the program. More data may be collected, but that data cannot really be used to challenge the private sector's prerogative to manage JTPA. As John Donahue put it,

> The heart of JTPA is payment for results. But the information and monitoring systems essential to put such an ideal into effect were rejected as unduly expensive and intrusive. JTPA's contractual provisions,

accordingly, are far too loosely drawn, allowing ample opportunity for covert waste and abuse. It is rather as if Medicaid physicians were presented with a large population of patients suffering complaints ranging from tendonitis to brain tumors, invited to choose two or three percent of them for treatment, and paid on the basis of how many of them were still breathing when they left the hospital.[47]

The cumulative effect of these flaws shows in the most recent JTPA evaluation. In this study, the General Accounting Office reviewed the employment and earnings of participants five years after they passed through JTPA. Once again, the results were disappointing. Although there were some positive results in the years immediately following their participation, these results faded so much by the fifth year that they could have just as easily occurred by chance.[48] Undoubtedly, the results fade because as with other employment programs, one short period of training cannot compensate for a long-standing deficit of skill. At the same time, however, perhaps JTPA participants would get a bigger boost if the training they experienced was designed more with their interests in mind.

As the premier training program, JTPA reflects many of the obstacles facing employment training in the United States. Job training in the United States suffers from the fragmentation of American social policy, the belief that individuals are ultimately responsible for their own success in the labor market, and the notion that training programs without job creation constitute a sufficient remedy. JTPA's explicit orientation to the private sector compounds these problems, because it skews the benefits of the program so decisively toward the employer. Employers do need some incentives to hire and train less-skilled workers. Unfortunately, with JTPA, all the attentiveness to employers means that a real training program for workers got lost in the bargain.

The implications of this analysis are depressing. Although Americans are wary of employment programs in the abstract, they do believe that if circumstances justify overcoming their wariness, that the exception should be successful. Yet there is little in this analysis to prevent those hopes from being dashed. The consensus is correct: employment programs have had at best modest success, so modest in fact that without some significant changes, they are unlikely to be of much use in arresting the downward mobility of the typical American worker.

A National Employment Policy

The establishment of an effective national employment policy demands that we address the fragmentation in the current system. Instead of a random and duplicative array of federal programs, job training policy in the United States should consist of an integrated set of programs that parallel and intersect with the educational system. This system will, at long last, produce a greater number of skilled workers. Still, since supply-side strategies to improve wages do not reflect the way the market actually works, a program of job creation is going to be necessary. Administered by the federal government and universalistic in its approach, this program will increase the supply of jobs for both more and less skilled workers. For all the talk about work, the history of the twentieth century suggests that genuine full employment requires another strategy besides going to war.

Permanence and integration distinguish this approach to training. By comparison with other countries, Americans are relatively undertrained. To catch up, we need a stable training network, locally based, without vouchers or separate administrative structures for each program. The strategy should focus on the transition between high school and work, but be sufficiently universal in its concept to offer an opportunity for reskilling to currently employed workers. Funded by the federal government, it would nonetheless be administered by the states, in either community colleges or stand-alone programs. Departing from the practice of JTPA, it would not provide training subsidies to firms for work that they would ordinarily conduct as a part of their business. Yet it would offer training to small and medium businesses that could not otherwise afford it, especially when that training stressed general as opposed to specific skills and explicitly sought to adhere to a high-wage strategy that could help to transform the workplace.[49]

Vertical integration is the key to the success of this model. In its present form, job training consists of a jumble of programs, with much duplication and no order or sequence. Unlike in the educational system, participants do not graduate from a training program that teaches one level of skill to a training program that teaches another. If they are lucky, they may get a job, but in the absence of a training ladder, there is no organized way they can further refine their skills and gain some traction in the labor market.

The path upward in the job market must therefore become systemic. Beginning at the bottom with short-term training of fifteen to thirty weeks for those with little experience or skill, this model would enable participants either to obtain a job or enter another training program at the next skill level, where a certificate would prove their mastery. By permitting trainees to shift easily back and forth from introductory programs in community-based organizations to more formal kinds of instruction at community colleges, participants who initially failed in school would get another chance to succeed in the labor market. With workplace training and classroom education adequately sequenced, they could even continue on to a bachelor's degree.

School and work, work and school: interlocking these stages is crucial to the success of the program. Inevitably, this kind of sequencing depends on several components. Just as some community colleges are commonly known to "feed" students to a particular university, so each training program should be clear about where it takes its participants from as well as where they might go after graduation. To smooth this process, requirements should be specific at every stage; when those requirements are met, official credentials should be earned. In short, the goal is to create a system of quality training and education that mirrors the natural progression of the academic track from grammar school to high school and on to college.[50]

Although there are a variety of possibilities for funding such a system, a dedicated payroll tax seems like the most plausible option. During his 1992 presidential campaign, Clinton at first proposed a 1.5 percent tax levy and then backed away from it. Others have advocated a 1 percent training levy, which the firm would either spend on its own employees or pass on to the government.[51] While employers often say that they desire a more skilled workforce, they do not want to fund the transition to it; for them, the benefits of the low-wage, low-skill strategy are simply too great. Employers are plainly going to contest any campaign for a dedicated training tax. Yet despite this opposition, a tax dedicated to training a more skilled workforce belongs high on the list of policy proposals.

The next question is what should be done with all those trained workers. Economic mythology would have us believe that their mere existence will create jobs. This is a lovely wish, but in practice, it seems unlikely. An abundance of labor has never spurred employment: the unemployment rate is consistent proof of that. Yet the illusion persists—if only the unemployed consisted of more rather than less skilled workers, unemployment would disappear. This view romanticizes why workers get hired. They are not hired because they are available; they are hired because employers in the private sector believe that the value of their contribution to the business exceeds their cost. Nothing in the history of economics suggests that a change in the skills workers possess is sufficient to alter this equation.

We venerate work in this country. Those who do not work are presumed lazy or morally deficient. Yet as long as the private sector is primarily responsible for providing work, there will always be a shortage of jobs. That is why genuine full employment—meaning full employment at half the 5 to 6 percent that is most often cited as the natural employment rate—necessitates the active intervention of the federal government. The problem is that although this intervention is necessary, it is potentially full of pitfalls.

One source of these pitfalls derives from stigmatization. If a full employment program run by the federal government is not open to everyone, then both the jobs in this program and the people who get them will be marked as the less employable. This mark occurs regardless of whether the program exists for a smaller group—for example, just for welfare recipients—or a somewhat larger one such as poor people. Either way, those who get the job are going to be stigmatized by it. As a consequence, some neighbors and many prospective employers will always see the job as a form of public aid just one step up from welfare.

Another pitfall relates to the perception that a government job program must necessarily be make-work. This criticism arises out of the policy conflict inherent in any public job program. Employees can neither perform work potentially profitable to a private employer nor can they labor at make-work tasks like raking leaves. There is really only one kind of public project that can slip between these prohibitions, and that is investment in the public infrastructure. Such investment is most likely to win public approbation because it is visible, improves the lives of many people, and produces efficiencies that benefit the business community. Following in the path of the great public works programs like the WPA, this program would construct new buildings, repair roads and bridges, and maintain parks and other public facilities. Wherever possible, this construction should also try to nurture the growth of civic life by broadening the arena of public space. With skillful coalition-building, investments in the social infrastructure could complement investment in the physical, through the provision of jobs as day care workers, teaching assistants, and preventive health technicians. Although any expansion of the public sector is sure to draw objections, at least the design of this employment program presents a smaller target to the charge that the jobs it funds are simply make-work.

Then there is the question of administration. In the past, whenever the federal government has implemented a job program and handed responsibility for its administration to the states, the states have merely substituted federal money for their own. As a result, the program did not actually create new jobs.[52] Since the proposed program's goal is both to create new jobs and in the process build up the federal government's operational capacity, it alone must retain administrative responsibility. That is the only way to prevent the states from simply shuffling the money around.

The final pitfall is the issue of salary. Here again, there is not too much room to maneuver. If the salary is set too low, then the job holder may be working, but the job both stigmatizes and fails to raise the worker out of poverty. If the salary is set too high, some poorly paid employees in the private sector will gravitate to the program, and between them and the already unemployed, the cost will become exorbitant. The solution to this dilemma is to pay participants the market rate for workers in comparable circumstances. In their last job, unemployed workers usually receive about four-fifths of the average hourly rate for all nonagricultural workers. That is therefore what they would be paid in the program. Guided by the same principle, part-time workers, discouraged workers, and welfare recipients would receive about two-thirds of this figure. To avoid problems of worker discipline, it should be clear that workers have a right to employment but not necessarily the right to any specific job. Those who misbehave would be demoted to less desirable jobs, including perhaps sheltered workshops.[53]

Properly calculated, the costs of this program start high, but then turn surprisingly low. There are essentially four categories of program expenses: the cost of direct compensation, the government's share of social security taxes, health insurance, and an amount for tools and materials. These costs mount up, but once they are totaled, many other items can be subtracted. For starters, the taxes collected on the salaries can be subtracted from the cost, and so can the reductions in outlays from benefit programs such as public assistance, food stamps, and Supplemental Security Income. Then there is the expense—less quantifiable perhaps, but still pervasive and substantial—of crime and other manifestations of social insecurity. These can be subtracted, too. In purely monetary terms, when everything is added up, the program still spends more than it saves. The net deficit, however, seems like a very small price to pay for all the economic, social, and political benefits of a full-employment society.

Of course, concerns about inflation would dog this full employment program. These concerns usually have two sources. One involves the inflationary effects of a budget deficit; the other alleges that the program's higher wages would trigger a new inflationary cycle. As we have seen, however, while the initial expenditures on the program would be significant, the net addition to the budget would be comparatively small—so small in fact that, if it were a simple matter of waging a war or rescuing some savings and loan, no one would contend the amount was inflationary.

The effect of the program on wages is more disputable. A full-employment program will boost the income of the poor and lead to increases for other workers. In this respect, any inflation that occurs merely represents the fallout from a renewed conflict over income shares. Yet once this period of adjustment is over, there is no inherent, technical reason amid the new equilibrium why inflation should persist. Besides, with the existence of a full-employment program addressing the issue of employment, policy makers would be freed from the conflicting responsibility of balancing inflation and unemployment. They could then more easily adopt other measures to combat whatever inflation might arise. These measures might begin with the publication of guidelines, but could conceivably progress from the use of government's taxing power to modify wages to serving as a mediator or a full-fledged participant in private wage talks.[54]

For these measures, as with a full-employment policy generally, the issue is political rather than technical. We can have full employment; policies to bring it about can be formulated easily. The obstacle to it arises from the distinct shift of power that full employment represents. Since that shift has not yet happened, Americans confront a very strange paradox: opposition against employment for too many people, juxtaposed to unrelenting sermons about the importance of work. This paradox affects everyone who wants to regain some upward mobility. Yet no group is so powerfully affected as those who receive welfare.

7

Poverty and Welfare: Market as Cure or Market as Cause?

Personal responsibility must be willed, precisely because it can no longer be assumed.

—*Lawrence Mead*

How does calling welfare mothers unmotivated and irresponsible build their self-esteem, encourage employers to hire them, or motivate the taxpayers to pay the bills?

—*Mimi Abramovitz*

Of all the recent market-based initiatives ostensibly intended to halt further downward mobility, none is more remarkable than the Personal Responsibility and Work Opportunity Reconciliation Act of 1996. Signed into law by President Clinton, the act terminated the old program of Aid to Families with Dependent Children (AFDC) and replaced it with a bill that relies on the market to fortify the work ethic and moral backbone of the poor—mostly, of poor women. The law ended the federal entitlement to assistance that dated to the Social Security Act of 1935. It requires that by 2002, 50 percent of one-parent families, and 90 percent of two-parent families, participate in work activities. It also limits the maximum allowable time for receipt of public assistance to a total of five years. Had these provisions been put forth during the Reagan administration, most Republican conservatives would have admired their forthrightness but viewed them as wistfully impractical. Just one decade transformed the politics of welfare reform. By then, even though his own Department of Health and Human Services declared that it would propel another 1.1

million children into poverty, it was William Jefferson Clinton, a Democratic president, who signed the bill into law.[1]

Background

The 1996 act reflects the convergence of many political forces. First, of course, there was the unrelenting pressure from conservatives, who saw welfare as sapping the nation's moral and financial vitality. Convinced that the act would reduce dependency, promote marriage, and restrict the number of out-of-wedlock children, they believed it was, as Newt Gingrich put it, "our best chance to restore hope and opportunity to our nation's neediest citizens."[2] Then, there was Clinton's promise "to end welfare as we know it." Tested out during his 1992 presidential campaign, this slogan meant something different to everyone, and soon became one of his most popular applause lines. The rhetoric was disingenuous at best, because it drew on moderate policy reforms proposed by Harvard University professor David Ellwood. In his 1989 book *Poor Support,* Ellwood had proposed time limits, but time limits with supports such as minimum wage jobs, day care, medical coverage, and expansion of the earned income tax credit (EITC).[3] Clinton appointed Ellwood assistant secretary for policy in the Department of Health and Human Services with the explicit purpose of turning his proposals into law.

In fact, given the history of the previous welfare reform, the Family Support Act of 1988, it was easy to predict what would happen to Ellwood's proposal. In exchange for demanding work from a higher percentage of welfare recipients, the Family Support Act had offered one year of transitional day care and medical coverage. Over the next five years, the insistence on work intensified, and the federal government provided the promised health coverage through the Medicaid program. The states, however, were perennially deficient in funding enough day care.[4] In this political environment, the outcome of Ellwood's proposal was hardly a mystery. The supports would vanish, but there would be a time limit on welfare.

The fate of the Ellwood proposal illustrates the naivete of a rationalistic, technocratic approach to welfare reform. As a professor at the Kennedy School, Ellwood embodied a "good government" approach to politics. This political model gives enormous credence to experts. It assumes that once a skilled reformer enters the fray with a measured, well-wrought proposal, the very rationality of the policy will calm the crowd. Insulated from political pressures, the proposal can then be fine tuned through a legislative process that looks suspiciously like a policy seminar. It is, frankly, a sterile, somewhat antiseptic concept of politics, and as Ellwood soon discovered, there are few subjects less likely for it than welfare reform.[5]

Ironically, Ellwood's analysis of the contradictions of welfare is one of the major strengths of *Poor Support.* In his book, Ellwood carefully delineated the "conundrums" that bedevil public assistance: between security and work; between assistance and the growth of single-parent families; and between the targeting and isolation of the poor.[6] Time limits tried to resolve these conundrums by limiting their duration. Yet the very prospect of a limited time on welfare raised the possibility of a more drastic approach. If the conundrums Ellwood identified could be partly resolved by limiting welfare, then doing away with it completely would resolve them even more. This reasoning had a certain logic. Unfortunately, it also meant that once Clinton dangled time limits in front of an inflamed electorate, there was no turning back.

Ellwood's proposal may have been badly misconceived, and Clinton's decision to sign the bill highly questionable. By themselves, however, neither of these explanations clarifies why the storm about welfare intensified so rapidly. It is one of those instances in public policy where facts do not matter, and none of the usual explanations make much sense. It is not that Americans are stingy: support for the "assistance to the poor" typically runs 40 percent more than assistance for "welfare."[7] Nor, as many advocates have pointed out, is it the cost of public assistance programs: AFDC and food stamps together represented less than 3 percent of the entire federal budget. If the issue is purely a matter of concern about fraud, then it is difficult to explain the estimated $150 billion of fraud we perpetrate upon ourselves each year by cheating on taxes. And if the issue is "dependency," then what is to be made of the $51 billion in direct subsidies to business, the rental of public lands to ranchers at 25 percent of the market rate, and the sale of mining rights for $4500 when, according to a General Accounting Office study, the minerals on the land were actually worth between $14 and $48 million? Plainly, since many similar practices are willingly indulged, the rage about welfare must have other explanations.[8]

Perhaps the underlying reason is the transition from an industrial to a post-industrial society. This transition is crucial, because the response to need within a market economy has always been specific to the stage of economic development. Since assistance establishes a minimum standard of living below the labor market, the definition of need, as well as the method of providing assistance, is periodically modified to remain consistent with the dominant mode of production. Assistance in an agricultural economy is therefore going to take a different form from assistance in an economy dominated by large industries.

From this perspective, the AFDC program had unquestionably outlived its usefulness. AFDC fitted in a broader world of industrial capitalism, where the family relied on the man's income from work. The result was a two-tier structure of assistance. There were social insurance programs like unemployment insurance and Social Security for men, and then there was welfare—meaning AFDC—for women who had lost their source of male financial support, presumably as a result of their widowhood. The government took the absent father's role. In a post-industrial economy, ever fewer men earn a family wage, a majority of women work, and single parenthood has proliferated. The AFDC program simply came into increasing conflict with this new system of social and economic reproduction.[9]

There are many historical precedents for this kind of shift. As the industrial revolution swept through England in the late eighteenth century, the rural gentry adopted the Speenhamland plan, which tied the rate of assistance for the poor to the cost of bread. Designed to provide a year-round minimum income and thereby prevent seasonal workers in the countryside from migrating to the factory towns, Speenhamland represented the last gasp of the old agrarian system. Yet, as its expense grew, so did the clamoring for a new poor law more in keeping with England's emerging industrial base. No wonder then that just two years after the Reform Bill of 1832 admitted the commercial classes to Parliament, the government enacted the Poor Law Reform of 1834, which barred assistance in the family's own home and required that workers either accept the prevailing wage or enter a workhouse. The novels of Charles Dickens and many histories of the period all bear painful witness to the subsequent impoverishment of the English working class.[10]

The termination of the AFDC program mirrors the English experience. Like Speenhamland, AFDC turned into an entitlement that many perceived as excessively generous. Like the Poor Law Reform of 1834, it vanished amid paeans about the importance of work once the new economic system was firmly established. There are not yet enough data to determine whether the insistence on work regardless of pay in the new welfare law will bring about a similar impoverishment of American workers. As part of a larger downward trend in wages, however, the parallels that do exist are already quite frightening.

This transformation of the labor market opens up another dimension about the rage toward the AFDC program. There was always one part of the population—usually described as working poor or lower middle class—that was angry at welfare recipients because they believed that recipients who did not work nonetheless managed a standard of living that was uncomfortably close to their own. Now that economic insecurity has spread to other sectors of the labor market, these feelings have spread, and they take a familiar form. The assumption that welfare clients should be allowed to stay home is no longer acceptable to the broad mass of employees who work every day at an unreliable and insecure job. So popular is this viewpoint that by a 64 to 22 percent margin, the public favors recipients working over staying at home.[11]

Two other ingredients underlie the insistence on work. One ingredient grows out of feelings of powerlessness and the consequent desire to control *something*. The powerlessness arises out of the inability of most American workers to affect their economic destiny in the face of the global forces that are buffeting their lives. If, however, more powerful people and more powerful institutions cannot be controlled, then control must be exercised in the only places where it can be exercised—namely, over welfare recipients and other weaker, more vulnerable people.

Still, from another perspective, the veneration of work is rather curious. After all, in one sense at least, much work has been devalued—that is, many people are paid less for it. The insistence that welfare recipients engage in devalued work reflects a desire to revalue it, to make it once again worthwhile. This desire is understandable, but doomed, because the more welfare recipients flood the lower rungs of the labor market, the more the value of work as reflected in the wages paid will continue downward.

Anger about the changing status of women also contributed to the rage against welfare recipients. In 1937, widows accounted for 43 percent of the welfare caseload. By 1990, however, 54 percent of the children on AFDC had mothers who had never been married to their father.[12] This growth in single-parent families entangled modern public assistance in the irreconcilable tension between the state as a substitute for a husband and the state as a resource enabling a woman to leave her husband. Popular discussions of welfare usually misrepresent this conflict, because only one poor child in fifty-six is African-American, born of an unmarried teen mother who dropped out of school and lives in the central city.[13] Nevertheless, the need to misrepresent itself reflects exactly how powerful the conflict has become.

The AFDC program traced its origins to the Social Security Act of 1935 and the presumptions about women's roles that informed the New Deal. Still influenced by Victorian ideology, these presumptions held that women should remain economically dependent on men, whose wages, alone, would be enough to support a family. Protected against potential demands for a double work day, women could then devote themselves solely to household work. To be sure, the family wage might not be very widespread. When there was a shortfall, however, the preferred policy called for government supplementation, rather than shared housework, female economic independence, and a drastic change in women's roles.[14]

This drastic change took place anyway, stretched out over the next sixty years. Yet while working women today provide almost half of their families' financial support, and women earn more than men in 15 percent of the married couple families where both partners work, welfare mothers are the only women for whom paid work is an unambivalently assigned social responsibility. Further up the income scale, many still revere the notion of women as homemakers. When Congress discussed the possibility of establishing independent retirement accounts to provide a tax deduction for wives, the bill's sponsor, Senator Diane Feinstein of California, declared that the law "says to every woman that's at home and takes care of the family that this is a job and is recognized as a job. It puts an imprimatur on the ability of women to take pride in being a homemaker." Despite their obvious relevance, words like these are rarely used any more to describe the work at home of women on welfare.[15]

Proponents of the new welfare law seem only vaguely aware of the paradoxes inherent in women's dual roles. At the same time, they both deplore the growth of single-parent families *and* want to push women into the workforce. Yet the conflict in women's roles cannot be dispatched quite so easily. Women's growing economic independence is a major cause of single motherhood. A larger number of economically independent women is therefore likely to produce more single mothers. Although proponents of the new welfare law may not appreciate the conflict, their desire to improve the morality of welfare mothers clashes rather starkly with their desire to expand the workforce.[16]

Then too, the anger about welfare is infused with feelings about race as much as it is infused with feelings about gender. Once again, as with much of the discussion about public assistance, the facts do not justify the presumptions. Although African-Americans are popularly thought to dominate the welfare program, the actual percentage of African-Americans is only slightly higher than whites (37.2 to 35.6, with Hispanics at 20.7). Other racially cast aspersions are equally dubious. Despite belief to the contrary, some two-thirds of all female-headed African-American families were poor before the event in the family that made a woman a single mother. And, while the rate of out-of-wedlock births among African-American women (births per thousand unmarried women) is higher than among whites, most of the increase in the "illegitimacy rate"—births to unmarried women as a percentage of all live births—comes from a reduction in the fertility of married couples. In fact, among African-Americans, the incidence of live births among unmarried women has declined for most of the last twenty-five years.[17]

In a public debate where facts mattered, these data would have at least partly calmed the discussion. After the passage of the 1996 welfare law, however, the truly interesting question is why they mattered so little. The linkage of race and public assistance is a well-established phenomenon in this country, but the intensity of feelings about this linkage rises and falls over time, only rarely combining with other factors to produce dramatic changes in the law. In the 1990s, the linkage of race and public assistance became explosive.

AFDC was an entitlement. To be entitled to something means that it is secure and guaranteed to you as a matter of right. In the 1990s, this concept of an entitlement collided with the increasing insecurity of the labor market, raising the difficult question of why the right to public assistance should be guaranteed when the right to a job was not. Coming on top of the perception that racial minorities not only dominated the AFDC program but had benefited disproportionately from the "rights revolution" of recent years, the notion of AFDC as an entitlement loosed a visceral anger. It capped a quarter century of feeling that "those people had gone too far."

Put another way, racial distinctions mark difference. They may be socially constructed differences, but they are differences nonetheless. Differences arm people. When people are secure, they matter less; when they feel besieged, they matter more. Since taxpayers who have access to fewer resources feel besieged, it is hardly surprising that the racial component of AFDC gained prominence as a method of drawing the line between those to whom aid would, and would not, be given. As their empathy withers away, emphasizing racial distinctions becomes too handy a method of aiding only their own kind.

Racial distinctions also fueled a selective application of the concept of reciprocity as the final ingredient of welfare reform. Proponents of reciprocity argue that while welfare recipients get benefits, they, alone among U.S. citizens, return nothing to the society. Recipients should therefore work for their benefits in order to give something back. It is a crafty and seductive argument: drawing on a deep reservoir of racial stereotypes, it evokes images of shiftless, freeloading mothers from the inner city.[18] A little analysis suggests, however, that the whole theory of reciprocity is badly misconceived and selectively applied.

The concept of reciprocity derives from the theory of contracts. In the law, contracts represent a binding set of mutual obligations. It says "you do this and I will do that." Because a contract usually stipulates what happens when one party to the agreement fails to uphold its terms, it is fairest when the signatories possess relatively equal power—two neighbors who enter into contract about a piece of land, for example. When the relative power of one party substantially exceeds the power of the other party, however, it becomes harder to enforce its terms. That is why even though there are protections written into the law, landlords have leverage over tenants, and the odds still favor a large corporation sued by a single employee.

The putative contract between a welfare mother and the government reflects an even greater disparity of power. In this contract, the welfare recipient is supposed to work in exchange for the government's provision of benefits and services. If, however, there are no jobs, or the government fails to provide enough day care, a mother on welfare is left without any effective recourse. The government can even unilaterally change the terms of the contract, and the welfare mother can do nothing. In circumstances where the difference in power is so wide, the whole concept of reciprocity in a contract is fraudulent.[19]

If the theory underlying reciprocity is badly flawed, its practice is not much better. The principle of reciprocity is selectively applied. It suggests that women raising poor children are not doing real work: even after they devote a day to child care, they still owe taxpayers something. By contrast, in the innumerable instances where other people get government benefits, no genuine reciprocation is demanded. U.S. farm policy gave Helen Pinnell, who lives in one of Chicago's most affluent suburbs and is heir to Texas's 87,000-acre King Ranch, $1.5 million over ten years; with $558,000, it made Henry Warren, a Fifth Avenue psychotherapist and absentee farmer, the biggest recipient of agricultural subsidies on the island of Manhattan. When U.S. taxpayers gave Bristol-Myers-Squibb $32 million to develop the anticancer drug Taxol, it reciprocated by charging $986, or an estimated six to eight times the cost of producing it, for a three-week supply. The government spends $150 million to build roads in national forest so that private companies can harvest timber, offers $128 million in low-interest loans through the Rural Electrification Administration to reduce the cost of running ski resorts in Aspen, Colorado and casinos in Las Vegas, Nevada, and contributes $333 million to American auto manufacturers for a new generation of clean cars. The Cato Institute, a libertarian policy group, estimates that direct subsidies to business exceed $86.2 billion; the Progressive Policy Institute of the Democratic Leadership Council calculates that the tax benefits conferred on business may be even larger. Now and then, there may be brief stirrings of indignation about these subsidies, but in a society that only stigmatizes some benefits, the principle of reciprocity is never seriously applied.[20]

These five factors then—the transformation of the economy, plus the anxiety about work, the role of women, race, and the concept of reciprocity—underlie the drift to the right on welfare policy. Together, they galvanized a movement that turned the fanciful reverie of conservatives into an actual law. The law's provisions confuse the interests of the top and bottom fifth of the income distribution. They assume that minimalist government and a market orientation will combine to end the "dependency" of the poor. The act cannot possibly achieve this goal, but before most Americans learn the right lessons from its failure, its provisions will drive many more people into poverty.

The Personal Responsibility and Work Opportunity Reconciliation Act of 1996

The Personal Responsibility and Work Opportunity Reconciliation Act of 1996 ended the AFDC program and gave the states responsibility for administering public assistance. The old AFDC law provided funding for cash assistance to families with children. The law was a federal entitlement. Families were supposed to be assured of food, clothing, and housing, though, in practice, the courts were always reluctant to inject themselves into debates about the quality and quantity of these items.[21] Replacing AFDC with Temporary Assistance to Needy Families (TANF), Title 1 of the 1996 law completely repealed this entitlement.

Under TANF, the states have virtually total discretion to establish eligibility rules and assistance levels. States can provide cash assistance, but if they wish, may offer vouchers and services instead. While the law sets a maximum time-limit of five years' assistance, it both allows states to fix an even shorter period and permits hardship exemptions for up to 20 percent of the total caseload. The work requirement is equally strict. Although it excludes single parents caring for a child under one year of age from calculation of the participation rate, it sets a goal of 90 percent participation by 1999 for two-parent families on top of the 50 percent expected by 2002 for all families. Participation is defined as twenty hours a week for a single parent of a child under six, thirty hours a week for single parents with a child over six, and thirty-five hours for all two-parent families. If a state does not meet these goals, it is subject to a reduction of between 5 and 21 percent in its TANF grant.

While the federal government matched the states to increase AFDC funding during a recession, block grants freeze the allocation of TANF money through the year 2002. Typically, a state will receive the amount of money that it collected in fiscal year 1994. It must continue to spend 75 percent of this amount on welfare programs, but, in keeping with the principle of local discretion in a block grant, it can shift 25 percent to other purposes. TANF does set aside a $2 billion contingency fund for the fiscal years 1997 to 2001. Intended for states that experience high unemployment or increased food stamp participation, this fund will help to cushion the effect of a short regional downturn. In the case of a nationwide recession, however, $2 billion represents just a small fraction of what has usually been needed.[22]

In addition to TANF, the Personal Responsibility Act saved money by cutting food stamps $27.7 billion over six years. This cutback, which accounts for half of the $55 billion of the act's planned savings, reduces the average food stamp benefit from 80 to 66 cents per person per meal. It is not, however, the harshest measure in the food stamp portion of the act. That designation belongs to the provision which restricts food stamps for unemployed single individuals between the ages of 18 and 50 to three months out of every thirty-six. Once this limit is reached, these recipients are only eligible to receive food stamps if they work half-time or participate in a workfare program. A 1995 federal study showed that almost 60 percent of these recipients had no income during the period that they received food stamps. But since only ten states have workfare programs for food stamp recipients not on public assistance, the Congressional Budget Office has estimated that in an average month, this provision will deny food stamps to one million jobless individuals.[23]

The third major target of the Personal Responsibility Act is Supplemental Security Income (SSI). Since its enactment in 1972, one part of this program had always provided assistance to disabled children. In 1990, however, the Supreme Court ruled in *Sullivan v. Zebley* that the eligibility standards for disabled children should be the same as for adults. This decision caused the program to grow fivefold in six years. Children could now qualify for benefits with a combination of several disabilities that prevented normal functioning, even though no single disability was particularly severe. Rejecting both the allegations of inappropriate allowances and the alleged need for sharp cuts in the current rolls, a National Academy of Sciences study merely proposed some measures to clarify the eligibility standards. The Personal Responsibility Act ignored this advice. Eliminating the assessment procedure that combined several moderate disabilities, it cut the program by 25 percent. By 2002, the Congressional Budget Office projects that this change will deny aid to some 308,000 children.[24]

The final crucial provision of the act slashed $22 billion over six years by denying federal assistance to legal immigrants. Although immigrants were supposed to be ineligible for TANF, SSI, Medicaid, and food stamps, the 1997 budget agreement restored SSI funding for immigrants who were already here at the time of the law's signing, and Clinton has twice asked for an allocation to provide some money for food stamps.[25] The states have led the lobbying for this restoration. In the meantime, many continue to fund some social programs for immigrants. Twelve states, including California and New York where half the legal immigrants live, now fund local food stamp programs; every state but Alabama allows immigrant residents as of August 1996 to receive cash payments; and immigrants already in the country remain eligible for Medicaid everywhere, except Wyoming and Louisiana.[26]

The motivation for this change of heart is doubtlessly mixed. Partly, the change springs from humanitarian reasons; partly, it comes from a desire to maintain the supply of low-wage foreign labor. Nevertheless, it is encouraging to see that so many people have had second thoughts about assisting immigrants. Under the 1996 act, older legal immigrants whose age and condition effectively bar them from work or citizenship would be prohibited from obtaining benefits for the rest of their lives. For still others, the Personal Responsibility Act prescribed zero tolerance for "dependency," from the time they arrive to the time at least five years later when they become citizens. In effect, the United States, that "nation of immigrants," adopted a standard of zero tolerance that many of our own ancestors could not have met.[27]

By comparison with the other provisions, however, the retreat on immigrant benefits has been unusual. Since the states all had to submit their plans for implementing the new welfare law to the federal government, many opponents initially hoped it would soften some of the act's harsher provisions. Clinton, after all, had agonized quite publicly about whether he should sign the bill, and it seemed entirely possible that he would steer it in a gentler direction. These hopes have proved illusory. Having already waived some regulations in forty-three states for AFDC, the Clinton administration adopted a laissez-faire policy toward the state plans, intervening only to make the regulations tighter. Eighteen of the first forty states submitted plans with lifetime limits of less than five years. Indiana and North Carolina set two-year limits, Montana has a two-year limit for single parents, and Louisiana will pay for no more than two years of public assistance in a five-year period. Similarly, sixteen states do not intend to wait two years before demanding that recipients work. In Florida, Texas, and Tennessee, adult recipients are expected to work immediately; Massachusetts at two months and Virginia at three months are only slightly less insistent. And, finally, nineteen of the forty states will not pay more to mothers on public assistance who give birth to additional children.[28]

The Clinton administration's posture toward these plans has been to approve them when they are strict, even if the proposed practice—limiting travel by paying recipients the benefit rate of their prior state—has been declared unconstitutional.[29] When the states' interpretation of the law was not so stringent, the administration brought them quickly back into line. In these cases, it set a higher target for job placements, required an end to assistance for mothers who refuse to identify the father of their children, and increased the amount of data that states should send to Washington. It even closed a loophole that would have permitted assistance to children, but not the adult caretaker, beyond the five-year limit. The Clinton administration contended that these measures were necessary because the law still used federal money. That is true, if a little tendentious: the federal government could still allow the law to be interpreted more gently. With this posture, however, the outcome seems predetermined: either the states harshly interpret the law, or the federal government will do it for them.[30]

The meaning of welfare reform is therefore clear: fecund and dependent for too long, welfare recipients are to receive no leeway. Leeway suggests coddling, and coddling connotes an open-ended entitlement like AFDC. Instead of an entitlement, the new social policy prescribes that recipients be punished for their failure to obtain a job. Because the Personal Responsibility Act is authoritarian in its approach to the poor, it includes plenty of punishment. Yet, for poor people who already receive public assistance, it is very doubtful that more punishment is precisely what they need.

Why It Won't Succeed

Proponents of welfare reform believe it will encourage work and family responsibility. To them, any prediction of imminent disaster clashes with deeply held personal beliefs about how the market functions and families should behave. The early returns even support their contentions: from a high of 14.4 million people in 1994, the number of people on public assistance dropped 30 percent to under ten million by 1997. It was the first time since 1971 that the rolls have dipped below that level.[31]

This decline has sparked a vigorous debate. President Clinton attributed the decline in equal measure to changes in the welfare regulations and the improving economy. Once the president set the limits of the discussion, his Council of Economic Advisors fleshed out his analysis with statistical precision: economic growth accounts for 44.1 percent of the decline, while 30.9 percent derives from recent changes in the laws. An appendix in the CEA report, however, suggests that the role of welfare waivers might be as low as 13 percent.[32] Other studies have established that the changing demand for workers during the course of the business cycle can swing the number of welfare recipients from 15 to 20 percent in either direction.[33]

Certainly, at the extremes, unemployment rates in the states with the biggest decline attest to the economy's larger role. In Wisconsin and Indiana, where the welfare rolls plunged at least 40 percent, the unemployment rates dropped to 2.7 percent and 3.3 percent, respectively.[34] The Federal Reserve Bank has tried for many years to keep the national unemployment rate from going down to these levels. Although the governors of these states like to boast about their strict new welfare laws, it would be more consistent with the evidence if they took credit for a successful experiment with the "welfare effects" of a full-employment policy.

This is not to deny that the new laws have influenced some people's behavior. Surely, there are recipients who, in the face of an ever more burdensome set of regulations, decided to leave welfare. Since, however, there are no provisions for tracking what has happened to such people, we do not know if they are actually supporting themselves, the jobs they got, or the wages they received. The presumptive success of the policy therefore rests solely on program data, indicating that a smaller number of people receive welfare. Since those who do obtain a job often lose their health insurance and see their modest material gains go for work-related expenses such as meals, child care, and transportation, few of the newly employed actually improve their standard of living. Hence, despite claims to the contrary, there is actually very little evidence that a decrease in spending on "welfare" necessarily translates to a greater degree of well-being.[35]

Ultimately, it is the validity of the proponents' assumptions about people, government, and the marketplace that will determine the effectiveness of the Personal Responsibility Act. Some evidence about the validity of these assumptions is already available from among the waivers the Clinton administration issued to the states. We can test other hypotheses by asking some hard-nosed questions. In our more nostalgic moments, we might well prefer that everyone stay married, work, prosper, and be governed locally. The issue is whether a state-administered law specifically targeting poor people can enforce these preferences in the twenty-first century.

Managing Women and Poor Families

The first assumption underlying the demand for reform attributes growth of marital instability and single parenthood among the poor to the receipt of welfare. The correlation is evident: in 1995, largely due to administrative hurdles, only 12.1 percent of all AFDC families had both parents present. By contrast, in almost 83 percent of all AFDC families, the parent was absent because of divorce, separation, or the absence of any marital tie.[36]

We could blithely dismiss concerns about this correlation. After all, policy makers explicitly designed AFDC as a program for single mothers, so complaining about their prevalence in AFDC is roughly comparable to alleging that Social Security assists too many retired people. To be fair, however, those who are anxious about these trends are making a subtler argument. They contend that the existence of welfare is itself an incentive for the trends they decry. The trouble is, of course, that these trends do not merely exist among the poor, but are, in fact, national and even global in their scope.

Between 1980 and 1991, the number of births to unmarried women rose by 82 percent to a total 1.2 million births, or 30 percent of all the births in that year. The most dramatic part of this phenomenon has been the sharp rise among adult white women, especially those who are college graduates and work in professional jobs. Once again, this trend is not as simple as it is usually portrayed. From 1960 to 1975, when welfare benefits were going up, marital fertility rates went down from 157 to 92 births per 1000 married women, while nonmarital births remained constant at 23 births per 1000 unmarried women. The increase in the "illegitimacy rate" between 1960 and 1975 was therefore due to two factors—the decline in the fertility of married women and the delay in marriage, which increased the number of women at risk of having a nonmarital birth. In the 1970s, however, marital fertility rates stopped declining, nonmarital fertility rates began to climb, and the age at first marriage continued to rise. Thus, from 1960 to 1975, the decline in marital births keyed the changing "illegitimacy ratio," and it was not until the late 1970s and 1980s that an actual increase in nonmarital fertility drove the ratio upward.[37]

Although these statistics may be uniquely American, the broader trends are global. According to a study by the Population Council, many countries experienced a doubling of divorce rates between 1970 and 1990. In less-developed countries, about a quarter of first marriages end by the time women reach their forties, and unwed motherhood is ever more common. In northern Europe, nonmarital births account for about one-third of all births, but the phenomenon does not imply single parenthood, because almost all the children are born to cohabiting couples.[38]

The combination of these national and global trends point to a single fact: the presence of welfare has contributed very little to the changing composition of families. Not only are two-thirds of the young women who give birth outside of marriage not poor in the year prior to their pregnancy, but it is extremely difficult to argue that the proportion of children born outside marriage has risen because of "dependency" when the value of the putative incentive—welfare benefits—sank 50 percent between 1970 and 1997. Then there is the inconvenient fact that the incidence of teenage mothers seems to vary inversely with benefits. The five states with the highest birthrate among 18–19-year-olds—Arizona, Arkansas, Mississippi, Nevada, and New Mexico—all have benefits below the national median, while the four states with the lowest birthrate—Massachusetts, New Hampshire, North Dakota, and Vermont all have AFDC benefit rates above it. This pattern even extends to other countries, which despite their lower birthrates, have higher welfare benefits.[39]

Nevertheless, these data have not prevented policy makers from including a family cap at the state's option in the Personal Responsibility Act. Such proposals are hardly new; the first mention, in fact, dates to the second edition of Thomas Malthus's *Essay on the Principle of Population,* published in 1803. Despite this lineage, the Clinton administration had previously granted a number of waivers for family caps to New Jersey, Indiana, Virginia, and Wisconsin, and about half the states appear likely to include one as part of their plan. The New Jersey experience has received the most complete, though still preliminary, evaluation; it showed no statistically significant difference between the experimental and control groups. Puzzled by this result, New Jersey officials have contended that because the birthrate declined in both groups by 12 percent, knowledge of the experiment affected the behavior of the control group. Though birthrates rise and fall for many reasons besides the family cap, let us momentarily accept this explanation for the sake of a larger argument about proportionality. A 12 percent reduction means that New Jersey, with 360,000 welfare recipients, reduced its caseload by 124 fewer births per month, or about one-third of 1 percent in a year. In order to exclude these 124 births, however, the state did not pay for 5496 newborns annually; estimates suggest it may have also resulted in 240 more abortions. The real issue, then, is not the reason that both groups experienced declines in their birthrates, but rather why New Jersey is willing to pursue such infinitesimal savings at the risk of imperiling so many more children over the longer term.[40]

The family cap, it is alleged, ensures that people on welfare are treated just like those who work. Since workers' wages do not get adjusted for family size, neither should public assistance recipients. This view is right about wages, but wrong about benefits. Although employers do not raise the wages of workers when they have more children, the federal government does offer an indirect benefit in the form of a tax exemption for every new dependent. In the median state, when a mother on AFDC had a third child, she received an additional monthly benefit of $78, or $936 annually. Taxpayers get an exemption of $2600 for each additional child, or the equivalent of $728 for someone in the 28 percent tax bracket (roughly $36,900–$89,000). In the case of both the welfare recipient and the taxpayer, we provide aid because we believe that child-rearing is an important social task. Yet no one alleges that a taxpayer conceives a child in hot pursuit of the tax exemption.[41]

Once a child is born, the welfare reform act continues to allow state experiments like Wisconsin's Learnfare program that try to make mothers assert greater control over their children. In the Learnfare program, a mother could lose her welfare benefits if her children did not attend school. Other than an unconditional commitment to state waivers, it is not altogether clear why such experiments would be incorporated into the act. A 1992 evaluation by a team of researchers at the University of Wisconsin at Milwaukee found no improvement in attendance for the students subject to Learnfare in any of the six school districts studied. In fact, Milwaukee AFDC teens showed a slight, but statistically significant increase in absences under the Learnfare policy.[42]

Perhaps even more important, the very premise of Learnfare defies common sense. The one intervention that parents on public assistance do not need is state lawmakers giving obstreperous teens the power to determine whether their family eats.

The welfare reform bill holds a misguided conception of families. It wrongly assumes that people would all be able to support their children if they would only stay in school and delay parenthood until they are in their twenties and married. Yet, because there are not enough good jobs around, and few husbands earn a family wage, a substantial minority of women will never be able to support their children without government assistance. As a consequence, unless society is willing to tell this substantial minority of the population that it can never have children, and devise a way to enforce this prohibition, the need for something more generous than the 1996 Personal Responsibility Act will persist.[43]

Welfare and Work

The 1996 act's misconceptions about welfare and work parallel the act's misconceptions about families. In reality, all the volumes of research about work among welfare recipients come down to two simple points. The first is that some recipients are simply unable to work, because they lack either skills or the capacity to hold a job. Although people of different political viewpoints might disagree about the exact proportions, most people are, in principle, willing to accept this notion. After all, despite its harshness, even the 1996 act itself exempts 20 percent of all single-parent families. The second point is equally straightforward, but somehow has always been harder to grasp: welfare recipients represent part of a group of poor people who regularly cycle in and out of the labor market. While this interpretation sounds unremarkable, it is foreign to most American social science research. Instead this research talks about "spells"—the length of time that recipients are on public assistance—and uses words like "dependency." The distinction is crucial. To speak of spells and dependency is to focus on welfare independent of the job market. It makes welfare seem purely volitional, a bad decision that one lazy person made.

There is, however, a whole other method of understanding the interplay of work and welfare. It is to assert that "time on welfare" reflects changing conditions in the labor market, which shapes the determination of large numbers of poor people to seek, or not to seek, work. All that is required to see the pattern from this perspective is a willingness to acknowledge that for the poor, work has not always been available or minimally worthwhile. Too often in the American social sciences, that acknowledgment has not been forthcoming.

Without this acknowledgment, research about recipients has yielded sophisticated, albeit flawed, studies about the length of time people spend on welfare. These studies are helpful, but they are also confusing. The confusion stems from all the true, yet seemingly contradictory statements that can be made about welfare. At one and the same time, it was true that 35 percent of all recipients had been on welfare for two years, and only about 20 percent had been on for 10 years or less; that half of all spells lasted less than two years, but only 14 percent lasted ten years or more; and that less than 15 percent of all current recipients would be on welfare for two years or less, while 48 percent would be on for ten years or more.[44] Perhaps, amid this welter of apparently conflicting data, it is just a whole lot easier to think of the time spent on welfare as a simple matter of dependency.[45]

Still, by paying greater attention to the phenomenon of cycling, some recent research comes closer to explaining these patterns. In La Donna Pavetti's study of welfare, 45 percent of all women leave public assistance for work, and 60 percent of these departures occur within one year. Yet typically, 40 percent of those who leave for work return to welfare within one year. Moreover, by the time five years have passed, fully two-thirds of all women who have left welfare for work will go back to the welfare system. Very similar results emerged from another study, which found that in a two-year period, 43 percent of AFDC recipients did paid work for a total of 900 hours a year. These women averaged 1.7 jobs, mostly in food service, as maids, or as janitors. They were more likely to work if they had a high school education, job training, twice the typical number of years of work experience, lacked a serious disability, and lived in a state with a low unemployment rate.[46] There are no surprises in these studies. Almost half of the women on public assistance cycle back and forth between welfare and the working poor, and those who do so have precisely the characteristics one would expect.

Nevertheless, over the last quarter century, an ever larger number of people have looked at these patterns and expressed first surprise and then outrage. Instead of seeing a group of poor women who, despite low pay and difficult circumstances, work whenever they can, they perceive the same fitful job pattern as evidence of a disturbing laziness. Their remedy follows closely. If these women will not get a job, then government social policies should do everything they can to make them. As a result, from WIN, the first welfare-to-work program in 1967, to the Family Support Act of 1988, and the Personal Responsibility Act of 1996, their strategy has been to enforce steadily more onerous work requirements.

This enforcement has occurred in spite, rather than because of, much evidence about the success of welfare-to-work programs. The outcomes from these programs have been, at best, ambiguous. Forced into the job market, a small percentage of the welfare population have improved their living standard. An equal or even larger number of people have been severely immiserated. Following the economy, welfare rolls have gone both up and down.[47] When the economy deteriorates, many people have difficulty finding work;

when it prospers, getting a job may be easier, but high unemployment rates often persist among some groups.[48] In either circumstance, there is little in the record to support the notion that compelling people to work succeeds on its own terms, and much less that it produces any real enhancement of their standard of living.

Observe, by contrast, among workfare programs, the fairly long list of very small gains or outright failures. Both The Wisconsin Work Experience and Job Training Program and Community Work Experience Program were not successful in increasing AFDC family earnings or reducing AFDC dependency rates. For one-parent AFDC families, the program showed no impact on AFDC reduction in fourteen counties and an impact on the measure of increased earnings in only one county; for two-parent AFDC families, it yielded an impact on AFDC reduction in two counties, but just one county showed an effect on earnings. Similarly, two years after Michigan ended its General Assistance Program in 1991, only 35 percent of the nondisabled recipients were doing as well as they had been. Since the benchmark for upward mobility involved no more than the equivalent of a state medical program, food stamps, and $160 a month in cash, this outcome is especially dismal. And, finally, in the much-touted California GAIN experiment, Riverside, the most successful county program, still had only an 11 percent differential in employment between the experimental and control groups after two years. The Riverside program achieved this result not with employment training but through a single-minded emphasis on jobs. As a consequence, even this difference faded over time.[49]

In the aftermath of welfare reform, the returns have been consistent with these outcomes. When the New York State Office of Temporary and Disability Assistance compared a list of people whose benefits ended in 1996–97 with the wages employers reported to the state, it found that just 29 percent of former recipients had earned more than $100 in the next quarter. Admittedly, this study did omit several categories of employees including the self-employed and those who work off the books. Its outcome is, however, so consistent with the other studies that nothing really augurs well for the success of compulsory work.[50]

In other times and in other places, results like these would puncture the infatuation with work as an all-purpose remedy for the perceived ailments of the welfare system. Because this is not such a time, the implementation of work programs has continued apace. In New York City, Mayor Rudolph Giuliani has pushed 35,000 welfare recipients into work programs, where they replaced downsized civilian servants in a variety of municipal agencies at a fraction of the cost. Employers in Alabama benefited, too. Faced with the prospect of reduced benefits or a malodorous job in a catfish processing plant, seven of the fourteen recipients in a rural county promptly found other work. In general, when women leave welfare voluntarily, 40 percent are still poor five years later, and only 20 percent manage the next five years without using any means-tested program. When larger numbers of less skilled women are forced off welfare, it stands to reason that the results will surely be worse.[51]

With few positive outcomes for welfare recipients themselves, the primary effect of workfare programs will be to flood the bottom tier of the labor market with a large pool of compliant employees working under duress. Their sheer numbers and willingness to work will depress wages, undermine trade unions, and exacerbate the odds against getting a job. These effects are already evident. In Baltimore, nine public schools hired welfare recipients at $1.50 an hour, rather than renew contracts with agencies that supply cleaning people for $6.00 an hour. Likewise, in Salt Lake City, SOS Staffing Services, a provider of temporary workers in the western states, acknowledged that without the availability of welfare recipients, it would have to raise wages 5 percent.[52]

Even when they do not get the job, the mere presence of welfare recipients will intensify the competition for work. In New York City, where the jobless outnumber the available positions by ten to one, it is estimated that at the 1992–1996 rate of job creation, it would take twenty-one years to provide jobs for just the 470,000 adults on welfare. Of course, this calculation makes no attempt to match skills and education of welfare recipients to the new, and likely more technically advanced, positions. Nor does it account for the fact that while 13 percent of the New York City population receives public assistance, even more do so in other cities (Cleveland, Miami, Milwaukee, Chicago, and Philadelphia), and proportionately, twice as many do in Detroit. Unless these cities create jobs at many times the rate of New York, there is no reason to believe that their obligatory work programs will be any more successful.[53]

Although job prospects may be gloomy for welfare recipients, the outlook for private interests seeking to cash in on the new welfare program is quite rosy. Ross Perot's Electronic Data System, Andersen Consulting, sister of the Arthur Andersen accounting firm, and Lockheed Martin already have contracts in many states for a variety of data management tasks in public welfare. With the possibility of privatizing the welfare system in states such as Wisconsin, Florida, and Texas, these firms could significantly enrich themselves: the Texas contract alone is worth $563 million annually. Lockheed's bid for these contracts has an especially bizarre twist. Lockheed has lobbied the Department of Defense for $1.6 billion in subsidies to help pay for mergers with two of its competitors, Loral and Martin Marietta. Since the mergers are tied to the dismissal of 30,000 workers, this payoff-for-layoffs scheme could put Lockheed in the enviable position of collecting one public subsidy to fire its workers and another to manage their subsequent receipt of welfare. Besides such double-dipping, the "dependency" of a recipient with a few spells on public assistance looks pretty paltry indeed.[54]

Devolution to the States

Managing the family and enforcing work are the two primary substantive changes in the welfare law. Yet the law also mandates a major shift in welfare administration. This shift returns administration of the welfare program to the states and block-grants the funding. Favored in one public opinion by 55 to 39 percent, this turnabout grows out of the old American belief that the government nearest to "the people" is the one which governs best. Fueled by a sense that both the welfare program and the federal government were spinning out of control, the Personal Responsibility Act proposes to replicate the kind of state plans for administration of relief that existed before the Great Depression.[55]

In reality, the states are not more efficient than the federal government, nor do they govern better. This is not to suggest that the federal government is a model of administrative competency. The efficiency of its programs varies, depending on the clarity of their mission and the conflicting demands on them. Within the field of social welfare, for example, there are sectors such as housing riddled with bureaucracy and red tape, as well as those such as social security, which pay more than $370 billion annually in benefits while keeping administrative costs to less than 1 percent.[56] By comparison, although some states operate model programs, few possess the financial resources or the depth of technical skill that the federal government can command. And, despite all the talk of lobbying and influence-peddling in Washington, state governments from Louisiana to Delaware are also far more susceptible to bribery and corruption. Just as in wartime, we do not devolve responsibility for military affairs from the Department of Defense to the state national guard, so too in peacetime we should not vest the responsibility for national domestic matters with fifty different state governments.

The states' capacity to take care of their poor varies widely. The four most affluent states—Connecticut, Alaska, Hawaii, and New Hampshire—have median incomes almost twice as high as the four poorest—Mississippi, West Virginia, Louisiana, and Tennessee. At more than 3–1, the difference between the states with the highest (22.5 percent) and the lowest (6.7 percent) poverty rates is even greater. A still more accurate gauge of financial capacity—median income for each 1 percent of poverty—tops out at a 7–1 ratio: it contrasts states like Mississippi and Louisiana that have high poverty rates and low median incomes, with states like Connecticut and New Hampshire, where the median income is high, but the poverty rate is low. Proponents may wish otherwise, but if the money is not there, it makes little sense to speak of the domestic policy "choices" that states make.[57]

Regressive state tax systems further compound these inequities. The average state and local tax on the most affluent 1 percent of families is 7.9 percent, considerably less than either the middle fifth—9.8 percent—or the bottom fifth—12.5 percent—of families pay. In fact, in the ten most regressive states, the middle fifth pays taxes that, as a share of income, average nearly 200 percent higher than the top 1 percent. It is even worse for the bottom fifth. Calculated as a share of income, their taxes average more than 300 percent of the top group.[58] These statistics bespeak a form of fiscal Social Darwinism: now that welfare administration is a state responsibility, redistribution will become more difficult, and the poor—those with the least capacity—must pay taxes to care for themselves.

Block grants are supposed to provide the funding for this state administration of welfare. In the abstract, at least, they are a relatively neutral method of providing such funds. After many experiments, however, it is evident that their effectiveness with any particular constituency depends on factors like the total amount of money and the allocation formula. Certainly, as a funding mechanism for poor people, block grants suffer from several well-known problems. Block grants are capped and cannot provide the additional funds needed during a recession. Block grants may also shortchange the poorest people, as other, more powerful constituencies the block grant targets lobby for funds to be spent on their own needs. Lastly, because block grants make blanket provisions for a broad category of people, they rarely go beyond federal law to collect performance data, evaluate programs, or suggest improvements.[59]

Much of the concern about block grants stresses their inadequacy during a recession. For purposes of illustration, the 1990 recession epitomizes the most likely scenario. Had a block grant been enacted in 1989 for AFDC, the actual federal funding for the recession of 1990 would have been $1.2 billion less, a reduction of more than 10 percent. The block grant would have provided less funding in all but five states. While the maximum state gain in federal funding would have been 14 percent, the maximum state loss would have been almost 30 percent. All told, nine states would have experienced shortfalls of more than 20 percent, and in California alone, the shortfall would have risen to $460 million. By 1993, the shortfall would have totaled $3.7 billion.[60] As expected in a recession, the flexibility block grants confer on the states becomes merely permission to reduce assistance to the poor.

Between the problems inherent in block grants and the inequities embedded in state tax systems, it seems as if an early twentieth-century policy—the administration of welfare by the states—has come back to haunt the poor one hundred years later. If the return to the states is not quite one of those instances in welfare where facts do not matter, it is nonetheless an example where a persuasive and ultimately more convincing argument was simply swept away. For, in truth,

> state and local governments are actually the worst possible levels of government for service and benefit programs that intend to redistribute money through taxes and spending from the better off to help the

poor. . . . the smaller the governmental jurisdiction, the greater the likelihood of a mismatch between needs and resources, with jurisdictions with the most poor having the fewest taxable resources to help them. Federal funding of safety net programs for the poor means that the cost of helping the disadvantaged can be shared by taxpayers throughout the country, as are the costs of major floods, hurricanes, and other natural but very expensive disasters.[61]

The difference is, of course, that while natural disasters are inflicted upon us, the return of welfare to the states is a disaster in the making, and it is one that the nation chose.

Acceding to some of this criticism, proponents of the welfare reform bill have developed a second line of defense. Yes, they acknowledge, there will be pain; yes, they admit, there will be a period of adjustment. Eventually, they contend, it will all work out for the best, and welfare recipients will no longer be mired in a state of virtually perpetual dependency. This explanation can succeed as an excuse for the present, but only if we ignore the trends of the past twenty-five years and the most likely projections for the future.

The early 1970s were the high point of both wages and welfare in the United States. Since then, the 50 percent decline in the value of public assistance has enabled wages to decline, too. After all, wages are not allowed to slip below the level of public assistance, or they would nullify the whole purpose of work. The 1996 welfare law expedites, rather than reverses, these trends. By driving down the value of welfare, it drops the floor underneath the labor market that would otherwise prevent wages from sinking still further.

With that floor gone, the projections are bleak. The Urban Institute estimates that 2.6 million more people, including 1.1 million children, will fall below the poverty line, and the income of over one-fifth of all families with children will decline by $1300 per year. Similarly, according to a study by the Economic Policy Institute, the absorption of almost one million new low-wage employees will effect an 11.9 percent decline in the pay of the bottom 30 percent of workers—the 31 million men and women who earned less than $7.19 an hour in 1994.[62] This is Economics 101, a simple matter of supply and demand. It is therefore altogether disingenuous for proponents of the welfare law who pride themselves on understanding the marketplace to contend that wages will rise. Either they believe the labor market is the only market institution exempt from the law of supply and demand, or, more likely, they hold no such belief at all.

Although it is easy to understand why business-oriented conservatives would be so enthusiastic about the 1996 Personal Responsibility and Work Opportunity Reconciliation Act, it is—on purely economic grounds, at least—far more difficult to comprehend the enthusiasm of most other working Americans. Their enthusiasm endures as the saddest part of the whole saga. Angry about rising taxes and anxious about their own declining standard of living, they seized on welfare reform in the hope of regaining some upward mobility. In reality, they could not be more wrong. By insisting on a reduction in the value of welfare, they drive down wages; by forcing more workers into the labor market, they collaborate in attacks on their own standard of living. In short, they badly miscalculated their economic self-interest. Given the tenor of modern American politics, it is probably too much to expect them to ally with the poor. Until recently, however, it would have still been surprising to see how delighted they were to join an alliance that is partly directed at themselves.

Reforming "Welfare Reform"

Now that welfare is "reformed," it will be even more difficult to get it right. At the outset, the political opposition to changes is well-entrenched; until the early twenty-first century when the casualties begin to mount, it will undoubtedly hold firm. Then there are all the problems with the law itself. From such a poor starting point, any amendments will surely be more like damage control than reform of welfare. Most of all, major welfare legislation in England and the United States has a long history. The Elizabethan Poor Laws (1601–1834), the British Reform Bill (1834–1909), and AFDC (1935–1996) all share one distinctive historical fact. Once they have the weight of law behind them, these policies tend to last.

Still, anything that can be done should be done to minimize the damage. Since Congress abolished AFDC with such enthusiasm, it is not going to relax the demand for work after two years or extend the five year maximum time limit. Yet some changes might protect children and soften the law's harshest effects. Instead of exempting just 20 percent of a state's caseload from the law, the exemption might be 25 or 30 percent. Amendments could also limit the states' flexibility to use the block grant for other purposes, most likely by restricting the percentage of money that can be transferred out of the block. For those parents who exhaust their benefits, vouchers should permit them to provide their children with basic necessities. And, even though it is not an entitlement, it is reasonable to expect that a law predicated on the notion of reciprocal responsibilities might specify—in sufficient detail to be legally enforceable—exactly what responsibilities the states bear. Finally, the 1996 law does not require the states to explain what they do with the money they receive. They do not have to describe benefits and services they provide, the number of people assisted, or the effects of the assistance. Since this information is essential to an accurate evaluation of every major government program, the reporting requirements in the act must be strengthened substantially.[63]

While these changes would certainly improve the 1996 act, they do not address its most fundamental premise about the necessity of work. Here is where some real reporting should be required. To certify that sufficient jobs are in fact available, Congress should initiate a monthly survey of job vacancies. If the number of jobs becomes inadequate, or their qualifications too demanding, then the work requirements of the act would be suspended. To ensure that welfare recipients do not displace other workers, the wages and benefits in these jobs would have to be the same. Because this proposal goes to the core of the Personal Responsibility Act, it is sure to be rebuffed in the immediate future. Nevertheless, the welfare reform act has thrown down the gauntlet. As the evidence of displacement in the public sector grows, and workers in the private sector encounter former welfare recipients who must underbid them on wages, its job requirements could trigger a new round of organizing.[64]

Beyond the new welfare law lies political terrain which, if not quite uncharted, is still a place where ambiguity reigns. Political scientist Hugh Heclo has mapped this terrain well:

> Americans are typically ill at ease with comprehensive ideological justifications for national action in social policy. . . . Norms of democratic equality and solidarity are accepted in the realm of political affairs, while norms of inequality, individual competition, and the like are applied to what are regarded as economic matters. Questions of social relations are the terrain on which these diverging views are puzzled over and never resolved. Social policy inevitably requires choices among applications of social values that are criss-crossed by considerations of political realities, economic incentives, and personal caring about one's own versus the claims of unknown untrusted strangers. Comprehensive theories of social policy, whether of the rightist libertarian or the leftist social solidarity variety, seem to resolve too many things that Americans do not want to be clear about in their own minds.[65]

This is the crux of the issue. Any welfare reform worthy of its name would provide jobs, child care, and an opportunity for education and training. Yet in a political culture where these options are not universally available, they constitute special treatment. They are, in essence, simply too comprehensive.

If many Americans do indeed bristle at the notion that those on public assistance are people with special needs, then most descriptions of those needs inevitably sound like special pleading. Yet unless other people find these needs compelling, no meaningful welfare reform can be achieved. The task, then, is to link the minority on public assistance to a larger group of people, because only then can the additional difficulties facing the poor get special attention. This proposal combines the appeal and political stability of a universalistic approach to social welfare with the focus of a more categorical program. The basic premise is that even if we cannot at first realize the complete universalism of the European countries, political success in the United

States demands that any effective social policy provide some benefits to the working poor.[66]

The policies that would help welfare recipients are familiar, and this principle applies across their entire range. Jobs just for welfare recipients constitute workfare. Punitive toward recipients and competitive with other employees, these jobs isolate and stigmatize those who hold them. The alternative is clear. Instead of disciplining the supply of labor, we need to increase the demand. The needs are there—in health care, day care, education, and community development: some have become steadily more insistent. If we spend money on these social needs and make work worthwhile with decent wages and adequate social supports, then the lives of the working poor would improve, while the supposed resistance to work among welfare recipients would vanish.

A demand strategy would also transform the whole enterprise of job training. Training without jobs is the softer version of a supply-side labor policy. While raising expectations, it implicitly places the blame on workers when those expectations go unrealized. Imagine instead job training for a broad sector of workers in an expanding labor market. Participation in a job training program would no longer stigmatize workers, and best of all, they could actually get and keep a job. Although some technical problems would undoubtedly continue to beset training programs, these problems would seem far less daunting in an environment where the jobs were available, and the compensation was materially as well as morally rewarding.

Since several studies have demonstrated the effect of college on income and upward mobility, access to education is equally vital. The data suggest that for every twenty-four degrees of college credit, the income of welfare recipients rises by 4 to 5 percent. Moreover, studies in five states show that an average of 81 percent of AFDC recipients who went on to get a college degree have been employed since their graduation. These figures are much higher than with other methods of intervention, and they lead to a dramatic decline in public aid, from 80 percent before college to 21 percent after in Illinois, and from 70 to 11 percent in Tennessee.[67] Of course, it is neither wise nor necessary for everyone to go to college. Still, for welfare recipients and the working poor, the availability of money should not be the decisive factor in determining who gets to go.

Because women compose almost 90 percent of the adult caretakers in the public assistance program, no meaningful reform of welfare can occur without provision of day care and child support enforcement. Subsidizing child care would have a dramatic effect on the employment of low-income mothers. Although employment would increase among all three income groups—poor, near-poor, and nonpoor—it would increase the most among low-income mothers, both poor and near-poor. It is estimated that a 100 percent increase in child care subsidy would result in 90 and 158 percent increases in the respective probability of nonpoor and poor mothers getting a job. Put another way, the number of low-income mothers who would be working if they did not have to pay anything for child care could rise from 43 to 81 out of every 100 near-poor mothers and from 29 to 74 out of every 100 poor mothers. Despite these figures, a shortage of child care has been one of the states' most troubling failures. After the 1988 Family Support Act, the states were supposed to put up money for child care, and the federal government was to match this sum. Yet in one study of child care for welfare recipients in seven states, the United States General Accounting Office found that five suffered from insufficient funds.[68]

Although enforcement of child support would have a less dramatic effect on the living standards of welfare recipients, it too represents an opportunity to construct a broad-based coalition around a well-established social need. Child support is hardly a panacea. Many fathers are poor, the enforcement mechanisms are costly, and the best possible child support enforcement program would probably only reduce childhood poverty by 12 percent. Fathers, however, should be financially responsible for their children, and making them so just might help lessen the demonization of single motherhood, especially among the poor. At the same time, however, because the most rapid growth within the Office of Child Support Enforcement has been among non-AFDC cases, child support can help poor mothers and their children without becoming marked by the stigma that stamps a welfare program.[69]

Ideally, then, the best reform of welfare would sidestep the issue of welfare itself. Reform welfare directly, and what we get is a harsh, program-specific measure that enforces work with inadequate pay and family accountability with too little social support. This comes naturally from our veneration of the market: when we judge people by its standards, we will devalue, scapegoat, and punish those who fail. The 1996 welfare reform act will quickly produce many casualties. It will take a while, however, to count these casualties, and longer still for the American electorate to second-guess what it has done. We can only hope that when this second-guessing finally does occur, the issue of the downward mobility of the poor will not be so completely severed from the downward mobility of so many other Americans.

Part 3

Both Workers and Citizens

The Route to Economic Security

8

Democracy
in the Workplace?

It has been a curious feature of democratic thought that it has
not faced up to the private corporation as a peculiar organization
in an ostensible democracy.

—*Charles Lindblom*

To separate labor from other activities of life and to subject it to
the laws of the market was to annihilate all organic forms of existence and to replace them by a different type of organization, an
atomistic and individualistic one.

—*Karl Polanyi*

Americans want to renew their economic prospects. They want to regain a
sense of possibility and recover a sense of control. Although market-based
reforms of education, job training, and welfare are supposed to help realize
these aspirations, they are highly unlikely to do so. This failure is sure to cause
bitterness, because most Americans believe in the "free market," and do not
know how to respond when, in a very personal way, the market fails them.
Having looked to market-based reforms to reverse their declining standard of
living, they are ill-prepared to recognize that the new, global market channels
most of its benefits toward the top fifth of the population. Not so incidentally,
their inability to grasp this fact explains a good deal of recent political history.
Campaigns against poor people, campaigns against gays, campaigns against
women, immigrants, and racial minorities: over the last twenty-five years,
Americans have expended an enormous amount of political energy feverishly
searching for other culprits.

In reality, many of these campaigns will be explicitly counterproductive,
and none will yield any significant positive results. The reform of welfare will

lower wages and produce more poverty; the backlash against women breeds domestic violence; and the hostility toward racial minorities leads to the construction of prisons, rather than investment in jobs, education, or other social services. These campaigns will inevitably have perverse consequences. By failing to solve the problems they purport to solve, they will heighten the sense of government as impotent, and of social problems as truly beyond control. This is a recipe for hyperindividualism. It leaves its adherents nothing but a dismal choice between civic disengagement and tilting at other political windmills.

More effective solutions lie elsewhere, in measures that promote economic security and democratic accountability. Economic security means well-paying jobs and adequate social provisions; democratic accountability means greater control over the institutions of government and the market. These measures do not target welfare, immigrants, or a narrowly defined population of substance abusers: in this respect, at least, they have the virtue of addressing the real sources of our political and economic troubles. At the same time, however, the size and scale of both government and markets make accountability difficult. For these reasons alone, they will be hard to bring under democratic control.

The task, however, must be undertaken, because the split between democracy in the economic and political spheres has simply become too great. Even though the political realm is ever less shielded from the economic, it remains nominally democratic: each person has one vote. In the economic realm, however, the power of the private corporation has vastly increased the disparity between the typical business enterprise and the average citizen. Small businesses with roots in the community could be subjected to some controls; the multinational corporation cannot. The wealth, mobility, and political leverage of the multinational corporation denies the typical citizen an effective remedy. As a consequence, it also drains the concept of meaningful democracy of any plausible theory.

Yet healing the split between economics and politics is not a matter of the market versus the government. That is an important debate, but no longer is the crucial issue. Instead the crucial issue is giving people control over their lives. In essence, this criterion makes everything a matter of democratic accountability. Democratic accountability is not fake populism. It does not pretend that taxes and government bureaucracy, rather than private decisions about employment and investment, determine the framework of our lives. On the other hand, it does acknowledge that for a unique set of political and historical reasons, Americans often experience their government as distant and uncaring. The standard of democratic accountability must therefore be applied to it, too.

The standard of democratic accountability has yet another virtue. What ails the body politic ails the body social—a sense of disconnection and disempowerment that finds its most frequent expression in all sorts of antisocial behavior. The slightest evidence of personal disrespect can start a fight: brush up against somebody on the subway, or cut in front of them on the highway, and what once would have passed as an annoyance provokes a dangerous confrontation.[1] Violence in the United States has many causes, but surely one cause of the readiness to take another human life is the feeling of those who are violent that somehow they, in their lives, have not been respected. Although it would enormously overburden politics to expect that it alone could bind these wounds, an insistence on democratic accountability could at least start the process of healing.

We begin then by applying this principle to the market, seeking ways for employees to exercise power in the businesses where they work, as well as in the marketplace generally. Unlike the political sphere, which has usually reserved a place for the forms of democracy, markets have generally been inhospitable to democratic aspirations. Hierarchy is, after all, essential to them; whoever has the money determines the nature of the investment, including the size and composition of the labor force. Once, when small businesses made most of these decisions, even bad social consequences were relatively contained. Now, however, large businesses make them, and their effects—political, economic, social, and environmental—shape every aspect of our lives. Gradually, as these effects become more pervasive, it gets ever more difficult to justify the existence of a separate economic sphere impervious to the most rudimentary democratic principles.

The Accountability of Markets

Markets set prices. Whether it is the price of goods at the store, the price of labor in the form of wages, or the price of money in the form of interest, much of the market's claim to virtue comes from its capacity to adjust—and constantly readjust—prices in some rough correlation with the laws of supply and demand. This ability seems especially prized after the collapse of the Soviet Union, where a command economy failed at this, and several other, critical tasks. Prices influence the behavior of buyers, sellers, and investors. When buyers and sellers are brought together at the "right" price, investors want to invest, and the economy is supposed to function efficiently.

This claim describes allocative efficiency. In truth, however, there are three other kinds. Allocative or static efficiency exists either when a given level of benefits cannot be achieved at a lower cost, or a given level of costs cannot yield greater benefits. Allocative efficiency is what managers pursue when they try to finetune their current business operations. In this respect, it is clearly distinguishable from dynamic efficiency, which involves the market's capacity to promote new technology and thereby create better products at a lower cost. The steadily declining price of computers is a good example of dynamic efficiency. Then there is x-efficiency, which involves the capacity of markets to raise the productivity of a given technology by stimulating organizational improvements such as downsizing, training workers, and reengineering the flow of work. Visions of greater x-efficiency have driven many of the 1990s' biggest corporate shake-ups. Finally, there is the Keynesian concept, which seeks to address the issue that the efficiencies each individual firm pursues may result in a level of unemployment inefficient for the economy as a whole.[2]

Except for Keynesian efficiency, which is macroeconomics and largely silent on the issue, the other concept of efficiency have all served as microeconomic arguments against participation. Participation, it is avowed, would wreak havoc with efficiency. It would claim for workers an expertise they do not possess, usurp management's prerogative to run the firm, and violate the most basic principles of private enterprise. Once again, the corporation is a bulwark, with boundaries clearly separating it from the rest of the social order. The corporation crosses those boundaries to market its goods; it traverses them each time its products have a social and/or environmental impact; and it ventures far beyond them to influence the political process. For such purposes, the boundaries are all quite porous. When, however, nonmanagerial employees want to participate, or people outside the firm seek to exercise control over corporate behavior, a wall goes up, and cries of interfering with "efficiency" ring out from behind the wall. In effect, the boundary only operates to stop traffic going one way.

Actually, even on microeconomic grounds, the efficiency argument is certainly too narrow and probably just wrong. Workers possess expertise, and studies have consistently demonstrated an increase in productivity when they are allowed to use it. By comparison, the private sector in other countries such as Japan and Germany does not take nearly as hard a line against the influence of other stakeholders. Their systems of corporate governance are much less rigidly closed.

The separation of ownership and control is still the hallmark of corporate governance in the United States. First highlighted by Adolf Berle and Gardiner Means in their 1932 book *The Modern Corporation and Private Property,* this separation makes stockholders effectively passive and limits their ability to modify the behavior of managers except by selling stock.[3] The subsequent history of the corporation in the United States really consists of two distinct periods. In the first period, from the 1930s to the 1970s, when the industrial sector was still dominant, managers retained relatively unchallenged control over corporations. While corporations certainly borrowed from banks, and bank directors sat on many corporate boards, the banking industry acquiesced in a fundamentally advisory role. This was the period of value-creation, the pinnacle of American economic power. Not so surprisingly, it was also the time when workers and communities were recognized as implicit stakeholders in the corporate enterprise.[4]

That all changed during the second period, beginning in the mid-1970s. Once the end of the Bretton Woods agreement terminated fixed exchange rates, the proliferation of computers enabled speculators to extract profits from the slightest differential. These developments increased the velocity of money and enabled the financial sector to challenge the corporation. Amid a host of buyouts and hostile takeovers, "the right to manage a large corporation [began] to be seen as a market just like any other."[5] Wall Street's top guns always claimed that they were conducting these raids on behalf of shareholders. Although this claim may have provided some cover, most noninstitutional investors exercised very little influence in these gambles. Indeed, their power diminished steadily, as institutional investors increased their share of the U.S. stock market from 38 percent in 1981 to more than 53 percent by 1993. Aided by the Reagan administration's policy of financial deregulation, many U.S. corporations modified their practice. Instead of creating value, they tried ever more zealously to extract it.[6]

By comparison, in Germany and Japan, the system of corporate governance seeks to promote the firm's long-term interests. Since the market for corporate control is much less of a factor in both countries, firms do not have to show quick profits necessary to satisfy investors or pay off the debt accumulated in a takeover.[7] Instead of a fluid marketplace where the price of all but the largest firms could conceivably be put into play, both German and Japanese models of corporate governance rely on their business elite to steward the nation's economic future. The new global capitalism does threaten this system. Yet even under these contemporary pressures, both Japan and Germany retain a commitment to recognize the existence of other stakeholders.

There are, of course, some significant differences. Because Japanese corporations are organized into industrial groups with broad, cross-sectoral holdings, the success of each company is woven into the nation's economic life. In the Japanese system, the stakeholders are, in order of priority, employees, customers, and shareholders. Unlike in the United States, profits may therefore be sacrificed to maintain either wages or employment. As a consequence, the system values a more varied range of interest groups than just stockholders and management.

In the German system of corporate governance, banks play a still more active role. Although they own just 10 percent of all corporate stock, their ability to vote proxy shares significantly enhances their influence, so that it may well extend beyond the 42 percent of shares that are owned by other enterprises. They wield this influence within a system that allows continuous monitoring of company performance by all stakeholders who have a long-term connection with the firm. This system includes a board of managing directors, a supervisory board, and the shareholders' general meeting. While the board of managing directors is responsible for operating the firm, the supervisory board functions as a controlling body that oversees the managing board without direct involvement in the firm's day-to-day activities. The shareholders then elect members to the supervisory board. By law, the principle of codetermination requires that employee representatives in all German companies with more than two thousand workers must constitute one half of the supervisory board.[8]

From a conventional economic perspective, the Japanese and German models have some serious problems. Both are more corporatist than the United States. Since corporatism often involves nationwide negotiations between powerful sectors—a national business coalition negotiating with a national coalition of labor unions—it tends to raise the stakeholders' profile. Yet it can also make a system sluggish and inhibit change. Instead of simply downsizing like most U.S. firms, for example, Japanese companies reassign their white collar workers to production. As a result, it is estimated that by orthodox economic criteria, Japan may be employing as many as two million unnecessary workers, or 3 percent of its workforce. Similarly, while German engineering remains strong, it has been slow to shift to services and lags behind other countries in the development of some hi-tech products. Mainstream American economists have no problem explaining these problems. They are an incontrovertible reflection of "supply-side rigidities," which arise when, contrary to U.S. business practices, corporations cannot simply dismiss employees at will.[9]

Obviously, the debate here is between concept of economic and social efficiency. By the conventional economic criteria, corporations are not charities, and it vitiates their effectiveness when they get sidetracked in pursuit of objectives other than their own financial success. From this perspective, downsizing would improve the efficiency of both Japanese and German companies. Firms in Japan should fire their nonessential people, and firms in Germany should streamline so that its economy can be modernized: otherwise, they will never gain a foothold in the booming hi-tech market. These are the standard arguments, very familiar to the American ear.

These arguments are wrong, or at least sadly inadequate, for several reasons. The Keynesian concept of efficiency offers a first clue. When a large segment of the employable population remains unemployed, the unused labor demonstrates that the putative efficiency of the individual firm is poorly related to the efficiency of the economy as a whole. This social concept of efficiency points in turn to a parallel argument that applies to every individual. With the exception of business owners and the small percentage of the population that is self-employed, working for somebody else represents most people's only satisfactory means of support. To be sure, some social welfare programs do exist, but in the United States at least, these programs generally push people toward a fairly minimal level of survival. The public sector pays for these programs. As a result, when the business sector does not employ people, it displaces the responsibility for their survival on to the public. This is keeping two sets of books at once: as long as the social costs of maintaining the unemployed are public while the profits remain private, the efficiencies that business claims for itself do not benefit the society as a whole.

The modern corporation is a social institution. It determines investment and employment, has a significant impact on the environment, and shapes patterns of culture and consumption. Modern organizational theory recognizes these effects. It acknowledges that in a complex business environment, corporations must deal with a multiplicity of interests—stockholders, certainly, but also with employees, government regulatory agencies, and the public at large. Although all this strategizing clearly represents an implicit acknowledgment of the corporation as a social institution, it is strategizing solely in pursuit of financial success. In the United States, at least, stockholders and corporate management are the only stakeholders, and profit is the only goal.

Yet other stakeholders need to be enfranchised, and other goals invoked. Private business corporations are the dominant contemporary institutions. As their primary stakeholders, however, corporate management and the major stockholders represent a tiny fraction of the total population. As long as the political system caters to this fraction's interests and bars genuine participation by other potential stakeholders in the economic sphere, it abandons ever more completely any claims to a democratic practice that has both content and meaning.

The only possible remedy for this deficit is, at long last, to apply the principle of democratic accountability to the economic sphere. Democratic accountability means participation by employees. Participation would yield economic benefits; it would raise, rather than lower, productivity. Every kind of efficiency would gain. Input from the shop floor would surely boost allocative efficiency. In addition, if employees' participation reduced the fear that the adoption of new technology would cost them their jobs, there would also be an improvement in dynamic efficiency. And certainly the knowledge that only employees can bring to bear on the organization of the work would increase x-efficiency, too. Most significantly, as genuine participation began to engender feelings of respect and affirmation, these feelings would spill over into the political and social spheres.

Participation

At the outset, any discussion of participation demands several important qualifications. The first is the usual stipulation about comparative social policy. Most innovative practices arise in a particular institutional context. This means that whatever appeal a particular practice has may not travel so easily. The relationship between state and society is very different in the United States than, for example, in Germany or Japan. In the United States, business is usually strong enough to outflank labor and the government. By contrast, the German government is also relatively weak, but both business and labor are strong, while in Japan, strong business and government sectors combine to dominate a weak labor movement.[10] The multitude of these variations define the limits of comparative social policy. They suggest both why we must look overseas and why it would be pointless for our gaze to turn into a naïve envy.

Participation in the workplace is itself a rather amorphous concept. Participation can be simply advisory—the appearance of consultation as a strategy to cement the ties between management and its employees—or it can be the path to exercising real power. Only the latter is a worthwhile objective. Genuine participation will enhance productivity and employee motivation, but it does so best when it is linked to the power to make decisions. Since that decision-making power, rather than a simple increase in productivity, is key to nurturing greater democracy in the workplace, it should be the standard for judging all such innovations.[11]

By these standards, then, the previous American experiments with participation have been very limited. In the past, U.S. companies have adopted a series of methods to promote togetherness and improve workplace performance. Initially, there was the human relations model of the 1930s, the first to acknowledge that workers were more than automatons. In the 1960s and early 1970s, sociotechnical models stressed teams. Quality circles (in late 1970 and early 1980s) and total quality management (the middle to late 1980s) then followed in rapid succession, but neither provided employees with more power over their workplace or tied improvements in productivity to compensation. Both presupposed disempowerment of employees in the workplace. Recently, they have given way to a belief in networks and the model of flexible specialization. Once again, the consultation presumed here is more horizontal than vertical—less with management and more with fellow employees.[12]

Real participation goes to the heart of American labor law. It challenges management rights, shifts decision-making power over issues central to firm profits such as workers' income and employment security, and requires the union to play a political rather than a strictly economic role in the production process. Since none of the previous efforts measure up, it is hardly surprising that an estimated 40 to 50 million workers want to participate in decisions at their workplace, but lack the opportunities to do so. Then again, though the possibilities for participation are quite varied, only a few of them are genuinely democratic and empowering.[13]

Strategies for Democratizing the Workplace

Let us start at the most basic: better human resource practices correlate closely with better firm performance. In a study analyzing this hypothesis, Mark Huselid of Rutgers University examined 700 publicly held firms from all major industries. Utilizing a series of measures, he defined best human resource practices by a variety of indicators, including use of employment testing, linkage of compensation to performance appraisals, an active information-sharing program, and existence of an employee participation program. The study found that the top 25 percent of human resource practices yielded a 9.4 percent annual shareholder return, while the bottom 25 percent yielded 6.5 percent. Gross return on capital investment reflected a similar pattern: the top 25 percent of firms returned 11.3 percent, while the bottom 25 percent made just 3.7 percent.[14] Apparently, quite apart from any real power to make decisions, it paid to treat people better.

Of course, the possibilities for employees' involvement in the firm extend far beyond improved treatment of workers. Some of these possibilities include profit-sharing, employee stock-option plans (ESOPs), gain-sharing plans, codetermination, and worker cooperatives. Profit-sharing and ESOPs confer financial benefits. They are usually designed to secure the employee's interest in the firm without giving much decision-making power or control. The last three options link participation and financial success. They represent a more purposeful effort to democratize the workplace.

Profit-Sharing

Profit-sharing is most common in nonunion workplaces. Approximately one-sixth to one-quarter of American businesses and their employees already participate in some form of profit-sharing; it is also mandatory in thirteen foreign countries, though the enforcement mechanisms sometimes undercut the law. Studies suggest that profit-sharing usually correlates with small but consistent productivity increases in the range of 3.5 to 5 percent.[15] Since, however, most of these studies fail to distinguish between nondeferred and deferred compensation plans, the implications for productivity are actually more ambiguous than they first might seem.[16]

Proponents of profit-sharing argue that it is a profits tax rather than a salary. If the firm pays $9 an hour and the profit share is $1 an hour, the firm will retain workers as long as their output exceeds $9 an hour, because $1 comes out of the company's profits. By contrast, a firm with a fixed wage of $10 an hour will lay off workers when their output drops below that figure. This is the reason that proponents contend profit-sharing enhances employment stability.[17]

Perhaps employment stability is enhanced, but the financial benefits of profit-sharing often prove illusory. Wal-Mart's profit-sharing plan illustrates the way that benefits tend to vanish. Wal-Mart employs 490,000 people, more than any other private employer except General Motors and Manpower. Although the company pays a few dollars above the minimum wage, it generally keeps the time worked down to about thirty hours a week, so shifts can be lengthened when necessary without resorting to overtime. Wal-Mart's profit-sharing plan provides 6 percent of a workers' pay in company stock. That sounds good, but with minimal pay and the constant turnover, just 7018 of Wal-Mart's employees have accumulated stock worth more than $50,000.[18]

Closer analysis suggests that even the claim of productivity gains is open to question. While the gains may be real, economists do not really know whether profit-sharing raises productivity, or merely attracts the most productive workers to a company that will reward their efforts. In the latter case, profit-sharing may be good for the company, but society experiences no net productivity gains. There is also the question of whether productivity pays for itself. If productivity rises 5 percent in a company with a 10 percent profit-sharing plan, the company is still losing money. In short, for profit-sharing to succeed even on its own terms, there must be a long-term commitment to link workers' extra effort and concern with a tangible reward. Where the benefits are little more than a pot of gold at the end of the rainbow, or workers have reason to fear that more efficiency will lead to the loss of their own jobs, the economic benefits of profit-sharing evaporate quickly.[19]

The political difficulties of profit-sharing are even more apparent. Every social theory imagines its most typical citizen. In free market capitalism, it is the small businessman; in social democracy, it is the committed trade unionist; and in communism, it is the worker who, together with other workers, owns the means of production. Proponents of profit-sharing had someone in mind, too. Like free market capitalism, this person was also a small capitalist. Yet this individual did not own a small business. Instead, through profit-sharing, he or she possessed a small stake in the larger corporate order. Implicit in their vision was the hope that if enough people owned such stakes, the larger corporate order could be purged of trade unions.[20]

This political vision, however, not only excluded trade unions, but also foreclosed any other effective means of political participation. Indeed, profit-sharing sometimes seems to have been designed with that purpose in mind. Focused on the individual rather than the group, it conveys the clear message that it is enough for a person to possess a purely economic stake in society. Its basic premise is that once you have a piece of the pie, you will no longer act like a union member and make trouble. Profit-sharing is therefore supposed to secure political quiescence by transferring the naturally self-correcting tendencies of the marketplace to the political realm. Ultimately, it is a vision of an economics so perfect that employees completely displace citizens, and politics become unnecessary.

Employee Stock Option Plans

Employee stock option plans (ESOPs) are another variation on profit-sharing. In ESOPs, shares in the company's financial success take the form of payments in the company's own stock. This stock usually becomes the employee's pension plan, with all the risks that such a pension entails. In the United States, there are approximately 9500 companies with ESOPs. These companies include Avis, Hallmark, and United Airlines and cover ten million employees, who in turn control some $150 billion in corporate stock.[21] To establish an ESOP, a company sets up a trust fund for employees and then borrows money to purchase shares. When the company makes a cash contribution to the trust fund, the contribution is tax-deductible. It is this tax deduction, rather than any philosophical commitment to employee ownership, that has spurred the growth of ESOPs. Undoubtedly, it has also helped that this tax deduction enabled companies to raise money for the purchase of their own stock.

Together, these two incentives offer the most accurate insight into the real function of ESOPs. Proposed by an investment banker in 1974 and subsequently incorporated into the Employee Retirement and Income Security Act, ESOPs represent an even bigger diversion than profit-sharing. Both profit-sharing and ESOP cater to the belief in upward mobility of the individual rather than the active participation or the power of the group. Yet at least with profit-sharing, companies can distribute profits as they accumulate. When a profit-sharing pension plan becomes an ESOP, however, the employer receives the tax deduction immediately, but the employee's receipt of the pension lies far in the future, at which time it may, or may not, possess real value.[22]

Quite apart from these concerns about values, perhaps the decisive argument against ESOPs is that they do not really work. Since most ESOPs distribute the greatest part of their assets to senior management, few line employees receive enough to create an incentive. In addition, while some ESOPs allow for participation, many do not. Although stock ownership combined with participation has sometimes yielded marginally positive outcomes, the mix of participation and incentives is usually too thin to produce a measurable result. For this reason, it is probably more accurate to classify ESOPs as a potential fringe benefit than as a serious stratagem for changing the organization of the workplace.[23]

Gain-Sharing

Another option often put forward is gain-sharing. Unlike profit-sharing which ties rewards to profits, gain-sharing awards bonuses based on a formula that specifically measures growth in productivity, usually defined as an increase in the difference between inputs and outputs. Unions tend to prefer gain-sharing plans because they have greater control over the formula and measurement of the results; the calculation of profits, by contrast, is more easily manipulated. Moreover, since gains are typically allocated at the level of the department or work unit, employees can see a direct connection between bonuses and any increase in their productivity, which is often boosted by an explicit emphasis on participation.[24]

These distinguishing features of gain-sharing have yielded some surprisingly positive results. In a 1981 study, the U.S. General Accounting Office found that firms with five or more years of gain-sharing experienced a 29 percent reduction in labor costs. Gain-sharing is said to produce these results because it encourages teamwork and recognizes employees' social needs. As a result, employees work smarter rather than just harder or faster. Confident that they will benefit from any improvements in efficiency, they contribute ideas, insist on better management, and embrace new technologies. Better relationships between labor and management often materialize in this environment. Gain-sharing played an important role in the remarkable fifteen-year-long contract that Magma Copper, an Arizona company with a lengthy history of antagonistic labor relations, signed in 1992 with the United Steelworkers of America. The contract formally recognized the cooperation with the union that between 1989 and 1995 yielded an 86 percent increase in productivity.[25]

The disadvantages of gain-sharing are less obvious but nonetheless real. Serious questions have been raised about the quality of the gain-sharing research studies. Most are essentially anecdotal: they lack comparison sites, measure only selected features within the organization, and do not examine longitudinal data. Even the claims of success are underelaborated. Although the studies often describe specific features of a program, they fail to account for how these features explain its success. Without a clear sense of which features produce results, gain-sharing may benefit different companies for different reasons. This makes replication difficult.

In fact, gain-sharing has been difficult to implement in some companies. Gain-sharing may fail if the initial threshold for payment of a bonus is set so high that adoption of the new system does not yield a prompt reward. Problems have also arisen in companies where lower level management interprets questions about the organization of work as a direct challenge to its competence and authority. Even more broadly, gain-sharing is no panacea in a company whose management fundamentally opposes participation. If the participative structures are not already in place, gain-sharing becomes little more than another incentive pay plan. Then, it is just too weak an intervention.

Finally, there is the larger question of whether even the successes of gain-sharing are sufficient. In essence, gain-sharing formalizes the capital-labor accord of the post-war era, when most major corporations tacitly agreed to pay workers for improvements in productivity. Now that this era is gone, gain-sharing only promotes participation in some selected companies. More finely calibrated than profit-sharing, gain-sharing's span of influence is nevertheless restricted to improvements in the organization of work. It is estimated that only 2 percent of all American workers labor in such high performance systems. Yet because they do not consult on investments, and really do not help to manage the company, the role they play continues to reflect a rationing of democracy in the workplace. Gain-sharing may constitute one small step, but Americans still need something more.[26]

Codetermination

The fourth option worth considering is some variation on the German system of codetermination. Codetermination in Germany dates back to 1920. Although the Nazis abolished it, and the minimum firm size has undergone several changes since its reintroduction for the coal, iron, and steel industries in 1951, codetermination remains the distinctive feature of the German corporate-trade union relationship. Under current German law, representatives of the workers must constitute half of the supervisory board in all companies with more than 2000 workers. Two-thirds of these worker representatives are employees of the firm; the other one-third are external trade union officers. For companies with 500 to 2000 employees, the law requires one-third of the supervisory board to consist of worker representatives.[27]

Codetermination systematizes participation; it offers workers a real voice in operating the firm. Codetermination certainly does not end conflict between labor and management. Trade unions and companies continue to fight about issues such as wages, which the German system, unlike the American, usually handles at the national or regional level. Yet by providing a forum where management and labor can work together to improve productivity, codetermination channels and contains conflict. Instead of an adversarial relationship between management and labor, it establishes a structure to nurture cooperation and prevent the conflicts that do exist from contaminating everything.

Nothing remotely comparable to codetermination has ever arisen in the United States. From time to time, union membership on corporate boards has capped the brief spurts of labor-management cooperation—Douglas Fraser of the United Auto Workers in the late 1970s and former Labor Secretary Ray Marshall of the United Steel Workers in the late 1990s. But this representation has always been token—a single, well-known labor leader on a major corporate board, rather than a system of electing multiple labor representatives. In a corporate culture where the attitude toward labor unions is at best begrudging, businesses have always resisted anything more.

The obstacles facing codetermination are therefore considerable. There is the opposition of business, which will acquiesce to labor-union partnerships when its economic prospects are shaky, but rejects the slightest hint of shared governance. There is the enormous disparity in political culture, a disparity that contrasts the orderly, corporatist, and systematic methods of German politics with the disorderly, fragmented, and decentralized approach that prevails in the United States. And there is the rightward drift of American politics, where democracy is a central tenet, so long as it is excluded from the places where people work and from the market relations that have come to so dominate American political life.

Still, if American politics were to break sharply with its recent history, some form of codetermination warrants consideration. Codetermination has the considerable merit of going beyond mere participation to establish a genuine system of governance. The power that governance confers may be limited, and the system itself neither extends beyond the workplace into the community nor provides a ready linkage for doing so. Unlike the previous options, however, codetermination does grant a measure of control over the workplace, and this reason alone is enough to nudge it across the minimum threshold.

Cooperatives

Of course, the most thoroughgoing—and therefore rarest—method for employees to exercise control over their workplace is for workers to run businesses cooperatively. Currently, there are about 150 worker-owned cooperatives in the United States. This figure excludes consumer-owned coops, mostly for food, but it does include a variety of other business enterprises such as manufacturing and the retail trades, as well as services like restaurants and health care. In the Bronx, Cooperative Home Care Associates (CHCA) employs some 300 Latina and African-American women in a home care company: 80 percent of these women used to receive some aid. Based on this success, home care cooperatives have also been franchised in Boston, Philadelphia, and rural Connecticut.

The ICA Group, a Boston-based firm that provides technical assistance to cooperatives, has analyzed the industries with the greatest opportunities for low-income people. Applying the criteria of growth, minimal barriers to entry, access to capital, and potential for significant employment, it identified five kinds of businesses: retail franchises, temporary agencies, environmental products and services, child care, and private security.[28] This is not a glamorous list, but it does suggest that even in poor communities, worker-owned cooperatives can be a real alternative to the harsher versions of workfare.

Both within poor communities and higher up the income scale, worker-run businesses face some consistent difficulties. Investors are generally wary about such enterprises; in the absence of a conventional management structure, they usually doubt that the firm will make money. Banks are unwilling to lend funds for similar reasons. It is, moreover, often difficult to find competent executives who are prepared to adapt to the cooperative style of a worker-run business. After all, in the American economy, managers are supposed to manage, and workers are supposed to work. The historical division between these roles is so deeply embedded that even when the political and economic hurdles are overcome, a whole host of sociopsychological obstacles quickly replace them.

Perhaps foremost among these obstacles is the depoliticization of the U.S. workplace. Most American workers have been socialized into an understanding of the trade-off that used to underlie their jobs. This trade-off exchanged access to paying work for a depoliticization of their views about how that work should be organized. In essence, the message was: come to work, do the job well, and take your check home without looking back over your shoulder. Over time, this understanding led many American workers to accept the existing structures at their jobs. Never seeing that these structures might possibly rank among their concerns, they disengaged from these issues at work and focused their political energies elsewhere.[29]

In retrospect, developments over the last quarter century have illuminated the key to this arrangement: it presupposed a stable and secure workplace. As long as the business was running smoothly and workers were paid well for their disengagement, their interest in self-management was limited, and most preferred to take the time as leisure. By now, though, the stable and secure workplace is long gone, and all U.S. workers are left with is their legacy of depoliticization. With the world of work spinning out of its old orbit, the rationale for this depoliticization must be reexamined.

Despite all these obstacles, the experiment with worker-owned cooperatives needs to be expanded. And it could be easily, through technical assistance offered by an agency in the federal government, as well as the establishment of a national cooperative bank. Such a bank would provide funds for start-up and some working capital. The federal government already provides subsidies that recognize the contribution of home ownership and the family farm to the social fabric. Measures to increase democracy in the workplace could make just as great a contribution.[30]

Democratic Accountability

Of all these strategies for democratizing the workplace, then, only codetermination and worker-owned cooperatives make real progress toward greater participation and democracy. Profit-sharing and ESOPs cater to the belief in the upward mobility of the individual, but they stint on participation and fail to offer a true system of governance. Gain-sharing elicits better performance on behalf of a group, but its mechanisms for participation are uneven, and it also lacks a system of governance. That leaves codetermination and worker-owned cooperatives—by conventional political standards, the least palatable options—as the only meaningful methods of extending the principle of democratic accountability into the workplace.

Democratic accountability is crucial, because it offers the possibility of workers exercising real control. The labor process produces things; work itself helps to define people—who they are and what skills they possess, as well as their economic position in American society. When this labor process comes undone, as it has over the last quarter century, the psychic damage is enormous. Lacking control over their work lives, people direct their anger at teenage pregnancy, sexuality, drugs, welfare, and the federal bureaucracy. Their belief that something has gone badly awry is quite palpable. Yet look carefully at this list: impose abstinence on teenagers, eliminate welfare, reduce drug usage, and streamline the federal government—either as strategies to give people greater control or as measures for improving the standard of living, these issues are trivial beside the centrality of democratic accountability in the workplace.

Powerful forces have always ensured that the principles of democracy in the United States stopped at the office door. These forces will oppose any assertions about the inherent value of economic democracy, and they will greet claims about its potentially therapeutic effects on our political culture with equally intense cynicism. There are essentially two dimensions to their argument, one about efficiency and the other about power. Participation is supposed to be inefficient, because it involves delegation from managers to workers, who in turn require greater supervision. This contention seems plausible only if we assume a hierarchical model. As David Gordon has argued, this model leads inevitably to the antagonistic labor relations we have in the United States today, where monitoring workers to extract more work is the prime function of a huge, and hugely inefficient, corporate bureaucracy.[31]

Yet another, more cooperative set of assumptions is also possible. Workers possess enormous knowledge about how to get their jobs done. Put that knowledge in the service of the corporation, and its business will be conducted more, rather than less, efficiently. Disposing of this issue does not speak to the issue of power, or to the question of who gets what share of corporate finances. But it does puncture the assumption that participatory methods will automatically diminish total output.

Go beyond mere participation to issues of control, accountability, and ownership, and the powerful forces that exclude democracy from the workplace get less susceptible to argument. Arguments do not matter in quite the same way when issues shift from questions of productivity and efficiency to conflicts about shares of income and wealth. The matter is further complicated, because democratization of the workplace cannot stand alone, and in fact, represents just one of a broader array of policies needed to democratize the economy. This democratization includes measures such as a sharp increase of the minimum wage to $7.50, subsequently indexed to inflation; ready community access to capital; support for trade unions, especially through reforms to facilitate organizing; and perhaps, as Robert Reich has suggested, granting the right to incorporate only upon the express promise of good corporate behavior.[32] Like democratization of the workplace, these policies would significantly improve the lives of the bottom four-fifths of the U.S. population. To everyone but a small elite, that, in itself, would seem like a good enough argument. To be successful with them, however, is going to take much more political power.

9

The Government:
From Client
to Customer to Citizen

The American people know how to spend [their] money better
than the government.

—*Bob Dole*

The commonest trick is this: of people's individual spending,
mention only the prices they pay. When they buy a private car
and a public road to drive on, present the car as a benefit and the
road as a tax or cost. Tell how the private sector is the productive
sector which gives us food, clothing, houses, cars, holidays, and
all goods things, while the public sector gives us nothing but red
tape and tax demands.

—*Hugh Stetton*

Although democratization of the workplace may be vital for reasons both of
efficiency and equity, it will only help those who already have jobs. Those
who do not have jobs, or whose jobs pay too little, need some other means of
support. Over the last hundred years, the usual form of support has been
social protection from the government. For those who prize the market, this
development violates the natural order. Determined to reduce or even eliminate social provision, they have pursued it to its source.

A quarter century of these assaults has had its effects. Subjected to a steady
drum beat of criticism about its purposes and functioning, the public sector
has pursued a timid politics in which deference to the marketplace distinguishes every policy initiative. The most obvious example is existing social
programs. Because they provide an alternative to work, the value of their ben-

efits has been racheted steadily downward. Yet the same principle also applies elsewhere. That one-sixth of the U.S. population lacks health care is one of the system's most serious deficiencies. Nevertheless, policy makers do not take any reform seriously unless it caters to the very institutions within the health care delivery system—hospitals, insurance companies, and health mainte-nance organizations—whose profit orientation prompts them to ration care. In the politics of deference, the same market institutions that have so clearly failed get to decide what constitutes an acceptable policy proposal.

Crippled by this decision-making process, the policies that emerge are likely to be ineffectual, and the field of policy options tilts ever more toward the market. It is just what conservatives have long desired: the more ineffec-tual government policies get, the more they feed the sense that government cannot do anything. As a consequence, if anything needs to be done, only the market is left to do it, and only the market is authorized to judge exactly how much more deferential the next round of policy initiatives have to be.

This downward spiral may seem like an inexplicable reversal from the height of confidence in government that flourished in the 1960s. Then, gov-ernment appeared assured of further growth. From Medicaid to Medicare, from VISTA to affirmative action, the Great Society added social programs; their appeal was such that even a Republican conservative like Nixon continued this growth, implementing the Comprehensive Employment Training Act and expanding Social Security. In retrospect, however, the reversal is not so inex-plicable. After all, the expansion rested on the shaky edifice of American atti-tudes toward government. Those attitudes did not make a reversal inevitable, but once a reversal did occur, it is not hard to trace its historical antecedents.

Actually, Americans do not dislike government. If they did, they would not have created over 85,000 of them. The federal government, the fifty states, and governments for every incorporated city or town represent the most obvi-ous part of this total, but there are also a horde of county commissions, school boards, and water districts. Illinois alone has 6500 governmental bodies with power to tax. Similarly, New Jersey's many small governments include 567 municipalities, 611 school districts, 400 local authorities and fire districts, and 21 governments for the counties. In fact, 75 percent of the state's municipali-ties have fewer than 5000 people, equivalent to providing schools, police, fire protection, and town government for every six blocks in Manhattan.[1]

Nationwide, these governments elect more than 511,000 officials. With all the governments and elected officials, it is quite clear that the vision of the government in the United States remains profoundly local. Americans do not want to be ruled by a distant power, and they take particular umbrage when that distant power is their own government. At the root of this mindset lurks the fantasy of small town America: in American myth, if you can talk to your elected official over a white picket fence, the government is benign. This is why the most epigrammatic description of the American attitude toward government comes not from a political science textbook, but rather from that great repository of theories about governing, the *Godfather II* movie. Like Michael Corleone, we like our friends close, but we like our enemies closer.

This wariness about governmental power has shaped the decentralization and fragmentation of the government structure that persists to the present day. Within the federal government, we have the legacy of checks and balances and of separation of powers; between the federal government and the states, we have the extraordinary fragmentation of governmental power and a two-century long battle about states' rights. In the absence of capable central government, political patronage became the dominant method of delivering federal largess. It was this system of political patronage that reformers seeking to modernize the government had to bypass in the Progressive Era.[2]

Not so incidentally, the project of modernizing government also meant taking power back from the patronage and corruption of predominantly immigrant political machines. Andrew White, the first president of Cornell University, was only slightly more explicit than other reformers when he said, "The work of a city being the creation and control of city property, it should logically be managed as a piece of property by those who have created it, who have a real title to it, and or a substantial part in it . . . [and not by] a crowd of illiterate peasants, freshly raked in from the Irish bogs, or Bohemian mines, or Italian robber nests."[3] Partly designed to end corruption, the effort to develop bureaucracies with administrative capabilities in the Progressive Era quickened the process of detaching the American people from their government.

After the Progressive Era, few of the ways that Americans related to the federal government built an enduring relationship. Some people depended on the individual patronage of a local political boss, while others condemned such corruption. Still others felt detached from the expanding administrative apparatus. In Europe, working class parties demanded services from the national government for the collective benefit of their members. Without such a party in the United States, no mechanism existed to fill this political void.[4]

The New Deal reenforced this trend. During the New Deal, however, it was the power of social movements in the 1930s, and not so much the issues of patronage and corruption, that propelled the development of the administrative state and speeded the decline of the party apparatus. It is one thing to go to the local political boss and get a job paving city streets; it is quite another to apply for a job at the Civil Conservation Corps, the Works Projects Administration, or any other agency in the alphabet soup of New Deal creations. The size and complexity of the administrative apparatus in every modern state tends to weaken its ties to the citizenry. Nevertheless, because the United States possessed neither the unifying symbol of a monarch nor the European tradition of a centralized, administratively capable bureaucracy, New Deal domestic policies put some extra distance between the government and those it governed.[5]

The racial focus of Great Society programs in the 1960s accentuated this distance. The civil rights movement forced the issue. Domestically, migration of southern blacks to the northern cities changed the electoral equation; in foreign affairs, a world power fighting for the allegiance of new, predominantly nonwhite nations found official policies of segregation ever more difficult to explain. Although, originally, poverty among whites in places like Appalachia received national attention, race soon replaced class as the staple of Great Society politics. After all, except for Medicare, which provided health coverage for the elderly, most Great Society programs were either race-specific in intent, like affirmative action, or in their practical effects, like Model Cities. As a result, racial minorities came to feel connected to the federal government, but whites who were neither rich nor poor felt increasingly excluded and ignored.

The Great Society set the contemporary political stage. The cynicism about Washington, the resistance to taxation, and the new localism with its retreat into largely white suburban enclaves all express a sense of the federal government as either counterproductive or uncaring. Conservatives have taken these feelings and magnified them skillfully. Yet the fact is that even with some racial skewing of programs for the poor, 49 percent of all families still receive at least one form of entitlement benefit.[6] Curiously, figures like these barely register in the current political climate. Quite to the contrary, what people get, they feel entitled to, and what they do not get, they are angry that someone else is receiving. Either way, the federal government continues to loom alien and distant, and little that it does seems to connect it with the populace.

This history follows a consistent pattern in American culture. Although Americans believe in self-government, the tension in this belief has persisted throughout American history. Sometimes, self-government means that Americans elect their own government. In other, more wide-eyed versions, however, it means that Americans do not need a government to rule themselves. This concept of self-government matches the idyllic vision of the self-regulating market. In both cases, grand forces, impersonal but always beneficent, work their good without conscious human intervention.

Unfortunately, the myth of perfect self-government periodically clashes with the reality of human imperfection. In the face of patronage and corruption in the Progressive Era, the collapse of the economy in the Depression, and the exclusion of racial minorities in the 1960s, reforms were plainly indispensable. Nevertheless, because of the American ambivalence toward the very idea of government, the reforms enacted always made government more cumbersome and unwieldy. In effect, government rarely got the political authority to do what needed doing. Instead, belief in the magic of self-government burdened it with ill-defined mechanisms of political accountability on the one hand and a ponderous bureaucracy on the other. An authoritative, efficient government could have been more accountable to its citizens, but this understanding of self-government requires people to delegate responsibility to elected representatives with the expectation that they will really govern. That Americans have never been willing to grant this authority is hardly surprising, since the self-government of their dreams has always outperformed the government they actually have.[7]

While distrust of government has deep roots in American social philosophy, the most recent outbreak comes at a particularly inopportune time. Like all human institutions, governments are imperfect, and governments make mistakes. Nevertheless, for all their imperfections, government remains the only institution that is capable of countering the market's increasing power. Left unchallenged, the market would atomize everyone. The solitary worker, the solitary consumer, the solitary citizen: none commands any effective remedy against the market. Solitary workers can do nothing about their "natural" wages and working conditions; solitary consumers cannot oppose dishonest businesses and defective products; and solitary citizens are doomed to political isolation and ineffectuality. Amid all the talk of market outcomes, it behooves us to remember *these* market outcomes, because without government power to prevent them, they are the market outcomes that are, in fact, most likely.

Enfeebling Government

As long as government retains some potential to counter the market, proponents of an unregulated economy will put forth policies to undermine its power. In recent years, these policies have taken several different forms. They include less explicitly ideological efforts to increase the efficiency of government, as well as direct attacks, through deregulation, privatization, and a balanced budget, on its function and capacity. Even in the guise of greater efficiency, these policies have taken their toll.

The most reasonable critique of government functioning spotlights changes that occur in all large organizations. This is the analysis that Vice President Albert Gore put forth in his capacity as chair of the National Performance Review.

> From the 1930s through the 1960s, we built large, top-down centralized bureaucracies to do the public's business. They were patterned after the corporate structures of the age: hierarchical bureaucracies in which tasks were broken into simple parts, each the responsibility of a different layer of employees, each defined by specific rules and regulations. With their rigid preoccupation with standard operating procedure, their vertical chains of command, and their standardized services, these bureaucracies were steady—but slow and cumbersome. And in today's world of rapid change, lightening-quick information technologies, tough global competition, and demand customers, large, top-down

bureaucracies—public or private—don't work very well. Saturn isn't run the way General Motors was. Intel isn't run the way IBM was.[8]

Operating upon these assumptions, the National Performance Review set out to save $108 billion between 1995 and 1999. These savings were supposed to come from a variety of sources: $36 billion from agencies, $40 billion from streamlining bureaucracy, $22 billion from a 5 percent annual savings in procurement, and $5 billion from improved information technology. As a result of these cutbacks, the National Performance Review hoped to reduce the civilian nonpostal workforce by 12 percent, or a total of 252,000 workers, over the next five years.[9]

There are several easy criticisms of these plans. The savings projections are surely inflated, in part because the plan simply advocates shifting functions from one office to another. Hence, while it might be wise in the abstract to break up the monopolies of the Government Printing Office and the General Services Administration, it is not altogether clear how much money can be saved if these functions are reallocated to agency procurement staffs themselves targeted for cutbacks. Without sufficient contract monitoring, outsourcing services can make even the least efficient government administration look cheap by comparison. This is one reason why the Congressional Budget Office estimated that in its first phase, the National Performance Review will actually realize just 5 percent of its projected $6 billion in savings.[10]

Although we are used to discounting projections of what a policy will accomplish, we are less accustomed to engaging the premises of a plan that promises to reduce the size of government. A more efficient government is something everyone desires. Nevertheless, the Gore plan seems to embody the principle of reflexive downsizing, where cuts are good because they shrink government, but no one has really asked the fundamental question: What is government for? If the role of government is merely to enforce law and order, stabilize the economy, and act as a service center for the marketplace, then, in the name of efficiency, it should be smaller still. Yet there has always been another conception, one that imagines government as more than merely the night watchman state in the information age. Tarnished in its practice by the realities of class, race, and gender, this conception nonetheless envisioned a government that ensures a decent standard of living, promotes an active civic life, and fosters a sense of community. Firmly rejecting this vision, Al Gore and the National Performance Review have instead elevated efficiency experts to their current position as the preeminent guardians of our public life.

Deregulation

While the National Performance Review targets government efficiency, deregulation directly attacks its authority. Some seemingly absurd tales of government abuse give considerable aid and comfort to this effort.[11] David McIntosh, a Republican congressman from Minnesota, campaigned against excessive regulatory oversight by citing what sounded like a truly sublime example of bureaucratic stupidity: the government's insistence that buckets have holes in them. Yet like many such tales, there was actually a lot more to this story. Over the last ten years, 500 babies have drowned in the large plastic containers used for dry wall construction, including 36 in 1994. The Occupational Safety and Health Agency (OSHA) solicited comments from manufacturers about designing a bucket that would tip over or be otherwise childproof. Few budged. Faced with an unrelenting campaign for deregulation, OSHA then had to settle for a voluntary educational effort within the industry.[12]

This vignette underscores a key issue about deregulation: regulations are not issued unless something bad has occurred before. This seems like such a basic fact that it hardly requires reiteration. In the current political climate, however, it may help us to regain a little perspective if we remember that the need for regulation did not spring solely from the fevered imaginings of government bureaucrats. Yes, it is true: businesses have discriminated against black workers, short-weighted consumers, and dumped toxic chemicals in residential neighborhoods. To be sure, only a small number of individuals in any industry do these things. Yet despite the fundamentally laissez-faire attitude many Americans have toward business, the government has regulated these practices because they angered enough people to threaten the stability of the marketplace.

As the premier business newspaper, *The Wall Street Journal* presents the best case for the merit of business regulation. While its editorial page rages about the intrusiveness of "liberal" government, its reporters use the most sober and circumspect language to document white collar crime. Investigative journalist Robert Sherrill followed this trail for just one year. During this time, he found articles about $170 million worth of price-fixing by Archer Daniel Midland, the "supermarket to the world"; a thirteen-year-long deception by Prudential Insurance Company that duped thousands of customers and required $1 billion of restitution; the mysterious case of money-laundering at Citibank, which unquestioningly sent $100 million of Raul Salinas's money overseas, when he, as the brother of former Mexican President Carlos Salinas, never earned more than $190,000 in a single year; the 1000 current investigations about health care fraud that are reckoned to have cost the government some $100 billion; and the misrepresentations of hazardous conditions by Kentucky mining executives, which subsequently led to an explosion that killed ten men. All these actions *The Wall Street Journal* reported because, as the newspaper of the corporate world, business people need to know what other business people do. Nevertheless, those concerned with matters other than the possible effects of these actions on the company's stock might well read these articles and welcome some additional regulation.[13]

Social regulation of business invariably provokes arguments about proportionality. Yes, critics acknowledge, some business people do commit crimes, and some of these crimes may even endanger people's health. In their view, however, the regulations to prevent such actions are expensive, disruptive to process of price-setting, and completely disproportionate to the risk.[14] To prove these points, they often resort to that mighty dispatcher of policy disputes, the cost-benefit analysis. The trouble is that especially in matters of regulatory importance, cost-benefit analysis is itself seriously flawed.

Every public policy has costs and benefits. Cost-benefit analysis errs because it presupposes a classless society in which the costs and the benefits are both randomly distributed. In the workplace, it may be corporate policy to handle a poisonous substance, but the corporate executive who orders it handled and the workers who actually do the handling run very different kinds of risk. And if the cumulative risk to a worker is life-threatening, cost-benefit analysis then introduces still another bias into the calculations: it appraises a life based on an estimate of the worker's future earnings. In a cost-benefit analysis, the methodology determines the outcome, because only the market can decide what anybody is worth.

In addition to the critique of social regulation, the campaign against government has also targeted government regulation of specific industries like the airlines. As with deregulation of the telephone system, deregulation of the airlines aspired to substitute the perfect market imagined by conservatives and the mainstream of the economic profession for the imperfect market managed by the government. With this substitution, they supposed, new airlines would proliferate, competition would increase, and cheap fares would abound. Any recent airline passenger can testify that these projections missed by a wide margin.

Government regulation of the airline industry managed a stable, reasonably well-ordered oligopoly. Deregulation produced a brief period of fierce competition that drove out upstarts like People Express, and then a tighter oligopoly nationally, with effective monopolies at many hubs. Thus, between 1985 and 1989, the four largest airlines increased their share of the national market from 42 to 75 percent, while, by 1996, monopoly shares rose above 80 percent in numerous metropolises, including Atlanta, Cincinnati, Detroit, Memphis, Minneapolis, Pittsburgh, St. Louis, and Salt Lake City.[15] As Mark S. Kahan has written, these outcomes occurred because the deregulators misunderstood some fundamental economic concepts.

> Deregulators believed that airline size was not critical to efficient operation. The marketplace, to the contrary, has ruled that bigger is better. Deregulators believed that the barriers to entry are low in the airline business. Experience has demonstrated that they are very high. Deregulators believed that increased competition would produce low unrestricted fares. In fact, it has produced a bewildering array of discriminatory prices. Deregulators believed that travel agencies were obsolete as well as potentially misleading channels of information and

distribution. But travel agencies became more powerful than ever. A fifth assumption, that the antitrust laws would restrain competitive abuses, has been negated by the policy default of two administrations.[16]

Proponents of deregulation continue to insist that because prices have declined, the consumer is better off. Yet prices were declining even more rapidly before deregulation. Moreover, most discounted fares are reduced from high levels and come with severe encumbrances, such as a ticket purchase well in advance and the obligation to stay over on a Saturday night.

The meaning of deregulation is obviously much broader than the specifics of what happened in the airline industry. It makes an ongoing statement that no sector of the economy can remain in the government's hands. Conventional theory held that the elegance of the market's price-setting mechanisms would put the clumsiness of government regulation to shame. In fact, the principle of yield management dictates that depending how and when they made their reservations, passengers flying cross-country in a 747 pay many different fares. With such a crazy quilt of a pricing structure, perhaps a critique of government is not the most emphatic statement that deregulation makes.

Privatization

Privatization has complemented deregulation to strip government of its economic functions. In the normal course of development, the increasingly social nature of production tends to promote an increase in the proportion of public goods. Privatization is therefore a political attempt to reverse what would otherwise become a steady process of encroachment on the private sector. The airwaves are a good example: as an inherently public good, they constitute a key sector of any modern economy. Nevertheless, if the private sector did not earn money from them, the terrain open to business would shrink.[17] This dynamic explains part of the economic desire that drives privatization. Just as the Federal Communication Act of 1934 assured private ownership of the airwaves, the current effort to privatize government reflects a desire to recapture many of the new government functions that have arisen since the 1960s.

By the early 1990s, this effort was well along. Within the federal government, the Department of Energy had 165,000 employees, but only 16,000 were government civil servants: most of the rest were contractors and consultants. A similar pattern occurred in urban areas. When the Mercer Group, an Atlanta management consulting firm, surveyed the status of privatization in 1997, it found that a sizable component of local government functions had been reprivatized, including 22 percent of street sweeping, 32 percent of health care, 44 percent of building maintenance, 54 percent of solid waste management, and 73 percent of janitorial services.[18]

A mischievous blend of faith and number crunching promotes privatization. In the aftermath of deindustrialization and middle-class flight to the suburbs, privatization encourages the belief that services can continue on a shrinking tax base. Soon, however, privatization stumbles on the issue of public sector productivity, which is inherently labor intensive. More students per teacher may mean less education; more patients per nurse in a municipal hospital may mean poorer health care. Since a shift in management from public to private cannot change these realities, the only recourse is to drive down wages. The perception of public work aids in this effort. Although public workers are paid less than private sector workers in comparable occupations— only 20 percent of private sector workers have a college degree compared with 40 percent of public employees—taxpayers generally minimize the importance of work by government employees, and when it involves most social welfare programs, see it as detracting from their own standard of living. This receptivity to privatization creates a political opening. It means that even if the number crunching fails, privatizers can fall back on the wisp of a promise that better services will still be forthcoming. It is for this reason that William Weld, former governor of Massachusetts, opposed a state law mandating strict cost studies. As his governor for administration explained, "privatization may make sense if it delivers better services, even if there is no cost savings."[19]

The most popular manual for the privatization movement is David Osborne and Ted Gaebler's *Reinventing Government*. Osborne and Gaebler want the government to steer, not row—to provide the direction, but not the actual service. In the belief that greater entrepreneurialism is the best path to this goal, they make what has become a fairly standard argument. Bureaucracies, they contend, were developed for tightly knit neighborhoods and towns in a slower-paced society, for people who worked with their hands, not their minds; they still work if the environment is stable, the task is simple, every customer wants the same service, and the quality of performance is not critical. In most cases, however, communities are the most appropriate mechanism for solving problems because their commitment to residents surpasses the commitment of service delivery systems to their clients. While institutions offer services, communities offer care. In addition, communities are more flexible and creative than large service bureaucracies; are cheaper; enforce standards of behavior; and focus on capacities, instead of on deficits. Osborne and Gaebler believe that if we are resourceful, drop our reliance on bureaucracy, and draw upon the natural assets of communities, we can turn clients into citizens.[20]

The goal is noble, but it cannot be attained because it is based on a such a reified concept of community. Without government as a countervailing force, the market will ever more dominate communities, and it is just as likely to let communities wither away as it is to build them up. Markets are not as sentimental as Osborne and Gaebler. They are not interested in communities that cannot provide workers or consumers. Historically, we have placed some values outside those of the market: care of the sick, the aged, and yes, sometimes even the poor. Osborne and Gaebler use the word "community" when what they really mean is the marketplace. Yet once marketplace is substituted for community in their analysis, the likelihood that everyone will actually receive the promised services plummets sharply.

Osborne and Gaebler also make much of the failure of bureaucracies, and their descriptions of these failures are vivid. These descriptions, however, mask a deeper analytic problem: they endow bureaucracies with too much autonomy. Bureaucracies do not create themselves. Rather, they are, in the American context at least, usually the outcome of complex political struggles that seek to limit the power of government. In other words, Osborne and Gaebler never ask the truly important question: Who benefits when bureaucracies fail? Many of the techniques that they favor, such as the introduction of computers and the reengineering of bureaucracy, could make government more effective. Among conservatives and in the business community, however, the widespread perception of government ineffectuality furnishes too large a payoff.

Finally, despite all their efforts, Osborne and Gaebler never completely succeed in reassuring those who are not true believers on the issue of accountability. Their inability to do so takes two forms. First, their judgment is questionable. In specific areas like employment policy, they praise the Private Industry Councils, which link job trainees to well-connected local businesses and are one of the features of the Job Training Partnership Act, where accountability has been most lacking.[21] Second, there is the more general issue of the relationship between the market and the government. If, in their terms, government steers and the market rows, government will never be able to go anywhere the market does not want to take it. In principle, this means that no service will ever be provided unless the provider is assured of a profit. Education, job training, health care, and day care: we are not yet all so prosperous that the receipt of every essential service should be conditioned upon this premise.

This is not to say that privatization has failed completely. Cost-savings may indeed be possible where the private sector possesses a readily accessible technology that the public sector can purchase. The government may also save money if there is preexisting competition, and the public agencies can define the job, conduct an evaluation of the contractor's performance, and fire those who fail. This is the reason privatization of garbage collection, street repair, and vehicle maintenance has been successful in some cities. All involve tasks where there are measurable results, and the terms of the contract can be adequately specified.[22]

Indianapolis is probably the leading city in the movement to privatization. During a three-year period from 1992 to 1995, Mayor Stephen Goldsmith cut $100 million from the city budget, keeping union workers but eliminating hundreds of jobs in middle management. Total employment dropped about 25 percent to 3870, the lowest number of city employees in twenty years.

Goldsmith's approach is different. Unlike others who are ideologically committed to privatization regardless of circumstance, he frames the issue as a matter of competition. For him, "the issue is not public or private. The problem is monopolies. If you bring in a private contractor with a monopoly, you are not going to be any better off—maybe worse." When Goldsmith first became mayor, he asked how much it cost to fill a pothole. The answer was $425 per ton of asphalt. Goldsmith put it up for bid; city workers won, with a bid of $307 per ton. This outcome was hardly atypical. In fact, in those cases where services go up for a bid, public workers won a majority of times.

Not surprisingly, when the movement to privatization is ideologically driven, the outcome has often been much less commendable. In one such venture, New Jersey Governor Christine Whitman tried to sell two of the four state-operated marinas. The original deed to the state barred one sale, so the $7 million price for two marinas quickly turned into a sale of the remaining one for $1.7 million. Unhappily, the only bid was for $900,000, out of which $608,000 had to be repaid to the Green Acres fund for two adjoining acres of land. In addition, the state will still need to pay $279,000 a year in rent for use of the maintenance building on the property. Hence, though it recently spent $1.6 million on capital improvements, the state made only $13,000 on the sale of the property. Proponents may try to dress it up, but this kind of privatization is little more than a fire sale of state assets.[23]

The Denver Regional Transportation District was supposed to be a more conventional example of privatization. In 1989, the agency privatized one-fifth of its routes to save money. But just the opposite happened: $8 million a year in projected savings rapidly became $8 million a year of additional costs. Opponents had previously criticized the public sector's monopoly of transportation. Yet once the Regional Transportation District divided the privatized segment of the system and awarded contracts to three different bus companies, the private oligopoly that it created became an essential part of Denver's infrastructure and had to be supported regardless of the cost.[24]

The federal government has occasionally recognized exactly how much privatization can enrich private interests. In a report prepared for the Office of Management and Budget, even the Bush administration admitted that privatization in the form of cost-plus contracts had wasted billions of dollars. With federal agencies failing to supervise expenditures, private companies were paid for tickets to sporting events, lavish cruises, and high salaries for executives. Lockwood Greene Engineers' $38 million contract with the Energy department's Oak Ridge Laboratory included $3.5 million of disallowed costs such as liquor, travels for the spouses of employees, and golf tournament registrations. Likewise, CH2M Hill, an Oregon company that cleans up toxic wastes for the Environmental Protection Agency, billed the government for parties, country club fees, and use of a corporate airplane. Costs spiraled out of control because the federal government privatized many functions in these agencies at the same time it slashed the staff in charge of contract-monitoring.[25]

In sum, privatization has been vastly oversold. The savings that can be extracted are, at best, likely to be small, and even these may vanish upon closer examination. Prisons for profit typify the bookkeeping techniques of privatized institutions. Despite management practices that try to shift medical costs to outside specialists paid for by the federal government, they have not saved money. No wonder that a careful analysis of privatization so readily illustrates its limits. Although 60–75 percent of public sector costs pay for employees, only one-half to two-thirds of this total involves direct service provision, with the rest spent on management and materials. Hence, only one-third to one-half of total public spending is even amenable to short-term privatization. Moreover, since education, police, and fire are hard to privatize, the real fraction of the budget open to privatization is actually about one-fifth. At their most enthusiastic, proponents of privatization anticipate savings of 50 percent. Under textbook conditions, then, privatization would only save about 10 percent of the whole budget. In reality, that means it would probably be a wash.[26]

Privatization's success, then, has been more in damaging the idea of government than in actually delivering services. Like campaigns for efficiency and against regulation, privatization seeks to empower the market at the price of disempowering government. Some privatizers are explicit about this goal and do not care if government is weakened. Yet for those like Osborne and Gaebler who claim to value government, this trend is devastating. They know their arguments for privatization are vulnerable on the issue of accountability: hence, the constant reassurance that privatization does not imply a loss of government control. But they cannot have it both ways, enfeebling government through privatization, while insisting an enfeebled government will nonetheless enforce controls on a strengthened private sector. In a classic example of the jujitsu effect, privatization inevitably stumbles because the stronger the movement becomes, the weaker its promise of accountability.

Deficits and the Balanced Budget

For the first time since 1969, the federal government had a balanced budget in fiscal year 1998. Very modest surpluses are expected for several years thereafter, until early in the twenty-first century when the surplus is projected to grow, climbing sharply until at least 2008. Of course, these totals include Social Security, which is flush from taxes on the earnings of baby boomers. Without this artificial boost, deficits ranging from $116 billion to $60 billion would still be posted during this period.[27] The symbolism is nonetheless powerful. Politically and ideologically, conservatives have won, because it is they who finally forced the government of the United States to live within its means.

If campaigns for efficiency, deregulation, and privatization seek to modify the behavior of government, then the insistence on a balanced budget presents a conscious effort to starve it. A tight financial straitjacket restricts the range of possible government interventions and further limits its role in our public life. In addition, with less capacity to regulate, government is more likely to privatize, and these privatizations will occur, despite a receding ability to monitor the performance of those who assumed its old functions. Campaigns to modify the behavior of government are certainly potent political weapons, but for its pure power to disrupt, nothing can quite compare with an insistence on a balanced budget.

Three primary arguments drove the balanced budget campaign. Mainstream economists and those particularly concerned about the financial markets are most likely to make the argument about "crowding out," which claims that borrowing by the federal government competes with borrowing by the private sector to drive up interest rates. A second, more populist contention completely ignores the issue of interest rates. Relying instead on a homey comparison between the federal government and the typical American household, it insists that since most Americans have to balance their budgets, their government should have to do so, too. With its call for restraint in both the public and private realms, this comparison evokes an older vision of the American family, one that possesses the moral authority to shame the federal government. Finally, in the third kind of argument, state government replaces the nuclear family as the model of budgetary rectitude. Once again, by comparison with the balanced budgets of many state governments, it spotlights the federal government's financial profligacy.

Though popular, none of these arguments can bear careful examination. On the issue of crowding out, even the Reagan administration in its 1985 *Economic Report of the President* acknowledged that "the extent of upward pressure on real interest rates and on the dollar through [expanded federal budget deficits] is uncertain, and numerous studies have failed to uncover significant effects." Designed to elbow the federal government out of the way, the crowding-out argument assumes, in essence, that only public borrowing contributes to inflation. By this reasoning, money borrowed for Amtrak is inflationary, but if Amtrak is privatized, and the private operator took on some debt to keep it in operation, the loan would not be inflationary. The assumption of these inflationary effects is an artifact of classical economics, where a fixed amount of productive resources can only be depleted by government spending. The catch here, of course, is that in a slack economy, the likelihood of future profits may well depend more on aggregate demand than it does on the price of money in the form of interest rates. In sum, although the cost of borrowing funds is certainly one part of any investment decision, the argument about "crowding out" seizes it as a primary weapon to bludgeon the public sector.[28]

Nor does the family with its frugal moral economy make for a better argument. Consumers owe $1.2 billion for the purchase of goods; they owe another $4.2 billion in mortgages on noncommercial properties; and in 1997, a record 1.3 million households filed for bankruptcy.[29] Few families therefore survive on what is literally a balanced budget. Just like the federal government, they assume long-term debt as an investment in their future—to buy a house, start a business, or finance a college education. Contentions about the superiority of family finances hearken back to a distant time when the economy really was rooted in the nuclear family, and debt, both familial and governmental, was not so fundamental a part of the modern U.S. economy. Although deploying "the family" in this campaign draws skillfully on an American archetype, its political potency far exceeds its value as an economic or moral indicator.

And the comparisons with state governments? They are equally illusory. True, most states are constitutionally obligated to balance their budgets. Yet in the context of all state government activities, this obligation captures just 48 percent of their total finances. The distortion occurs because unlike the federal government, most states distinguish between capital budgets and annual operating expenditures. Hence, whether it is parks, stadiums, or convention centers, they usually pay for major public works projects out of capital funds. In addition, aided by earmarked user fees, off-budget or special funds in the states have grown significantly during the last twenty years. In California, special funds rose from 13 percent of all state funding in fiscal year 1983–84 to 28 percent in 1994–95. Similarly, in New York, special funds have grown 154 percent over the last decade until they constitute 42 percent of total state spending. Without a separate category for capital expenditures, the federal government is already obligated to extract money for large projects out of annual operating funds. Operating within a balanced budget, it will be pushed even further toward the margins of American public life.[30]

Besides, in addition to these fundamental flaws in the insistence on a balanced budget, the whole debate rests on some fairly dubious calculations. Because the government borrows in current money and repays its debts in future money, the $3.75 trillion debt must be corrected for inflation. At 3 percent a year, this inflation tax is worth about $112 billion dollars. With this offset, the 1996 deficit of $107 billion instantly becomes a $5 billion surplus; even without it, our 1996 deficit constituted just 1.4 percent of the national income. By comparison in 1983, we ran a deficit equal to 6.3 percent of our national income; in national emergencies such as wartime, the percentage has risen as high as the 25 percent figure reached in 1944. Since most state and local governments already run surpluses, a moderate federal deficit still means that the total cost of operating all major governmental units remains well within acceptable bounds.

We must also remember that as the deficit becomes the debt, it is—except for the 28 percent payable to foreigners—money owed to ourselves. The interest on this debt represents income paid to individuals, mutual funds, banks, insurance companies, and private pension funds. Although one could have a debate about who benefits more—the constituents of the programs that the deficit helps to fund, or the generally affluent recipients of this income—the larger point is to redeem the deficit from ceaseless demonization. It may be taboo to say this in the United States, but the deficit offers benefits as well as costs.[31]

Indeed, the reverence for a balanced budget is somewhat diversionary, because the real issues are investment, aggregate demand, and the opportunities for profit. A stress on these factors implies that people should have enough money to buy things, while the attack on government that accompanies the deficit clears the field of competitors and gives a freer rein to capital. This is not to suggest that the deficit should be open-ended or that it cannot be too high. Keeping the deficit as a percent of the gross domestic product below the overall rate of economic growth constitutes a reasonable target, especially if the extra money is used for long-term public investment rather than current spending. Thus, a deficit equal to 2 percent of the GDP, or about $160 billion, would conform to these guidelines, as long as it was outdistanced by a 3 percent growth rate. Numbers like these would have the additional benefit of bringing down the debt to GDP ratio by 1 percent a year.[32]

The practical consequences of the campaign for deficit reduction are clearest in cuts of programs for the poor. In the 104th Congress (1995–96), 93 percent of the budget reductions in entitlements ($61 billion of $65.6 billion) came from programs for low-income people. These cutbacks occurred even though these programs accounted for just 37 percent of total expenditures for entitlements other than Social Security and only 23 percent of all entitlement spending. Similarly, among nonentitlement spending, 34 percent of the cutbacks targeted low-income people, a proportion that was one and half times their actual share of these programs. Although the Congressional Budget Office regularly identifies other options for reducing the budget, these options get no attention. Reduce the number of nuclear warheads from 3500 to 3400; cancel a variety of new weapon programs such as the attack destroyer and the Commanche helicopter; and limit the deductibility of interest on mortgages to $300,000: all these proposals violate the accepted principle that in contemporary political parlance, a balanced budget means a budget balanced primarily by cutting programs for poor people.[33]

Another way the budget crusaders have tried to slash the deficit is by declaring that the Consumer Price Index significantly overestimates inflation. The best known of these efforts was the commission chaired by Michael Boskin of Stanford University, who was formerly chairman of the Council of Economic Advisors under President Bush. Many government programs including Social Security are indexed to inflation. The Boskin Commission therefore projected that by 2008, correction of the estimated 1.1 percent over-statement of inflation would save the federal government more than $1 tril-lion. In particular, it contended that because the Bureau of Labor Statistics underestimates changes in the quality of life, purchase of a given product means that consumers are actually buying more of that product—the more energy-efficient car of the 1990s over the gas-guzzlers of the 1970s, or the power of modern computers compared to the first PCs of the early 1980s.

Initial applause soon yielded to a host of criticisms about these judgments. The Commission, it turned out, was not as ideologically impartial as many first thought. Although fifteen economists had testified before Congress about possible errors in the Consumer Price Index, the members of the Commission consisted of five of the six with the highest estimates of inflation bias. More-over, on the question of improvements in the quality of life, the Commission ignored Bureau of Labor Statistics calculations that in 1995 had already incor-porated this factor to discount inflation by 2.2 percent. The Commission not only failed to analyze any offsetting degradation in the quality of life—traffic congestion, overcrowding on airplanes, and the deterioration of public ser-vices—but its judgments of what affects the quality of life also seems quite class-bound. Contrary to its assumptions, the availability of "imported beers, microbreweries, and a greatly improved system of imported wines from all over the world" simply does not touch most Americans' experience of infla-tion. Indeed, broadly applied, this class-prejudice is perhaps the most decisive criticism of the whole study. To reach its conclusions, the Commission relied heavily on the well-known "substitution effect," where chicken may replace steak when steak gets too expensive. The Boskin Commission assumed that everyone could easily make this substitution. Yet substitution downward may not be quite so effortless for those who already struggle to afford the most basic necessities. Battered by all these criticisms, budget negotiators ultimately decided to discount inflation by 0.15 percent beginning in 1999, less than one-seventh of what the Commission had recommended.[34]

All these budget-cutting forays suggest that the infatuation with a bal-anced budget should be viewed with much apprehension. Not only is there a long history of the program cuts that budget balancing actually entails, but there is also the potential loss of the deficit as an economic stabilizer. The 1990–91 recession illustrates these effects. If a balanced budget had been enacted, the unemployment rate would have reached 9 percent instead of 7.7 percent, and an unemployed worker who collected $12,000 in unemploy-ment benefits would instead have received just $7000. Overall, according to the Treasury Department, the deficit helped to cushion the recession with $65 billion. Without this money, between 20 cents from falling tax revenue and 7 cents from higher spending, every 73 cent drop in the national income would have become one dollar, and the effects of the recession would have been sharply exacerbated.[35]

Although these factors are disturbing, they are not the most unnerving feature of the balanced budget campaign. There is also a frightening historical pattern. In a remarkable reworking of conventional wisdom, Frederick J. Thayer has demonstrated that when we seek to balance the budget, a major depression has often followed. Thus, from 1817 to 1821, debt decreased $127 million to $90 million, but the first depression occurred in 1819. Similarly, between 1823 and 1836, over fourteen consecutive years, debt was reduced by 99.7 percent to $38,000. The second real depression began in 1837. Likewise, over six consecutive years from 1852 to 1857, the debt was reduced by 59 percent to $28.7 million. The third depression occurred in 1857. Then, between 1867 and 1873, the debt was reduced in seven consecutive years by 27 percent, to $2.2 billion. The fourth significant depression occurred in 1873. Subsequently, between 1880 and 1893, over fourteen consecutive years, the debt was reduced by 57 percent to $1 billion. The fifth real depression began in 1893. Lastly, between 1920 and 1930, the debt was reduced over eleven consecutive years by 36 percent to $16.2 billion. The Great Depression began in 1929. All together, these six periods constitute fifty-seven of the ninety-three years in which debt has been reduced, compared to 112 years in which it has been increased. The historical record therefore deflates what everyone has recently been taught. Although it certainly does not prove that debt reduction causes depression, neither is there any empirical evidence to support the notion that balancing the budget leads to sustainable prosperity.[36]

Taxes

If deficit reduction has sought to limit federal government spending, tax policy has tried to limit the government's income. Although overall taxes—federal, state, and local—have not increased much since 1973, three major changes have affected the composition of the effective tax burden which, at 30 percent of the gross domestic product, remains one of the lowest in the industrialized world. These changes involve a reduction in corporate taxes, a cut in the effective tax rates paid by the wealthy, and a shift to higher taxes in the states.

The corporate tax burden has declined significantly. In 1962, corporate taxes accounted for about 21 percent of all federal revenues. By 1997, however, this proportion had dropped to 11.5 percent. Loopholes in corporate tax policy combined with increased business mobility caused this reduction. Within the pattern of federal revenue collection, this development represents perhaps the most dramatic example of burden-shifting. In fact, one estimate suggests that had corporate taxes continued to yield the share of federal revenue they did in the 1950s, they would have raised an additional $2600 billion between 1960 and 1993, or more than fourth-fifths of the cumulative federal deficit during these years.[37]

Wealthy families have gained from a parallel reduction. Changes in the tax code between 1977 and 1985 left the top 1 percent of families paying an average of $97,250 less per family, while the bottom 80 percent of families saw their taxes rise $221. After two subsequent modifications of the tax laws in 1986 and 1993 partly mitigated these changes, tax breaks for the wealthiest 1 percent of families dropped by an average of $36,710. Over the coming decade, however, the 1997 law reducing the capital gains tax is likely once again to give the wealthiest families large tax savings. With luck, the top 1 percent may even be able to return to the halcyon days of 1979 to 1989, when changes in the tax laws enabled them to capture 70 percent of all the growth in post-tax income.[38]

A similar pattern has developed in the states, where the sharpest rise has occurred. Between 1959 and 1997, the total tax burden increased by 6.7 percent of the gross domestic product, but about half of this increase derives from higher state and local taxes. Admittedly, one part of these higher taxes has gone for services like police, schools, and recreation that all local communities require, but another derives from the deliberate federal policy of devolving services to the states. The financing of services has gradually been shifted. Unfortunately, as a matter of equity, state tax policy is even more regressive than the federal government's. Including state and local taxes, the effective tax rate nationally for an average family exceeds, by 37 percent to 36 percent, the tax rate for those with an annual income of $1 million. In fact, in some jurisdictions, it is even higher; 38 percent to 34 percent in Pennsylvania, 37 percent to 32 percent in Texas; and 40 percent to 34 percent in Illinois. Recent tax cuts in the states have done little to reverse these inequities. When fully implemented after three years, New Jersey Governor Christine Whitman's tax cut would save a married couple with a gross income of $10,000 only $30 in state taxes. At the $45,000 level, however, a couple would save $270, a sum that would balloon even further to $1671 in savings for families earning $200,000. In the constellation of American politics, the federal government is far too distant and alienated from the electorate to get away with state tax policies like these.[39]

The Consequences of Enfeebled Government

Twenty-five years of attacks have significantly diminished government's power. Calls for efficiency seek to reduce its size; calls for privatization and deregulation strip it of important functions; calls for a balanced budget deprive it of funds. In the meantime, changes in the tax laws seek to shift the financial burden for those functions that remain. Understandably, then, the government left over is not very appealing. True, it provides roads and schools and some broad-based entitlement programs such as Social Security. Yet compared to the advantages it offers the wealthy or even to the ever less generous programs specifically designed for the poor, its costs often seem to exceed its benefits. In short, the output of government appears either so rudimentary or so irrelevant that many people try to rid themselves of its expense. Enveloped by the marketplace, they can only hope that somehow they will then be better able to make their own way.

This is, ultimately, the great paradox of the attack on government. So many people have acquiesced in its enfeeblement that those who look to it next to counteract the market will not find much there. Yet unless we completely accede to the market, we will need government again. Most Americans need government to ensure economic security; all Americans need government to ensure democratic accountability. The task is, then, to restore the government's image and recover some of its power. It will be a slow, arduous process, but the goal can nonetheless be achieved if we design public policies that connect the government to a much larger number of people.

Reconstituting the Government

Twice in the twentieth century—in the midst of the major social upheavals of the 1930s and the 1960s—many people felt connected enough to the federal government to demand its intervention. Although the legacy of both periods is hardly unambiguous, this history is instructive enough to provide guidelines for the government's reconstitution. These guidelines suggest that in order to win popular support, the federal government must be able to act, it must be effectual, and it must be accountable.

The capacity to act means an end to the politics of deference. By declaring that social policies do not require business approval, this guideline would substantially expand the scope of government activities. From national standards in education, to full employment in labor policy, and noncategorical benefits in income assistance, the "capacity to act" nullifies the private sector's prohibition against governmental legislation of policies that would benefit most of the American people.

The standard of effectuality has similar import. Effectuality does not imply a centralized monolithic state, because the new American state could either operate programs itself, or with proper assurance of accountability, contract them out directly to groups in the community. Under this model, it could also be the source of funds for local or regional development. Although a federal government that performed these functions would doubtlessly play a larger role in the economy than it does today, it would still have a lower profile than in many European countries. The test, then, is not the size of the federal government, but whether it is allowed to shed its reputation for incompetence and be successful.

Lastly, the state, like the private sector, must be held accountable. The principle of democratic accountability is relatively simple. Having been granted greater latitude for their actions, governmental institutions must be equipped with sufficient financing, expertise, and authority—indeed, with all the tools to do what needs to be done. If they succeed, they retain responsibility for the task; if they fail, voters can make the necessary changes. Ideally, then, to ensure that money has less influence on these results, democratic accountability assumes campaign reform.

Of course, in the future, the possibility of reconstituting the federal government hinges on one of those great paradoxes of social change. The demand for a more effective federal government presupposes the existence of a large and probably disruptive social movement. Yet no such movement is likely either to arise or make this demand unless people first change their perceptions of government. Like many such horse-and-cart dilemmas, this contradiction is one of those that, while it does not seem solvable in the present, the future will somehow resolve.

10

The Next Deal

Economic dependency—whether in the form of the financial dependency of women on men, unemployment induced deliberately by macroeconomics policy to discipline the labor force, or the instrumental use of the threat of capital flight—arbitrarily limits individual choices and erodes democratic accountability even where it is formally secured. Economic dependency is thus antithetical to both liberty and popular sovereignty.

—Samuel Bowles and Herbert Gintis

What people do about the government depends upon what they think the government is able to do.

—E. E. Schattschneider

For the moment, the shift toward the market both reflects and extends the disconnection of American citizens from their government. This shift sets most of the citizenry up for a terrible fall. Markets do bring benefits—to the more affluent under virtually all circumstances and to the nonpoor in periods of economic recovery. Although these benefits are sometimes just enough to persuade a majority of the population that they might be better off going it alone, they are rarely sufficient or sufficiently long-lasting to provide a firm foundation for economic security. Usually, when markets fail, government provides a cushion. Next time, however, the political success of markets means that the cushion is much less likely to be there. And there will be another downturn. But this time, without new government policies to assure the economic well-being of every citizen, that economic downturn will be the first absent a safety net since the Great Depression of the 1930s.

To gain sufficient public support, these new policies must speak to the daily, lived experience of a majority of people. They must impart a feeling that the government is on their side. When the U.S. government is not upbraided for its opposition to the interests of most working Americans, it is upbraided for either its paternalism or its indifference. The best rebuttal to all these criticisms can only come in the form of policies that enable Americans to regain some control over their economic lives. The only controversial question is what form this control should take.

For conservatives, individuals can only regain control over their economic lives if they get to keep more of the money they make. This is a seductive, but ultimately illusory, appeal to the individualistic tradition in American life. It is illusory because both its theory and its practice are so badly flawed. The theory is wrong because large institutions, not individuals, dominate the U.S. economy: they determine the levels of investment and employment, what is produced as well as who works and how much these workers get paid. Although several hundred or even several thousand extra dollars might be nice to have, no tax decrease can empower the average American worker enough to change these facts: after the new TV, VCR, or PC is bought, the money is gone. Either as individual consumers or as individual workers, they are still dwarfed by the economic forces with which they must contend, and as a result, there is very little leverage they can exercise.

If the theory is wrong, the practice of conservatives has been even worse. The bipartisan 1997 tax agreement was typical. In the guise of returning money to the average citizen, it gave the median American taxpayer a reduction of exactly $148, or less than $3 per week. At this rate, their path to economic independence and prosperity is going to be interminable.[1] Harsh social policies are the natural analogue of such fraudulence.

In order to be successful in the twenty-first century, then, economic policy must move beyond social archetypes from the nineteenth century. Admittedly, archetypes die hard, and images of both the diligent, penny-saving worker and the resourceful small entrepreneur can still be easily summoned into popular consciousness. Their evocativeness, however, is ever more out of joint with economic realities: the modern American economy has largely disempowered the individual worker, and the few thriving entrepreneurs featured in magazine profiles hardly offset the high rate of small business failures.[2] There is, then, an actual economic base for other, saner public policies.

Inevitably, these policies will have their roots in government and in government-sponsored social programs. Although this conclusion runs against the current political tide, government is still the only institution strong enough to counter the market and empower workers to regain some control over their economic destiny. That government has this power is the subject of a virtually unanimous consensus: conservatives certainly agree with this judgment, or they would not have labored so long and hard in the last quarter century to bring it to heel. Their concept of government, however, is paternalistic and deprives most people of liberty. Neither is true of the concept proposed here.

The heart of the conservative vision is the autonomous individual, able to retain the maximum freedom of action without encumbrances by others. And naturally, since government represents the biggest encumbrance, it is to be shunned above all. This vision shatters on a paradox. When conservatives speak of freedom, they refer mostly to freedom of economic action. Yet freedom of economic action is assured only for those with significant capital. Poverty, impoverishment, dependency—call it what you will—all diminish the capacity to act unimpaired, as a fully sensate human being. Those without capital, then, must depend on government intervention to expand their range of freedom. Without it, they have very little freedom at all.

Besides, the critique about paternalism and violations of liberty falls wide of the mark. To be sure, the existence of a government program establishes a source of income and services on which people can depend. Indeed, if it could not be depended upon, it would not be much of a program. Yet, historically, that has been exactly the most distinctive characteristic of U.S. social welfare. Time and again, we established programs where the conditions placed on them would hamstring the assistance the programs are supposed to provide. This ambivalence about social provision has two immediate consequences. The first consequence is a matter of program design: programs where giving is so conditional provide less help to people than those where social provision is unencumbered. The second consequence dovetails with the first. Those with many conditions require more intrusive monitoring, and it is monitoring, rather than the giving itself, that is paternalistic. Hence, the real paternalism is not social protection, but social protection with so many strings attached.

Concerns about violations of personal liberty are equally overwrought. As Michael Lind has argued, conservatives consistently confuse the alleged dangers of big government with the real dangers of arbitrary government. Welfare states are not, and have never been, police states:

> Neither the United States nor any other democratic welfare state with a strong central government has become a police state. Sweden did not move from welfare-state egalitarianism toward authoritarian rule. The adoption of universal health care by Britain after 1945 did not lead to a reign of terror in the British Isles. The Civil Rights Act of 1964 did not lead to an American equivalent of the Gestapo.[3]

Welfare states do not overthrow democracies. In fact, the record shows they have consistently extended democracy in the nation-state. Rather, where democracy has been overthrown, it is the agents of the old regime—in particular, the police and the military—who have always taken the leading role.[4]

Once we dispose of the concerns about paternalism and violations of liberty, the policy options converge. This is because, in practice, the three major tasks—restoring the role of government in American public life, reconnecting it to people, and enabling them to regain some measure of control over their economic life—all require the same cluster of policies. Emphasizing the issues of jobs and social welfare, these policies seek to share the costs of a market economy, so that their full burden falls more equally.

Within the labor market itself, there are several policy issues of compelling importance. These policies involve full employment, unions, and the campaign for minimum, maximum, and living wages. The American economic system has become wildly unbalanced, with rich and poor at the extremes bracketing the spread of economic insecurity in the middle. The purpose of these policies is to provide a greater measure of economic security for a decisive majority.

That advocacy of such policies is now rare only reaffirms how cut off we are from our own historical legacy. Perhaps the most famous expression of this legacy is the Second Bill of Rights set forth by Franklin Roosevelt in his 1944 State of the Union message. Roosevelt said, "We have come to a clear realization of the fact that true individual freedom cannot exist without economic security and independence." A Second Bill of Rights should therefore include two crucial additions, "the right to a useful and remunerative job," and "the right to earn enough to provide adequate food and clothing and recreation."[5] Full employment at adequate wages, then, is the policy umbrella under which all these other policies stand.

Curiously, despite all the doubts about the federal government, the goal of full employment—even full employment with a job by the government provided for everyone who needed it—has remained popular. Public opinion polls favored the policy by a 79 to 16 percent margin in 1969. Even under President Reagan in 1987, the margin stayed at 71 to 26 percent.[6] Outcomes like these reflect the more appealing side of Americans' respect for the work ethic. Thoroughly convinced of the value of work, they are even willing to support interventionist government policies that would guarantee a job.

The public's opinion of full employment is one thing; the political and economic elite's is quite another. The prospect of full employment makes them blanch. Attuned to its primary constituency of bond holders and institutional investors, the Federal Reserve fears inflation; corporations object to the higher wages that a tightened labor market would bring; and most mainstream economists assume that, except for the deepest trough of the business cycle, the current unemployment rate already constitutes full employment, because it is the best the market can do. As the unemployment rate dipped below 5 percent in 1997, James K. Galbraith captured their fears well:

Natural rate devotees remain cautious. For them, the metaphor of a labor market where supply just balances labor market demand, is too strong: they cannot give it up. True, the equilibrium wasn't 6 percent: We passed that point and disaster didn't happen. And probably wasn't 5.5 percent. We passed that point too, and again no disaster happened. But it must be somewhere, they think, and we only have 5 percentage points left to go.[7]

The contrast between the political popularity of full employment and the elite's doubts about its prudence make this issue one of the policy matters where the gap between the two is the widest. Full employment becomes all the more imperative for this very reason, both for its own merits and as a means of democratizing the economy.

Unemployment is, in fact, one of the most compelling reasons why the economy needs to be democratized. Unemployment has both costs and benefits. Among the costs are the growth in social spending to keep people alive, the loss of the taxes the unemployed would otherwise pay if they were working, and the missing goods and services that will never be produced. In addition, there are all the collateral effects of unemployment—crime, the loss of health insurance coverage, and the additional stress on families. The putative benefits include lower wages, lower prices, and a reduced risk of inflation. Looking at this list, it is clear that the costs and benefits line up fairly neatly. Lower prices and less inflation may benefit the majority of Americans, but then they also shoulder most of the costs. The benefits, on the other hand, largely accrue to a smaller number of employers and significant holders of stocks and bonds. That the path to full employment has been so consistently obstructed suggests it is not the vast majority of Americans who are leaning most heavily on the policy scales.

The path to full employment begins with faster economic growth. From 1999 to 2007, the Congressional Budget Office estimates growth rates that begin at no higher than 2.2 percent and gradually drift downward to 1.9 percent.[8] Without the Federal Reserve keeping its foot on the economic brakes, we could do considerably better. Moreover, given the scale of the whole U.S. economy, even small differences in annual growth yield large differences in the total gross domestic product. At 3 percent a year, for example, the economy would benefit from an additional $340 billion annually. That is enough to pay down some debt, eliminate the appearance of imminent crisis in the Social Security system, and have money left over to reconstruct cities and repair the environment.[9]

Although faster growth will bring down the unemployment rate, it will not by itself be sufficient to ensure full employment. Some people will stay unemployed, either because they have skills that do not match the available jobs, or because they lack skills entirely. These workers will need a government employment program. Designed on the scale of the New Deal's Works Progress Administration, this program would rely on three distinctive features to avoid the difficulties associated with previous employment initiatives. It would, in short, be targeted broadly, pay decently, and address the problem of "fiscal substitution."[10]

Each of these features has a compelling rationale. Any job program that is targeted just to poor people becomes a welfare program, and the political support for welfare programs is notoriously unstable over time. For this reason, employment programs must be open to anyone who wants a job, with only wage rates and the nature of the work determining their appeal. Since the work would be largely public sector labor that remains undone, and the wages would be set at a level adequate to support a family—say, $9 an hour by the year 2000—the program would absorb enough of the unemployed to reach full employment. That leaves job displacement as the primary administrative obstacle.

Job displacement is a problem because in the past, employment programs like the Comprehensive Employment Training Act (CETA) that were funded by the federal government but administered by the states made little headway against unemployment. Instead, states and localities used federal money to replace their own: although the source of funding changed, few new workers were added. It is only when a federal program can hire workers directly that this outcome can be avoided.[11]

We return finally to the question of costs. There is no mincing words: a large-scale government job program will be expensive. In fact, simply totaling up the outlays, it might cost as much as $200 billion, or slightly less than Medicare in 1997. The point is, however, that offsetting benefits immediately discount this outlay. First, there is the 20 percent of the outlay that is immediately recapturable in taxes to government. Then, there is another 60 percent that would have otherwise been spent on unemployment insurance and other means-tested benefits. Lastly, there are the savings to be gained by internalizing other costs. A comprehensive job program could easily provide free day care to other workers. The existence of this option would reduce the cost of going to work for employees who now pay for child care as well as for employers and governments who currently subsidize it. Benefits like these would cut actual outlays to about 20 percent of the total, or about 2.5 percent of the federal government's budget in 1998 and half a percent of the $8 trillion U.S. economy. Factor in other potential gains, such as a likely reduction in crime and domestic violence, and compared to all the costs associated with joblessness, full employment seems cheap. Unfortunately, political and economic elites do not follow this logic. Instead they make another calculation, one which leads them to prefer unemployment with all its costs to a genuine full-employment policy that would weaken them economically and politically.[12]

While the existence of a full employment program would undoubtedly have a beneficial effect on wages, the real push is going to have to come from a reenergized union movement. There are signs of this movement already. Since the election of John Sweeney as president of the AFL-CIO in 1995, trade unions have obtained a hike in the minimum wage, defeated the "Fast Track" legislation, organized the successful 1997 strike by 185,000 United Parcel workers, and won the biggest single private sector election in a decade when 10,000 employees of U.S. Airways voted to join the Communication Workers of America. Nevertheless, the percentage of workers in trade unions continues to slide. Trade unions, which had organized about 38 percent of the workforce in 1954, by 1997 represented just 14.1 percent of the total workforce and a mere 9.8 percent of the workforce in the private sector. Although the movement is gearing up for a breakthrough, the decline of its power currently tracks rather too closely with the declining wages of many American workers.[13]

It is not that employees do not want to join unions. In fact, surveys usually show that another 25 to 30 percent of them would like to belong.[14] The addition of these workers would drive the total proportion of unionized workers to about 40 percent, a level that approximates the degree of unionization in Canada. Although Canada has experienced a similar rise in market-generated inequality, its social programs have kept its poverty rates to about half of those in the United States. As a political and economic force, trade unions have played a vital role in this outcome.[15]

But how can American unions exercise that kind of power if they do not already possess it? The "retail" approach to organizing certainly will not work, because just to maintain the current level of unionization in the private sector, trade unions must add 250,000 members a year. An influx of workers will only happen with a major political and economic jolt, like the effect of the Wagner Act and the Depression on the mass of workers who joined the Congress of Industrial Organizations in the late 1930s. In the meantime, trade union supporters should first identify some changes that would facilitate organizing and then keep the pressure up in the hope that there might be a window of opportunity during which they could be turned into law. The reforms best able to fulfill these criteria are card check, first contract arbitration, and the restriction of employer campaigns.[16]

These reforms are all designed to remove impediments to the organizing process. Under current procedure, bargaining does not begin until enough cards have been signed *and* a formal election has been held. Card check would authorize the National Labor Relations Board (NLRB) to order bargaining as soon as a majority of workers have signed a union card. With this law in place, management would no longer have the time to replace union sympathizers and delay the vote. Similarly, first contract arbitration is designed to ensure that when a union wins the right to represent workers, a contract results. As the law is now written, management must bargain, but it does not have to bargain in good faith. That is undoubtedly why about one-third of the workplaces voting to be represented by a union do not obtain a collective bargaining contract with their employer. First contract arbitration would alter this outcome. For a law that permits management to propose wages below the preunion level, it would substitute an arbitrator's award of wages consistent with the prevailing pattern in the industry.[17]

Finally, a multitude of anti-union campaign practices demand careful scrutiny. Management consultants, for example, are legally entitled to ban known and suspected union supporters from company meetings, so that statements critical of the union can go unchallenged. A variety of reform measures could remedy such challenges to open debate about the benefits of unionization, including granting union representatives access to company property during an organizing drive and prohibiting supervisors from meeting with workers to disparage unions during paid working hours. The purpose of these reforms is not merely to level the playing field. It is, rather, to create an environment in which employees join unions because unions raise their wages, increase their political and economic power, and provide representation of workers that helps to democratize the workplace.

In addition to unions, three other campaigns could make a significant contribution to the effort to raise wages. These campaigns involve efforts to address respectively, the issues of a minimum, maximum, and living wage. The three campaigns are linked because despite two increases in the 1990s, the minimum wage continues to lag behind its historic high. Campaigns have therefore arisen for both maximum and living wages, which are, in light of the failure of the minimum wage, essentially alternative methods of ensuring that workers are paid enough to support their families.

The two increases in the minimum wage during the 1990s (from $3.35 to $4.25 in 1991, and then to $5.15 in 1997) raised its value 53 percent in eight years. These hikes nonetheless failed to compensate for the precipitous decline of the minimum wage leading up to 1989, when it sank to a 1997 inflation-adjusted value of just $4.34 an hour. The 1997 increase did little to rectify this trend, since by the year 2000, inflation will have once again reduced its value to $4.38. This figure represents an 18.1 percent decline in value since 1979 and suggests why, if the minimum wage had kept pace with inflation since 1965, it would now exceed the current earnings of nearly 30 percent of American workers.[18]

With the minimum wage losing its utility as a tool to ensure decent wages, proponents of higher wages have shifted tactics. Instead of simply targeting the bottom of the wage scale, some have campaigned for a maximum wage that links the bottom of the income scale to the top. Others have pushed for a living wage that pays something closer to the actual cost of survival. The maximum wage campaign is more visionary; the living wage campaigns have had more success. Either or both would have a beneficial effect on wages.

The maximum wage is based on a simple premise: no one should earn more than twenty-five times the amount of the lowest paid worker. Introduced into Congress by Martin Sabo (D-Minnesota) with thirty cosponsors, the maximum wage bill would prohibit companies from deducting any portion of an executive's compensation that was above this ratio. A company where the chief executive received $500,000 a year would suddenly discover a new and absolutely imperative reason why the lowest paid worker should receive more than $20,000.

Of course, such a law might also produce a number of other consequences. Demand for real estate in the most affluent communities might diminish, and new methods of hiding income would likely proliferate. Companies, for example, could easily modify their methods of compensation so that executives could take their money in deferred stock payments rather than in current salary. Nevertheless, if tax policies were altered to capture these funds, the fundamental principle would be worth upholding. After all, the maximum wage's proposed ratio of highest to lowest salary does not differ very much from salary differentials in Japan, which has witnessed no noticeable loss of entrepreneurial initiative.[19]

Although the maximum wage is a long way off, living wage bills have already been adopted in a number of cities. Baltimore, New York, Minneapolis, and Milwaukee have all enacted laws requiring a living wage for employees of companies that conduct business with the local government. In Baltimore, the city had already spent $2 billion in direct subsidies for its Inner Harbor Development. Pointing to such subsidies, BUILD, a local community organization, together with the Industrial Areas Foundation and the American Federation of State, County, and Municipal Employees (AFSCME) successfully contended that simple fairness and proportionality demanded the payment of a living wage. They got $6.60 an hour, which has since been raised to $7.70.[20]

Some of the objections to the living wage are identical to those directed at minimum wage campaigns. At one time or another, it has been asserted that like the minimum wage, the living wage kills jobs, forces companies to raise their prices, and goes beyond what the market will bear. The most recent work on the minimum wage suggests that none of these assertions is true. The minimum wage increase in 1991 did not kill jobs, had no significant impact on prices, and established a more level playing field by forcing nonunion employers to pay wages that approximate those of union shops. A strong argument can also be made that when people earn more, they spend more, increasing the demand for consumer goods in low-income neighborhoods. And, despite allegations to the contrary, there is no credible evidence to substantiate the claim that employers will not do business with cities that insist on a living wage. Cities must provide other forms of assistance to compensate for any deficiency in wages. That is why, finally, they have every right to insist on the adequacy of salaries paid out of city funds.[21]

The Public's Capital

Unions, along with the campaigns for minimum, maximum, and living wages, all seek to boost the income of workers. Still, unless there is also an increase in the demand for labor, these efforts will be less than completely successful. An investment in the public's capital must therefore constitute an essential part of any full-employment program. The economic stimulus from such infrastructural investment will certainly increase the number of jobs and enhance the productivity of private capital. In addition, if the projects are well chosen, they will also improve the quality of life.

Like so many of the other policy recommendations, an investment in the public's capital will require reversal of the trends of the last thirty years. Public sector investment fell sharply in the years after 1965. In fact, by 1980, even though the U.S. economy had grown another 60 percent, overall public construction had already fallen to just three-quarters of its 1965 level. Most of the public investment involved water, sewer, and mass transit projects: there was very little direct investment in industry. Faced with a fiscal crisis in major cities, the Northeast simply stopped investing. In the South and West, governments consistently refused to invest.[22]

According to economist David Alan Aschauer, more than half of the decline in our productivity growth over the past two decades can be explained by lower public infrastructure spending. Aschauer contends that if the same rate of investment in infrastructure relative to GNP had been maintained from 1970 to 1990 as had been maintained from 1950 to 1970, the rate of return to private capital would have averaged 9.6 percent instead of 7.9 percent, and the average annual rate of private sector productivity would have been 2.1 instead of 1.4 percent. Not everyone agrees with Aschauer about the size of this effect: other economists such as Alicia Munnell think it is actually about 25 percent smaller. Nevertheless, with the exception of those economists who proclaim that nearly every dollar spent by the public sector wastes resources, most believe that the effect is positive.[23]

Certainly, the need exists. The Department of Transportation has estimated that one-fifth of the nation's highways have poor or mediocre pavement; among bridges, an equal proportion are structurally deficient.[24] Since this nation is so dependent on the automobile as a means of delivering goods, improvements in these structures will bring about measurable improvements in productivity. At the same time, dependence on the automobile has a deleterious effect on the environment. For this reason, public investment should also wean us from this dependence with environmentally sound projects such as mass transit and high speed trains.[25] Together with other major projects such as land reclamation and park maintenance, these investments will employ workers, produce clearly visible benefits, and renew peoples' sense that government can have a positive effect on their lives.

To carry it out well, a program of public investment probably requires a separate federal budget for capital spending. Such a budget does not now exist. Instead, the government lumps together all federal spending, mixing money for current expenses with money for major capital projects that will only pay off over the longer term. The very notion of a longer term is the nub of the problem, because refusing to create a separate budget for capital spending is really just another way of keeping the government on a very short leash. The evidence suggests that other forms of federal investment have paid off well indeed—between 33 and 66 percent a year from federal research in agriculture, 27 percent per year for spinoffs to commercial aviation, plus substantial returns from the research within the National Aeronautics and Space Administration that led to the development of products such as the cardiac pacemaker and the nickel-zinc battery. Yet these outcomes make few inroads against the deep-rooted cynicism about the value of federal programs. Perhaps it is true, as Rudolph Penner, former director of the Congressional Budget Office, has argued, that if a budget is established specifically for capital spending, then many items will soon be seeking that designation. Nevertheless, the purpose of creating a separate capital budget is not to make one kind of federal spending more worthy than another. It is, rather, to demonstrate that among the various kinds of public spending, some simply take longer to pay off.[26]

Universalism

Even under full employment, not everyone will work. For the unemployable, the very young, and the very old, some forms of social assistance will still be necessary. The most fundamental question about these programs is the extent to which they are universalistic—that is, available to everyone, regardless of income. The answer is, in brief, that although they should be universal, some weaknesses in the universal approach to social policy must be taken into consideration.

The main argument for universalism endures. Without coverage for everyone, it is difficult to retain the political support of those who are taxed for the benefit of others. Admittedly, universalism is hardly the only issue: to some extent, the effectiveness of the program and the "deservedness" of the recipient do have an effect, especially if the benefit targets people who work.[27] Still, more than any other factor, this aspect of universalism matters.

Yet universalism's potential obscures a minefield. The real issue is the question of difference. In a society fractured by differences of race and sharply divided by extremes of wealth and income, universalism merely offers an equal measure of remedy. This implicit assumption of equality is problematic. It may persuade people in their role as taxpayers, but it does not specifically address racial injustice, and it does not bring the bottom much closer to the top. The best solution to this dilemma is to demand universalism as the first form of social protection, but then provide extra benefits for those whose needs are especially acute. In effect, while the first form of social protection secures political support, the second takes some of that political support and tries to channel it into areas where it will do the most good.[28]

Obviously, it is easier to apply these principles to some forms of social protection than it is to others. If job training were available to everyone, it would be easy to design programs based on level of skill and direct people to the appropriate agency—more extensive training for those with poor skills, refresher courses for those who just needed a brush-up. Similarly, a network of preventive clinics for poor children in the inner cities fits naturally into a system of national health care. In other universal kinds of policies, however, especially those involving cash, the existence of different benefits to compensate for lack of income complicates the administrative process and may sap political support for the program. A supplemental minimum income benefit plainly falls into this category.

To avoid this loss of political support, we need to find other ways of providing some additional income. One is surely children's allowances, a monthly sum that most other countries give for each child from birth to age eighteen. Children's allowances help parents of every income level care for their families. Like other universal programs, however, they also have the wonderful knack of converting equal benefits into political durability, because what makes life tolerable for poor people also ties the affluent to the program. Universal programs will not do all that needs to be done to overcome the deficits of poverty and race. Nevertheless, in an age when some Americans bristle at the notion of any entitlement, their capacity to cultivate political support still distinguishes them as our best chance for coping with economic insecurity in the twenty-first century.[29]

Entitlement Spending

Before universal programs can be advanced, entitlement spending must be defended. The attack on entitlement spending began with a campaign against AFDC. The success of this campaign has, in turn, established a beachhead for a more general critique of entitlements, particularly those that provide some measure of social support for the middle class. The campaign's political fallout breeds governmental studies with titles like *Reducing Entitlement Spending*. The meaning of these efforts could not be less ambiguous: now that the old federal system of public assistance has been dismantled, the economic insecurity brought about by a loss of government social support will creep steadily up the income ladder.[30]

The Concord Coalition is probably the leading advocate of entitlement cutbacks. Founded by financier Peter Peterson, together with former senators Warren Rudman (R-New Hampshire) and the late Paul Tsongas (D-Mass), and now chaired by former Democratic Senator Sam Nunn, the Concord Coalition fears that our current entitlement spending is totally profligate. Eighty percent of entitlements, they argue, goes to the elderly without regard to need; entitlements are even paid to the 30 percent of all families who earn more than $100,000. It is indeed because such a big percentage of entitlements go to the elderly that the prospect of aging baby boomers frightens the members of the Concord Coalition. Seeing a large, demanding constituency about to make a substantial claim on the federal budget, they warn that the anticipated level of entitlement spending cannot be sustained.[31]

Like so many other attacks on federal spending, this critique wraps a small kernel of truth in a lot of fear-mongering. The retirement of aging baby boomers will alter the proportion of workers for each retiree, from 3.2 workers per retiree in the year 2000 to 2.4 workers per retiree by the year 2020. In that same period, however, the total dependency ratio (the number of youth plus the number of aged compared to the number of workers—an index of the total burden on the working population) rises only from .695 to .699. By comparison, at the height of the baby boom in 1960, the dependency rate reached .904. Surely, if the country flourished with such a high level of dependency then, it can manage a much lighter burden on the working population in the first quarter of the twenty-first century.[32]

It is true that the increasing number of retirees will alter the pattern of federal spending—broadly speaking, from money spent on the education of children to money spent on the health care and survival of the elderly. Yet a real crunch will only occur if we persist in choosing policies from the same paltry repertoire. Perhaps the best example is the growth in health care costs, which contribute mightily to the sense of impending doom. A national health care system is widely recognized as administratively efficient and hence a potential moneysaver. Yet despite projected growth in the Medicare program of about 19 percent per year through 2006, debate about a national health care system is taboo because so much of the waste is actually profit for the private sector. Similarly, if, like most other countries, the United States used money from general revenues to supplement the financing of Social Security or pushed up the cap on taxable income ($68,400 in 1998), its future costs would be easy to handle. And, most important of all, it would help if a more progressive tax system ended the perpetual deprivation of the federal government by providing it with some additional money.[33]

Critics of entitlement spending, however, will not touch any of these policies. Their primary goal is to constrict the federal government, deprive it of funds, and diminish it as a factor in peoples' lives. This goal rests on the superficially plausible premise that social benefits should be carefully targeted so that they only go to those most in need. In the kindest possible interpretation, this premise merely suffers from a very basic misconception about means-tested benefits. It assumes that if money is withheld from those who are not poor, the benefits the poor receive will still be adequate. Yet, as the entire history of American social welfare demonstrates, and as the last thirty years have particularly dramatized, means-tested programs attenuate the political links between the poor and the rest of society. And once these links have vanished, neither the current poor nor those who might become poor in the future will have much to fall back on.

Privatizing Social Security

The centerpiece of the critique of entitlements is the effort to privatize Social Security. Long a dream of conservatives, this effort got its first real entree into the national political debate with the 1996 report of the Social Security Advisory Council. Although members of the commission reached no consensus, all three subgroups recommended that trust funds should be invested in the stock market. The groups diverged, however, about exactly what form this investment would take. One group headed by former Social Security Commissioner Robert Ball advocated keeping the current benefit structure, but investing 40 percent of the trust fund in the capital markets. A second group led by commission chairman Edward M. Gramlich want to reduce benefits, raise taxes by 1.6 percent, and funnel the new tax revenues into individually defined retirement accounts. Lastly, the five most business-oriented members of the Advisory Council seek to replace the current Social Security system with Personal Security Accounts (PSAs). Although their proposal would provide a small ($410 a month) flat benefit independent of earnings, its main focus is really on PSAs, which constitute their primary means of transforming the Social Security system. Funded by 5 percent of the 12.4 percent that currently goes into the Social Security Trust Fund, PSAs would allow individuals to invest the most in the capital markets. In the past, the Social Security program has functioned as a somewhat redistributive defined benefit. Dispensing with its redistributive function, this proposal would leave the sufficiency of a worker's retirement income to the capriciousness of the market.[34]

Proponents of this shift, such as the libertarian Cato Institute, would like to replicate the Chilean Social Security system. Implemented under the military dictatorship of General Augusto Pinochet, it has boosted the Chilean stock market, but has left half of the future retirees with projections of little more than a poverty level pension. The privatized Chilean system is also full of administrative inefficiencies. Between the cost of the sales force for the competing mutual funds and fees for their managers, administrative expenses have been running at about 30 percent, compared to 1 percent under the American Social Security system.[35] What will happen, then, if the U.S. Social Security system steps into the quagmire of managing the financial records of 160 million separate Personal Security Accounts? In this instance at least, the market cannot compete with superior governmental administration.

Besides, the whole notion of superior stock market performance is very much open to question. The stock market boom of the 1990s has distorted the recent average; the knowledge required for profitable investing casts doubt on whether a slew of first-time investors could even obtain a more historically average return. There is also the issue of the long-term economic projection. Supporters of privatization project a total annual return of 7 percent a year, which is the rate the stock market has yielded over the last seventy-five years, when economic growth averaged 3.5 percent. Their prediction of economic growth over the next seventy-five years is slightly under 1.5 percent. If nothing else changes—that is, corporations continue to get the same share of total income and a speculative bubble does not push price-earnings ratios to absurdly high levels—there is no way that a significantly lower rate of economic growth can sustain the same rate of annual return.[36]

A more likely scenario suggests that this new Social Security system would soon experience a bigger and much more genuine crisis. After expenses are considered and PSAs are divided equally between investment in stocks and investment in bonds, annual returns range from 2.2 percent for high-income workers in the optimistic projection to just 0.8 percent for low-income workers in the pessimistic prediction. While the high-income worker would have accumulated a total of about $239,000, the low-income worker would have set aside less than $43,000. At 30 percent of their old income, these numbers would support the high-income worker for eleven and half years and the low-income worker for little more than eight. Social Security currently pays high-income workers 31 percent, and low-income workers almost 57 percent, of their final wage, but it pays these benefits for the rest of their lives. Despite the assertions of the Advisory Council, no privatized system can guarantee anything like this degree of economic security.[37]

Although this comparison reflects unfavorably upon proposals for a privatized system, it is still not as damning as the lack of provision for people who exhaust their funds because they invest unwisely or live too long. Supposedly, these retirees are to fall back on the flat benefit of just $410 a month. At more than $2000 a year below the poverty rate for a single elderly person, this amount speaks volumes. In essence, it says that you had better make it on your own, or dependence on the public sector will consign you to poverty. Such a political philosophy makes a terrible mistake. A single individual may be able to make some provision for the future, but a system that burdens each individual with the responsibility for this provision will fail the great majority of them. Ultimately, the only truly satisfactory form of social insurance requires that we all, through the public sector, assume collective responsibility for the elderly's well-being.

The current Social Security program therefore represents the first line of defense against the erosion of entitlement programs. Besieged by the call for individual entrepreneurship in all matters, it will not be easy to protect. Still, as the single most prominent triumph of universalism in U.S. social policy, it must be protected nonetheless. Without it, it will be hard to reconnect the

American people to their government. Without it, it will be impossible to demonstrate that adequate social provision can convey a sense of caring.

International Linkages

The new, post-Keynesian market thrives not on greater aggregate demand, but on economic insecurity. From a defense of entitlements to full employment and universalistic social programs, any increase in economic security therefore heightens the risk of capital flight. Capital mobility has intensified as an ordinary part of doing business. Nevertheless, faced with a secure, confident, and ever-more demanding labor force, many more U.S. businesses might pick themselves up and move overseas.

The prospect of such capital flight brims with serious economic and political consequences. When international economic disparities become severe, they distort investment and trade flows. As manufacturing emigrates from high- to low-wage countries, it lowers wages and reduces consumption. Workers in countries with cheap labor cannot buy the goods they produce; soon, an ever-larger proportion of workers in the better-off countries may not be able to do so, either. It is a very slippery slope, this race to the bottom, one which increased capital flight would incline even more steeply.[38]

The political implications of capital flight are equally portentous. For the immediate future, workers have been outflanked, and a nascent international labor movement is scrambling to catch up. The first signs of such cooperation are already evident. Since Japanese interests own the New Otani Hotel in Los Angeles, the hotel workers union sent members to Tokyo to protest and elicit support from Japanese labor. The leadership of the AFL-CIO has been trying to establish contacts, too. In 1998, AFL-CIO president John Sweeney became the first AFL-CIO leader to seek alliances with labor unions in Mexico.[39]

Outside the organized trade union movement, a host of transnational worker networks have also proliferated. International labor organizations have existed for over one hundred years; their leadership, which tends to be male, white, and older, has generally focused on the manifest difficulties of contracts across borders. The new groupings are entirely different. Often female, and organized as networks rather than as hierarchies, they rely on coalitions that encompass but are not necessarily rooted in unions to address a broader range of issues. Mujer a Mujer is typical of these new worker networks. Founded in 1986 after a group of Mexican housing activists toured the southern United States, Mujer a Mujer organized the "First International Union Women's Exchange of Experiences" in Mexico City, which brought together women from Guatemala, Korea, Mexico, and the United States. Soon, there were "Global Strategies Schools," a Trinational Conference of

Women Workers on Continental Integration, and throughout, a concerted effort to nurture feelings of solidarity between Mexican and American workers who confront the same problems.[40]

Admittedly, all these efforts are in the very early stages, and it may be years before they are strong enough to influence public policy. The goal, however, is clear: because wage differentials, especially wage differentials including fringe benefits, are higher than productivity differentials, we need international labor standards for the production of internationally traded goods. These international labor standards should include prohibition of child labor, a minimum wage appropriate to a nation's development, and the right of workers to organize and bargain collectively. In other words, we need to establish a global social market, where pay approximates productivity and both the environmental and labor standards of products exported to the United States mirror U.S. norms. These measures will help to increase purchasing power in the third world, while simultaneously reducing the incentive for corporations to go elsewhere for cheap labor.[41]

Capital flight remains a distinct possibility. Given the dynamics of the international economy, corporations will always try to play the labor force of one country against the labor force of another. Yet capital flight creates its own opportunities. When capital flees, it is the management and the money, and not the runaway shop, that moves to greener pastures. Since management and money do not produce output—that comes only from machines and labor— the real issue is the political question of whether workers will yield to their dependency on the good will of the business or get angry at it for abandoning their community and seek to implement a more democratic economic program. In the latter case, with public investment at local levels to compensate for some investment shortfalls, and selected subsidies to private investment in strategic sectors, capital flight could become a manageable problem.[42]

Campaign Reform

Like the threat of capital flight, the issue of campaign reform hovers over the prospects for economic reform and democratic renewal. If one person, one vote is the American ideal, something approximating one dollar, one vote is gradually becoming the standard American practice. Of course, from the fear of "factions" in James Madison's *Federalist Papers* to the present day, American political theorists have labored to contain the ever-present conflict between the power of the purse and the power of the ballot. The Constitution sought to contain this conflict by establishing a system of checks and balances. These checks and balances ensured that any faction—especially those factions with little property—would have to control all the branches of government before they could truly threaten the wealthiest's power and privilege.

In recent years, however, the long-standing and uneasy tension between purse and ballot has dissolved in favor of the purse. Surely, the consequent skewing of national political dialogue is partly responsible for the absence of 50 percent of the electorate from participation in presidential elections. Among voters themselves, the association between wealth and contributions is especially clear: the richest 9 percent account for 55 percent of the money, while the poorest 19 percent provide just 2 percent of the financing.[43] These distortions of the democratic process came together with particular force in the 1996 election campaign. All told, some $2.2 billion was spent on the presidential election and the accompanying congressional races, with business interests outspending organized labor by a 7–1 ratio, $242 million to $35 million. Just 235,000 Americans—one-tenth of 1 percent of the public—gave $1000 or more. Not surprisingly, the richest geographic lode of contributions was the $12.4 million mined from three zip codes on Manhattan's affluent East Side.[44] In the aggregate, these numbers confirm the impression that the political marketplace resembles any other business enterprise, where the largest shareholders make the largest investments.

The legal justification for this position is the Supreme Court's 1976 decision in *Buckley v. Valeo*. Rejecting the argument that big contributions distort the democratic process, it interpreted limitations on private money as a constraint on freedom of speech. Like the 1896 Supreme Court decision in *Plessy v. Ferguson*, which established the doctrine of separate but equal and impeded progress on racial relations for the next sixty years, *Buckley v. Valeo* privileges the rights of property and constitutes a major obstacle to campaign reform. Nevertheless, some activists have begun to find ways around it. In the 1996 election, Maine voters approved a Clean Money Election initiative that provides full public financing to those who accept limits on spending and voluntarily reject large private contributions.[45] Conservatives are usually concerned that such initiatives cost too much and unduly empower the public sector. Although they are correct that the initial public costs may be higher, these costs quickly recede besides the long-term dependency of large contributors who, once they buy access, can easily usurp public policy for private ends.

Paying for It

New programs necessitate new sources of financing. The potential sources are plentiful. They include steeper taxes on the affluent, an annual wealth tax, the Tobin tax on foreign exchange speculation, military spending, and reform of state and local taxes. With the exception of military spending, which involves the reallocation of current funds, all the new tax initiatives can be crafted to increase revenues without affecting more than a tiny percentage of American taxpayers. This targeting will not only make the system more progressive, but it should also help to shield the proposals from the inevitable cries of outrage.

When Bill Clinton became president in 1993, he raised the highest tax rate to 39.6 percent. The House of Representatives passed his tax bill by just one vote. Even with this increase, however, the marginal tax rate is still well below its historic norm. From World War II to 1964, the rate was set at 91 percent. In 1964, the rate was cut to 70 percent, and it stayed at that level until the Reagan administration, with two "tax reforms" in 1981 and 1986, reduced it first to 50 percent and then to 28 percent.[46] Raising taxes on the wealthy has been proposed so often and rejected (by the wealthy) so often that the proposal has acquired a pro forma air. Yet, despite the opposition to it, it remains a key component of any progressive tax legislation.

A tax on wealth constitutes another possible source of revenue. A wealth tax is already well established in some countries: in fact, eleven members of the OECD currently tax wealth, including Spain, Germany, and Switzerland. Usually, the rate is set low—a few percent at most, with flat rates in some countries and graduated ones in others. In addition, all the existing wealth taxes have thresholds, and most exclude some assets such as pensions, life insurance, and personal/household effects. The Swiss system, for example, exempts the first $100,000, and then applies graduated rates of .05 percent on $100,000 to $200,000, .10 percent on $200,000 to $350,000, and on up to .30 percent above one million dollars. In the United States, it is estimated that a wealth tax modeled after the Swiss system would raise $40 billion, with just 3 percent of the population experiencing tax increases of more than 10 percent. In the aftermath of the 1997 reduction in the capital gains tax, it offers a useful antidote to the increasing inequity of the tax system.[47]

Then there is the Tobin tax, named after the Yale economics professor, James Tobin. Tobin has proposed a .5 percent tax on foreign currency transaction.[48] Designed to raise the cost of currency speculations, it meshes well with the paper entrepreneurialism of the new global economy. Predictably, the very specter of such a tax triggers fulminations on Wall Street. Who can tell, opponents contend, what part of the swing in currency rates is normal price-setting, and what part is irrational speculation?[49] They are right: it would be foolish indeed to try to make this distinction. That is why the tax doesn't. Instead, it simply tries to reassert the primacy of government over the international currency markets. For this reason alone, it is worth supporting.

New social programs could also be financed through the reallocation of military spending. The military budget is projected at $284 billion for the year 2000.[50] The United States has no military rivals. During the Cold War, many speculated that continuation of the Cold War served an essential economic function, because it kept unemployment down and assured profits for industries such as aerospace that might otherwise lack for customers. Although this proposition was difficult to test as long as the Cold War lingered, it is now indisputably right: the Soviet Union collapses, but after a brief dip, the spending continues. The United States, it is said, must be always prepared to fight wars in two different places at one time, though against whom and for what remains alarmingly murky. The Congressional Budget Office regularly offers a range of options to reduce military spending without endangering the national security: cut the number of aircraft carrier groups from twelve to ten, forgo purchase of a CVN-77 nuclear carrier in 2002, and cancel the new attack submarine—the first to be less capable than its predecessor. Just these three options would save $15.5 billion by 2002.[51] Both in their own right and as a downpayment on a broader retrenchment, these reductions would be a good place to start.

Lastly, there are the state and local tax systems, the soft underbelly of American public finance. As services devolve to the states, it becomes critical to assure more equitable methods of financing. While the regressiveness of state taxation often exceeds the federal government's, there are also some hopeful signs, such as Vermont's plan to make the property tax income-based. Regressive state systems cater to the fragmentation of government power: the smaller the governmental unit, the greater the inequity that is likely to be perpetuated. Minimize the role of property and sales taxes as the basis for essential state services like education, and inequities can be reduced through progressive income taxes that promote consolidation. In this way, it will not cut quite so deeply when social welfare programs are brought closer to home.

These proposals constitute just a few of the possible methods of paying for programs that offer greater economic security. Separately or in combination, they demonstrate that funds are available. The United States is the world's wealthiest country, but it defines most of this wealth as private and/or sacrosanct, even though workers, communities, and the public infrastructure play a decisive role in its creation. The issue, then, is not the absence of funds. Rather, it is the absence of the political will to make those funds available for overarching public goals.

Civil Society and Community

In addition to their apprehensions about economic security, many Americans are greatly troubled by what they perceive as a noticeable decline in the sense of community. This concern has found its most prominent expression in a widely discussed article by Harvard professor Robert Putnam entitled, "Bowling Alone: America's Declining Social Capital." In this and several subsequent articles, Putnam used statistics on membership in volunteer organizations to argue that over the last three decades, Americans have reduced the extent of their community involvement.[52]

Controversy quickly engulfed Putnam's thesis. Some critics questioned his data, contending, for example, that the decline he observed in PTA participation was merely a reflection of lower school enrollments. Others upbraided him for his failure to distinguish among groups: presumably, the League of Women Voters and the Montana Militia do not contribute equally to the existence of a vibrant civil society. And, many added, whatever the vitality of community life in the mid-twentieth century, few would want to return to a time when most groups were narrowly based, relied on the labor of unemployed wives and mothers, and had such exclusionary practices.[53]

In truth, while Putnam has identified a very real phenomenon, his analysis of causes leaves something to be desired. Putnam is surely right to rebut conservatives who blame the welfare state, since other, larger welfare states have much higher levels of civic engagement. Nor can residential mobility be faulted, because people moved more frequently during the suburbanization of the 1950s. Yet something in his analysis seems unbalanced, especially when Putnam deemphasizes the economic context for civic disengagement in order to focus on television and technology. Summarizing the economic changes in just one sentence, he writes:

> Moreover, the changes in scale that have swept over the American economy in these years—illustrated by the replacement of the corner grocery by the supermarket and now perhaps of the supermarket by electronic shopping at home, or the replacement of community-based enterprises by outposts of distant multinational firms—may perhaps have undermined the material and even physical basis for civic engagement.[54]

Certainly, television has made its own profound contribution to the decline of civic life. Nevertheless, it seems quite asymmetrical to compress discussion of the U.S. economy to this extent while holding forth for many pages on the effects of television. Technological determinism need not take us quite that far.

Besides, there is a better explanation. Health policy analysts have recently underscored the close linkage between inequality, social capital, and mortality. Focusing primarily on the connection between mortality rates and networks of social support, they have noted that high rates of inequality tend to destroy social capital and undermine community life.[55] It is a provocative hypothesis with particular implications for Putnam's work, because it shows exactly how the new, market-generated inequality contributes to the loss of a vital community life. Although Putnam's instincts may point elsewhere, the turn to the market can rightfully claim our attention on this issue just as much as television and technology.

This economic explanation has its social correlate. Short of time, money, and a sense that they matter, many Americans have fallen back on their core roles as workers and consumers. Their self-concept dovetails nicely with both the ideology underlying the market economy and the radical individualism that pervades much of the middle class. This combination produces an impoverished self that has civic disengagement as one of its primary by-products.[56] Inevitably, the war of all against all must take its toll.

In the American model of a market economy, economic security is the pot of gold at the end of the rainbow: a few reach it, but most spend their life in ceaseless pursuit. To ensure economic security for all, this book has proposed democratization of the economy, universal social provision, and full employment in jobs with sufficient pay. Not so incidentally, these are precisely the measures that would provide what Putnam describes as "the material and physical basis for civic engagement." In short, they are a big part of the remedy for both our economic and social ills. If only Americans were assured of their economic security, if only they did not have to worry so obsessively about their material well-being, then they would be freed to direct their energies to the world outside. There, they could once again engage in the gratifying work of community-building.

Getting There

It is now time to acknowledge the 800-pound gorilla that looks over the shoulder of everyone who reads this book: Even if these proposals have merit, how can they possibly be enacted in the face of the conservative tide? One answer is that they cannot be, if political sentiment remains unchanged. As every 1960s' retrospective demonstrates, however, the center that rules American politics is not stationary. For this reason, it is equally plausible to argue that while the short-term prospects are not good, over the next generation, nothing here should be foreclosed.

Conservatives have plainly transformed U.S. politics. They have cut taxes, ended the federal entitlement to public assistance, and firmly established the values of the market as the benchmark for most public policies. The New Deal and the Great Society provided more government support for people, but they also offered imperfect legacies. Now that conservatives have either modified these legacies or completely swept them away, the slate is clean, and we can begin again. The political implications of this opportunity are enormous, because it means that the old system of social provision is not going to be reconstructed. Put bluntly, it is all right to mourn the loss of a federal entitlement to public assistance, as long as we remember that when some welfare recipients begin to reach the end of their five-year cap in 2002, no one is going to propose the revival of AFDC.

The end of the old system of social provision constituted a clear conservative triumph. Yet oddly enough, it may turn out to represent the high point of the conservative tide. For conservatives, the 1994 elections were what 1968 was for liberal Democrats: a time when their political power was at its height, and they had considerable influence in the media, but they could not elect a president, and splits began to show in the ranks. Humphrey fought off Kennedy and McCarthy, just as Gingrich fought off the militants on his right, brought to Congress in the class of 1994. There is in this analogy a close parallel between how fast the U.S. should have gotten out of Vietnam and how fast contemporary conservatives should push their agenda. Indeed, the parallel extends even further to the victorious presidents, because Nixon managed the anti-war movement in much the same way that Clinton managed the attack on social provision. In ending the war as well as in ending welfare, both granted just enough to preserve their own political power, despite a hostile media and a Congress the opposing party controlled.

If 1994 through 1996 was the high point of the conservative tide, then the victories of conservatism have to be described as significant but not complete. Conservatives shredded the safety net; they destroyed the old system of social provision. Yet the triumph of conservatism may come back to haunt it. Had we limped along with a fragmented system of employment policies and a passel of means-tested programs, their existence would have muddied the fight for universal social policies. The next time, however, something new will undoubtedly be proposed, and that something new might well include precisely the kind of universalism that conservatives most fear.

Ultimately, of course, decisions about the direction of U.S. politics will depend upon the broad middle of the American electorate. This part of the population is neither rich nor poor, but for the moment at least, it has bet both its current and future well-being on the capacity of markets to satisfy its most basic needs. Certainly, there are social forces trying to get this vast middle to act in its own economic interest. In these struggles, the reinvigorated labor movement and a number of dynamic local coalitions have made some progress. Looking back on the last hundred years, however, it is clear that the six years of this century's most important social legislation—1933–1935 and 1964–1966—occurred in the midst of the century's greatest periods of mass social protest. These protests triggered widespread social disorder, reshaped electoral politics, and expanded the state's role in reducing inequality. Until some significant part of the population helps to generate such a protest movement, the efforts of others to bring about social reform will be largely contained.[57]

This containment is likely to last until market-based policies lose their allure. Although this prediction may sound reassuring, no one who believes in the American version of free markets should get too comfortable. Markets have always been unstable; their benefits have always been skewed. Now, after twenty-five years of conservative policy, their benefits are even more skewed, and fewer social supports exist to offset the resulting inequities. For all these reasons, the appeal of markets is not sustainable over the long term. Americans need greater economic security. They require more democratic accountability. Once they discover that they cannot obtain these things from the market, they will then have to decide how much of a correction they want to make.

Notes

Notes to Chapter 1

1. For Mobil Oil, see Matt Murray, "Amid Record Profits, Companies Continue to Layoff Employees," *The Wall Street Journal*, May 4, 1995; for the Chemical-Chase merger, see Saul Hansell, "Chase and Chemical Agree to Merge In $10 Billion Deal Creating Largest U.S. Bank," August 29, 1995, as well as Floyd Norris "You're Fired! (But Your Stock Is Way Up)," *The New York Times*, September 3, 1995; and for Kimberly-Clark, see Bloomberg Business Service, "Acquisition Done, Kimberly Plans to Eliminate 6,000 Jobs," *The New York Times*, December 14, 1995, and Dana Canedy, "Kimberly-Clark To Dismiss 5,000 Workers and Eliminate 18 Plants," *The New York Times*, November 22, 1997.

2. U.S. Department of Labor, Bureau of Labor Statistics, *Worker Displacement During the Mid-1990s*, October 25, 1996.

3. See Bureau of the Census, *Income and Poverty 1996*, for the data about quintiles. The 97 percent figure comes from Louis Uchitelle and N. R. Kleinfield, "On the Battlefields of Business, Millions of Casualties," *The New York Times*, March 3, 1996. Others who have come to similar conclusions about the top 20 percent include Robert Reich, *The Work of Nations* (New York: Vintage, 1992); John Kenneth Galbraith, *The Culture of Contentment* (New York: Houghton-Mifflin, 1992); Wallace Peterson, *Silent Depression* (New York: W.W. Norton, 1994); and Lawrence Mishel, Jared Bernstein, and John Schmitt, *The State of Working America, 1998–99*, Economic Policy Institute Series (Ithaca, New York: Cornell University Press, 1999). On p. 321, the latter is also the source of the figure about the number on new jobs.

4. Robert Reich, *The Work of Nations*, p. 58.

5. United States General Accounting Office, *Competitiveness Issues: The Business Environment in the United States, Germany, and Japan* (Washington, D.C.: Government Printing Office, 1993), p. 12.

6. Not so incidentally, this change in the nature of the market is also the major weakness of David Osborne and Ted Gaebler's book, *Reinventing Government: How the Entrepreneurial Spirit is Transforming the Public Sector* (New York: Plume, 1993). Osborne and Gaebler want to return government in the form of market-oriented services to communities. The problem is that they want to do this at the very moment in history when market institutions are ever less community-based.

7. See Kenneth De Meuse, "The Tie That Binds—Has Become Very, Very Frayed," *Human Resource Planning* 13 (3): 203–213, 1990, especially pp. 205 and 208.

8. See Jill Quadagno, *The Color of Welfare* (New York: Oxford University Press, 1994) for a succinct history of the period.

9. The 1967 figure comes from Lawrence Mishel and Jared Bernstein, *The State of Working America, 1994–95*, Economic Policy Institute Series (Armonk, New York: M.E. Sharpe, 1994), p. 101; the 1996 figure comes from United States Congressional Budget Office, *The Economic and Budget Outlook* (Washington, D.C.: September, 1997), p. 31.

10. Kevin Phillips, *Arrogant Capital* (Boston, Massachusetts: Little, Brown, 1994), pp. 80–81.

11. See Bloomberg News, "Investors Moved $24.5 Billion Into Stock Funds Last Month," *The New York Times*, May 29, 1998, and Sara Calian, "As Mutual Funds Face Growing Competition, Wholesalers Struggle," *The Wall Street Journal*, March 16, 1995.

12. Lawrence Mishel, Jared Bernstein, and John Schmitt, *The State of Working America, 1998–99*, p. 260; Jeremy Siegel, *Stocks for the Long-Run* (Chicago: Irwin, 1994), p. 11, along with Siegel's updated data cited in David Barboza, "Bull Market's Glitter May Be Blinding

Investors," *The New York Times,* October 22, 1997. The 6.99 percent figure covers the period from 1802 to 1997. See also David Barboza, "Another Bull Year of the Bull; Dow Up 22%," *The New York Times,* January 1, 1998, and Gretchen Morgenson, "90s Mantra: Bull Market to Carry On," *The New York Times,* January 4, 1999.

13. See Lester Thurow, "The Crusade That's Killing Prosperity," *The American Prospect* 25: 54–59, March–April, 1996. Interest rates were raised seven times between early 1994 and early 1995.

14. U.S. Census Bureau, *Income and Poverty 1996,* and Organization for Economic Cooperation and Development, *The OECD in Figures: 1997* (Paris: OECD), pp. 48–51.

15. For an analysis of the development of managed care, see Arnold Birenbaum, *Managed Care: Made in America* (Westport, Connecticut: Greenwood, 1997).

16. William Kristol, "Memorandum to Republican Leaders: Defeating President Clinton's Health Care Proposal" (Washington, D.C.: Project for the Republican Future, December 2, 1993), p. 4, as cited in Theda Skocpol, *Boomerang: Clinton's Health Security Effort and the Turn Against Government in U.S. Politics* (New York: W. W. Norton, 1996), pp. 145–146.

17. In "What Happened to Health Care Reform," *The American Prospect* (20): 20–32, 1995, Paul Starr identifies a number of other factors that affected the outcome. First, the administration initially ignored Congress, violating the old political precept "in on the takeoff, in on the landing." Second, Starr argues, the legislation received a 70 percent favorable rating in focus groups when it was simply identified as a "health reform bill"; when it was *Clinton's* health reform bill, the ratings dropped to 30 to 40 percent. Third, Starr insists—probably correctly—that single-payer got off easy, because the Clinton legislation acted as a lightning rod. For her part, Hillary Clinton admits that the complexity of the legislation hurt it and stresses the extent to which the opposition outfinanced proponents—$120 to $300 million spent opposing the bill, compared to the $12 to $15 million spent supporting it. Adam Clymer, "Hillary Clinton Says Adminstration Was Misunderstood on Health Care," *The New York Times,* October 3, 1994. For a somewhat different understanding of what happened, see Theda Skocpol's *Boomerang.*

One could also imagine another scenario. Compare what the Clinton administration did with the strategy advocated by union organizer Ray Rogers. Rogers is well known for his corporate campaigns, in which he pressures every major institution including banks and other businesses with members on the board of directors who have links to his target. When Clinton came out with his plan, the Business Roundtable, led by the insurance companies, immediately attacked it. The Chamber of Commerce, which had originally favored a more moderate plan, saw what was happening and quickly withdrew support. Some reform groups then said that they had to get behind the president, but once they did, the debate shifted immediately to one between the center and the right. In the preferred scenario, the movement for health reform, or even better, a president with real ties to a movement for health reform, would have campaigned against individual insurance companies such as Prudential and made them fight for a place at the bargaining table. In the case of Prudential, the most effective way of conducting this campaign would have been to run alternative slates for their board of directors and to attack their corporate links to businesses like Pepsi that sell products directly to American workers and sit on the Prudential board. The movement for national health care was not powerful enough to defeat the combined opposition, but in a shrewd organizing campaign, it could have emerged with some fairly strong legislation if it had picked that opposition apart one by one. See Ray Rogers, "Make Them Fight For a Place at the Table: How To Take On the Insurance Industry," *Social Policy* 24 (4): 31–39, Summer, 1994.

18. Louis Uchitelle, "Long March of the Arms Contractors," *The New York Times,* April 19, 1995; Council of Economic Advisors, *Economic Report of the President,* 1994 (Washington, D.C.: Government Printing Office, 1994), p. 76; *Business Week,* "High-Tech Jobs All Over the Map," January 13, 1995, p. 113; Jaclyn Fierman, "What Happened to the Jobs?" *Fortune,* July 12, 1993, pp. 40–41.

19. Iris Lav, Edward B. Lazere, and Jim St. George, *A Tale of Two Futures: Restructuring California's Finances To Boost Economic Growth* (Washington, D.C.: Center on Budget and Policy Priorities, 1994), p. x; Seth Mydans, "Orange County Begins Pain of Cutbacks," *The New York Times*, March 10, 1995. Obviously, the role of growing income inequality within the state should not be underemphasized. For a useful monograph on this subject, see Deborah Reed, Melissa Glenn Haber, and Laura Mameesh, *The Distribution of Income in California* (San Francisco, California: Public Policy Institute of California, 1996).

20. Vincent Schiraldi, *Trading Books for Bars: The Lopsided Funding Battle Between Prisons and Universities* (San Francisco, California: Center on Juvenile and Criminal Justice, 1994). Of course, California is hardly alone in this use of public monies: the trend toward imprisonment is a national one. From the early 1980s to 1997, the prison population grew from 400,000 to 1.7 million people, and money spent on crime control increased at twice the rate of defense spending. The twelve million people who spend at least one night in jail each year is greater than the population of the fourteen least populous states. And yet, despite media portrayals to the contrary, just 10 percent of all arrests are for violent crime, and only 3 percent are for violent crime resulting in injury. See Steven R. Donziger, "Fear, Crime, and Punishment in the United States," *Tikkun* 12 (6): 24–27, 77, November–December, 1997.

21. These examples comes from Allen R. Meyerson, "O' Governor, Won't You Buy Me a Mercedes Plant," *The New York Times*, September 1, 1996; Fred Bleakley, "Many States Press for Concessions," *The Wall Street Journal*, March 8, 1995; and Louis Uchitelle, "Corporate Spending Booms, But Jobs Stagnate," *The New York Times*, June 16, 1994.

22. Frank Rich, "Disney's Bull Run," *The New York Times*, May 22, 1994.

23. Lawrence Mishel, Jared Bernstein, and John Schmitt, *The State of Working America, 1998–99*, pp. 262–263, and Edward Wolff, *Top Heavy: A Study of the Increasing Inequality of Wealth in America* (New York: The Twentieth Century Fund, 1995), p. 10. Similar data are also reported in Eril Hurst, Ming Ching Luoh, and Frank P. Stafford, *Wealth Dynamics of American Families, 1984–1994* (University of Michigan at Ann Arbor, Department of Economics and Institute for Social Research, 1996), which found that the top 10 percent of American families held 61.1 percent of the nation's wealth in 1989 and 66.8 percent in 1994.

24. The *Fortune* prediction is cited in Paul Krugman, *The Age of Diminished Expectations* (Washington, D.C.: The Washington Post Publishing Company, 1994), p. xi; William Greider, *Who Will Tell the People?* (New York: Touchstone Books, 1992), p. 397.

25. Jaclyn Fierman, "When Will You Get a Raise?" *Fortune*, July 12, 1993, pp. 34–36. The study was conducted by William H. Mercer, Inc., compensation consultants in New York City.

26. Richard May and Kathryn Porter, *Poverty and Income Trends: 1994* (Washington, D.C.: Center on Budget and Policy Priorities, 1996), p. 66; Center on Budget and Policy Priorities, *Only High-Income Households Have Recovered Fully from the Recession* (Washington, D.C.: Center on Budget and Policy Priorities, October 24, 1995), pp. 1–3; and Lawrence Mishel, Jared Bernstein, and John Schmitt, *The State of Working America, 1998–99*, p. 5.

27. See Kathryn Larin and Elizabeth C. McNichol, *Pulling Apart: A State-By-State Analysis of Income Trends* (Washington, D.C.: Center on Budget and Policy Priorities, 1997).

28. Lawrence Mishel, Jared Bernstein, and John Schmitt, *The State of Working America, 1998–99*, p. 127, and Keith Bradsher, "Americans' Real Wages Fell 2.3% in 12-Month Period," *The New York Times*, June 23, 1995.

29. Lawrence Mishel, Jared Bernstein, and John Schmitt, *The State of Working America, 1998–99*, pp. 157–158 and 132; Chinhui Juhn, Kevin Murphy, and Robert H. Topel, "Why Has the Natural Rate of Unemployment Increased Over Time?" *Brooking Papers on Economic Activity* (2): 100, 1991.

30. Center for Study of Social Policy and the Philadelphia Children's Network, *World Without Work: Causes and Consequences of Black Male Joblessness*, 1994, p. 15.

31. Bureau of Labor Statistics, *Union Members Summary 1997*, January, 1998; Council of Economic Advisors, *Economic Report of the President 1994*, p. 120; and Martin Neil Baily, Gary Burtless, and Robert E. Litan, *Growth with Equity: Economic Policymaking for the Next Century* (Washington, D.C.: The Brookings Institution, 1993), p. 63. Of course, union membership is

not the only factor in the pay differential. For a discussion of this issue, see Kay E. Anderson, Philip M. Doyle, and Albert E. Schwenk, "Measuring Union–nonunion Earning Differences," *Monthly Labor Review* 113 (6): 26–38, June, 1990.

32. Louis Harris & Associates for the Families and Work Institute, *Women: The New Providers* (New York, 1995), p. 33; Wallace Peterson, *The Silent Depression*, p. 39; Maria Cancian, Sheldon Danziger, and Peter Gottschalk, "Working Wives and Family Income Inequality Among Married Couples," in Sheldon Danziger and Peter Gottschalk, eds., *Uneven Tides: Rising Inequality in America* (New York: Russell Sage, 1994), pp. 195–221; Joint Economic Committee, *Families on a Treadmill in Staff Study of the Joint Economic Committee*, January 13, 1992, p. 18, cited in Kevin Phillips, *Boiling Point* (New York: Random House, 1993), p. 159. For an analysis of the effect of women's employment by ethnic group, see also Peter Cattan, "The Effect of Working Wives on the Incidence of Poverty," *Monthly Labor Review* 121 (3): 22–29, March, 1998.

33. William Lazonick, "Creating and Extracting Value: Corporate Investment Behavior and American Economic Performance," in Michael A. Bernstein and David E. Adler, eds., *Understanding American Economic Decline* New York: Cambridge University Press, 1994), p. 102; *Business Week*, "Executive Pay: Special Report," April 21, 1997, p. 58–66; AFL-CIO, *Executive Pay Watch*, 1997.

34. Holman Jenkins, "Paying Off CEOs Is Worth It," *The Wall Street Journal*, January 9, 1996.

35. See Derek Bok, *The Cost of Talent* (New York: The Free Press, 1993), pp. 98–99, and Charles A. O'Reilly, Brian G. Mein, and Graef S. Crystal, "CEO Compensation as Tournament and Social Comparison: A Tale of Two Theories," *Administrative Science Quarterly* (33): 257, 1988, cited in Bok, p. 113.

36. Derek Bok, *The Cost of Talent*, p. 71.

37. Lawrence Mishel, "Capital's Gain," *The American Prospect* 33: 71–73, July–August, 1997. For comparison's sake, the entire gain in hourly compensation from 1989 to 1996 was only 2.8 percent, so this shift would have more than doubled it. By contrast, according to the Congressional Budget Office, after seven years, a balanced budget would yield just a 0.5 percent increase.

38. Cited in Sylvia Nasar, "Rich and Poor Likely to Remain So," *The New York Times*, May 18, 1992. For a more sophisticated defense of this position contending that growing social equality compensates for the necessary inequality of income that the market produces, see Irving Kristol, "Income Inequality Without Class Conflict," *The Wall Street Journal*, December 18, 1997.

39. See Peter Gottschalk, Sara McLanahan, and Gary Sandefur, "The Dynamics of Intergenerational Transmission of Poverty and Welfare Participation," p. 91, in Sheldon H. Danziger, Gary D. Sandefur, and Daniel H. Weinberg, eds., *Confronting Poverty*; Richard V. Burkhauser, Douglas Holtz-Eakin, and Stephen E. Rhody, *Labor Earnings Mobility and Inequality in the United States and Germany During the Growth Years of the 1980s*, Maxwell School of Citizenship and Public Affairs, Syracuse University, 1996, p. 10.

40. Peter Gottschalk, *Policy Changes and Growing Earnings Inequality in Seven Industrialized Countries*, The Luxembourg Income Study, 1994, pp. 7 and 14; see also Peter Gottschalk and Timothy M. Smeeding, *Empirical Evidence on Income Inequality in Industrialized Countries*, Luxembourg Income Study Working Paper No. 154, 1997, for similar conclusions.

41. Organization for Economic Cooperation and Development, *The OECD Jobs Study: Unemployment in the OECD Area, 1950–95* (Paris: OECD, 1994), p. 23; Sheila Collins, Helen Lachs Ginsberg, and Gertrude Schaffner Goldberg, *Jobs for All* (New York: Apex Press, 1994) p. 41. The proportion of single mothers with income below 50 percent of the median income is 53 percent in the U.S., 45 percent in Canada, 25 percent in Germany, 18 percent in the United Kingdom, 16 percent in France, 7 percent in the Netherlands, and 6 percent in Sweden. See Irwin Garfinkel and Sara McLanahan, "Single Mother Families, Economic Insecurity, and Government Policy," in Sheldon H. Danziger, Gary D. Sandefur, and Daniel H. Weinberg, eds., *Confronting Poverty*, p. 209.

42. See Timothy Smeeding, with A. B. Atkinson and L. Rainwater, *Income Distribution in the OECD Countries: The Evidence from the Luxembourg Income Maintenance Study* (Paris: OECD, 1995). This research relied on data from the Luxembourg Income Study to analyze income distribution in fifteen nations. It is the most comprehensive study of its kind ever done. The study found that not only is the income ratio of the tenth and ninetieth percentiles more than twice (5.94 to 2.59) Finland's, the country with the smallest differential, but it is also significantly larger than Italy (4.04), Canada (4.03), and Britain (3.80). For a good summary of the data, see Gary Burtless and Timothy Smeeding, "America's Tide: Lifting the Yachts, Swamping the Rowboats," *Washington Post*, June 25, 1995.

43. For a succinct overview of these causes, see Barry Bluestone, "The Inequality Express," *The American Prospect* (20): 81–93, Winter, 1995. The literature on these causes is plentiful, but the following are among the most helpful: Martin Neil Baily, Gary Burtless, and Robert E. Litan, *Growth with Equity*, especially chapter 3 on "Inequality"; Sheldon Danziger, Gary Sandefur, and Daniel Weinberg, eds., *Confronting Poverty*, especially chapter 2 on the historical record; Sheldon Danziger and Peter Gottschalk, eds., *Uneven Tides;* Wallace Peterson, *The Silent Depression;* Lawrence Mishel, Jared Bernstein, and John Schmitt, *The State of Working America, 1998–99;* and Robert H. Frank and Philip J. Cook, *The Winner-Take-All Society* (New York: The Free Press, 1995).

44. For example, in the above list, the only exception is Barry Bluestone, "The Inequality Express."

45. See the articles in *U.S News and World Report*, January 22, 1996, pp. 44–54.

46. Quoted in Dennis Farney, "Even U.S. Politics Are Being Reshaped By a Global Economy," *The Wall Street Journal*, October 28, 1992.

47. Paul Kennedy, *The Rise and Fall of the Great Powers* (New York: Vintage, 1989), p. 533.

48. This figure is calculated from United for Fair Economy, *Born on Third Base: The Sources of Wealth of the 1997 Forbes 400* (Boston: United for a Fair Economy, 1997). The number of billionaires has risen from 50 in 1990. Derek Bok, *The Cost of Talent*, p. 2.

49. See Benjamin Ginsberg and Martin Shefter, *Politics by Other Means* (New York: Basic Books, 1990), especially pp. 2 and 162.

50. From a different but complementary perspective, see David Wagner, *The New Temperance: The American Obsession With Sin and Vice* (Boulder, Colorado: Westview Press, 1996), which describes this search as one of those periodic "moral panics" Americans have had and, from the drug wars to sex and obesity, questions our sudden need to pathologize everything.

51. Richard B. Freeman and Joel Rogers, *Worker Representation and Participation Survey: Report on the Findings* (Princeton, New Jersey: Princeton Survey Research Associates, 1994), p. 49.

52. Reported by Proudfoot, USA, an international consulting firm, and cited in Barbara Presley Noble, "Workaday Visions of Sugar Plums," *The New York Times*, December 25, 1994.

53. Rebecca Blank has done some useful research on this issue. For example, the historical record of poverty data and economic growth thru 1983 would have suggested a poverty rate of 9.3 percent in 1989. The actual rate was 12.8 percent, suggesting that poverty can no longer be diminished so easily by a growth strategy. See Rebecca M. Blank, *Growth Is Not Enough: Why the Recovery of the 1980s Did So Little to Reduce Poverty* (Washington, D.C.: Paper Prepared for the Joint Economic Committee, Congress of the United States, September 26, 1991).

54. George Peterson and Wayne Vroman, "Urban Labor Markets and Economic Opportunity," in George Peterson and Wayne Vroman, eds., *Urban Labor Markets and Job Opportunity* (Washington, D.C.: The Urban Institute, 1992), p. 5.

55. See Council of Economic Advisors, *Economic Report of the President 1997*, Table B-48, p. 355 for the 1990–1995 data, and the U.S. Department of Labor, Bureau of Labor Statistics, *Employment Cost Trends*, Table 1, as well as *Quarterly Labor Productivity*, Nonfarm Business Sector, Table-2, March 9, 1998, for 1996 and 1997 data.

56. The two best books on the history of the way we talk about the poor are Herbert Gans, *The War Against the Poor* (New York: Basic Books, 1995), and Michael B. Katz, *The Undeserving Poor* (New York: Pantheon, 1989).

57. For a useful discussion of this issue, see S. M. Miller, "Many Americas," *Social Policy* 28 (1): 19–29, Fall, 1997.

Notes to Chapter 2

1. See Karl de Schweinitz, *England's Road to Social Security* (New York: A.S. Barnes, 1961). The first major piece of social legislation was the Statute of Laborers (1349), which barred alms to able-bodied beggars. When this law proved insufficient, another law was enacted two years later (the Statute of Laborers, 1351) that limited the movement of workers. This law was the first in a more than six-hundred-year-long legislative tradition that saw movement, vagrancy, begging, and the price of labor as different dimensions of the same fundamental issue.

2. Eileen Appelbaum and Rosemary Batt, *The New American Workplace* (Ithaca, New York: ILR Press, 1994), p. 3.

3. Josh Clark, "No Good Jobs," *Mother Jones*, March/April, 1994, p. 36.

4. *Business Week*, "The Triple Revolution," January 24, 1995, p. 23; J. David Richardson, Geza Feketekuty, C. Zhang, and A. E. Rodriguez, "U.S. Performance and Trade Strategy in a Shifting Global Economy," in Geza Feketekuty with Bruce Stokes, eds., *Trade Strategies for a New Era* (New York: Council on Foreign Relations, 1997), p. 39; for the 40 percent projected for 2006, see Charles Bowman, "BLS Projections to 2006—a summary," *Monthly Labor Review* 120 (11): 3–5, November, 1997; Council of Economic Advisors, *Economic Report of the President* (Washington, D.C.: Government Printing Office, 1994), pp. 206–207.

5. Peter Passell, "U.S. and Europe Clear the Way for a World Accord on Trade, Setting Aside Major Disputes," *The New York Times*, December 15, 1993.

6. *Business Week*, "Borderless Finance: Fuel for Growth," Special Issue on 21st Century Capitalism, January 24, 1995, pp. 50 and 44; for the $2.5 trillion figure, see Thomas Friedman, "Where's the Crisis?" *The New York Times*, May 23, 1998; for the description of the Bournemouth facility, see "Technobanking Takes Off," in the same special issue of *Business Week*, p. 53. The estimate of 80 percent comes from Jorge Mariscal, manager of Latin American equity research for Goldman Sachs & Co. and is cited in Tim Carrington, "Private-Capital Flow Can Hurt Poor Nations," *The Wall Street Journal*, January 30, 1995.

7. Michael R. Sesit, "Global Capital Crunch Is Beginning To Punish Some Weak Economies," *The Wall Street Journal*, January 12, 1995.

8. *Business Week*, "The Lesson from Barings' Straits," March 13, 1995, p. 30.

9. Erik Leaver and John Cavanagh, "Controlling Transnational Corporations," Interhemispheric Resource Center and the Institute for Policy Studies, *Foreign Policy in Focus* 1 (6): 1, November, 1996, and Sheila Collins, Helen Lachs Ginsberg, and Gertrude Schaffner Goldberg, *Jobs for All* (New York: Apex Press, 1994), p. 11.

10. *Business Week*, "Borderless Finance: Fuel for Growth," p. 4.

11. See Scott Jacobs, "Why Governments Must Work Together," *OECD Observer*, 186, February/March, 1994, pp. 13–16, citing John Braithwaite, *Prospects for Win-Win International Rapprochement of Regulation* (Paris: OECD, 1993); Paul Kennedy, *Preparing for the Twenty-First Century* (New York: Random House, 1993), pp. 131–134; Robert Reich, *The Work of Nations* (New York: Vintage, 1992), p. 9; Jean-Marie Guehenno, *The End of the Nation-State* (Minneapolis, Minnesota: University of Minnesota Press, 1995); Walter Russell Mead, "Forward to the Past," *The New York Times Sunday Magazine*, June 4, 1995, pp. 48–49; Dennis Farney, "Even U.S. Politics Are Being Reshaped By a Global Economy," *The Wall Street Journal*, October 28, 1992; and Sally Washington, "Globalisation and Governance," *OECD Observer*, 199, April–May, 1996, pp. 24–27.

12. For the role of this concept in the development of the Republican party, see Eric Foner, *Free Soil, Free Labor, Free Men: The Ideology of the Republican Party Before the Civil War* (New York: Oxford University Press, 1970).

13. Nicholas Vanston, "How Trade Affects Jobs," *OECD Observer*, 195, August/September, 1995, p. 11.

14. Paul Krugman, *Pop Internationalism* (Cambridge, Massachusetts: The MIT Press, 1996). The quotation on international trade comes from page 120. The books that Krugman criticizes include Robert Reich, *The Work of Nations;* Lester Thurow, *Head to Head: The Coming Economic Battle Among Japan, Europe, and America* (New York: William Morrow, 1992); and Clyde Prestowitz, *Trading Places* (New York: Basic Books, 1988).

15. J. David Richardson, Geza Feketekuty, C. Zhang, and A. E. Rodriguez, "U.S. Performance and Trade Strategy in a Shifting Global Economy," pp. 51 & 55. For a critique of Krugman from this perspective, see, for example, Dani Rodrik, *Has Globalization Gone Too Far?* (Washington, D.C.: Institute for International Economics, 1997), pp. 13–14.

16. See Robert Kuttner, *The End of Laissez-Faire* (Philadelphia: University of Pennsylvania, 1992), p. 118 for a review of the classical theory, and William Lazonick, *Business Organization and the Myth of the Market Economy* (New York: Cambridge University Press, 1993), pp. 3–5 for a discussion of how Britain's superior political power stifled the development of the Portugese textile industry.

17. See Paul Barioch, *Economics and World History: Myths and Paradoxes* (Chicago: University of Chicago Press, 1995); James Fallows, "How the World Works," *Atlantic Monthly* 272 (6): 61–87, December, 1993; McKinsey Global Institute, *Manufacturing Productivity* (Washington, D.C.: McKinsey Global Institute, 1993), pp. 4–5; Kevin Phillips, *Arrogant Capital* (Boston, Massachusetts: Little, Brown and Company, 1994), p. 206.

18. See Ian Robinson, "Globalization and Democracy," *Dissent* 42(3): 373–380, Summer, 1995.

19. Bennett Harrison, *Lean and Mean* (New York, Basic Books, 1994), pp. 8–9, and *Business Week*, "Hired Guns Packing High-Powered Know-how," January 24, 1995, pp. 92 and 96.

20. William Greider, *One World, Ready or Not* (New York: Simon & Schuster, 1997), p. 214.

21. Robert Reich, *The Work of Nations*, p. 112.

22. Laura Tyson, "They are Not Us: Why American Ownership Still Matters," *American Prospect,* 37–49, Winter, 1991. For a helpful summary of this issue, see Bennett Harrison, *Lean and Mean*, pp. 27–28.

23. Robert Kuttner, *The End of Laissez-Faire*, p. 135.

24. Michael Borrus and John Zysman, "Industrial Competitiveness and American National Security," in Wayne Sandholtz, Michael Borrus, John Zysman, Ken Conca, Jay Stowsky, Steven Vogel, and Steve Weber, eds., *The Highest Stakes* (New York: Oxford University Press, 1992), pp. 49–50, as well as Stephen S. Cohen and John Zysman, *Manufacturing Matters* (New York: Basic Books, 1987), pp. 109–110. Before he rebelled against the way it was implemented, Paul Krugman was also an advocate of strategic trade. See his *The Age of Diminished Expectations* (Washington, D.C.: The Washington Post Company, 1994), p. 132.

25. Walter Russell Mead, *The Low-Wage Challenge to Global Growth* (Washington, D.C.: Economic Policy Institute, 1990), p. 37.

26. Stephen S. Cohen and John Zysman, *Manufacturing Matters,* p. 11.

27. James K. Galbraith and Paulo Du Pin Calmon, "Industries, Trade, and Wages," in Michael Bernstein and David Adler, eds., *Understanding American Economic Decline* (New York: Cambridge University Press, 1994), pp. 188–189.

28. Ian Robinson, "Globalization and Democracy," *Dissent* 42 (3): 378, 1995.

29. As chapter 3 explains, this growth in wage inequality has been most evident among male workers. See Richard B. Freeman and Lawrence F. Katz, "Rising Wage Inequality: The United States vs. Other Advanced Countries," in Richard Freeman, ed., *Working Under Different Rules* (New York: Russell Sage, 1994), pp. 29–62.

30. See Peter Applebome, "South Raises Stakes in Fight for Jobs," *The New York Times,* October 4, 1993, and Peter Applebome, "In Race to Outrun Recession, Southeast Sets Dazzling Pace," *The New York Times,* November 27, 1993, as well as Robert W. Crandall, *Manufacturing on the Move* (Washington, D.C.: The Brookings Institution, 1993).

31. Kirk Johnson, "By Pratt & Whitney's Math, Connecticut Costs Too Much," *The New York Times,* April 23, 1993.

32. Lawrence Mishel, Jared Bernstein, and John Schmitt, *The State of Working America, 1998–99* (Ithaca, New York: Cornell University Press, 1999), p. 347, and Peter T. Kilborn, "For High School Graduates, A Job Market of Dead Ends," *The New York Times,* May 30, 1994.

33. Kate Bronfenbrenner, *Final Report: The Effects of Plant Closing or Threat of Plant Closing on the Right of Workers to Organize,* Submitted to the Labor Secretariat of the North American Commission for Labor Cooperation (Ithaca, N.Y.: Cornell University School of Industrial and Labor Relations, 1996).

34. See Barry Bluestone, "The Inequality Express," *The American Prospect* (20): 91, Winter, 1995.

35. *Business Week,* "The Triple Revolution," p. 24.

36. See Richard W. Stevenson, "U.S. to Report to Congress NAFTA Gains Are Modest," *The New York Times,* July 11, 1997; David Bonior, "I Told You So," *The New York Times,* July 13, 1997; Jesse Rothstein and Robert E. Scott, *NAFTA's Casualties: Employment Effects on Men, Women, and Minorities* (Washington, D.C.: Economic Policy Institute, 1997), p. 2; the United States General Accounting Office, *Dislocated Workers: An Early Look at NAFTA Transitional Adjustment Assistance Program* (Washington, D.C.: Government Printing Office, 1994), which expresses concern about the transitional assistance office's capacity to process petitions efficiently; and Bill Richards, "Layoffs Not Related to NAFTA Can Trigger Special Help Anyway," *The Wall Street Journal,* June 30, 1997, says that it has certified job losses that have nothing to do with NAFTA.

37. See the Public Citizen's Global Trade Watch, *NAFTA's Broken Promises* (Washington, D.C.: Public Citizen, 1995).

38. See Sidney Weintraub, *NAFTA At Three: A Progress Report* (Washington, D.C.: The Center for Strategic and International Studies, 1997), and Raúl Hinojosa Ojeda, Curt Dowds, Robert McCleery, Sherman Robinson, David Runsten, Craig Woolf, and Goetz Wolff, *North American Integration Three Years After NAFTA: A Framework for Tracking, Modeling and Internet Accessing the National and Regional Labor Market Impacts* (Los Angeles, California: UCLA School of Public Policy and Social Research, 1996).

39. "Editorial," *In These Times* (19) 5: 2, January 23, 1995.

40. Allen Meyerson, "Out of a Crisis, an Opportunity," *The New York Times,* September 26, 1995.

41. Richard J. Barnet and John Cavanagh, *Global Dreams: Imperial Corporations and the New World Order* (New York: Simon & Schuster, 1994), p. 318.

42. Sarah Anderson, John Cavanagh, David Ranney, and Paul Schwab, editors, *NAFTA's First Year* (Washington, D.C.: U.S. Citizens' Analysis, 1994), p. 4.

43. Sarah Anderson, John Cavanagh, David Ranney, and Paul Schwab, *NAFTA's First Year,* p. 7.

44. Raúl Hinojosa Ojeda et al., *North American Integration Three Years After NAFTA,* p. 15.

45. Craig R. Whitney, "West European Companies Head East for Labor," *The New York Times,* February 9, 1995; *Business Week,* "Finally, Germany Is Paring the Fat," October 17, 1994, p. 65.

46. Richard J. Barnet and John Cavanagh, *Global Dreams: Imperial Corporations and the New World Order,* pp. 285–286.

47. See UNICEF, *Crisis in Mortality, Health, and Nutrition: Central and Eastern Europe in Transition,* Monitoring Report No. 2, August, 1994; Jane Perlez, "Fast and Slow Lanes on the Capitalist Road," *The New York Times,* October 7, 1994; and Michael R. Gordon and Celestinne Bohlen, "But Twilight Cloaks Russia," *The New York Times,* January 3, 1999.

48. William Greider, *One World, Ready or Not,* p. 62.

49. *Business Week,* "The Triple Revolution," pp. 17 and 24.

50. Andrew Pollack, "Companies Rediscovering Indonesia," *The New York Times,* December 6, 1994.

51. For Western Digital, see Louis Uchitelle, "Dim Asian Economies Casting Shadows in U.S.," *The New York Times,* December 14, 1997; for Hewlett Packard, see G. Pascal Zachary, "High-Tech Firms Shift Some Skilled Work To Asian Countries," *The Wall Street Journal,* September 30, 1994.

52. See Floyd Norris, "In Asia Stocks Melt Faster Than in '29," *The New York Times,* January 11, 1998; Mark Landler, "Goodbye World!," *The New York Times,* September 12, 1998; Joseph Kahn and Michel Schuman, "Korea's Past Policies Are Unable to Remedy Today's Economic Ills," *The Wall Street Journal,* November 24, 1997; David P. Hamilton and Bill Spindle, "Yamaichi Folds in Japan's Biggest-Ever Failure," *The Wall Street Journal,* November 24, 1997; and Sheryl WuDunn, "Japan Says Unemployment Has Reached Record High," *The New York Times,* May 30, 1998.

53. Paul Krugman, "The Myth of Asia's Miracle," in *Pop Internationalism,* pp. 167–187. The Singapore data are on p. 175. The article originally appeared in the November–December, 1994 issue of *Foreign Affairs.*

54. Jeff Gerth and Richard W. Stevenson, "Poor Oversight Said to Imperil World Banking," *The New York Times,* December 22, 1997.

55. *The Economist,* "The enlightened welfare-seeker's guide to Europe," *The Economist,* vol. 330, no. 7854, p. 57, March 12–18, 1994.

56. Organization for Economic Cooperation and Development, *New Orientations for Social Policy* (Paris: OECD, 1994), p. 59.

57. See the Organization for Economic Cooperation and Development, *New Orientations for Social Policy,* pp. 59–61; Sheldon H. Danziger and Daniel H. Weinberg, "The Historical Record: Trends in Family Income, Inequality, and Poverty," in Sheldon Danziger, Gary Sandefur, and Daniel Weinberg, eds., *Confronting Poverty* (Cambridge, Massachusetts: Harvard University Press, 1994), pp. 29–30, Gary Burtless, "Public Spending on the Poor: Historical Trends and Economic Limits," in *Confronting Poverty,* p. 82; and Irwin Garfinkel and Sara McLanahan, "Single Mother Families, Economic Insecurity, and Government Policy," in *Confronting Poverty,* p. 210.

58. See Richard Stevenson, "Smitten By Britain, Business Rushes In," *The New York Times,* October 15, 1995; Sveinbjorn Blondal and Stefano Scarpetta, "The OECD Jobs Strategy Under Scrutiny," *OECD Observer* 209, December 1997/January 1998, pp. 5–10, contains both the 36 million and 10+ percent figures. The Spanish unemployment number comes from *The OECD in Figures, 1997 Edition,* p. 13, and is for 1994; the German and French figures are from Roger Cohen, "The Cries of the Welfare States Under the Knife," *The New York Times,* September 19, 1997.

59. Organization for Economic Cooperation and Development, *The OECD Jobs Study: Unemployment in the OECD Area, 1950–1995* (Paris: OECD, 1994), pp. 12–13.

60. See Phineas Baxandall, "Jobs vs. Wages: The Phony Trade-Off," *Dollars & Sense,* #206: 8–11, 42, July/August, 1996; for calculation of the real unemployment rate, see Lester Thurow, "The Crusade That's Killing Prosperity," *The American Prospect* no. 25: 54–59, March–April, 1996.

61. Daniel Singer, "The Real Eurobattle," *The Nation* 263 (21): 20–23, December 23, 1996, and Phineas Baxandall, "Jobs vs. Wages," p. 9.

62. Nathaniel C. Nash, "Europeans Shrug as Taxes Go Up," *The New York Times,* February 16, 1995.

63. Alexandra Iwanchuk Bibbee, "Spotlight on Germany Overcoming Structural Hurdles," *OECD Observer,* 190, October/November, 1994, pp. 35–37.

64. See Alan Cowell, "German Workers Fear the Miracle Is Over," *The New York Times,* July 30, 1997; *Business Week,* "Finally, Germany Is Paring the Fat," "Rethinking Work," Special Issue, *Business Week,* October 17, 1994, pp. 64–66; Craig R. Whitney, "In Europe, Touches of Leanness and Meanness," *The New York Times,* January 1, 1995; Daniel Benjamin and Tony Horowitz, "German View: 'You Americans Work Too Hard—and For What?' " *The Wall Street Journal,* July 14, 1994; and Ferdinand Protzman, "Rewriting the Contract for Germany's Vaunted Workers," *The New York Times,* February 13, 1994.

65. *Business Week,* "Finally, Germany Is Paring the Fat," "Rethinking Work," Special Issue, *Business Week,* October 17, 1994, pp. 64–66; Alexandra Iwanchuk Bibbee, "Spotlight on Germany Overcoming Structural Hurdles," pp. 35–37; Alan Cowell, "Kohl Offers Plan for Big

Cuts in the German Welfare State," *The New York Times,* April 27, 1996; Edmund L. Andrews, "German Industry Agrees to Discuss Sick-Pay Cuts," *The New York Times,* October 9, 1996; and Walter Hanesch, "Poverty and Social Policy in Unified Germany," University of Wisconsin-Madison, Institute for Research on Poverty, *Focus* 17 (3): 49–54, Spring, 1996.

66. See Dani Rodrik, *Has Globalization Gone Too Far?,* pp. 41–44, for an analysis of the 1995 French strike, and Edmund L. Andrews, "German Industry Losing Appetite for Labor Struggle," *The New York Times,* December 10, 1996, for a description of the trade union response to Daimler-Benz's effort to implement the new sick law.

67. Wallace Peterson, *Silent Depression* (New York: W.W. Norton, 1994), p.189.

68. See *Business Week,* "High-Tech Jobs All Over the Map," January 24, 1995, p. 114; Keith Bradsher, "Skilled Workers Watch Their Jobs Migrate Overseas," *The New York Times,* August 28, 1995; and Allen Meyerson, "Need Programmers? Surf Abroad," *The New York Times,* January 18, 1998.

Notes to Chapter 3

1. Robert L. Rose and Emily Nelson, "Checkoff," *The Wall Street Journal,* January 9, 1996 describes the Challenger, Gray, and Christmas report. The International Survey Research Corporation conducted the other study, which is described in *Study Spanning 1992–1996 Reveals That Amid Increased Fears of Job Security, Employees Show Growing Optimism on Key Workplace Issues* (Chicago, Illinois: 1996), p. 1. The title is somewhat of a misnomer, since what it captures is primarily the lower expectation of U.S. workers: "U.S. employees are toughening to the realities of a global economy. People are living their lives in chapters now" (p. 2).

2. Jobs Now Coalition, *The Job Gap Study* (Minneapolis, Minnesota: Jobs Now Coalition, 1995), p. 5; Ruth W. Messinger, *Work to Be Done: Report of the Borough President's Task Force on Education, Employment & Welfare* (New York: Office of the Manhattan Borough President, 1995), p. 21.

3. Bernard Wysocki, Jr., "About a Million Men Have Left Work Force in the Past Year or So," *The Wall Street Journal,* June 12, 1996. Additional data about the long-term trend can be found in the Council of Economic Advisors, *Economic Report of the President* (Washington, D.C.: Government Printing Office, 1997), Table B-38, p. 344, which shows a drop of almost 6 percent (from 83.2 to 77.3 percent) among all male workers above age 20 between 1971 and 1996.

4. After rising from 68.4 percent in 1959 to 73.5 percent in 1979, labor's share dropped slightly to 70.8 percent in 1996. The small size of this drop reflects the offset from growth in the government sector; in the corporate sector alone, labor's share dropped from 82.6 percent in 1979 to 78.4 percent in 1997. It would have required a 5.4 percent increase in hourly compensation to recover the difference. See Lawrence Mishel, Jared Bernstein, and John Schmitt, *The State of Working America, 1998–99* (Ithaca, New York: Cornell University Press, 1999), pp. 66–68.

5. For 1959–1973 and 1973–1990 data, see George E. Peterson and Wayne Vroman, "Urban Labor Markets and Economic Opportunity," in George E. Peterson and Wayne Vroman, eds., *Urban Labor Markets and Job Opportunity* (Washington, D.C.: The Urban Institute, 1992), p. 5; for the 1990s data, see the Bureau of Labor Statistics, *Quarterly Labor Productivity,* Nonfarm Business Sector, Table-2, March 9, 1998, and the Council of Economic Advisors, *Economic Report of the President, 1997* Table B-45, p. 352.

6. The fullest treatment of the social model is contained in Samuel Bowles, David Gordon, and Thomas Weisskopf, *After the Wasteland: A Democratic Economics for the Year 2000* (Armonk, New York: M.E. Sharpe, 1990), pp. 98–99, and David Gordon, *Fat and Mean: The Corporate Squeeze of Working Americans and the Myth of Managerial "Downsizing"* (New York: Free Press, 1996), pp. 145–157.

7. David Levine and Laura D'Andrea Tyson, "Participation, Productivity, and the Firm's Environment," in Alan S. Blinder, ed., *Paying for Productivity* (Washington, D.C.: The Brookings Institution, 1990), pp. 183–243.

8. McKinsey Global Institute, *Manufacturing Productivity* (Washington, D.C.: McKinsey Global Institute, 1993), p. 2, and Erik Hornell, *Improving Productivity for Competitive Advantage* (London: Pitman, 1992), pp. 239–252.

9. A more detailed examination of this data can be found in chapter 10. See David Alan Aschauer, *Public Investment and Private Sector Growth: The Economic Benefits of Reducing America's Third Deficit* (Washington, D.C.: Economic Policy Institute, 1990), p. 1; David Alan Aschauer and W. David Montgomery, "Point-Counterpoint—Public Capital Investment: Rx for Productivity," in *The Public's Capital* 1 (3): 4–6, 1990; Alice Munnell, "Productivity and Public Investment," *New England Economic Review*, January–February, 1990, pp. 3–22.

10. Ray Marshall, "Work Organization, Unions, and Economic Performance," in Lawrence Mishel and Paula B. Voos, eds., *Unions and Economic Competitiveness* (Armonk, New York: M.E. Sharpe, 1992), pp. 288–289, and Eileen Appelbaum and Rosemary Batt, *The New American Workplace* (Cornell, New York: ILR Press, 1994), pp. 147–148.

11. See Michael Harrington, *Socialism Past and Future* (New York: Arcade, 1989), p.137; United States General Accounting Office, *Competitiveness Issues: The Business Environment in the United States, Japan, and Germany* (Washington, D.C.: Government Printing Office, 1993), pp. 14–15; the estimates of German and Japanese productivity by industry come from the McKinsey Global Institute, *Manufacturing Productivity*, p. 1. The seven industries where Germany lags behind are autos, auto parts, computers, consumer electronics, food, beer, soap and detergent.

12. McKinsey Global Institute, *Manufacturing Productivity*, chapter 3, pp. 333–334; United States General Accounting Office, *Competitiveness Issues: The Business Environment in the United States, Japan, and Germany*, p. 3.

13. Alan S. Blinder, "Introduction," in Alan Blinder, ed., *Paying for Productivity*, p. 2.

14. See David Gordon, *Fat and Mean*, pp. 206–211, and Joel Blau, *The Visible Poor: Homelessness in the United States* (New York: Oxford University Press, 1992), pp. 40–41.

15. Lawrence Mishel and Jared Bernstein, *The State of Working America 1994–95* (Armonk, New York: M.E. Sharpe, 1994), p. 165; Thomas Karier, "Trade Deficits and Labor Unions: Myths and Realities," in Lawrence Mishel and Paula B. Voos, eds., *Unions and Economic Competitiveness*, p. 35; and Richard Freeman, "How Much Has De-Unionization Contributed to the Rise in Male Earnings Inequality," in Sheldon Danziger and Peter Gottschalk, eds., *Uneven Tides: Rising Inequality in America* (New York: Russell Sage Foundation, 1994), p. 133.

16. Dale Belman, "Unions, the Quality of Labor Relations, and Firm Performance," in Lawrence Mishel and Paula B. Voos, eds., *Unions and Economic Competitiveness*, p. 70, and the United States Department of Labor and the United States Department of Commerce, *Fact-Finding Report, Commission on the Future of Worker–Management Relations* (Washington, D.C.: U.S. Department of Labor and U.S. Department of Commerce, 1994), p. 79. For a full review of studies about the effects of unions on a variety of factors, see the list in Belman, pp. 76–107.

17. For a review of these experiments, see chapter 6 of Eileen Appelbaum and Rosemary Batt, *The New American Workplace*, pp. 69–97.

18. G. Pascal Zachary, "Service Productivity Is Rising Fast—and So Is the Fear of Lost Jobs," *The Wall Street Journal*, June 8, 1995. The more academic version of this sentiment appears in the Council of Economic Advisors, *Economic Report of the President 1994* (Washington, D.C.: Government Printing Office, 1994), p. 44: "Since the dawn of the industrial revolution, alarmists have argued that technology and automation threatened jobs. Such claims are still heard today. But history shows that they have never been right in the past and suggests that they are wrong again. Time after time, in epoch after epoch and country after country, technological advancement has produced higher wages and living standards, not mass unemployment. That is exactly what we expect to happen again in the 21st century." For a good journalistic overview from the same perspective, see George Papaconstantinou, "Technology and Jobs," *OECD Observer*, no. 194, June–July, 1995, pp. 6–9.

For the contrary view, see the Jack Rehm quote in Louis Richman, "CEOs to Workers: Help Not Wanted," *Fortune*, July 12, 1993, p. 42. Lawrence Siefert is cited in Louis Uchitelle, "Job Extinction Evolving Into a Fact of Life in U.S.," *The New York Times*, March 22, 1994.

19. Nathan Rosenberg, *Inside the Black Box: Technology and Economics* (New York: Cambridge University Press, 1982), pp. 117–118; Council of Economic Advisors, *Economic Report of the President*, 1994, p. 194; Ray Marshall, "Work Organization, Unions, and Economic Performance," in Lawrence Mishel and Paula B. Voos, eds., *Unions and Economic Competitiveness*, p. 290.

20. John Holusha, "Why American Steel Is Big Again," *The New York Times*, July 21, 1994; John Holusha, "Big Steelmakers Shape Up," *The New York Times*, April 16, 1996.

21. Stephen J. Davis, John C. Haltiwanger, and Scott Schuh, *Gross Job Flows in U.S. Manufacturing* (Washington, D.C.: U.S. Department of Commerce, Center for Economic Studies, 1994), chapter 4, pp. 24–27, and Peter Kilborn, "A City Prepares for Life After Steel," *The New York Times*, December 6, 1994.

22. John Holusha, "First to College, Then the Mill," *The New York Times*, August 22, 1995, and Stanley Aronowitz and William DiFazio, *The Jobless Future* (Minneapolis, Minnesota: University of Minnesota Press, 1994), pp. 305–306.

23. Paul Kennedy, *Preparing for the Twenty-First Century* (New York: Random House, 1993), p. 85, and *Business Week*, "Custom-Made, Direct From the Plant," January 24, 1995, p. 159.

24. John Holusha, "Industrial Robots Make the Grade," *The New York Times*, September 7, 1994.

25. Paul Kennedy, *Preparing for the Twenty-First Century*, pp. 86–88.

26. Paul Kennedy, *Preparing for the Twenty-First Century*, p. 88, and Lester Thurow, *Head to Head: The Coming Economic Battle Among Japan, Europe, and America* (New York: Warner Books, 1992), p. 139.

27. Council of Economic Advisors, *Economic Report of the President*, 1994, p. 59, and Jaclyn Fierman, "What Happened to the Jobs?" *Fortune*, July 12, 1993, p. 40.

28. *Business Week*, "Custom-Made, Direct From the Plant," p. 158.

29. G. Pascal Zachary, "Service Productivity Is Rising Fast—and So Is the Fear of Lost Jobs"; Aaron Bernstein, "Who Says Job Anxiety Is Easing?" *Business Week*, April 7, 1997, p. 38, and Sana Siwolop, "Vending-Machine Technology Pushes Electronics Frontier," *The New York Times*, July 17, 1994.

30. Steve Rattner, "If Productivity Is Rising, Why Are Jobs Paying Less?" *NYT Magazine*, September 19, 1993, p. 97, and G. Pascal Zachary, "Service Productivity Is Rising Fast—and So Is the Fear of Lost Jobs."

31. Doron P. Levin, "Compaq Storms the PC Heights From Its Factory Floor," *The New York Times*, November 13, 1994.

32. Philip Harvey, *Securing the Right to Employment* (Princeton, New Jersey: Princeton University Press, 1989), p. 75.

33. Shoshana Zuboff, *The Age of the Smart Machine* (New York: Basic Books, 1988), cited in Michael Harrington, *Socialism Past and Future*, p. 193.

34. *Business Week*, "The New World of Work," Rethinking Work, Special Issue, October 17, 1994, p. 76.

35. See Rob Buchanan, "Brave New Work," *Details*, (13) 9: 94–99, 141, February, 1995, and Thomas R. King, "How a Hot Ad Agency, Undone By Arrogance, Lost Its Independence," *The Wall Street Journal*, April 17, 1995. Chiat-Day represents Nissan, but after losing the American Express account in 1992 and the Reebok account in 1993, it was sold to the Omnicom Group in 1995.

36. Rob Buchanan, "Brave New Work," p. 97 for the quotation, and p. 99 for "Chiat/Day and Night."

37. "Can You Afford a Paperless Office?" *International Spectrum*, May/June, 1993, pp. 16–17; *Business Week*, "The Technology Payoff," June 14, 1993, p. 60; and "Advances in Networking and Software Push Firms Closer to a Paperless Office," *The Wall Street Journal*, August 5, 1993, all as cited in Jeremy Rifkin, *The End of Work* (New York: Jeremy Tarcher/G.P. Putnam, 1995), p. 147.

38. United States General Accounting Office, *Management Reforms: Examples of Public and Private Innovations to Improve Service Delivery* (Washington, D.C.: Government Printing Office, 1994), p. 37.

39. Ronald Smothers, "Slopping the Hogs, the Assembly-Line Way," *The New York Times,* January 30, 1995.

40. Michael Williams, "Some Plants Tear Out Long Assembly Lines, Switch to Craft Work," *The Wall Street Journal,* October 24, 1994.

41. See *Business Week,* "Custom-Made, Direct From the Plant," p. 158; B. Joseph Pine, Bart Victor, and Andrew C. Boynton, "Making Mass Customization Work," *Harvard Business Review,* September/October, 1993, pp. 116–118; and Michael Piore and Charles Sabel, *The Second Industrial Divide* (New York: Basic Books, 1984), p. 17.

42. Glenn Rifkin, "Digital Blue Jeans Pour Data and Legs into Customized Fit," *The New York Times,* November 8, 1994; *Business Week,* "Custom-Made, Direct From the Plant," p. 158; and John Holusha, "Producing Custom-Made Clothes for the Masses," *The New York Times,* February 19, 1996. For a discussion of mass customization, see B. Joseph Pine, *Mass Customization: The New Frontier in Business Competition* (Cambridge, Mass: Harvard University Press, 1992).

43. Patrick Dubarle, "The Coalescence of Technology," *OECD Observer* 185: 4–8, December/January, 1993/1994.

44. Steven J. Davis, John C. Haltiwanger, and Scott Schuh, *Gross Job Flows in U.S. Manufacturing,* chapter 3, p. 7. The rate of job loss was 2.7 percent per year for plants in the top plant wage quintile, and 1.3 percent per year for plants in the second highest quintile. Although plants at the bottom contracted by almost 1 percent per year, plants in the middle quintiles were relatively stable. The study includes data from an early period—1973 to 1988, but shows relatively little change from the 1970s to the 1980s.

45. Council of Economic Advisors, *Economic Report of the President,* 1994, p. 114, and the Congressional Budget Office, *Displaced Workers: Trends in the 1980s and Implications for the Future* (Washington, D.C., Congress of the United States, 1993), p. 6.

46. Tony Horwitz, "Jobless Managers Proliferate in Suburbs, Causing Subtle Malaise," *The Wall Street Journal,* September 20, 1993; K. S. Cameron, S. J. Freeman, and A. K. Mishra, "Best Practices in White-Collar Downsizing: Managing Contradiction," *Academy of Management Executive* 5: 57–73, 1991, as cited in Kenneth De Meuse, Paul A. Vanderheiden, and Thomas J. Bergmann, "Announced Layoffs: Their Effect on Corporate Financial Performance," *Human Resource Management* 33 (4): 509–530, Winter, 1994; Louis Uchitelle, "The Humbling of the Harvard Man," *The New York Times,* March 6, 1994; and Julie Amparano Lopez, "Many Executives Are Now Being Discharged With Stunning Speed," *The Wall Street Journal,* March 4, 1994.

47. Louis Uchitelle, "Job Extinction Evolving Into a Fact of Life in U.S.," *The New York Times,* March 22, 1994.

48. Claudia H. Deutsch, "Kodak to Lay Off 10,000 Employees in a 10% Cutback," *The New York Times,* November 12, 1997; The Associated Press, "Retiring Boss Escaped Levi Belt-Tightening," *Newsday,* November 13, 1997; Seth Schiesel, "AT&T Maps Its Battle Plan for Escalating Phone Wars," *The New York Times,* January 27, 1998, and Barnaby J. Feder, "Motorola Says It Will Cut 15,000 Jobs," *The New York Times,* June 5, 1998.

49. For an overview, see Art Burdros, "The New Capitalism and Organizational Rationality: The Adoption of Downsizing Programs—1979–1994," *Social Forces* 76 (1): 229–249, September, 1997, as well as Kenneth P. De Meuse, Thomas J. Bergmann, and Paul A. Vanderheiden, "Corporate Downsizing: Separating Myth from Fact," *Journal of Management Inquiry* 6 (2): 168–176, June, 1997.

50. Tony Horwitz, "Jobless Managers Proliferate in Suburbs, Causing Subtle Malaise"; Joseph Berger, "The Pain of Layoffs for Ex-Senior I.B.M. Workers," *The New York Times,* December 22, 1993; and Daniel Rubin, "The Passing of a Way of Work," *The Philadelphia Inquirer,* May 2, 1993.

51. Kenneth De Meuse, Paul A. Vanderheiden, and Thomas J. Bergmann, "Announced Layoffs: Their Effect on Corporate Financial Performance," especially Table 1, pp. 513–514, summarizing the arguments for and against downsizing.

52. Eileen Appelbaum and Rosemary Batt, *The New American Workplace*, p. 23.

53. The data are from a *New York Times* poll. See N. R. Kleinfield, "The Company as Family, No More," *The New York Times*, March 4, 1996.

54. For a similar conclusion, based on a review of downsizing by the *Fortune* 100 between 1977 and 1993, see Nitin Nohria and Geoffry Love, *Adaptive or Disruptive: When Does Downsizing Pay for Large Industrial Corporations?* (Cambridge, Massachusetts: Harvard Business School Division of Research, 1996).

55. William Neikirk of the *The Chicago Sun-Times*, as quoted in *In These Times*, Editorial, "Clinton's Modest Step Toward A New America," March 8, 1993.

56. Steven Greenhouse, "Equal Work, Less Equal Perks," *The New York Times*, March 30, 1998, and Lawrence Mishel, Jared Bernstein, and John Schmitt, *The State of Working America, 1998–99*, pp. 247–248 for an analysis of involuntary employment among part-timers.

57. Richard S. Belous, *The Contingent Economy: The Growth of the Temporary, Part-Time, and Subcontracted Work Force* (Washington, D.C.: National Planning Association, 1989); Polly Callaghan and Heidi Hartman, *Contingent Work: A Chart Book on Part-Time and Temporary Employment* (Washington, D.C.: Economic Policy Institute, 1991), p. 5; Council of Economic Advisors, *Economic Report of the President*, 1994, p. 123; and U.S. Department of Labor, Bureau of Labor Statistics, *Contingent and Alternative Employment Arrangements*, August, 1995. For a study that places the total of all nonstandard work arrangements at 29.4 percent, see Arne L. Kalleberg, Edith Rasell, Naomi Cassirer, Barbara F. Reskin, Ken Hudson, David Webster, Eileen Appelbaum, and Robert M. Spalter-Roth, *Nonstandard Work, Substandard Jobs* (Washington, D.C.: Economic Policy Institute and the Women's Research & Education Institute, 1997).

58. Janet C. Gornick and Jerry Jacobs, *A Cross-National Analysis of the Wages of Part-Time Workers: Evidence From the United States, United Kingdom, Canada, and Australia* Luxembourg Income Study, Syracuse University, The Maxwell School, June, 1994, pp. 9–10, and Chris Tilly, "Short Hours, Short Shrift: The Causes and Consequences of Part-Time Employment," in Virginia duRivage, ed., *New Policies for the Part-Time and Contingent Work Force* (Armonk, New York: M.E. Sharpe, 1992), p. 22.

59. See Steven Greenhouse, "Equal Work, Less-Equal Perks," *The New York Times*, March 30, 1998; Barnaby J. Feder, "Bigger Roles for Suppliers of Temporary Workers," *The New York Times*, April 1, 1995, as well as Louis Uchitelle and N. R. Kleinfield, "On the Battlefields of Business, Millions of Casualities," *The New York Times*, March 3, 1996.

Compared to other English-speaking countries, the rapid growth of part-time workers yields some conflicting results. In part, due to the scarcity of child care, the rate of part-time employment among women in the United States—at 28 percent—is lower than the United Kingdom (54 percent), Australia (42 percent), or Canada (29 percent). But controlling for age, occupation, education, and industry, women in the United States did have the highest differential between part and full-time workers. The wage differential for men was not as severe, with a still larger differential in Australia. At about 10 percent, however, more men worked part-time here than in the other countries. For the most part, these differentials reflect the extent of unionization within these countries, government policies toward the presence of women in the workforce, and government willingness to establish wages and regulate mandatatory overtime. See Janet C. Gornick and Jerry Jacobs, *A Cross-National Analysis of the Wages of Part-Time Workers*.

60. Virginia duRivage, "New Policies for the Part-Time and Contingent Work Force," in *New Policies for the Part-Time and Contingent Work Force*, pp. 89–121.

61. Stanley Aronowitz and William DiFazio, *The Jobless Future*, p. 322, and Chinhui Juhn, Kevin Murphy, and Robert H. Topel, "Why Has the Natural Rate of Unemployment Increased Over Time," *Brooking Papers on Economic Activity* 2: 78, 1991.

62. See John Pawasarat, *Survey of Job Openings in the Milwaukee Metropolitan Area, Week of May 24, 1993*, Employment and Training Institute and Social Science Research Facility, University of Wisconsin at Milwaukee, 1993.

63. Council of Economic Advisors, *Economic Report of the President*, 1997, Table B-41, p. 347, and William Julius Wilson, *The Truly Disadvantaged* (Chicago: University of Chicago Press, 1987).

64. See, for example, James H. Johnson, Jr. and Mevin L. Oliver, "Structural Changes in the U.S. Economy and Black Male Joblessness," in George Peterson and Wayne Vroman, eds., *Urban Labor Markets and Job Opportunity* (Washington: D.C.: The Urban Institutte, 1992), pp. 113–147; Roberto M. Fernandez, "Demand-Side and Supply-Side Explanations of Black Male Joblessness," in George Peterson and Wayne Vroman, eds., *Urban Labor Markets and Job Opportunity*, pp. 155–159; and, for overviews, William Julius Wilson, *When Work Disappears* (New York: Alfred A. Knopf, 1996), as well as Doug S. Massey and Nancy A. Denton, *American Apartheid: Segregation and the Making of the Underclass* (Cambridge, Massachusetts: Harvard University Press, 1993).

65. Sam Roberts, "Black Women Graduates Outpace Male Counterparts," *The New York Times*, October 31, 1994.

66. Richard B. Freeman, "Employment and Earnings of Disadvantaged Young Men in a Labor Shortage Economy," in Christopher Jencks and Paul E. Peterson, eds., *The Urban Underclass* (Washington, D.C., The Brookings Institution, 1991), pp. 103–121.

67. Council of Economic Advisors, *Economic Report of the President*, 1997, p. 347.

Notes to Chapter 4

1. Richard McIntyre, *The Field of Dreams and Labor Market Outcomes in the 1990s*, Paper Presented to the Industrial Relations Research Association, Department of Economics and Labor Research Center, January 5, 1994, p. 5.

2. See David Wessel, "Strong Growth Brings Jobs to Cedar Rapids, But Many Pay Poorly," *The Wall Street Journal*, June 24, 1994; Robert D. Hershey, Jr., "Where Job Hunters Hit the Jackpot," *The New York Times*, June 30, 1994; and Peter T. Kilborn, "A City Built on $4.25 an Hour," *The New York Times*, February 12, 1995.

3. Tony Horwitz, "These Six Growth Jobs Are Dull, Dead-End, Sometimes Dangerous," *The Wall Street Journal*, December 1, 1994. Horowitz won a Pulitzer Prize for this article.

4. Richard McIntyre, *The Field of Dreams and Labor Market Outcomes in the 1990s*, p. 2.

5. For a typical example of this position, see Donald Deere, Kevin M. Murphy, and Finis Welch, "Sense and Nonsense on the Minimum Wage," *Regulation* 1: 47–56, 1994. For a summary and analysis of this view, see Edward Nell, *Prosperity and Public Spending: Transformational Growth and the Role of Government* (London: Unwin Hyman, 1988), pp. 148–149.

6. See, for example, Samuel Bowles, David Gordon, and Thomas Weisskopf, *After the Wasteland: A Democratic Economics for the Year 2000* (Armonk, New York, M.E. Sharpe, 1990), p. 209.

7. Lawrence Katz, Gary Loveman, and David G. Blanchflower, *A Comparison of the Changes in the Structure of Wages in Four OECD Countries* (Cambridge, Massachusetts: National Bureau of Economic Research, 1993), p. 3, and Dana Milbank, "Unlike the Rest of Europe, Britain Is Creating Jobs, But They Pay Poorly," *The Wall Street Journal*, March 28, 1994.

8. Martin Neil Baily, Gary Burtless, and Robert E. Litan, *Growth with Equity: Economic Policymaking for the Next Century* (Washington, D.C., The Brookings Institution, 1993), p. 61; Lawrence Mishel and Jared Bernstein, *The State of Working America, 1994–95* (Armonk, New York: M.E. Sharpe, 1994), p. 110; Lawrence Mishel, "Skill Requirements and the Work Force," in George Peterson and Wayne Vroman, eds., *Urban Labor Markets and Job Opportunity* (Washington, D.C.: The Urban Institute, 1992), p. 71; and Jeffrey Faux, "Clinton's Industrial Policy," *Dissent* (40) 4: 467–474, Fall, 1993, especially p. 470.

9. Lawrence Katz and Kevin Murphy, "Changes in Relative Wages, 1963–1987: Supply and Demand Factors," *Quarterly Journal of Economics* (107): 35–78, February, 1992, and Kevin M. Murphy and Finis Welch, "Industrial Change and the Rising Importance of Skill," in Sheldon Danziger and Peter Gottschalk, eds., *Uneven Tides: Rising Inequality in America* (New York: Russell Sage Foundation, 1994), pp. 101–132.

10. Chinhui Juhn, Kevin Murphy, Brooks Pierce, "Wage Inequality and the Rise in Returns to Skill," *Journal of Political Economy* 101 (3): 410–442, 1993, and Lawrence Mishel,

Jared Bernstein, and John Schmitt, *The State of Working America, 1998–99* (Ithaca, New York: Cornell University Press, 1999), Table 3.18, p. 156.

11. Arnold H. Packer and John G. Wirt, "Changing Skills in the U.S. Work Force: Trends of Supply and Demand," in George Peterson and Wayne Vroman, eds., *Urban Labor Markets and Job Opportunity* (Washington, D.C.: The Urban Institute, 1992), pp. 31–65.

12. George E. Peterson and Wayne Vroman, "Urban Labor Markets and Economic Opportunity," in George E. Peterson and Wayne Vroman, eds., *Urban Labor Markets and Job Opportunity*, p. 9; John Bound and George Johnson, "Changes in the Structure of Wages in the 1980s," *American Economic Review*, 82(3): 371–392, June, 1992; and G. Pascal Zachary, "High-Tech Explains Widening Wage Gaps," *The Wall Street Journal*, April 22, 1996.

13. Lawrence Mishel, Jared Bernstein, and John Schmitt, *The State of Working America, 1998–99*, p. 169.

14. The best critiques of the skills mismatch thesis are Lawrence Mishel and Jared Bernstein, *The State of Working America, 1994–95*, pp. 16–18, and David Gordon, *Fat and Mean* (New York: Free Press, 1996), pp. 178–187. This passage blends them both.

15. William Greider, *Who Will Tell the People?* (New York, Touchstone Books, 1992), pp. 344–345, and Lawrence Mishel and Ruy A. Teixeira, *The Myth of the Coming Labor Shortage* (Washington, D.C.: Economic Policy Institute, 1991), pp. 26–27.

16. Council of Economic Advisors, *Economic Report of the President* 1997 (Washington, D.C.: Government Printing Office, 1997), p. 167, and Peter Gottschalk, *Policy Changes and Growing Earnings Inequality in Seven Industrialized Countries*, Luxembourg Income Study, Syracuse University, The Maxwell School, February, 1994, p. 3. Contrary to economic convention, the addition of fringe benefits actually makes the differential larger. Between 1982 and 1996, the ratio of compensation (wages and benefits) for workers at the tenth and ninetieth percentile expanded from 4.56 ($35.15 vs. $7.72) to 5.43 ($36.89 vs.$6.65). See Peter Passell, "Benefits Dwindled Along With Wages for the Unskilled," *The New York Times*, June 14, 1998.

17. Lawrence Mishel, Jared Bernstein, and John Schmitt, *The State of Working America, 1998–99*, pp. 157–158.

18. Council of Economic Advisors, *Economic Report of the President, 1994* (Washington, D.C.: Government Printing Office, 1994), p. 108.

19. Marilyn Gittell and Sally Covington, *Higher Education in JOBS: An Option or An Opportunity? A Comparison of Nine States* (New York City: Howard Samuels State Management and Policy Center, City University of New York, 1993), p. 8, and Inge O'Connor, *A Cross-National Comparison of Education and Earnings*, Luxembourg Income Study, Syracuse University, The Maxwell School, July, 1994, pp. 3–4.

20. George T. Silvestri, "Occupational Employment Projections to 2006," *Monthly Labor Review* 120 (11): 58–83, November, 1997, especially p. 82; Wendy Bounds, "Graduates Learn Diplomas Aren't Tickets to Success," *The Wall Street Journal*, October 10, 1994.

21. David E. Rosenbaum, "The Minimum Wage: A Portrait," *The New York Times*, April 19, 1996.

22. David E. Rosenbaum, "The Minimum Wage: A Portrait," and Isaac Shapiro, *Four Years and Still Falling: The Decline in the Value of the Minimum Wage* (Washington, D.C.: Center on Budget and Policy Priorities, 1995), pp. 3–4.

23. David Card and Alan Krueger, *Myth and Measurement: The New Economics of the Minimum Wage* (Princeton, New Jersey: Princeton University Press, 1995), p. 11.

24. See David Card and Alan Krueger, *Myth and Measurement: The New Economics of the Minimum Wage*, especially the analysis of New Jersey in chapter 2, pp. 20–77.

25. Donald Deere, Kevin Murphy, and Finis Welch, "Sense and Nonsense on the Minimum Wage," p. 48; David Neumark and William Wascher, "Employment Effects of Minimum and Subminimum Wages: Panel Data on State Minimum Wage Laws," *Industrial & Labor Relations Review*, 46 (1): 55–81, October 1992; and Richard B. Berman, "Dog Bites Man: Minimum Wages Hikes Still Hurt," *The Wall Street Journal*, March 29, 1995. For an analysis of the conservative critique, see John Schmitt, "Cooked to Order," *The American Prospect*, 26: 82–85, May–June, 1996.

26. See Isaac Shapiro, *Four Years and Still Falling: The Decline in the Value of the Minimum Wage;* Richard Stevenson, "Clinton Is Reported Set to Propose Rise in the Minimum Wage," *The New York Times,* February 12, 1998; and David Gordon, *Fat and Mean,* pp. 211–219.

27. Isaac Shapiro, *Four Years and Still Falling,* pp. 4–5, and Michael Horrigan and Ronald Mincy, "The Minimum Wage and Earnings and Income Inequality," in Sheldon Danziger and Peter Gottschalk, eds., *Uneven Tides,* p. 272.

28. Jared Bernstein, *America's Well-Targeted Raise* (Washington, D.C.: Economic Policy Institute, 1997), Issue Brief No. 118.

29. For a discussion of the growing split among service jobs into high and low wage, see Arnold Packer and John G. Wirt, "Changing Skills in the U.S. Work Force: Trends of Supply and Demand," in George Peterson and Wayne Vroman, eds., *Urban Labor Markets and Job Opportunity,* p. 48. The changes on Wall Street are discussed in Stephanie Strom, "Two-Tier Wall St.," *The New York Times,* June 15, 1995.

30. Susan Denzter, "Secretaries Down the Chute," *U.S. News & World Report,* March 28, 1994, p. 65; George T. Silvestri, "Occupational Employment Projections to 2006," *Monthly Labor Review* 120 (11): 58–83, November, 1997; and Lawrence Mishel, Jared Bernstein, and John Schmitt, *The State of Working America, 1998–99,* p. 129.

31. Robert Reich, *The Work of Nations* (New York: Vintage, 1992), p. 48 supplies the data for the 1950s, between $4000 and $7500, in 1953 dollars. The other data comes from Lawrence Mishel, Jared Bernstein, and John Schmitt, *The State of Working America 1998–99,* p. 6l. The 1969 and 1996 comparisons are based on the percentage of families earning between $25,000 to $75,000 (in 1996 dollars).

32. A number of books have discussed this phenomena. Among the most useful are Katharine S. Newman, *Falling From Grace: The Experience of Downward Mobility in the American Middle Class* (New York: Free Press, 1988), as well as her *Declining Fortunes: The Withering of the American Dream* (New York: Basic Books, 1993), and Barbara Ehrenreich, *Fear of Falling* (New York: Harper, 1989).

33. See Gregory J. Duncan, Timothy M. Smeeding, and Willard Rodgers, "W(h)ither the Middle Class? A Dynamic View," in Dimitri B. Papadimitriou and Edward N. Wolff, eds., *Poverty and Prosperity in the USA in the Late Twentieth Century* (New York: Macmillan, 1995), pp. 240–271. In the 1980–1991 period, 27.1 percent of the top 10 percent slid to middle class, while 30.4 percent of the poor became middle class. Movement downward out of the affluent group therefore declined from 31.1 percent (in 1967–1979) to 27.1 percent (1980–1991), at the same time that movement upward out of the poorest group declined from 35.5 (1967–1979) to 30.4 percent (1980–1991).

Notes to Chapter 5

1. U.S. Department of Education, Office of Educational Research and Improvement, *National Excellence: A Case for Developing America's Talent* (Washington, D.C.: Government Printing Office, 1993), p. 7, and National Education Goals Panel, *National Education Goals Report: Building a Nation of Learners 1995* (Washington, D.C.: Government Printing Office, 1995), p. 22. For an extended discussion of Chicago school reform and the effort to improve student scores, see Michael B. Katz, *Improving Poor People* (Princeton, New Jersey: Princeton University Press, 1995), pp. 112–143.

2. Progress is better in math and science than in reading, but in the 1990s, the Scholastic Aptitude Test (SAT), American College Test (ACT), and the National Assessment of Educational Progress (NAEP) have all reported a slight upward trend in average scores. See Peter Applebome, "Students' Test Scores Show Slow But Steady Gains at the Nation's Schools," *The New York Times,* September 3, 1997.

3. Ethan Bronner, "U.S. Trails the World in Science and Math," *The New York Times,* February 25, 1998, and U.S. Department of Education, *National Excellence: A Case for Developing America's Talent,* 1993, p. 9.

4. U.S. General Accounting Office, *School Facilities: Conditions of America's Schools* (Washington, D.C.: Government Printing Office, 1995).

5. See The National Center on the Educational Quality of the Work Force, *The Other Shoe: Education's Contribution to the Productivity of Establishments*, The University of Pennsylvania, 1995.

6. Cited in Samuel Bowles and Herbert Gintis, *Schooling in Capitalist America* (New York: Basic Books, 1976), p. 162.

7. James W. Fraser, "Agents of Democracy: Urban Elementary Teachers and the Conditions of Teaching," in Donald Warren, ed., *American Teachers: Histories of a Profession at Work* (New York: Macmillan, 1989, p. 128), cited in Michael Apple, *Official Knowledge: Democratic Education in a Conservative Age* (New York: Routledge, 1993), p. 54.

8. See Linda J. Sax, Alexander W. Astin, William S. Korn, and Katharine Mahoney, *The American Freshman: National Norms for Fall, 1997* (Los Angeles, California: The Higher Education Research Institute at the University of California at Los Angeles, 1997).

9. Judith Rényi, *Going Public: Schooling for a Diverse Democracy* (New York: The New Press, 1993), p. 31.

10. The standard work on the issue of suburbanization is Kenneth T. Jackson, *Crabgrass Frontier: The Suburbanization of the United States* (New York: Oxford University Press, 1985).

11. Harvey Kantor and Barbara Brenzel, "Urban Education and the 'Truly Disadvantaged': The Historical Roots of the Contemporary Crisis, 1945–1990," in Michael Katz, ed., *The "Underclass" Debate: Views from History* (Princeton, New Jersey: Princeton University Press, 1993), pp. 369–70 and 376.

12. Gary Orfield, Mark D. Bachmeier, David James, and Tamela Eitle, *Deepening Segregation in American Public Schools* (Cambridge, Massachusetts: Harvard Project on School Desegregation, 1997), p. 2.

13. See Margaret Weir, "Urban Poverty and Defensive Localism," *Dissent*, (41) 3: 337–342, Summer, 1994.

14. Jonathan Kozol, *Savage Inequalities* (New York: Harper Perennial, 1992), p. 55.

15. National Education Goals Panel, *National Education Goals Report: Building a Nation of Learners (1995)*, revised addendum to page 34.

16. Jonathan Kozol, *Savage Inequalities*, pp. 207–209.

17. The summary of legal cases is drawn from James G. Ward, "Why Is School Finance Equity Such An Elusive Goal?" *Rethinking Schools* (10) 3: 6–7, 25, 27; the 1997 New Jersey decision is described in Abby Goodnough, "New Jersey's School Financing Is Again Held Unconstitutional," *The New York Times*, May 15, 1997, and Jennifer Preston, "Plan By Whitman on Urban Schools Backed By Court," *The New York Times*, May 22, 1998; and the Kentucky results are reviewed in Peter Galuszka, "Kentucky's Class Act," *Business Week*, April 7, 1997, pp. 90–91 and 94.

18. Carol Ascher and Gary Burnett, *Current Trends and Issues in Urban Education 1993* (New York: Columbia University Teachers College, ERIC Clearinghouse on Urban Education, 1993), p. 26; Carol Ascher, "Efficiency, Equity, and Local Control—School Finance in Texas," Columbia University Teachers College, ERIC Clearinghouse on Urban Education, No. 88, 1993; and Associated Press, "Court Upholds Texas Plan on Education," *The New York Times*, February 5, 1995.

19. William Celis 3d, "Michigan Votes for Revolution In Financing Its Public Schools," *The New York Times*, March 17, 1994, and "In Michigan, Uncertainty and Unhappiness Over New Method to Finance the Schools," *The New York Times*, January 18, 1995.

20. Cheryl Rivers, "The Equal Education Opportunity Act Helps Solve a Long-standing Problem," *Vermont Department of Education*, 1997.

21. Organization for Economic Cooperation and Development, *OECD in Figures: 1997* (Paris: OECD), pp. 52–53, and Gerald Bracey, "Debunking the Myth That the U.S. Spends More on Schools," *Rethinking Schools* 9 (4): 7, Summer, 1995.

22. United States Congressional Budget Office, *The Federal Role in Improving Elementary and Secondary Education* (Washington, D.C.: Government Printing Office, May, 1993), p. xii.

23. United States Congressional Budget Office, *The Federal Role in Improving Elementary and Secondary Education*, May, 1993, p. xiii, and Educational Issues Department, American Federation of Teachers, "Making Standards Good," *American Educator* 18 (3): 15 and 20–27, Fall, 1994.

24. National Education Goals Panel, *The National Education Goals Report: Building a Nation of Learners 1995*, pp. 22–23. The 1996 report showed a continuation of these trends. See National Education Goals Panel, *The National Education Goals Report: Building a Nation of Learners 1996* (Washington, D.C.: Government Printing Office, 1996).

25. United States Congressional Budget Office, *The Federal Role in Improving Elementary and Secondary Education*, p. 2, and William Taylor, "The New Title 1: Levers for Educational Change," *Poverty & Race Research Action Council* 4 (1): 3–4, January/February, 1995. In 1981, Title 1 was renamed Chapter I of the Educational Consolidation and Improvement Act.

26. Carol Ascher and Gary Burnett, *Current Trends and Issues in Urban Education, 1993*, pp. 29–30, and Richard J. Murnane, "Education and the Well-Being of the Next Generation," in Sheldon H. Danziger, Gary D. Sandefur, and Daniel H. Weinberg, eds., *Confronting Poverty: Prescriptions for Change* (Cambridge, Massachusetts: Harvard University Press, 1994), pp. 289–307.

27. Cited in Anne Wheelock, *Crossing the Tracks* (New York: The New Press, 1992), p. 9.

28. See Lester Thurow, *Head to Head: The Coming Economic Battle Among Japan, Europe, and America* (New York: Warner Books, 1992), pp. 54–55; William T. Grant Foundation Commission on Work, Family, and Citizenship, *The Forgotten Half: Non-College Youth in America* (Washington, D.C.: William T. Grant Foundation, 1988); and Jobs for the Future, *Essential Elements of Youth Apprenticeship Programs* (Cambridge, Mass: Jobs for the Future, 1991). For a comparative overview of the efforts by some other countries to connect education and work, see Abrar Hasan and Albert Tuijnman, "Linking Education and Work," *OECD Observer*, 199: 14–18, April–May, 1996.

29. U.S. General Accounting Office, *Transition from School to Work: States are Developing New Strategies to Prepare Students for Jobs* (Washington, D.C.: Government Printing Office, 1993), p. 2, and William Celis 3d, "Beyond Auto Shop: An Experiment in High School Training," *The New York Times*, March 9, 1994; and David Levine, "Souls or Dollars? How Wisconsin's Voc-Ed Program Will Change Our Schools," *Rethinking Schools* 7 (2): 1, 14–16, Winter, 1992–1993.

30. Center for Law and Education, "New Federal Law Brings Academics and Community Involvement to Vocational Education," *Newsnotes* 43: 2–5, December, 1991.

31. Lauren Jacobs, *The School-to-Work Opportunity Act of 1994* (Washington, D.C.: Center for Law and Education, 1995), pp. 1–4, and Michael Wines, "Senate Votes New Job-Training Program," *The New York Times*, April 23, 1994.

32. See Paul Osterman, *Employment Futures: Reorganization, Dislocation, and Public Policy* (New York: Oxford University Press, 1988); Alan Weisberg, "What Research Has To Say About Vocational Education and the High Schools," *Phi Delta Kappan* 64: 355–359, January, 1983; and Harvey Kantor and David Tyack, eds., *Work, Youth and Schooling: Historical Perspectives on Vocationalism in American Education* (Stanford, California: Stanford University Press, 1988).

33. For an excellent critique of the whole school-to-work strategy, see Harvey Kantor, "The Hollow Promise of Youth Apprenticeship," *Rethinking Schools* 8 (1): 1, 4–5, 24–27.

34. See, for example, John Chubb and Terry Moe, *Politics, Markets, and America's Schools* (Washington, D.C.: Brookings Institute, 1990). For the best critiques, see Jeffrey R. Henig, *Rethinking School Choice: Limits of the Market Metaphor* (Princeton: Princeton University Press, 1994), and Bruce Fuller and Richard F. Elmore with Gary Orfield, *Who Choses? Who Loses?: Culture, Institutions, and the Unequal Effects of School Choice* (New York: Teachers College Press, 1996). The Henig volume is particularly outstanding.

35. For an estimate of these effects, see Paul Teske, Mark Schneider, Melissa Marschall, and Christine Roch, *Evaluating the Effects of Public School Choice in District 4*, Department of Political Science, State University of New York at Stony Brook, Stony Brook, New York, 1997.

36. For a discussion of the East Harlem experiment from this perspective, see Jonathan Kozol, *Savage Inequalities*, pp. 62–63, and Donald Hirsch, "Schools: A Matter of Choice," *OECD Observer* 187: 12–15, April–May, 1994; for a much rosier view of the same issue, see David Osborne and Ted Gaebler, *Reinventing Government: How The Entrepreneurial Spirit Is Transforming the Public Sector* (New York, Plume, 1993), pp. 5–8.

37. The Carnegie Foundation, *School Choice: A Special Report* (Princeton, New Jersey: The Carnegie Foundation, 1992).

38. Bruce Fuller, *Who Gains, Who Loses From School Choice: A Research Summary*, National Conference of State Legislatures, 1995, p. 3.

39. Cited in David Osborne and Ted Gaebler, *Reinventing Government*, p. 94.

40. See Linda Darling-Hammond and Carol Ascher, *Creating Accountability in Big City School Systems* (New York: ERIC Clearinghouse on Urban Education, Columbia University Teachers College, 1991), p. 8; Derek Bok, *The Cost of Talent* (New York: Free Press, 1993), pp. 196–198; Charles Manski, "Systemic Educational Reform and Social Mobility: The School Choice Controversy," in Sheldon K. Danziger, Gary E. Sandefur, and Daniel Weinberg, eds., *Confronting Poverty*, pp. 308–329; and Gary Orfield, "Urban Schooling and the Perpetuation of Job Inequality in Metropolitan Chicago," in George Peterson and Wayne Vroman, eds., *Urban Labor Markets and Job Opportunity* (Washington, D.C.: The Urban Institute, 1992), pp. 161–199.

41. Interview with Linda Darling-Hammond, in "Choice Is a Smokescreen," *False Choices* (Milwaukee, Wisconsin: Rethinking Schools, 1992), p. 10.

42. "Fact Sheet on Vouchers: Argument and Evidence," *American Educator* 19 (3): 28, 31–33, Fall, 1995.

43. Barbara Miner, "What Can We Learn From Milwaukee's Voucher Program," in Robert Lowe and Barbara Miner, eds., *Selling Out Our Schools: Vouchers, Markets, and the Future of Public Education* (Milwaukee, Wisconsin: Rethinking Schools, 1996), pp. 30–31, and Kimberly J. McLarin, "Support for New Jersey School Vouchers Falters," *The New York Times*, December 24, 1994. In 1997, a State Supreme Court declared the Wisconsin voucher plan to be unconstitutional. See the Associated Press, "Wisconsin School-Voucher Plan Is Struck Down," *The New York Times*, Janaury 16, 1997.

44. Bob Davis, "Dueling Professors Have Milwaukee Dazed Over School Vouchers," *The Wall Street Journal*, October 11, 1996. Peterson has also coauthored a study of the Cleveland voucher system. The study, which found higher levels of parental satisfaction among a low-income minority population, most of whom attended Catholic schools, lasted only one year and was not a completely randomized experiment. See Jay P. Green, William G. Howell, and Paul E. Peterson, *An Evaluation of the Cleveland Scholarship Program* (Cambridge, Massachusetts: Harvard University Taubman Center for State and Local Government and the Center for American Political Studies, 1997).

45. Angela Dale and Dave DeSchryver, eds., *The Charter School Workbook* (Washington, D.C.: The Center for Education Reform, 1997), p. 11.

46. "Charter Schools: Potentials and Pitfalls: An Interview with Ann Bastian," in *Selling Out Our Schools*, pp. 45–49, and *The New York Times*, "Unions Consider Charter Schools of Their Own," September 22, 1996.

47. The quotation comes from *The New York Times*, "Unions Consider Charter Schools of Their Own." A report on the typical problems that a charter school faces appears in Peter Applebome, "Start of Charter School Shows Flaws in Concept," *The New York Times*, March 6, 1996. For other evaluations, see the U.S. General Accounting Office, *Charter Schools: New Model for Public School Provides Opportunities and Challenges* (Washington, D.C.: Government Printing Office, 1995), and Charles E. Finn and Diane Ravitch, *Education Reform 1994–1995* (Indianapolis: Hudson Institute, 1995).

48. These standards are adapted from those set forth in "Charter Schools: Potentials and Pitfalls, An Interview with Ann Bastian," in *Selling Out Our Schools*, pp. 46–47. See also Mark Walsh, "Declarations of Independence: The nation's 234 charter schools go their own way in striving to re-invigorate education," *Education Week*, November 29, 1995, pp. 3–7.

49. Peter Applebome, "Lure of the Education Market Remains Strong for Business," *The New York Times*, January 31, 1996.

50. For an overview of these failures, see Peter Schrag, "'F' Is for Fizzle: The Faltering School Privatization Movement," *The American Prospect* 26: 67–71, May–June 1996.

51. Carol Ascher, Norm Fruchter, and Robert Berne, *Hard Lessons: Public Schools and Privatization* (New York: The Twentieth Century Fund, 1996), pp. 44–59.

52. See George Judson, "Improved Schools at a Profit: Is a Private Effort Working?" *The New York Times*, November 14, 1994; William Celis 3d, "Hartford Seeking a Company to Run Its Public Schools," *The New York Times*, April 19, 1994; American Federation of Teachers, *How Private Managers Make Money in Public Schools: Update on the EAI Experiment in Baltimore* (Washington, D.C.: AFT, September, 1995), p. ii; Lois Williams and Lawrence Leak, *The UMBC Evaluation of the Tesseract Program in Baltimore City* (Baltimore, Maryland: Center for Educational Research, University of Maryland, 1995), p. 116; and George Judson, "Baltimore Ends Education Experiment," *The New York Times*, November 23, 1995.

53. George Judson, "Private Business, Public Schools: Why Hartford Experiment Failed," *The New York Times*, March 11, 1996.

54. See George Judson, "Hartford Plans to End the Private Management of Its Public Schools," *The New York Times*, January 24, 1996; Gary Putka and Steve Stecklow, "Do For-Profit Schools Work? They Seem to For One Entrepreneur," *The Wall Street Journal*, June 8, 1994; and Carol Ascher, Norm Fruchter, and Robert Berne, *Hard Lessons*, p. 78.

55. George Judson, "Private Business, Public Schools: Why Hartford Experiment Failed."

56. Cited in Barbara Miner, "For-Profit Firms Fail to Deliver," p.60.

57. Mark Walsh, "Brokers Pitch Education as a Hot Investment," *Education Week*, February 21, 1996, as cited in Carol Ascher, Norm Fruchter, and Robert Berne, *Hard Lessons*, p. 20.

58. William H. Honan, "Scholars Attack Public School TV Program," *The New York Times*, January 22, 1997, and Michael Apple, *Official Knowledge: Democratic Education in a Conservative Age* (New York: Routledge, 1993), pp. 94–101. The quotation comes from p. 94.

59. Chris Whittle and Mark Crispin Miller, "Debate: It's Not Just the Commercials," *MediaCulture*, July/August, 1993. The quotation appears on p. 3.

60. Stuart Elliott, "Whittle Communications' Fall Is Dissected," *The New York Times*, October 24, 1994. See also Sara Mosle, "The Wrong Box," *The New Yorker*, June 19, 1995, pp. 6–7.

61. Peter Passell, "Public Schools for Profit: Phase 2: The Sales Pitch," *The New York Times*, January 19, 1994, and Peter Applebome, "Class Notes: The Reason Behind For-Profit Management's Appeal Are Clear? But Will It Really Work?" *The New York Times*, November 2, 1994.

62. Peter Applebome, "Grading For-Profit Schools: So Far, So Good," *The New York Times*, June 26, 1996.

63. Peter Applebome, "For-Profit Education Venture to Expand," *The New York Times*, June 2, 1997, and Peter Applebome, "A Venture on the Brink: Do Education and Profits Mix?" *The New York Times*, October 30, 1994. In 1998, Edison received a $25 million grant from a new foundation established by the owners of the GAP clothing chain, Donald and Doris Fishman. The Fishman's son owns a 4 percent share of Edison, which may partly explain why the grant establishes a new form of charity by giving money to what is still—despite its failure so far—a for-profit enterprise. See Somini Sengupta, "Edison Project Gets Aid To Open New Schools," *The New York Times*, May 27, 1998.

64. Benjamin Barber, "America Skips School: Why We Talk So Much About Education and Do So Little," *Harper's* 287: 39–46, especially p. 44, November, 1993.

65. Benjamin Barber, *An Aristocracy of Everyone* (New York: Oxford University Press, 1994), p. 204.

66. The perspective of a number of authors has converged around the same goal. In addition to Benjamin Barber's previously cited *An Aristocracy of Everyone*, these authors include Amy Gutmann, *Democratic Education* (Princeton: Princeton University Press, 1987); Ann Bastian, Norm Fruchter, Marilyn Gittell, Colin Greer, and Kenneth Haskins, *Choosing Equality:*

The Case for Democratic Schooling (Philadelphia: Temple University Press, 1986); and Michael Apple, *Official Knowledge*.

67. This is the position of Albert Shanker and the American Federation of Teachers, as expressed in their magazine *The American Educator*, as well as of those like E. D. Hirsch, who, in books such as *What Every American Needs to Know* (Boston: Houghton Mifflin, 1988), argue for cultural literacy.

68. Judith Rényi, *Going Public: Schooling for a Diverse Democracy*, p. 238.

69. Peter Schrag, "The New School Wars: How Outcome-Based Education Blew Up," *The American Prospect* (20): 53–62, Winter, 1995, and The Educational Issues Department, American Federation of Teachers, "Making Standards Good," *American Educator*, 18 (3): 15 and 20–27, Fall, 1994.

70. See Sara Mosle, "A City School Experiment That Actually Works," *New York Times Sunday Magazine*, May 28, 1995, pp. 26–32 and 49–52.

71. See Derek Bok, *The Cost of Talent*, p. 180, and The International Association for the Evaluation of Educational Achievement, *Third International Mathematics and Science Study* (Boston College: Chestnut Hill, Massachusetts, 1996).

72. Derek Bok, *The Cost of Talent*, p. 180.

73. Anne Wheelock, *Crossing the Tracks*, pp. 149–190.

74. Deborah Meier, "A Talk To Teachers," *Dissent* 41 (1): 83–84, Winter, 1994.

75. Judith Rényi, *Going Public: Schooling for a Diverse Democracy*, p. 15.

76. Peter Schrag, "The New School Wars: How Outcome-Based Education Blew Up," p. 56.

77. This point is made by Benjamin Barber, *An Aristocracy of Everyone*, p. 200.

78. See Cornell West, *Race Matters* (Boston: Beacon Press, 1993), p. 3 for a discussion of this point, as well as Lawrence W. Levine, *The Opening of the American Mind: Canons, Culture, and History* (Boston: Beacon Press, 1996).

79. Harvey Kantor and Barbara Brenzel, "Urban Education and the 'Truly Disadvantaged': The Historical Roots of the Contemporary Crisis, 1945–1990," in Michael Katz, ed., *The "Underclass" Debate*, pp. 367–402.

80. Norm Fruchter, "Rethinking School Reform," *Social Policy* 20 (1): 16–25, Summer, 1989.

81. See Michael Apple, *Official Knowledge*, p. 41 on this point.

82. See United States Congressional Budget Office, *The Federal Role in Improving Elementary and Secondary Education*, p. 63, and Linda Darling-Hammond and Carol Ascher, *Creating Accountability in Big City School Systems*, p. 14.

83. The number of school districts comes from Alan Altschuler and Christopher Howard, "Local Government and Economic Development in the United States," John F. Kennedy School of Government Conference Report, July, 1991, pp. 40–41. For a description of the Clinton plan, see Alison Mitchell, "Clinton Promotes Education Testing Gingrich Opposes," *The New York Times*, September 9, 1997.

Notes to Chapter 6

1. Philip Harvey, *Securing the Right to Employment* (Princeton, New Jersey: Princeton University Press, 1989), p.15, and the Council of Economic Advisors, *Economic Report of the President* 1997 (Washington, D.C.: Government Printing Office, 1997), p. 346.

2. Philip Harvey, *Securing the Right to Employment*, p. 14.

3. The classic work on this recession is William Greider, *Secrets of the Temple* (New York: Simon and Schuster, 1987).

4. *The Economist*, "The Trouble with Success," March 12, 1994, p. 78.

5. For a description of this pattern of institutional dynamics, see James Morone, *The Democratic Wish: Popular Participation and the Limits of American Government* (New York: Basic Books, 1990).

6. See, for example, Benjamin Ginsberg and Martin Shefter, *Politics by Other Means* (New York: Basic Books, 1990), pp. 164–165, and Kevin Phillips, *Arrogant Capital* (Boston, Massachusetts, Little, Brown, 1994), pp. 115–118. Political scientists also paid a lot of attention to this issue during the bicentennial. Some examples include Committee on the Constitutional System, *A Bicentennial Analysis of the American Political Structure* (Washington, D.C., 1987), and the debate in *Presidential Studies Quarterly,* especially J. L. Sundquist, "Response to the Petracca Bailey Smith Evaluation of the Committeee on the Constitutional System," 20: 533–545, 1990.

7. Margaret Weir, *Politics and Jobs* (Princeton, New Jersey: Princeton University Press, 1992), p. 43.

8. For a discussion of the Full Employment Act of 1946, see Stephen Kemp Bailey, *Congress Makes a Law* (New York: Vintage, 1964). For an analysis of the limitations of the Council of Economic Advisors in the making of employment policy, see Margaret Weir, *Politics and Jobs,* p. 21, and Margaret Weir, Ann Shola Orloff, and Theda Skocpol, "The Future of Social Policy in the United States: Political Constraints and Possibilities," in their book *The Politics of Social Policy in the United States* (Princeton, New Jersey: Princeton University Press, 1988), pp. 424–425.

9. Adam Seitchik and Jeffrey Zornitsky, *From One Job to the Next* (Kalamazoo, Michigan: W.E. Upjohn Institute, 1989), pp. 122–123. After taking control of the House in 1994, the Republicans renamed some House committees. Education and the Workforce is its current name.

10. See Margaret Weir, Ann Shola Orloff, and Theda Skocpol, "The Future of Social Policy in the United States: Political Constraints and Possibilities," p. 431, and Stephen Skowronek, *Building a New American State: The Expansion of National Administrative Capacities, 1877–1920* (New York: Cambridge University Press, 1982).

11. Policy analysts like Theda Skocpol and Margaret Weir deserve a good deal of credit for developing the institutional-political approach, which demonstrates how particular governmental structures influence the development of social policy. In recent years, however, their treatment of this issue, which once coexisted with a recognition of business influence, has become so exclusive that it has pushed this recognition aside. Political structures then become as much of an explanation of social policy as the old simplified version of conflict between classes that they sought to replace. Margaret Weir's *Politics and Jobs* exemplifies this approach. Although it is otherwise a fine analysis, it underestimates the role of business opposition to a comprehensive employment policy. See also Theda Skocpol, *Boomerang: Clinton's Health Security Effort and the Turn Against Government in U.S. Politics* (New York: W. W. Norton, 1996).

12. For a view that stresses some but not all of these same highlights, see Lauri J. Bassi and Orley Ashenfelter, "The Effect of Direct Job Creation and Training Programs on Low-Skilled Workers," in Sheldon H. Danziger and Daniel H. Weinberg, eds., *Fighting Poverty: What Works and What Doesn't* (Cambridge, Mass: Harvard University Press, 1986), pp. 133–151.

13. Nancy Rose, *Put To Work: Relief Programs in the Great Depression* (New York: Monthly Review Press, 1994), pp. 12–13, and James Patterson, *America's Struggle Against Poverty, 1900–1980* (Boston: Harvard University Press, 1981), pp. 63–67.

14. Saul J. Blaustein, *Unemployment Insurance in the United States* (Kalamazoo, Michigan: W.E. Upjohn Institute, 1993), pp. 214–215; James Patterson, *America's Struggle Against Poverty,* p. 142; Margaret Weir, *Politics and Jobs,* p. 93; and Jill Quadagno, *The Color of Welfare* (New York: Oxford University Press, 1994), pp. 67–69.

15. Duane Leigh, *Does Training Work for Displaced Workers* (Kalamazoo, Michigan: W.E. Upjohn Institute, 1990), p. 7, and Margaret Weir, *Politics and Jobs,* p. 110.

16. U.S. General Accounting Office, *Multiple Employment Training Programs: National Employment Strategy Needed,* June 18, 1994 (Statement of Clarence C. Crawford, Associate Director, Education and Employment Issues, Human Resources Division), p. 3, and U.S. General Accounting Office, *Multiple Employment Training Programs: Overlapping Programs Can Add Unnecessary Administrative Costs,* 1994, p. 4. Nor are these the only programmatic confusions. Employment programs are troubled by conflicting eligibility requirements. The programs

targeting the economically disadvantaged use different standards for measuring income level, for defining family or household, and for defining what income includes. Programs targeting older workers create confusion because they define older differently. Programs targeting youth define both the lower and upper age limit differently. Dislocated worker programs differ in their standard for what constitutes an eligible job loss such as in recognition of pending layoff notices, definitions of dates of employment, voluntary separations, and reduced hours or wages. U.S. General Accounting Office, *Multiple Employment Training Programs: Conflicting Requirements Hamper Delivery of Services*, 1994, p. 3.

17. See Robert Kuttner, *The End of Laissez-Faire* (Philadelphia: University of Pennsylvania Press, 1992), p. 270, for discussion of this point.

18. U.S. General Accounting Office, *Unemployment Insurance: Program's Ability to Meet Objectives Jeopardized* (Washington, D.C.: Government Printing Office, 1993), pp. 2–3; Marion Nichols and Isaac Shapiro, *Unemployment Insurance Protection in 1994* (Washington, D.C.: Center on Budget and Policy Priorities, 1995), p. 7; Committee on Ways and Means, U.S. House of Representatives, *1998 Green Book: Background Material and Data on Programs Within the Jurisdiction of the Committee on Ways and Means* (Washington, D.C.: Government Printing Office, 1998), p. 332; and Congressional Budget Office, *Displaced Workers: Trends in the 1980s and Implications for the Future* (Washington, D.C.: Congress of the United States, 1993), p. 30.

19. U.S. General Accounting Office, *Unemployment Insurance*, pp. 4 and 43.

20. See Saul J. Blaustein, *Unemployment Insurance in the United States*, p. 45. This book also provides a useful summary of the history of unemployment insurance.

21. Saul J. Blaustein, *Unemployment Insurance in the United States*, pp. 336–337.

22. The best case for this model is W. Norton Grubb, *Learning to Work: The Case for Reintegrating Job Training and Education* (New York: Russell Sage Foundation, 1996).

23. Towers Perrin, *The People Strategy Benchmark Awareness and Attitude Study*, 1995.

24. The National Center on the Educational Quality of the Workforce, *The Other Shoe: Education's Contribution to Productivity of Establishments*, The University of Pennsylvania, 1995.

25. Louis Uchitelle, "Workers Scarce but So Are Raises," *The New York Times*, October 4, 1994.

26. Adam Seitchik and Jeffrey Zornitsky, *From One Job to the Next*, p. 121; Louis Jacobson, Robert LaLonde, and Daniel Sullivan, *The Costs of Worker Dislocation* (Kalamazoo, Michigan: W.E. Upjohn Institute, 1993), pp. 7 and 137; and Paul Osterman, "The Possibilities of Employment Policy," in *Workforce Policies for the 1990s* (Washington, D.C.: Economic Policy Institute, 1989), p. 43. On the estimate of the income gain, Rebecca Blank, "The Employment Strategy: Public Policies to Increase Work and Earnings," in Sheldon Danziger, Gary Sandefur, and Daniel Weinberg, eds., *Confronting Poverty* (Cambridge, Massachusetts: Harvard University Press, 1994), p. 190, comes to a similar conclusion. For a review of the results of various job training programs, see W. Norton Grubb, *Learning to Work*, as well as the U.S. General Accounting Office, *Self-Sufficiency: Opportunities and Disincentives on the Road to Economic Independence* (Washington, D.C.: Government Printing Office, 1993), pp. 47–53.

27. Louis Jacobson, Robert LaLonde, and Daniel Sullivan, *The Costs of Worker Dislocation*, p. 155; Robert Kuttner, *The End of Laissez-Faire*, p. 273; and Committee on Ways and Means, U.S. House of Representatives, *Background Material and Data on Programs within the Jurisdiction of the House Ways and Means*, pp. 1007–1009. The 35 percent decline combines JTPA, Summer Youth, and Job Corps programs.

28. Lisa M. Lynch, *Strategies for Workplace Training: Lessons from Abroad*, (Washington, D.C.: Economic Policy Institute, 1993), p. 7, and *The Economist*, "Training for Jobs," March 12, 1994, p. 26.

29. Lisa M. Lynch, *Strategies for Workplace Training*, pp. 18, 14, and 25, and Bennett Harrison, *Lean and Mean* (New York: Basic Books, 1994), p. 237. For a discussion of the German apprentice training system, see Bernard Casey, "Apprentice Training in Germany: The Experiences of the 1980s," in Katharine McFate, Roger Lawson, and William Julius Wilson, *Poverty,*

Inequality, and the Future of Social Policy (New York: Russell Sage Foundation, 1995), pp. 415–437.

30. Duane Leigh, *Does Training Work for Displaced Workers?*, p. 3, and W. Norton Grubb, *Learning to Work*, pp. 69–70 and p. 95.

31. U.S. General Accounting Office, *Multiple Employment Training Programs: Most Federal Agencies Do Not Know If Their Programs Are Working Effectively* (Washington, D.C.: Government Printing Office, 1994), p. 4, and W. Norton Grubb, *Learning to Work*, pp. 71–72.

32. U.S. General Accounting Office, *Dislocated Workers: Workers Adjustment and Retraining Notification Act Not Meeting Its Goals* (Washington, D.C.: Government Printing Office, 1993), pp. 4–6.

33. Congressional Budget Office, *Displaced Workers: Trends in the 1980s and Implications for the Future*, pp. 7–8.

34. Congressional Budget Office, *Displaced Workers*, pp. 12–13, and 30.

35. U.S. Department of Labor, Bureau of Labor Statistics, *Worker Displacement During the Mid-1990s*, October 25, 1996, p. 1.

36. See Robert Kuttner, *Everything for Sale* (New York: Alfred A. Knopf, 1996), p. 89.

37. Louis Jacobson, Robert LaLonde, and Daniel Sullivan, *The Costs of Worker Dislocation*, p. 13, and U.S. Department of Labor Office of the Inspector General, *Trade Adjustment Assistance Program: Audit of Program Outcomes in Nine Selected States* (Washington, D.C.: U.S. Department of Labor, 1993), pp. 1–2.

38. U.S. Department of Labor Office of the Inspector General, *Trade Adjustment Assistance Program: Audit of Program Outcomes in Nine Selected States*, pp. 1–2, 34, and 50, and Mathematica Policy Research, *International Trade and Worker Dislocation: Evaluation of the Trade Adjustment Assistance Program* (Princeton, New Jersey: Mathematica Policy Research, 1993), p. 154.

39. Peter T. Kilborn, "After the Jobs Went South: A Town Finds Pitfalls in a Retraining Effort," *The New York Times*, November 6, 1993.

40. Duane Leigh, *Does Training Work for Displaced Workers*, p. 4, and Louis Jacobson, Robert LaLonde, and Daniel Sullivan, *The Costs of Worker Dislocation*, p. 154.

41. U.S. General Accounting Office, *Job Corps: Where Participants Are Recruited, Trained, and Placed in Jobs* (Washington, D.C.: Government Printing Office, 1996); C. Mallar et al., *An Evaluation of the Economic Impact of the Job Corps Program* (Princeton, New Jersey: Mathematica Policy Research, 1980); and the U.S. General Accounting Office, *Job Corps: High Costs and Mixed Results Raise Questions About the Program's Effectiveness* (Washington, D.C.: Government Printing Office, 1995).

42. Howard S. Bloom and Larry Orr, *The National JTPA Study: Overview, Impacts, Benefits, and Costs of Title-IIA* (Bethesda, Maryland: Abt Associates, 1994).

43. Karen Blumenthal, "Job-training Effort, Critics Say, Fails Many Who Need Help Most," *The Wall Street Journal*, February 9, 1987.

44. John Donahue, *Shortchanging the Workforce: The Job Training Partnership Act and the Overselling of Privatized Training* (Washington, D.C.: Economic Policy Institute, 1989), p. 1.

45. Gary Orfield, "Urban Schools and the Perpetuation of Job Inequality," in George Peterson and Wayne Vroman, eds., *Urban Labor Markets and Job Opportunity* (Washington, D.C.: The Urban Institute, 1992), p. 175.

46. John Donahue, *Shortchanging the Workforce*, p. 14.

47. John Donahue, *Shortchanging the Workforce*, p. 1.

48. U.S. General Accounting Office, *Job Training Partnership Act: Long-Term Earnings and Employment Outcomes* (Washington, D.C.: Government Printing Office, 1996), pp. 2–3.

49. Paul Osterman, "The Possibilities of Employment Policy," in *Workforce Policies for the 1990s;* Rosemary Batt and Paul Osterman, *A National Policy for Workplace Training: Lessons from State and Local Experiments* (Washington, D.C.: Economic Policy Institute, 1993) and W. Norton Grubb, *Learning to Work*.

50. The most developed version of this model apears in W. Norton Grubb, *Learning to Work*, pp. 110–113, from which this version is adapted.

51. Jeffrey Faux, "Clinton's Industrial Policy," *Dissent* 40 (4): 469, Fall, 1993, and Lawrence Mishel and Ruy A. Teixeira, *The Myth of the Coming Labor Shortage* (Washington, D.C.: Economic Policy Institute, 1991), p. 41.

52. William Julius Wilson discusses this problem in his *When Work Disappears: The World of the New Urban Poor* (New York: Alfred A. Knopf, 1996), p. 232.

53. The most sophisticated plan for salaries in a full-employment program comes from Philip Harvey, *Securing the Right To Employment*, pp. 33–38.

54. See Philip Harvey, *Securing the Right to Employment*, pp. 75–78.

Notes to Chapter 7

1. For summaries of the law, see David Super, Sharon Parrott, Susan Steinmetz, and Cindy Mann, *The New Welfare Law* (Washington, D.C.: Center on Budget and Policy Priorities, August 1996), and the Center on Social Welfare Policy and Law, *Welfare News*, August 20, 1996, pp. 2–5; for discussion of the Health and Human Services analysis, see Alison Mitchell, "White House Held on to Study of Senate Bill's Harm," *The New York Times*, October 28, 1995.

2. Christopher Georges and Dana Milbank, "Sweeping Overhaul of Welfare Would Put Onus on the States," *The Wall Street Journal*, July 31, 1996. For a readable analysis of the conservative critique of welfare, see Mimi Abramovitz, *Under Attack, Fighting Back: Women and Welfare in the United States* (New York: Monthly Review Press, 1996).

3. David Ellwood, *Poor Support* (New York: Basic Books, 1989). For an inside political history of the bill in the months leading up to its signing, see Peter Edelman, "The Worst Thing Bill Clinton Has Done," *The Atlantic Monthly*, 279 (3): 43–58, March, 1997.

4. See the United States General Accounting Office, *Child Care: Working Poor and Welfare Recipients Face Service Gaps* (Washington, D.C.: Government Printing Office, 1994).

5. Since the enactment of the 1996 bill, there has been one major portrait of Ellwood's experience with welfare reform, and Ellwood himself has penned a short, autobiographical essay. See Jason DeParle, "Mugged By Reality," *The New York Times Magazine*, December 8, 1996, pp. 64–67 and 99–100, and David T. Ellwood, "Welfare Reform As I Knew It: When Bad Things Happen to Good Policies," *The American Prospect*, 26: 22–29, May–June 1996. Ellwood still seems somewhat bewildered about what happened to him. For some clues, Frances Fox Piven and Richard Cloward, "The Politics of Policy Science," in Piven and Cloward, eds., *The Breaking of the American Social Compact* (New York: The New Press, 1997), pp. 243–263, especially pp. 253–257.

6. David Ellwood, *Poor Support*, pp. 18–25.

7. Fay Lomax Cook and Edith J. Barrett, *Support for the American Welfare State* (New York: Columbia University Press, 1992), p. 27.

8. Sharon Parrott, *What Do We Spend on "Welfare"?* (Washington, D.C.: Center on Budget and Policy Priorities, 1995), p. 5; United States General Accounting Office, *Tax Administration: Increased Fraud and Poor Taxpayer Access to IRS Cloud 1993 Filing Season* (Washington, D.C.: Government Printing Office, 1993); Robert D. Hershey, "I.R.S. Finds Fraud Grows as More File By Computer," *The New York Times*, February 21, 1994; and James P. Donahue, "The Fat Cat Freeloaders—When American Big Business Bellys Up to the Public Trough," *The Washington Post*, March 6, 1994.

9. Nancy Fraser, "After the Family Wage: What Do Women Want in Social Welfare," *Social Justice* 21(1): 80–86, 1994. For a discussion of the political implications of the transition from an industrial to a postindustrial economy, see France Fox Piven and Richard A. Cloward, "Welfare and the Transformation of Electoral Politics," in Piven and Cloward, *The Breaking of the American Social Compact*, pp. 59–77.

10. Among the novels of Charles Dickens, *Oliver Twist* probably contains the best known portrayal of a workhouse. Some typical histories include Gareth Stedman Jones, *Outcast London: A Study in the Relationship Between Classes in Victorian Society* (Oxford: Oxford University

Press, 1971); Karl de Schweinitz, *England's Road to Social Security* (New York: A. S. Barnes, 1961); and Karl Polanyi, *The Great Transformation* (Boston, Massachusetts: Beacon, 1957).

11. Cited in Robin Toner, "G.O.P. Gets Mixed Reviews From Public Wary on Taxes," *The New York Times,* April 6, 1995.

12. Gwendolyn Mink, "Welfare Reform in Historical Perspective," *Social Justice,* (21) 1: 113, Spring, 1994, and Mary Jo Bane and David Ellwood, *Welfare Realities* (Cambridge, Massachusetts: Harvard University Press, 1994), p. x.

13. Thomas Corbett, "Child Poverty and Welfare Reform: Progress or Paralysis," University of Wisconsin-Madison Institute for Research on Poverty, *Focus* (15) 1: 8, Spring, 1993.

14. For a book-length treatment of this argument, see Linda Gordon's *Pitied But Not Entitled: Single Mothers and the History of Welfare* (Cambridge, Massachusetts: Harvard University Press, 1994); for the short version, see Linda Gordon, "Welfare Reform: A History Lesson," *Dissent* (41) 3: 323–328, Summer, 1994.

15. The data come from a 1995 Louis Harris & Associates poll prepared for the Families & Work Institute, *Women: The New Providers* (New York: Families & Work Institute, 1995), p. 33. The quotation is cited in Gwendolyn Mink, "Welfare Reform in Historical Perspective," *Social Justice* (21) 1: 121, Summer, 1994.

16. Sara McLanahan and Lynne Casper, *The American Family in 1990: Growing Diversity and Inequality,* The Luxembourg Income Study, July, 1994, pp. 3–4.

17. Committee on Ways and Means, U.S. House of Representatives, *Background Material and Data on Programs Within the Jurisdiction of the Committee on Ways and Means* (Washington, D.C.: Government Printing Office, 1998), p. 441; Mary Jo Bane, in "Household Composition and Poverty: Which Comes First?" in Sheldon H. Danziger and Daniel H. Weinberg, eds., *Fighting Poverty: What Works and What Doesn't* (Cambridge, Massachusetts: Harvard University Press, 1986), pp. 202–231; Kristin Luker, *Dubious Conceptions: The Politics of Teenage Pregnancy* (Cambridge, Massachusetts: Harvard University Press, 1996), p. 230; and Stephanie Ventura, *Births and Deaths: 1995,* National Center for Health Statistics, 1996.

18. The best known statement of this viewpoint is Lawrence Mead, *Beyond Entitlement* (New York: Free Press, 1986). For a good critique, see Michael Sosin's book review in *Social Service Review* 61 (1): 156–159.

19. This passage draws on Nancy Fraser and Linda Gordon, "Contract versus Charity: Why Is There No Social Citizenship in the United States?" *Socialist Review* 22 (3): 45–67, July–August, 1992. For a similar point about the failure of the state to uphold its part of the contract, see Evelyn Z. Brodkin, "Inside the Welfare Contract: Discretion and Accountability in State Welfare Administration," *Social Service Review,* 71 (1): 1–33, March, 1997.

20. Bruce Ingersoll, "As Congress Considers Slashing Crop Subsidies, Affluent Urban Farmers Come Under Scrutiny," *The Wall Street Journal,* March 16, 1995; James P. Donahue, "The Fat Cat Freeloaders—When American Big Business Bellys Up to the Public Trough," *The Washington Post,* March 6, 1994; Robert D. Hershey, "A Hard Look at Corporate Welfare," *The New York Times,* March 7, 1995; and Stephen Moore and Dean Stansel, *Ending Corporate Welfare As We Know It* (Washington, D.C.: The Cato Institute, 1995).

21. For a review of these cases, see Joel Blau, *The Visible Poor: Homelessness in the United States* (New York: Oxford University Press, 1992), chapter 7, and Michael Sosin, "Legal Rights and Welfare Change," in Danziger and Weinberg, eds., *Fighting Poverty,* pp. 260–283.

22. For a description of TANF, see *Welfare News,* a publication of the Center on Social Welfare Policy and Law, August 20, 1996, pp. 2–6.

23. See David Super et al., *The New Welfare Law,* pp. 17–19; Center on Budget and Policy Priorities, *Food Stamp Provisions of Welfare Law May Have Harsher Effects on Unemployed Adults Than Congress Intended,* October 17, 1996; the Congressional Budget Office, *Federal Budgetary Implications of the Personal Responsibility and Work Opportunity Reconciliation Act of 1996* (Washington, D.C.: Congressional Budget Office, 1996), p. 39. The 1997 budget agreement restored $1.5 billion of this funding, with $1 billion of this sum earmarked to create jobs for food stamp recipients.

24. The Committee on Ways and Means, *Overview of Entitlement Programs*, pp. 207–208; David Super et al., *The New Welfare Law*, pp. 29–30; and the Congressional Budget Office, *Federal Budgetary Implications of the Personal Responsibility and Work Opportunity Reconciliation Act of 1996*, p. 18. The 308,000 figure is calculated from the CBO's estimate of a 22 percent decline in the 1.4 million children who would have otherwise received SSI.

25. See Robert Pear, "Legal Immigrants Would Benefit Under New Budget Agreement," *The New York Times*, July 30, 1997, and James Dao, "Aliens Would Get Food Stamps Back in Clinton Budget," *The New York Times*, February 2, 1998.

26. The Associated Press, "States Keep Immigrant Benefits," October 19, 1997.

27. See David Super et al., *The New Welfare Law*, pp. 25–27. The most famous English "Law of the Settlement" was enacted in 1662, though laws restricting the mobility of paupers go back to fourteenth-century England and extend forward well into our own time. For the British antecedents, see Karl de Schweinitz, *England's Road to Social Security;* for the American, see Michael B. Katz, *In the Shadow of the Poorhouse* (New York: Basic Books, 1986).

28. Robert Pear, "Rewards and Penalties Vary in States' Welfare Programs," *The New York Times*, February 23, 1997.

29. See the Welfare Law Center's *Welfare News*, "States Seek to Pay Lower Benefits to New Residents; Advocates Respond With Litigation," 2 (2): 7–8, May, 1997. Although courts have already enjoined the California and New York statutes, thirteen states have adopted such policies.

30. Robert Pear, "State Officials Conclude Some Provisions of the Law May Be Unconstitutional," *The New York Times*, October 6, 1996; Robert Pear, "States' Authority May Be Disputed on the Use of Welfare Money," *The New York Times*, December 29, 1996; and Douglas J. Besharov, "Tightening the Welfare Noose," *The New York Times*, January 15, 1997.

31. Robert Pear, "Number on Welfare Rolls Dips Below 10 Million," *The New York Times*, January 21, 1998.

32. Jason DeParle, "Varied Reasons Found for Welfare Rolls' Drop," *The New York Times*, May 10, 1997, and Council of Economic Advisors, *Explaining the Decline in Welfare Receipt, 1993–1996*, May 9, 1997. The 13 percent figure can be found in the Appendix at Table 3.

33. See Hilary Williamson Hoynes, *Local Labor Markets and Welfare Spells: Do Demand Conditions Matter?* Burch Working Paper No. B96-22, Department of Economics, University of California at Berkeley. Thus, according to Hoynes, a 10 percent increase in employment growth combined with a 5 percent real increase in earnings would lead to a 16.2 percent reduction in the welfare caseload (p. 29).

34. Jason DeParle, "A Sharp Decrease in Welfare Cases Is Gathering Speed," *The New York Times*, February 2, 1997.

35. This point is made in summary form by Christopher Jencks in "The Hidden Paradox of Welfare Reform: Why Single Mothers May Earn More But Do Worse," *The American Prospect*, (32): 33–40, May–June, 1997. Jencks's argument is based on field research by Kathryn Edin and Laura Lein, the authors of *Making Ends Meet: How Single Mothers Survive Welfare and Low-Wage Work* (New York: Russell Sage Foundation, 1997). Edin and Lein found that working mothers spent $1243 monthly compared to $876 for welfare recipients: in other words, their expenses were 50 percent higher (p. 91).

36. Committee on Ways and Means, U.S. House of Representatives, *Background Material and Data on Programs Within the Jurisdiction of the Committee on Ways and Means*, p. 440.

37. Bureau of the Census, *Current Population Reports: Marital Status and Living Arrangements: March, 1993*, 1994, p. xii; Gwendolyn Mink, "Welfare Reform in Historical Perspective," p. 125; and Sara McLanahan and Lynne Casper, *The American Family in 1990: Growing Diversity and Inequality*, pp. 5–10. See also United States General Accounting Office, *Families on Welfare: Sharp Rise in Never Married Women Reflects Societal Trend* (Washington, D.C.: Government Printing Office, 1994).

38. Judith Bruce, Cynthia B. Lloyd, and Ann Leonard, with Patrice l. Engle and Niev Duffy, *Families in Focus: New Perspectives on Mothers, Fathers, and Children* (New York: The Pop-

ulation Council, 1995), and Sara McLanahan and Lynne Casper, *The American Family in 1990: Growing Diversity and Inequality*, pp. 11–12.

39. Sharon Parrott and Robert Greenstein, "Welfare, Out-of Wedlock Childbearing and Poverty: What is the Connection?," Center on Budget and Policy Priorities, Washington, D.C., 1995, pp. viii–xi; Committee on Ways and Means, U.S. House of Representatives, *Background Material and Data on Programs Within the Jurisdiction of the Committee on Ways and Means*, p. 431; and Gwendolyn Mink, "Welfare Reform in Historical Perspective," pp. 124–125. Compare the teen birthrate in the United States, 62 per 1000 women under 20 years in 1991, with 6 for the Netherlands, 9 for France, 10 for Italy, 17 Norway, 22 Australia, 25 Canada, and 33 for the United Kingdom. More recently, teen birthrates have declined 12 percent in the United States. See Stephanie J. Ventura, Sally C. Curtin, and T. J. Mathews, *Teenage Births in the United States: National and State Trends, 1990–1996* (U.S. Department of Health and Human Services, National Center for Disease Control, 1998).

For more general treatments of this issue, the following are helpful: Kristin Luker, *Dubious Conception: The Politics of Teenage Pregnancy* (Cambridge, Massachusetts: Harvard University Press, 1996); David Wagner, *The New Temperance: The American Obsession with Sin and Vice* (Boulder, Colorado: Westview Press, 1997), pp. 84–89; and Mary E. Corcoran and James P. Kunz, "Do Unmarried Births among African-American Teens Lead to Adult Poverty," *Social Service Review* 71 (2): 274–287, June, 1997.

40. See Gertrude Himmelfarb, *The De-Moralization of Society: From Victorian Virtues to Modern Values* (New York: Alfred A. Knopf, 1995), pp. 129–130 for the discussion of Malthus. The family cap is discussed in United States General Accounting Office, *Welfare Waiver Implementation: States Work to Change Welfare Culture, Community Involvement, and Service Delivery*, July, 1996, pp. 3 and 20; Michael Laracy, *The Jury Is Still Out: An Analysis of the Purported Impact of New Jersey's AFDC Child Exclusion Law* (Washington, D.C.: Center for Law and Social Policy, 1994), pp. 5–6. I have modified Laracy's data to reflect a 12 percent drop rather than the 9 percent which was first reported for the study. Tamar Lewin, "Report Tying Abortion to Welfare Is Rejected," *The New York Times*, June 8, 1998, says when a Rutgers University evaluation found an increase in the number of abortions, state officials claimed that the report needed to be revised because it was not "final."

41. Committee on Ways and Means, U.S. House of Representatives, *Background Material and Data on the Programs Within the Jurisdiction of the Committee on Ways and Means*, p. 420.

42. John Pawasarat, Lois Quinn, and Frank Stezer, *Evaluation of the Impact of Wisconsin's Learnfare Experiment on the School Attendance of Teenagers Receiving Aid to Families With Dependent Children* University of Wisconsin at Milwaukee, Employment and Training Institute, 1992. Five years later, in the State of Wisconsin Legislative Audit Bureau, *The Learnfare Program Final Report* (Madison, Wisconsin: Legislative Audit Bureau, 1997), the state's own evaluation agency reached the same conclusion.

Interestingly, upon receiving a draft copy of the 1992 report, the Wisconsin Department of Health and Social Services demanded that three sections be suppressed and that the methodology be altered. When the report was released without the changes, state officials attacked it as politically biased and canceled their evaluation contract with the University of Wisconsin at Milwaukee. Ever since this experience, the state Department of Health and Social Services has insisted on a "right to publish" clause in contracts with outside evaluators, specifying the need for prior written approval from the department. See Lois M. Quinn and Robert S. Magill, "Politics versus Research in Social Policy," *Social Service Review* (68) 4: 503–520, December, 1994. The whole experience is totally consistent with the research of Carol H. Weiss and Michael Bucuvalas, who found that 75 percent of the officials surveyed ignored research that did not correspond to their personal opinions. See their *Social Science Research and Decision-Making* (New York: Columbia University Press, 1980).

43. Christopher Jencks and Kathryn Edin, "Do Poor Women Have a Right to Bear Children?" *The American Prospect* 20: 43–53, Winter, 1995.

44. Mary Jo Bane and David Ellwood, *Welfare Realities*, p. 29.

45. Actually, a simple aphorism can clarify most of this confusion: while most spells on AFDC were short, most people were, at any given moment, in the midst of a long spell. The classic method of illustrating this statement is to think of a group home with thirteen beds. During the course of a year, 52 people use one of these beds for one week each. Twelve people occupy the other twelve beds for the entire year. Although most stays were short, because 52 of 64 people who lived in the group home remained for only one week, it is equally true that at any given time, 12 of the 13 residents were in the midst of a long stay. In essence, this pattern reflects exactly the way that AFDC operated.

46. La Donna Ann Pavetti, *The Dynamics of Welfare and Work: Exploring the Process By Which Women Work Their Way Off Welfare*, Ph.D. dissertation, John F. Kennedy School of Government, Harvard University, 1993, and Roberta Spalter-Roth, "The Real Employment Opportunities of Women Participating in AFDC: What the Market Can Provide," *Social Justice* 21 (1): 60–70, Spring, 1994.

47. See, for example, Daniel Friedlander and Gary Burtless, *Five Years After: The Long-Term Effects of Welfare-to-Work Programs* (New York: Russell Sage Foundation, 1995); James Riccio, Daniel Friedlander, and Stephen Friedman, *GAIN: Benefits, Costs, and Three-Years Impacts of a Welfare-to-Work Program* (New York: Manpower Demonstration Research Corporation, 1994). For a somewhat more optimistic overview of this research, see Dan Bloom, *After AFDC: Welfare-to-Work Choices and Challenges for the States* (New York: Manpower Demonstration Research Corporation, 1997), especially chapter 3.

48. See Jared Bernstein, *Low-Wage Labor Market Indicators by City and State: The Constraints Facing Welfare Reform* (Washington, D.C.: Economic Policy Institute, October, 1997). Bernstein emphasizes that while overall unemployment for a one-year period from 1996 to 1997 averaged 5.2 percent, unemployment among African-American women with a high school degree was 19.7 percent.

49. John Pawasarat and Lois Quinn, *Wisconsin Welfare Employment Experiments: An Evaluation of the WEJT and CWEP Programs* (Milwaukee, Wisconsin: University of Wisconsin-Milwaukee Employment and Training Institute, 1993), and Sandra K. Danziger and Sherrie A. Kossoudji, *When Welfare Ends: Subsistence Strategies of Former GA Recipients* (University of Michigan School of Social Work, February, 1995); Daniel Friedlander and Gary Burtless, *Five Years After: The Long-Term Effects of Welfare-to-Work Programs*.

50. Raymond Hernandez, "Most Dropped From Welfare Don't Get Jobs," *The New York Times*, March 23, 1998.

51. Annette Fuentes, "Slaves of New York," *In These Times* 21 (3): 14–17, December 23, 1996; Maureen Balleza, "One Motivator: The Catfish Plant," in Sam Howe Verhovek, "States Are Already Providing Glimpse at Welfare's Future," *The New York Times*, September 21, 1995; Daniel R. Meyer and Maria Cancian, *Life After Welfare: The Economic Well-Being of Women and Children Following An Exit From AFDC* (University of Wisconsin-Madison, Institute for Research on Poverty, 1996), p. 10.

52. Louis Uchitelle, "Welfare Recipients Taking Jobs Often Held By the Working Poor," *The New York Times*, April 1, 1997.

53. Ruth W. Messinger, *Work to Be Done: Report of the Borough President's Task Force on Education, Employment, & Welfare* (New York City: Manhattan Borough President's Office, 1995), p. 21, and Alan Finder, "Welfare Clients Outnumber Jobs They Might Fill," *The New York Times*, August 25, 1996.

54. Annette Fuentes, "Corporate Welfare Big Time," *In These Times* 21 (3): 16, December 23, 1996, and Nina Bernstein, "Giant Companies Entering Race to Run State Welfare Programs," *The New York Times*, September 15, 1996. For an overview, see The Welfare Law Center, "Ending Welfare As We Know It: Profit Seeking Companies Compete to Run Welfare Programs," *Welfare News* 2 (2): 1–4, May, 1997.

55. Robin Toner, "G.O.P. Gets Mixed Reviews From Public Wary on Taxes," *The New York Times*, April 6, 1995.

56. Committee on Ways and Means, *Background Material and Data on Programs Within the Jurisdiction of the Committee on Ways and Means*, pp. 81 and 4.

57. Demetrios Caraley, "Dismantling the Federal Safety Net: Fictions versus Realities," *Political Science Quarterly* 111 (2): 233–235. The actual numbers for median income per 1 percent of poverty are $949 (Mississippi) and $785 (Louisiana), compared to $6500 in Connecticut and New Hampshire. For a detailed analysis of state income trends, see Kathyrn Larin and Elizabeth C. McNichol, *Pulling Apart: A State-by-State Analysis of Income Trends* (Washington, D.C.: Center on Budget and Policy Priorities, 1997).

58. Citizens for Tax Justice and The Institute on Taxation and Economic Policy, *Who Pays? A Distributional Analysis of the Tax Systems in All 50 States* (Washington, D.C.: 1996), pp. 1–2. For another monograph making a similar point, see Center on Budget and Policy Priorities, *State Income Tax Burdens on Low Income Families in 1996: Assessing the Burden and Opportunities for Relief* (Washington, D.C.: Center on Budget and Policy Priorities, 1997).

59. See Demetrios Caraley, "Dismantling the Federal Safety Net: Fictions versus Realities," p. 237; Center on Budget and Policy Priorities, *Should Federal Food Assistance Programs Be Converted to Block Grants?* (Washington, D.C.: Center on Budget and Policy Priorities, 1995), p. 2; and Susan Rees and Maybelle Taylor Bennett, *Block Grants: Missing the Target, An Overview of Findings* (Washington, D.C.: Coalition on Human Needs, 1987).

60. Center on Budget and Policy Priorities, *How Would States Have Fared If The Personal Responsibility Act's Cash Assistance Block Grant Had Been Enacted in 1989 and in Place During the Recession?* (Washington, D.C.: Center on Budget and Policy Priorities, 1995).

61. Demetrios Caraley, "Dismantling the Federal Safety Net: Fictions versus Realities," p. 236.

62. Sheila Zedlewski, Sandra Clark, Eric Meier, and Keith Watson, *Potential Effects of Congressional Welfare Reform Legislation on Family Incomes* (Washington, D.C.: The Urban Institute, 1996), pp. 1–2, and Lawrence Mishel and John Schmitt, *Cutting Wages By Cutting Welfare* (Washington, D.C.: Economic Policy Institute, 1995), p. 1.

63. For an analysis of some possible amendments to the Act, see Peter Edelman, "The Worst Thing Bill Clinton has Done," p. 56, and Mary Jo Bane, "Welfare as We Might Know It," *The American Prospect* 30: 47–53, January–February, 1997.

64. Organizations like the National Jobs for All Coalition have already proposed a monthly survey of job vacancies. See, for example, their "Policy Statement on Welfare Reform," 1997. For the first signs of resistance to the job displacement brought about by the 1996 law, see Louis Uchitelle, "Welfare Recipients Taking Jobs Often Held by the Working Poor," *The New York Times*, April 1, 1997.

65. Hugh Heclo, p. 329 in "The Political Foundations of Antipoverty Policy," in Sheldon H. Danziger and Daniel H. Weinberg, eds., *Fighting Poverty,* pp. 312–340.

66. On this subject, see Theda Skocpol, "Politically Viable Policies to Combat Poverty in the United States," pp. 411–436, and Robert Greenstein, "Universal and Targeted Approaches to Relieving Poverty," pp. 437–459 in Christopher Jencks and Paul E. Peterson, eds., *The Urban Underclass* (Washington, D.C.: The Brookings Institution, 1991).

67. Arloc Sherman, *College Access and the JOBS Program* (Washington, D.C.: The Center for Law and Social Policy, 1990), cited in Marilyn Gittell and Sally Covington, *Higher Education in JOBS: An Option or An Opportunity? A Comparison of Nine States,* A Report to the Ford Foundation by the Howard Samuels State Management and Policy Center, City University of New York, 1993, p. 8, and Marilyn Gittell, Jill Gross, and Jennifer Holdaway, *Building Human Capital: The Impact of Post-Secondary School Education on AFDC Recipients in Five States,* Howard Samuels State Management and Policy Center, 1993, p. 13. For similar conclusions, see Roberta Spalter-Roth, "Welfare That Works: Increasing AFDC Mothers' Employment and Income," Institute for Women's Policy Research, Testimony Before the Subcommittee on Human Resources, Committee on Ways and Means, U.S. House of Representatives, February 2, 1995.

68. United States General Accounting Office, *Child Care: Current System Could Undermine Goals of Welfare Reform,* Testimony of Jane Ross Before the Subcommittee on Human Resources, Committee on Education and Labor, and Congressional Caucus for Women's Issues, September 20, 1994, p. 4, and United States General Accounting Office, *Welfare to Work: Child Care Assistance Limited: Welfare Reform May Expand Needs,* September, 1995, p. 4.

254 • Notes to Chapter 8

See also Marcia K. Meyers, "Child Care, Parental Choice, and Consumer Education in JOBS Welfare to Work Programs," *Social Service Review*, 69 (4): 679–702.

69. Elaine Sorensen and Sandra Clark, *A Child Support Assurance Program: How Much Will It Reduce Child Poverty, and At What Cost* (Washington, D.C.: The Urban Institute, 1994), and Joseph Delfico, *Child Support Enforcement*, Testimony Before the Subcommittee on Federal Services, Post Office, and Civil Service, Committee on Governmental Affairs, U.S. Senate, July 20, 1994. For a description of a child support assurance program, see Irwin Garfinkel and Sara McLanahan, "Single Mother Families, Economic Insecurity, and Government Policy," in Sheldon H. Danziger, Gary D. Sandefur, and Daniel H. Weinberg, eds., *Confronting Poverty* (Cambridge, Massachusetts: Harvard University Press, 1994), pp. 205–225, especially pp. 221–224, and Mary Jo Bane and David Ellwood, *Welfare Realities*, pp. 154–155.

Notes to Chapter 8

1. See, for example, Mathew Wald, "Temper Cited as Cause of 28,000 Road Deaths a Year," *The New York Times*, July 18, 1997.

2. Charles Wolf, Jr., *Markets or Governments: Choosing Between Imperfect Alternatives* (Cambridge, Massachusetts: The MIT Press, 1993), pp. 17–18, and Robert Kuttner, *Everything for Sale* (New York: Alfred A. Knopf, 1997), pp. 24–28.

3. See Adolf Berle and Gardiner Means, *The Modern Corporation and Private Property* (New York: The Macmillan Company, 1932).

4. William Lazonick, "Creating and Extracting Value: Corporate Investment Behavior and American Economic Performance," in Michael Bernstein and David Adler, eds., *Understanding American Economic Decline* (New York: Cambridge University Press, 1994), pp. 79–113.

5. For discussion of the growing dominance of the financial sector, see Kevin Phillips, *Arrogant Capital* (Boston, Massachusetts: Little, Brown and Company, 1994), pp. 81–91, and Doug Henwood, *Wall Street* (New York: Verso, 1997). The quotation is from Kuttner, *Everything for Sale*, p. 178.

6. United States General Accounting Office, *Competitiveness Issues: The Business Environment in the United States, Japan, and Germany* (Washington, D.C.: Government Printing Office, 1993), p. 42, and William Lazonick, "Creating and Extracting Value," p. 111.

7. On the market for corporate control, see the McKinsey Global Institute, *Manufacturing Productivity* (Washington, D.C.: McKinsey Global Institute, 1993), chapter 3, p. 34; on short-term horizons, see Bennett Harrison, *Lean and Mean* (New York: Basic Books, 1994), pp. 183–184.

8. United States General Accounting Office, *Competitiveness Issues: The Business Environment in the United States, Japan, and Germany*, pp. 33, 39–40, 109, and Jorgen Elmeskov, "Germany: The Structures of Corporate Governance," *OECD Observer*, 196: 46–47, October–November, 1995.

9. Andrew Pollack, "Japan Finds Ways to Save Tradition of Lifetime Jobs," *The New York Times*, November 27, 1993, and Alexandra Iwanchuk Bibbee, "Spotlight on Germany Overcoming Structural Hurdles," *OECD Observer*, 190, pp. 35–37, October–November, 1994. The estimate of unnecessary jobs in Japan comes from Peter Morgan, an economist at Merrill Lynch.

10. Jeffrey Hart, "A Comparative Analysis of the Sources of America's Relative Economic Decline," in Bernstein and Adler, eds., *Understanding American Economic Decline*, p. 199.

11. For a full list of studies on this issue, see David Levine and Laura D'Andrea Tyson, "Participation, Productivity, and the Firm's Environment," in Alan Blinder, ed., *Paying for Productivity* (Washington, D.C.: The Brookings Institution, 1990), pp. 183–241, especially pp. 191–194. Although some studies have yielded more ambiguous results, they have defined participation as a labor-management committee that is simply grafted on to a complex organization in a way that avoids controversial subjects and real problem solving. See, for example, Mary Ellen Kelly and Bennett Harrison, "Unions, Technology, and Labor Management

Cooperation," in Lawrence Mishel and Paula B. Voos, eds., *Unions and Economic Competitiveness* (Armonk, New York: M.E. Sharpe, 1992), pp. 247–286.

12. Eileen Appelbaum and Rosemary Batt, *The New American Workplace* (Cornell, New York: ILR Press, 1994), pp. 5 and 69.

13. Eileen Appelbaum and Rosemary Batt, *The New American Workplace*, p. 96, and United States Department of Labor and United States Department of Commerce, *Fact-Finding Report, Commission on the Future of Worker-Management Relations* (Washington, D.C.: Government Printing Office, 1994), p. 52.

14. Mark Huselid, *Human Resource Management Practices and Firm Performance*, Institute for Management and Labor Relations, Rutgers University, 1993.

15. Douglas J. Kruse, *Profit Sharing* (Kalamazoo, Michigan: The Upjohn Institute, 1993), p. 147; Kruse, p. 167, citing Gary W. Florkowski. "Profit Sharing and Employment: Growth and Stability Effects in American Companies," Draft, University of Pittsburgh, 1991; and Kruse, p. 68. Martin L. Weitzman and Douglas J. Kruse, "Profit-Sharing and Productivity," in Alan Blinder, ed., *Paying for Productivity*, includes a complete list of the econometric studies, pp. 128–130.

16. Adrienne E. Eaton and Paula B. Voos, "Unions and Contemporary Innovations in Work Organization, Compensation, and Employee Participation," in Mishel and Voos, eds., *Unions and Economic Competitiveness*, p. 214.

17. Douglas L. Kruse, *Profit-Sharing*, p. 3.

18. Louis Uchitelle, "'Good' Jobs in Hard Times," *The New York Times*, October 3, 1993. Although this article lists Wal-Mart as the second leading private employer, Manpower has since replaced it.

19. Alan Blinder, "Introduction," in *Paying for Productivity*, p. 4, and David I. Levine and Laura D'Andrea Tyson, "Participation, Productivity, and the Firm's Environment," in Blinder, ed., *Paying for Productivity*, especially pp. 210–211.

20. For a history of profit-sharing, see Daniel J. B. Mitchell, David Lewin, and Edward E. Lawler III, "Alternative Pay Systems, Firm Performance, and Productivity," in Blinder, ed., *Paying for Productivity*, pp. 15–94, especially pp. 33–35 and 42–45.

21. National Center for Employee Ownership, *Employee Ownership and Corporate Performance* (Oakland, California: National Center for Employee Ownership, 1997), and National Center for Employee Ownership, *An Overview of ESOPS, Stock Options, and Employee Ownership* (Oakland, California: NCEO, 1997).

22. See Rebecca Bauen, "Co-Ops, ESOPs, and Worker Participation," *Dollars & Sense*, #200, pp. 20–23, July–August, 1995, and Michael A. Conte and Jan Svejnar, "The Performance Effects of Employee Ownership Plans," in Blinder, ed., *Paying for Productivity*, pp. 143–181.

23. United States Department of Labor and United States Department of Commerce, *Fact-Finding Report: Commission on the Future of Worker-Management Relations*, pp. 43–44, and Adrienne E. Eaton and Paula B. Voos, "Unions and Contemporary Innovations in Work Organization, Compensation, and Employee Participation," pp. 214–215.

24. Douglas Kruse, *Profit Sharing*, p. 85; Adrienne E. Eaton and Paula B. Voos, "Unions and Contemporary Innovations in Work Organization, Compensation, and Employee Participation," especially pp. 184 and 213–214; and Eileen Appelbaum and Rosemary Batt, *The New American Workplace*, p. 79.

25. United States General Accounting Office, *Productivity Sharing Programs: Can They Contribute to Productivity Improvement?* (Washington, D.C.: Government Printing Office, 1981); Daniel J. B. Mitchell, David Lewin, and Edward E. Lawler III, "Alternative Pay Systems, Firm Performance, and Productivity," in Blinder, ed., *Paying for Productivity*, pp. 67–68; and Robert Kuttner, *Everything for Sale*, p. 79.

26. For a discussion of the capital-labor accord, see Joel Blau, *The Visible Poor: Homelessness in the United States* (New York: Oxford University Press, 1992), p. 37; for the 2 percent figure of Americans working in high performance systems, see Anthony Carnevale, "What Training Means in an Election Year," *Training and Development* 46: 45–53, October, 1992.

27. Katharine G. Abraham and Susan N. Houseman, *Job Security in America: Lessons from Germany* (Washington, D.C.: The Brookings Institution, 1993), p. 17, and United States General Accounting Office, *Competitiveness Issues: The Business Environment in the United States, Japan, and Germany,* p. 111.

28. Rebecca Bauen, "Co-Ops, ESOPS, and Worker Participation," p. 22.

29. For an exploration of these themes, see Ira Katznelson, *City Trenches: Urban Politics and the Patterning of Class in the United States* (Chicago, Illinois: University of Chicago Press, 1982).

30. Samuel Bowles, David Gordon, and Thomas Weisskopf, *After the Wasteland: A Democratic Economics for the Year 2000* (Armonk, New York: M.E. Sharpe, 1990), p. 214.

31. David M. Gordon, *Fat and Mean* (New York: The Free Press, 1996).

32. Robert Reich, "How to Avoid These Layoffs?" *The New York Times,* January 4, 1996.

Notes to Chapter 9

1. Associated Press, "511,039 Elected Officials," *The New York Times,* January 31, 1995. The Illinois figure comes from Kevin Phillips, *Arrogant Capital* (Boston: Little, Brown, 1994), p. 129; the New Jersey data is quoted in Iver Peterson, "In New Jersey, Links Between State and Local Tax Levels Aren't Clear-Cut," *The New York Times,* February 20, 1995. Interestingly, the number of government jurisdictions in the United States may be growing, but it is doing so in spite of the decline in school districts through consolidation. There were 108,579 school districts in 1942, compared to 14,721 in 1987. Over the same period, the number of special districts providing other services such as water, mass transit, and housing tripled from 8299 to 29,532. See Alan Altschuler and Christopher Howard, *Local Government and Economic Development in the United States Conference Report: Will Decentralization Succeed?,* Cambridge, Massachusetts, John F. Kennedy School of Government, 1991, pp. 40–41.

2. Margaret Weir, Ann Shola Orloff, and Theda Skocpol, "The Future of Social Policy in the United States: Political Constraints and Possibilities," in Margaret Weir, Ann Shola Orloff, and Theda Skocpol, eds., *The Politics of Social Policy in the United States* (Princeton, New Jersey: Princeton University Press), p. 431. As Theda Skocpol argues in *Protecting Soldiers and Mothers* (Cambridge, Massachusetts: Harvard University Press, 1992), fears about the distorting effects of patronage and corruption on Civil War pensions seriously impeded their transformation into a broader-based income security program.

3. Quoted in Peter Beinart, "The Pride of the Cities," *The New Republic,* June 30, 1997, p. 17.

4. For a comparison of the European and American experience, see Gosta Esping-Andersen, *The Three Worlds of Welfare Capitalism* (Princeton, New Jersey: Princeton University Press, 1990), as well as the excellent feminist critique by Ann S. Orloff, "Gender and the Social Rights of Citizenship: The Comparative Analysis of Gender Relations and Welfare States," *American Sociological Review* 58 (3): 303–328, June, 1993.

5. On this point, see H. Mark Roelofs, *The Poverty of American Politics: A Theoretical Interpretation* (Philadelphia: Temple University Press, 1992), p. 240, and Benjamin Ginsberg and Martin Shefter, *Politics by Other Means* (New York: Basic Books, 1990), p. 83.

6. U.S. Congressional Budget Office, *Reducing Entitlement Spending* (Washington, D.C.: Government Printing Office, 1994), p. x.

7. For an excellent analysis of these dynamics, see James Morone, *The Democratic Wish: Popular Participation and Limits of American Government* (New York: Basic Books, 1990).

8. Albert Gore, *Creating a Government That Works Better & Costs Less,* Report of the National Performance Review, 1993, p. 3. The sequel, *Businesslike Government: Lessons Learned from America's Best Companies,* comes complete with Dilbert comic strips by Scott Adams and is in much the same vein (The National Performance Review, October, 1997).

9. Al Gore, *Creating a Government That Works Better & Costs Less,* Preface, p. iii.

10. Robert Greenstein, "The National Performance Review," (Washington, D.C.: Center on Budget and Policy Priorities, 1993), p. 3, and Congressional Budget Office, *Review of Government Reform and Budget Savings Act of 1993,* November 15, 1993.

11. Phillip K. Howard, *The Decline of Common Sense* (New York: Random House, 1994) contains many such anecdotes.

12. John R. Cushman, "Tales From the 104th: Watch Out, or the Regulators Will Get You!" *The New York Times,* February 28, 1995.

13. See Robert Sherrill, "A Year in Corporate Crime," *The Nation,* April 7, 1997, pp. 11–20. Sherrill set out to verify Ralph Nader's comment that "*The Wall Street Journal* is the main reporter in our country of corporate crime. *The Wall Street Journal* has so much information on corporate crime it should be named *The Crime Street Journal.*"

14. See, for example, Charles Schultze and Allen V. Kneese, *Pollution, Prices, and Public Policy* (Washington, D.C.: The Brookings Institution, 1975).

15. Robert Kuttner, *Everything for Sale: The Virtues and Limits of Markets* (New York: Alfred A. Knopf, 1997), pp. 257–258. See also *Consumer Reports,* "How to Beat Sky-High Fares," 62 (6): 21–25, July, 1997, which reported that airports where one or two of carriers fly from 75 or more percent of the gates have substantially higher fares than airports where the gates are more evenly distributed.

16. Mark Kahan, "Confessions of An Airline Regulator," *The American Prospect* 12: 39 (Winter, 1992), cited in Robert Kuttner, *Everything for Sale,* p. 266.

17. Edward Nell, *Prosperity and Public Spending: Transformational Growth and the Role of Government* (London, England: Unwin Hyman, 1988), p. 175.

18. William Greider, *Who Will Tell the People?* (New York: Touchstone Books, 1992), p. 115, and The Mercer Group, *1997 Privatization Survey* (Atlanta, Georgia, 1997), pp. 14–15. The data were drawn from 84 municipalities, 26 county governments, and 10 special districts in 33 states.

19. Elliot Sclar, "Public Service Privatization: Ideology or Economics," *Dissent* 41 (3): 329–336, Summer, 1994; quote at p. 330.

20. David Osborne and Ted Gaebler, *Reinventing Government: How The Entrepreneurial Spirit is Transforming the Public Sector* (New York: Plume, 1993).

21. David Osborne and Ted Gaebler, *Reinventing Government,* p. 40.

22. John Donahue, *The Privatization Decision* (New York: Basic Books, 1990), and Paul Starr, "The Meaning of Privatization," National Conference on Social Welfare, Project on the Federal Social Role, 1985, p. 14.

23. Bob Herbert, "Marina Madness in New Jersey," *The New York Times,* February 8, 1995.

24. Elliot Sclar, "Public Service Privatization: Ideology or Economics," pp. 334–335.

25. Office of Federal Procurement Policy, *Summary Report of the SWAT Team on Civilian Agency Contracts: Improving Contracting Practices and Management Controls on Cost-Style Federal Contracts,* 1992.

26. Jeff Garth and Stephen Labaton, "Jail Business Shows Its Weaknesses," *The New York Times,* November 24, 1995, and Elliot Sclar, "Public Sector Privatizations: Ideology or Economics," p. 332.

27. The Congressional Budget Office and the Office of Management and Budget differ in their estimates. The CBO predicts virtually negligible deficits of between $5 billion and $2 billion from 1998 to 2000, followed by a period of surplus rising to a total of $138 billion by 2008. By contrast, OMB sees a surplus of $9.5 billion in 1999, rising to a total of $258.5 billion in the same year. See the Congressional Budget Office, *The Economic and Budget Outlook: Fiscal Years 1999–2008* (Washington, D.C.: Government Printing Office, 1998), p. 33, and Robert Pear, "Clinton Sees $1.1 Trillion in Excess Revenue in Decade," *The New York Times,* February 3, 1998.

28. Council of Economic Advisors, *Economic Report of the President* (Washington, D.C.: Government Printing Office, 1985), p. 105; Frederick J. Thayer, "Do Balanced Budgets Cause Depressions," *Social Policy* 25 (4): 54, Summer, 1995; and Robert A. Levine, "The Economic Consequences of Mr. Clinton," *Atlantic* 278 (1): 62, July, 1996.

29. Council of Economic Advisors, *Economic Report of the President* (Washington, D.C.: Government Printing Office, 1997), Tables B-73 and B-75, pp. 386 and 388, and Saul Hansell, "Battle Emerging on How To Revise Bankruptcy Law," *The New York Times,* October 19, 1997.

30. Karen M. Paget, "The Balanced Budget Trap," *The American Prospect* 29: 21–29, November–December, 1996; Iris Lav and Robert Greenstein, *State Balanced Budget Requirements Differ From Proposed Federal Balanced Budget Amendment* (Washington, D.C.: Center on Budget and Policy Priorities, January, 1997); and the General Accounting Office, *Balanced Budget Requirements: State Experiences and Implications for the Federal Government* (Washington, D.C.: Government Printing Office, 1993).

31. Robert Heilbroner, *The Devil Words: "Debt" and "Deficit"* (New York: Center for Democratic Values, 1997), and John Cassidy, "Hoover Rides Again," *The New Yorker,* December 9, 1996, pp. 9–10. The Trust Fund surplus comes from the Congressional Budget Office, *The Economic and Budget Outlook: Fiscal Years 1998–2007* (Washington, D.C.: Government Printing Office, 1997), p. 46.

32. This recommendation is made by Karen M. Paget, "The Balanced Budget Trap," p. 24. For a similar argument, see Robert Eisner, in William Schreyer et al., "Is the Deficit a Friendly Giant After All?" *Harvard Business Review* 71 (4): 140–148, July–August, 1993.

33. Robert Greenstein, Richard Kogan, and Marion Nichols, *Bearing Most of the Burden: How Deficit Reduction During the 104th Congress Concentrated on Programs for the Poor* (Washington, D.C.: Center on Budget and Policy Priorities, 1996), and the Congressional Budget Office, *Reducing the Deficit: Spending and Revenue Options* (Washington, D.C.: Government Printing Office, 1997).

34. Jeffrey Madrick, "The Cost of Living: A New Myth," *The New York Review of Books* 44 (4): 19–24, March 6, 1997; Marc Breslow, "Let Them Eat Pentium Chips," *Dollars & Sense,* no. 210, pp. 7–8, March–April 1997; and Louis Uchitelle, "The Negotiators Forgo a Cut in Inflation Index," *The New York Times,* May 3, 1997.

35. Louis Uchitelle, "The Pitfalls of a Balanced Budget," *The New York Times,* February 21, 1995.

36. Frederick J. Thayer, "Do Balanced Budgets Cause Depressions."

37. Congressional Budget Office, *The Economic and Budget Outlook: Fiscal Years 1999–2008* (Washington, D.C.: Government Printing Office, 1998), p. 114, Table E-6, as well as Marc Breslow and John McDermott, "Disappearing Corporate Taxes," *Dollars and Sense,* 194: 43, July–August, 1994.

38. Lawrence Mishel, Jared Bernstein, and John Schmitt, *The State of Working America, 1998–99* (Ithaca, New York: Cornell University Press, 1999), p. 4, and Paul Krugman, "The Rich, The Right, and the Facts: Deconstructing the Income Distribution Debate," *The American Prospect* no. 11: 19–31, Fall, 1992.

39. Lawrence Mishel, Jared Bernstein, John Schmitt, *The State of Working America, 1998–99,* p. 92; Kevin Phillips, *Boiling Point: Democrats, Republicans, and the Decline of Middle Class Prosperity* (New York: Random House, 1993), p. 104; and Iver Peterson, "Whitman Delivers Cuts Year Ahead of Schedule," *The New York Times,* June 27, 1995. For an overview of these trends, see Nicholas Johnson and Iris J. Lav, "Are State Taxes Becoming More Regressive?" (Washington, D.C.: Center on Budget and Policy Priorities, October, 1997).

Notes to Chapter 10

1. Center on Budget and Policy Priorities, *Distribution of Budget Agreement's Tax Cuts Far More Similar to Congressional Bills Than To President's Plan* (Washington, D.C.: Center on Budget and Policy Priorities, 1997), p. 5, citing Citizens for Tax Justice.

2. For data on the rate of small business failures, see the Council of Economic Advisors, *Economic Report of the President* (Washington, D.C.: Government Printing Office, 1997), Table B-94, p. 407. A useful dissection of some of the myths about small business can be found in Bennett Harrison, *Lean and Mean: The Changing Landscape of Corporate Power in the Age of Flexibility* (New York: Basic Books, 1994).

3. Michael Lind, *Up From Conservatism: Why the Right Is Wrong for America* (New York: Free Press, 1997), p. 232.

4. Michael Lind, *Up From Conservatism*, p. 232.

5. Cited in Philip Harvey, *Securing the Right to Employment* (Princeton, New Jersey: Princeton University Press, 1989), pp. 3–4.

6. Philip Harvey, *Securing the Right to Employment*, pp. 4–5.

7. James K. Galbraith, "Test the Limit," *American Prospect* 34: 66–67, September–October, 1997.

8. United States Congressional Budget Office, *The Economic and Budget Outlook: Fiscal Years 1998–2007* (Washington, D.C.: Government Printing Office, 1997), p. xvi.

9. This estimate is extrapolated from Barry Bluestone and Bennett Harrison, "Why We Can Grow Faster," *The American Prospect* no. 34: 63, September–October, 1997.

10. Other recent public employment programs include those found in Mickey Kaus, *The End of Equality* (New York: Basic Books, 1992); Sheldon Danziger and Peter Gottschalk, *America Unequal* (Cambridge, Massachusetts: Harvard University Press, 1995); William Julius Wilson, *When Work Disappears* (New York: Alfred A. Knopf, 1996); and Herbert J. Gans, *The War Against the Poor* (New York: Basic Books, 1995).

11. See William Julius Wilson, *When Work Disappears*, pp. 232–233 for a discussion of this issue.

12. See Philip Harvey, "Paying for Full Employment: A Hard-Nosed Look at Finances," *Social Policy* 25 (3): 21–30, Spring, 1995, and Congressional Budget Office, *The Economic and Budget Outlook: Fiscal Years 1998–2007*, pp. 18 and 36.

13. See Steven Greenhouse, "Union Strategy Results in Coup at US Airways," *The New York Times*, September 30, 1997. The 38 percent figure comes from Thomas Karier, "Trade Deficits and Labor Unions: Myths and Realities," p. 35, in Lawrence Mishel and Paula B. Voos, eds., *Unions and Economic Competitiveness* (Armonk, New York: M.E. Sharpe, 1992). The 1997 data on union membership comes from the Bureau of Labor Statistics, *Union Member Summary*, January, 1998.

14. The 25 percent figure comes from Richard B. Freeman and Joel Rogers, *Worker Representation and Participation Survey: Report on the Findings*, Princeton Survey Research Associates, 1994, p. 36. The University of Michigan surveys, as cited by William Greider in *Who Will Tell the People?*, p. 194, usually show 30 percent.

15. On Canada, see Sheldon Danziger and Daniel Weinberg, "The Historical Record: Trends in Family Income, Inequality, and Poverty," in Sheldon Danziger, Gary Sandefur, and Daniel Weinberg, eds., *Confronting Poverty* (Cambridge, Massachusetts: Harvard University Press, 1994), pp. 29–30; Peter Gottschalk, *Policy Changes and Growing Earnings Inequality in Seven Industrialized Countries*, Luxembourg Incomes Studies, 1994, p. 17; David Card and Richard B. Freeman, "Small Differences That Matter: Canada vs. the United States," in Richard B. Freeman, ed., *Working Under Different Rules* (New York: Russell Sage Foundation, 1993), pp. 189–222; plus the essays by various authors on different aspects of Canadian social policy in Katharine McFate, Roger Lawson, and William Julius Wilson, eds., *Poverty, Inequality, and the Future of Social Policy: Western Welfare States in the New World Order* (New York: Russell Sage Foundation, 1995).

16. The following recommendations draw on Richard Rothstein, "Toward a More Perfect Union: New Labor's Hard Road," *The American Prospect*, 26: 47–53, May–June, 1996.

17. United States Department of Labor and the United States Department of Commerce, *Fact-Finding Report, Commission on the Future of Worker-Management Relations*, 1994, p. 79.

18. Lawrence Mishel, Jared Bernstein, and John Schmitt, *The State of Working America, 1998–99* (Ithaca, New York: Cornell University Press, 1999), p. 189, and Barry Bluestone and Teresa Ghilarducci, "Rewarding Work: Flexible Antipoverty Policy," *The American Prospect* 26: 40–46, cited on p. 42, May–June, 1996.

19. See Sam Pizzagati, *The Maximum Wage* (New York: Apex Press, 1992); Stephen Greenhouse, "Corporate Greed, Meet the Maximum Wage," *The New York Times*, June 16, 1996; and Brian Snyder, "A Maximum Wage: How Much Is Enough?" *Dollars & Sense*, #200, pp. 30–31 and p. 42, July–August, 1995.

20. "Paychecks May Get Fatter," *The Wall Street Journal*, March 18, 1997; Alan Okagaki, *Developing a Public Policy Agenda on Jobs* (Washington, D.C.: Center for Community Change,

1997), p. 21; and Alisa Glassman, "Making Work Pay," *Shelterforce* 20 (3): 17–19, May–June, 1998.

21. Madeleine Janis-Aparicio, Steve Cancian, and Gary Phillips, "Building a Movement for a Living Wage," *Poverty and Race,* 5 (1): 6, January–February, 1996.

22. Edward Nell, *Prosperity and Public Spending: Transformational Growth and the Role of Government* (London: Unwin Hyman, 1988), p. 21; see also the data in Todd Schafer, *Still Neglecting Public Investment* (Washington, D.C.: Economic Policy Institute, 1994).

23. David Alan Aschauer, *Public Investment and Private Sector Growth: The Economic Benefits of Reducing America's Third Deficit* (Washington, D.C.: Economic Policy Institute, 1990), p. 1, and Alicia H. Munnell, "Is There Too Little Public Capital?" in *The Public's Capital* 3 (4): 4–5. Spring, 1991. By contrast, from a more conservative position, Dale Jorgensen, "Fragile Statistical Foundations," in *The Public's Capital,* pp. 6–7 says that public investment costs money because it uses resources that might be otherwise employed. For an overview, see Organization of Economic Cooperation and Development, *Infrastructure Policies for the 1990s* (Paris: OECD, 1993).

24. Council of Economic Advisors, *Economic Report of the President* (Washington, D.C.: United States Government Printing Office, 1994), p. 41.

25. Although Europe is well-known for its railroads, the public policy context for high-speed trains is different in the United States. Here the population is more spread out, domestic air travel is cheaper, the highway network is well developed, and gasoline is less expensive. These differences undoubtedly limit the development of high-speed trains to few major interurban connections less than 500 miles apart. By this standard, the most likely candidates are probably Houston, Dallas, and San Antonio; Anaheim, California to Las Vegas; and, of course, the Northeast corridor from Boston to Washington.
High-speed rail is expensive—so expensive, in fact, that the private sector will not do it. The most costly upgrades on already existing track include bridge repair and modification, electrification, grade crossings, added track (so very fast trains can pass freight), and new rolling stock. Altogether, these improvements push costs to about $10 million a mile for speeds of 125 miles an hour and $20 million a mile for speeds of 150 miles an hour. Amtrak has already ordered eighteen sets of trains with a top speed of 150 miles an hour for use on the Boston-Washington corridor. They will cut the Washington-New York run from three to two and half hours and reduce the New York-Boston trip from four and half to three hours. The trains, which will have outlets for lap tops, will be delivered in late 1999. This is the kind of project that would be competitive with air traffic on the other corridors. U.S. General Accounting Office, *High-Speed Ground Transportation: Issues Affecting Development in the United States* (Washington, D.C.: Government Printing Office, 1993), and Mathew Wald, "2 Builders Chosen For Speedy Trains on Northeast Run," *The New York Times,* March 16, 1996.

26. Robert Eisner and Rudolph Penner, "Point-Counterpoint: Should the Feds Adopt a Capital Budget?" *Governing* 6 (1): 57–59, October, 1992, and U.S. General Accounting Office, *Federal Budget: Choosing Public Investment Programs* (Washington, D.C.: Government Printing Office, 1993), p. 10, citing U.S. Congress Office of Technological Assessment, *Research Funding as an Investment: Can We Measure the Returns? A Technical Memorandum,* April, 1986. Charles Whalen, "Budget Deficits: Dead Ends and Sensible Directions," *Social Policy* 26 (3): 38–45, Spring, 1996, also comes down in favor of a separate capital budget.

27. Fay Cook Lomax, and Edith J. Barrett, *Support for the American Welfare State* (New York: Columbia University Press, 1992), pp. 226–227, and Robert Greenstein, "Universal and Targeted Approaches to Relieving Poverty: An Alternative View," in Christopher Jencks and Paul E. Peterson, eds., *The Urban Underclass* (Washington, D.C., The Brookings Institution, 1991), pp. 437–459.

28. For a review of the arguments on both sides of this issue, see Hugh Heclo, "Poverty Politics," in Sheldon Danziger, Gary Sandefur, and Daniel Weinberg, eds., *Confronting Poverty,* pp. 396–437, especially pp. 424–427.

29. For a treatment of a guaranteed income, see Herbert J. Gans, *The War Against the Poor* (New York: Basic Books, 1995), pp. 142–143, and Hugh Heclo, "The Social Question," in Kate

McFate, Roger Lawson, and William Julius Wilson, eds., *Poverty, Inequality, and the Future of Social Policy,* pp. 665–691.

30. See United States Congressional Budget Office, *Reducing Entitlement Spending* (Washington, D.C.: Government Printing Office, 1994).

31. Concord Coalition, "Sample Entitlements Speech," Washington, D.C., 1997.

32. Committee on Ways and Means, U.S. House of Representatives, *Overview of Entitlement Programs: 1998 Green Book,* p. 67.

33. For a nonpartisan treatment of the administrative savings in a national health plan, see the U.S. General Accounting Office, *Canadian Health Insurance* (Washington, D.C.: Government Printing Office, 1991). Information on the cap comes from the Committee on Ways and Means, U.S. House of Representatives, *1998 Green Book,* p. 3.

34. Joseph F. Quinn and Oliva S. Mitchell, "Social Security on the Table," *The American Prospect* 26: 76–81, May–June, 1996.

35. Doug Henwood, *Wall Street* (New York: Verso, 1997), p. 304.

36. Mark Weisbrot, *Unequal Sacrifice: The Impact of Changes Proposed by the Advisory Council on Social Security* (Washington, D.C.: Preamble Center for Public Policy, 1997), p. ii. This is also the problem with William W. Beach, *Social Security's Rate of Return* (Washington, D.C.: A Report of The Heritage Center for Data Analysis, 1998).

37. These calculations all come from Dean Baker, "The Privateers' Free Lunch," *The American Prospect* 32: 81–84, May–June, 1997. For a book-length treatment of this issue, see Dean Baker, ed., *Getting Prices Right* (Armonk, New York: M.E. Sharpe, 1997).

38. Walter Russell Mead, *The Low-Wage Challenge to Global Growth* (Washington, D.C., Economic Policy Institute, 1990), p. 37. For a similar perspective, see William Greider, *Who Will Tell the People?* (New York: Touchstone Books, 1992), p. 400.

39. Steven Greenhouse, "A.F.L.-C.I.O. Puts Recruiting at Top of Its Agenda," *The New York Times,* February 17, 1997, and Sam Dillon, "U.S. Labor Leader Seeks Union Support in Mexico," *The New York Times,* January 23, 1998.

40. Thalia Kidder and Mary McGinn, "In the Wake of NAFTA: Transnational Workers Networks," *Social Policy* 25 (4): 14–21, Summer, 1995.

41. Walter Russell Mead, *The Low-Wage Challenge to Global Growth,* p. 4, and Robert Kuttner, "The Corporation in America," *Dissent* 40 (1): 35–49, Winter, 1993.

42. Samuel Bowles, David Gordon, and Thomas Weisskopf, *After the Wasteland: A Democratic Economics for the Year 2000* (Armonk, New York: M.E. Sharpe, 1990), p. 226.

43. Sidney Verba, Kay Lehman Scholzman, and Henry E. Brady, "The Big Tilt: Participatory Inequality in America," *The American Prospect* 32: 74–80, May–June, 1997. See also their book, *Voice and Equality: Civic Voluntarism and American Politics* (Cambridge, Massachusetts: Harvard University Press, 1995).

44. Center for Responsive Politics, *Who's Paying For This Election* (Washington, D.C.: Center for Responsive Politics, 1996), p. 6 is the source of the 7–1 ratio. The number of donors comes from Center for Responsive Politics, *The Big Picture: Where the Money Came From in the 1996 Election* (Washington, D.C.: Center for Responsive Politics, 1997). The Center also performed the analysis of contributions by zip codes, which was cited by Leslie Wayne in "Hunting for Cash, Candidates Follow the Bright Lights," *The New York Times,* October 20, 1996.

45. Institute for Policy Studies, *A Fairness Agenda for America* (Washington, D.C.: Institute for Policy Studies, 1997), p. 11. In addition, for a discussion of all these issues, see the articles on campaign reform in the special issue of *Social Policy* 26 (1): Fall, 1995.

46. For a history of the marginal rate, see Kevin Phillips, *The Politics of Rich and Poor* (New York: Random House, 1990), pp. 76–78.

47. See Edward N. Wolff, *Top Heavy: A Study of Increasing Inequality of Wealth in America* (New York: The Twentieth Century Fund, 1995), chapters 7, 8, and 9. The OECD information is based on 1990 data. For an analysis of the 1997 tax bill, see Iris J. Lav, *The Final Tax Bill: Assessing the Long-Term Costs and the Distribution of Tax Benefits* (Washington, D.C.: Center on Budget and Policy Priorities, 1997).

48. See Doug Henwood, *Wall Street*, p. 318.

49. See Geoffrey Wood, "Currency Speculators Deserve Thanks, Not Taxes," *The Wall Street Journal*, November 28, 1997.

50. Congressional Budget Office, *The Economic and Budget Outlook: Fiscal Years 1999–2008* (Washington, D.C.: Government Printing Office, 1998), p. 64.

51. Congressional Budget Office of the United States, *Reducing the Deficit: Spending and Revenue Options* (Washington, D.C.: Government Printing Office, 1997), pp. 26–29.

52. Robert D. Putnam, "Bowling Alone: America's Declining Social Capital," *Journal of Democracy* 6 (1): 65–78, January, 1995. See also Robert D. Putnam, "Tuning in, Tuning Out: The Strange Disappearance of Social Capital in America," *PS: Political Science and Politics* 28 (4): 664–683, Winter, 1995.

53. Alexandro Portes and Patricia Landolt, "The Downside of Social Capital," *The American Prospect*, no. 26: 18–21, 94, May–June 1996; Frank Riessman and Erik Banks, "The Mismeasure of Civil Society," *Social Policy* 26 (3): 2–5, Spring, 1996; Rick Perlstein, "Blind Alley?" *Lingua Franca* 7 (1):12–13, December–January, 1997.

54. Robert D. Putnam, "Bowling Alone: America's Declining Social Capital," p. 75.

55. See Ichiro Kawachi, Bruce P. Kennedy, Kimberly Lochner, and Deborah Prothrow-Stith, "Social Capital, Income Inequality, and Mortality," *The American Journal of Public Health* 87 (9): 1491–1497, September, 1997, as well as Richard G. Wilkinson, "Comment: Income Inequality and Social Cohesion," *American Journal of Public Health*, 87 (9): 1504–1506, September, 1997.

56. The best discussion of this individualism is still Robert M. Bellah, Richard Madsen, William M. Sullivan, Ann Swidler, and Stephen M. Tipton, *Habits of the Heart* (New York, Harper & Row Perennial, 1986). See, for example, p. 65: "The notion that one discovers one's deepest beliefs in, and through, tradition and community is not very congenial to Americans. Most of us imagine an autonomous self existing independently, entirely outside any tradition and community, and then perhaps choosing one."

57. I draw here, of course, on two works of Frances Fox Piven and Richard Cloward about the history of American social reform, in particular, *Regulating the Poor* (New York: Random House, 1971), and *Poor People's Movements* (New York: Pantheon, 1977).

Index